The Austrian Dimension in German Intellectual History

The Austrian Dimension in German Intellectual History

From the Enlightenment to Anschluss

David S. Luft

BLOOMSBURY ACADEMIC
LONDON • NEW YORK • OXFORD • NEW DELHI • SYDNEY

BLOOMSBURY ACADEMIC
Bloomsbury Publishing Plc
50 Bedford Square, London, WC1B 3DP, UK
1385 Broadway, New York, NY 10018, USA
29 Earlsfort Terrace, Dublin 2, Ireland

BLOOMSBURY, BLOOMSBURY ACADEMIC and the Diana logo are trademarks of Bloomsbury Publishing Plc

First published in Great Britain 2021
Paperback edition published in 2022

Copyright © David S. Luft, 2021

David S. Luft has asserted his right under the Copyright, Designs and Patents Act, 1988, to be identified as Author of this work.

Cover image: Perthes Map of Bohemia and Austria © Getty Images / Sepia Times / Contributor

All rights reserved. No part of this publication may be reproduced or transmitted in any form or by any means, electronic or mechanical, including photocopying, recording, or any information storage or retrieval system, without prior permission in writing from the publishers.

Bloomsbury Publishing Plc does not have any control over, or responsibility for, any third-party websites referred to or in this book. All internet addresses given in this book were correct at the time of going to press. The author and publisher regret any inconvenience caused if addresses have changed or sites have ceased to exist, but can accept no responsibility for any such changes.

Every effort has been made to trace copyright holders and to obtain their permissions for the use of copyright material. The publisher apologizes for any errors or omissions and would be grateful if notified of any corrections that should be incorporated in future reprints or editions of this book.

A catalogue record for this book is available from the British Library.

Library of Congress Cataloging-in-Publication Data
Names: Luft, David S., author.
Title: The Austrian dimension in German intellectual history : from the Enlightenment to Anschluss / David S. Luft.
Description: First edition. | London ; New York : Bloomsbury Academic, 2021. | Includes bibliographical references and index. |
Identifiers: LCCN 2020055554 (print) | LCCN 2020055555 (ebook) | ISBN 9781350202207 (hardback) | ISBN 9781350202214 (ebook) | ISBN 9781350202221 (epub)
Subjects: LCSH: Austria–Intellectual life. | Austrian literature–History and criticism. | Philosophy, Austrian. | Learning and scholarship–Austria–History.
Classification: LCC DB30 .L84 2021 (print) | LCC DB30 (ebook) | DDC 943.6/04–dc23
LC record available at https://lccn.loc.gov/2020055554
LC ebook record available at https://lccn.loc.gov/2020055555

ISBN:	HB:	978-1-3502-0220-7
	PB:	978-1-3502-0224-5
	ePDF:	978-1-3502-0221-4
	eBook:	978-1-3502-0222-1

Typeset by Integra Software Services Pvt. Ltd.

To find out more about our authors and books visit www.bloomsbury.com and sign up for our newsletters.

Contents

List of Maps	vii
Preface	viii
Introduction	1
1 Austria and Bohemia before the Austrian State	15
2 The Developing Context of Austrian Intellectual Life: 1740–1938/1939	29
Modern German and the Austrian Enlightenment: 1740–1792	31
Josephinism and the Conservative Era: 1792–1866	38
The Liberal Era: 1867–1900	46
The Transformations of Modern Intellectual Life: 1900–1938/1939	51
3 Philosophy in Austria	59
Bernard Bolzano (1781–1848)	60
Franz Brentano (1838–1917)	66
Ernst Mach (1838–1916)	72
Ludwig Wittgenstein (1889–1951)	77
The Vienna Circle	81
Conclusion	83
4 German Literature in Austria	87
Grillparzer and Theater in Vienna	88
Adalbert Stifter and the Novel	94
The Writers of the Liberal Era	98
The Generation of 1905: Ethics and the Novel	102
Karl Kraus (1874–1936)	104
Robert Musil (1880–1942)	107
Hermann Broch (1886–1951) and Hugo von Hofmannsthal (1874–1929)	110
Rainer Maria Rilke (1875–1926)	111

5　The Human Sciences in Austria　　117
　　　In the Shadow of the State: From Cameralism to the
　　　　　Authoritarian State　　118
　　　Austrian Economics and Social Thought: From Menger
　　　　　to Hayek　　123
　　　Psychoanalysis and Intellectual History　　129

After Cisleithanian Austria　　137

Notes　　140
Bibliography　　199
Index　　222

Maps

1	Perthes Map of Bohemia and Austria	6
2	Austrian and Bohemian lands, *c.* 1871	8
3	Principalities of the Holy Roman Empire, *c.* 1547	20
4	Central Europe, *c.* 1780	25

Preface

For many years I have felt the need for a unified account of Austrian intellectual life. Most educated people in the English-speaking world have some notion of French intellectual history since the sixteenth century, of German intellectual history, of English or British intellectual history, or of the intellectual history of the United States. But this is not true of Austrian intellectual history except for a few familiar figures of the twentieth century such as Sigmund Freud and Ludwig Wittgenstein. For the most part, the history of Austrian thought since the eighteenth century disappears into conventional conceptions of German culture, or into contradictory assumptions about nationalism and the nation-state, or into the formlessness of Empire—whether Holy Roman or Habsburg. I want to provide a more specific sense of location for Austrian intellectual history, a context for reading important texts from Central Europe. I want to make more accessible ways of thinking that are not familiar to educated readers in Germany or in the English-speaking world. But an important part of my imagined audience is also readers who are already familiar with Freud or Wittgenstein, Franz Brentano or Ernst Mach, Robert Musil or Franz Kafka, the Austrian economists or social scientists—readers who want to make some sense of how to locate these figures historically. Placing these intellectuals accurately within their worlds has been made more difficult and more important by the history of Central Europe over the past two hundred years.

I want to thank the Horning Endowment in the Humanities, Fulbright/IFK, and Fulbright-Botstiber for their financial support for my work on this project, and I am also grateful to the many people who were gracious and hospitable to me while I was in Vienna doing research. I think particularly of Friedrich Stadler, Lonnie Johnson, Albert Müller, Sergius Kodera, Waltraud Heindl, and Susanne Hochreiter. Since the early 1960s many others have contributed to my Austrian education—from my *Pflegefamilie*, when I studied in Vienna in 1963, to Hilde Spiel, Wendelin Schmidt-Dengler, and Kurt Rudolf Fischer. Many colleagues and friends have supported my work over the years, especially Burton Pike, Allan Mitchell, and John Marino. I depended for years on the Central Library at the University of California, San Diego, and the melvyl system of the University of California. Since I began this project, I have enjoyed the support of Oregon

State University's Valley Library, including ILL and Summit. I have frequently worked at the *Nationalbibliothek* in Vienna, especially during my stays with the Institut für Kulturforschung and the Institut für Zeitgeschichte.

I am particularly grateful to Mason Tattersall, who was my graduate student and research assistant when I was in the early stages of designing this project. He has read many drafts of my chapters, and he was always encouraging and sensitive to my intent. In the final years of my writing, I was fortunate to discover another wonderful reader, Carl Findley, who had recently finished his doctorate at Chicago and happily made his energy and perceptiveness available to me as a critic. Both Mason and Carl read and commented on the whole of my book, and they were especially helpful with my chapter on philosophy and with my internal debates about my argument. I also want to thank the graduate students who helped me with the final stages of the manuscript: Ambika Natarajan, Lauren Stoneburner, Gus Paoli, and Emily Simpson. Finally, I want to thank the sandwich shops where I often worked: the Old World Deli, Panera in Corvallis, and University Hero.

A number of colleagues were kind enough to read my work in progress and provide me with thoughtful comments and suggestions. Katie Arens read the early chapters, and Rena Lauer read the introduction and Chapter 1. Erin Hochman and Don Wallace read Chapter 2; Brigitte Prutti, Geoffrey Howes, Michael Burri, and Craig Decker all read Chapter 4; and Janek Wassermann read Chapter 5. I am grateful to all of these colleagues who took the time to share their perspectives and their expertise. I also want to thank the readers at Bloomsbury Academic for their comments and suggestions and my colleagues at Oregon State University for their support for this project, especially Gary Ferngren, Chris Nichols, Kara Ritzheimer, and Anita Helle. Finally, I want to thank Frank Biess and Gerry Feldman for inviting me years ago to tell my Austrian story to the German historians of the UC system.

As I finish this book, I am conscious of those who will not have an opportunity to read it—from my parents and my brother to Allan Mitchell, Paul Saltman, John Marino, Chris Norris, and Rick Harmon. I hope that Jennifer, Cate, Gretchen, and Carole will all enjoy it.

Introduction

It is reality that awakens possibilities ....
—Robert Musil, *The Man without Qualities*

The Austrian Dimension in German Intellectual History: From the Enlightenment to Anschluss presents a new way of thinking about Austrian intellectual history—one that neither concentrates on Vienna nor encompasses the whole of the Habsburg Monarchy.[1] It is an intellectual history of German-speaking Austria between 1740 and 1938/1939, which aims to give historical shape to Austrian intellectual life by locating Austrian writers, philosophers, and other intellectuals within the wider context of language, culture, and politics in Central Europe. In order to make the Austrian dimension of German intellectual history more visible, I offer a contextual narrative for thinking about Austrian intellectual history in relation to the modern German language and modern thought. On the one hand, this means clarifying the place of Austria in relation to German intellectual history. On the other hand, it requires the clarification of the place of Austrian intellectual history in relation to the Habsburg Monarchy and its many linguistic and cultural traditions. The conventional separation of political history from the study of language, literature, and philosophy (a separation that is often even sharper in Europe than in the United States) has prevented certain issues from finding clear formulation; and the perspectives of history, philosophy, literature, and the human sciences are rarely brought together in a unified way. These pages present an historical narrative that includes an appreciation for what is Austrian in German intellectual life and a recognition of the nature of Austria's place *within* Central European German culture.[2] In this sense, the book is about German history though not about the history of Germany, and I hope it will be a contribution to seeing Europe and European intellectual history with fresh eyes. I criticize teleological, essentialist accounts of what is German by pointing to another "Germany." But my aim is not a competing Austrian essentialism or an idealization of what is Austrian, but rather a less reductive understanding of the European past.[3]

Eric Hobsbawm once asked why the intellectual histories "of Germany and Austria in the nineteenth century, [like those] of England and Scotland in the eighteenth century," were "so different, though linguistically and culturally … these countries belonged together."[4] This puzzle is close to my own concerns, but not identical with them. Austria in the nineteenth century was linguistically more complex than Scotland in the eighteenth century.[5] Moreover, I am concerned with the intellectual history of Austria over a longer historical period—from the eighteenth century to the twentieth, a period when the geographical and political forms of Austria and the Habsburg Monarchy repeatedly changed. After 1871 the new German Empire acquired firm political boundaries, but the context for German-speaking intellectual life in the Habsburg Monarchy is more difficult to define. After 1871, there was no longer any ambiguity about where Germany was, but for intellectual historians there has been a great deal of confusion about how to situate German intellectual history, especially German philosophy, literature, and the human sciences in Austria. Models of German culture and intellectual life, which have been designed for Bismarck's *Reich*, are often not adequate for understanding German-speaking intellectuals in Austria. As long as we are simply trying to understand Bismarck's Germany, these models of German intellectual life are at least reasonable points of departure that could of course be complicated in terms of regions, individual experience, or specialized fields. But for Austrian intellectuals, such models become a significant impediment. An Austrian response that tries to neatly separate Austria from Germany is also not adequate. It is important for intellectual historians to understand this intermediate context for Austrian intellectual history, that is, intellectuals who lived in Austria but wrote in German. But, as Marc Bloch reminded us in his classic essay on comparative history, "[b]efore phenomena can be interpreted, they have to be discovered."[6] Not only is the intellectual history of Austria unfamiliar to most readers in the English-speaking world, but this narrative is consistently obscured by the commonality of language between Germans and Austrians.

Discussions of intellectual history, philosophy, and literature often use the word "German" very loosely to refer both to modern German states and to German culture more widely. Meanwhile, scholars of Austria use the term "Austrian" to refer to very different periods and places, although for Austrian intellectual history scholars are nearly always thinking of work in German. Not surprisingly, this wide range of uses and meanings leads to many confusions.

For the most part, there are no "right" answers in these matters, but it is possible to make these issues more explicit so that the place of Austrian intellectual life in relation to a wider cosmopolitan German culture is not lost or submerged. At first glance the question seems to be a comparison between Germany and Austria, but it turns out not to be clear where or when Austria was, especially in the context of writing about Austrian intellectual history. My aim is not to compare Austria and Germany, but rather to clarify Austria's location within a broader German-speaking culture that emerged during the eighteenth century, more than a century before modern Germany came into being.[7] In this way, Imperial Germany and its canonical narratives are no longer privileged as the special proprietors of German intellectual life.

There has been a long history of arguments and narratives about what is distinctively Austrian, especially in contrast to Prussia. These accounts have variously emphasized the contrast of dynasties (Habsburg and Hohenzollern), of prominent political personalities (Maria Theresa and Frederick the Great), of religious styles and values (Baroque versus Protestant), or even of philosophical and literary styles. In this book, I am not attempting to characterize what is distinctively Austrian, and I am concerned primarily with intellectual history rather than popular views of political and cultural difference. I am not concerned with comparing Austria to other parts of German-speaking culture or with advocating the Austrian idea, but with understanding the intellectual life of this region.[8] This is not a book about the Austrian nation or Austrian identity. It is a way of thinking about Austrian intellectual history: a framework for understanding the intellectual history of Cisleithanian Austria between the Enlightenment and *Anschluss*, between 1740 and 1938–1939.

We must begin by clarifying the term "Austria," especially in the context of intellectual history. The diplomatic history of the nineteenth century has powerfully shaped our conventions about "Austria" as a term, and it is understandable that scholars of Austro-German literature, especially before the First World War, were inclined to follow the broadest understanding of these conventions.[9] Before the emergence of a modern state under Maria Theresa and Joseph II, the word had meant the Archduchy of Austria, or even just Lower Austria and Vienna, but usually Austria above and below the Enns.[10] Today, scholars of Austrian literature typically take the word to mean either the little Austria of the twentieth-century republics or the entire empire of the Habsburgs, while historians often use the term to refer to Cisleithanian Austria after 1867 (including Bohemia and Galicia). In his multinational account of the empire after 1848, Robert Kann decided to use the term "Austria" to mean

Cisleithanian Austria, that is, the non-Hungarian Habsburg lands after 1867. Here he followed constitutional usage under the arrangements of 1867, but he called this an expedient, even for the political history of the Dual Monarchy. On the other hand, Kann used the term "Habsburg" to refer to the empire as a whole,[11] as he did in his comprehensive narrative of the Monarchy: *A History of the Habsburg Empire, 1526–1918*.[12] Pieter Judson's recent account of the Habsburg Empire follows Kann's distinction; here Judson aims to set limits to nationalist narratives bequeathed in the twentieth century by the successor states and their advocates.[13] My book is doing something different. I want to understand Cisleithanan Austria as the core of German-speaking intellectual life in the Habsburg Empire and to clarify why this was the case between the mid-eighteenth century and the early twentieth century. I emphasize the achievements of the Austrian state in this region rather than its hopes and intentions for the Empire as a whole, and I emphasize the relatively greater success of efforts at centralization in Cisleithanian Austria and the importance of this for intellectual history. Most of the area of the Habsburg Empire was to the east of the Leitha River in the vast expanses of Transleithania and the much greater linguistic complexity of Hungary and Galicia and Bukovina. It is Cisleithanian Austria, the region to the West of the Leitha River, that I am concerned with here. I want to understand the intellectual history of this geographical space, which was not a nation and never a separate country, but the core of the Austrian state and Austrian intellectual history from the 1740s to 1938/1939—from the creation of the Austrian state to *Anschluss* (which by 1939 led to the absorption of both Austria and Czechoslovakia into the German *Reich*).[14]

As a field of knowledge, intellectual history usually stays close to the definition of intellectuals provided by Ralf Dahrendorf: those who are concerned with "the independent and deliberate use of the word."[15] In practice this means the history of literature, philosophy, and the human sciences. A broader definition would encompass everyone involved in culture and the symbolic world, including music, the arts, architecture, and science.[16] And such an approach would have appeal for a tradition in which the Baroque and music have been emphasized in cultural and even literary histories. For these fields, the broad, inclusive context of the Habsburg Monarchy has often worked very well, allowing scholars to emphasize aspects of cultural unity or commonality in the empire. But for fields that are concerned primarily with "the independent and deliberate use of the word," this conception of Austrian culture is more problematic—whether we think of an Austrian philosophy, an Austrian literature, or an Austrian economics and social science.[17] In fields such as philosophy, literature, and the human sciences, written texts are central, and this creative work is closely related to the spoken language. My aim is to understand these intellectuals and their texts.[18]

In *The Austrian Mind* William Johnston argued that, despite the linguistic variety within the empire, it was possible to understand the intellectual history of the Habsburg Monarchy by relying only on texts in German.[19] Johnston treated both Bohemia and Hungary as problematic national regions that were parts of a story that was centered in Vienna. He saved these sub-narratives for the end of his book and discussed them for a period when Bohemia and Hungary were institutionally quite different and separate from each other. His organization implied that the two regions were at once part of Austria and not part of it, whether politically or intellectually. At the same time, Johnston's account made clear that Hungarian intellectual history was very different from Austrian intellectual history, whereas Bohemia was deeply and closely related to Austrian thought. Other discussions of Austrian philosophy, literature, and the human sciences have often taken "Austria" to mean the Habsburg Monarchy as a whole, especially for the late nineteenth century. Such an approach would make sense if it were genuinely multilingual, that is to say, the prehistory of Eastern or Central Europe today, as in a book like Kann's *Multinational Empire*. But Austrian literature and philosophy nearly always turn out to mean texts in German, which can be located anywhere in the Habsburg Monarchy at any historical moment.[20] In his recent book on the cultural history of Austria and Hungary, Johnston pursues this question from a different point of view.[21] He emphasizes that Robert Musil's "Kakania" refers primarily to the Habsburg Monarchy to the west of the Leitha, and he explores the scholarly literature in English, French, and German on the intellectual and cultural history of the Monarchy as a whole (especially to the east of the Leitha), a project that is devoted to overcoming the boundary of the Leitha River. My book makes explicit and underscores the significance of this boundary for German-speaking intellectual life. Johnston also wants to elaborate forms of thinking and education that grew out of the Habsburg Monarchy and its elites, especially to the east of the Leitha. I am not trying to characterize an ethos, but to describe intellectual life west of the Leitha. The very existence of this region, let alone its long and rich history since the Middle Ages, often gets lost in political narratives of German nationalism and the Habsburg Monarchy. But this region is enormously important for understanding Austrian intellectual history. It is the historical core of German-speaking culture and social life in the Habsburg Monarchy and the basis for my study of the Austrian dimension in German intellectual history.

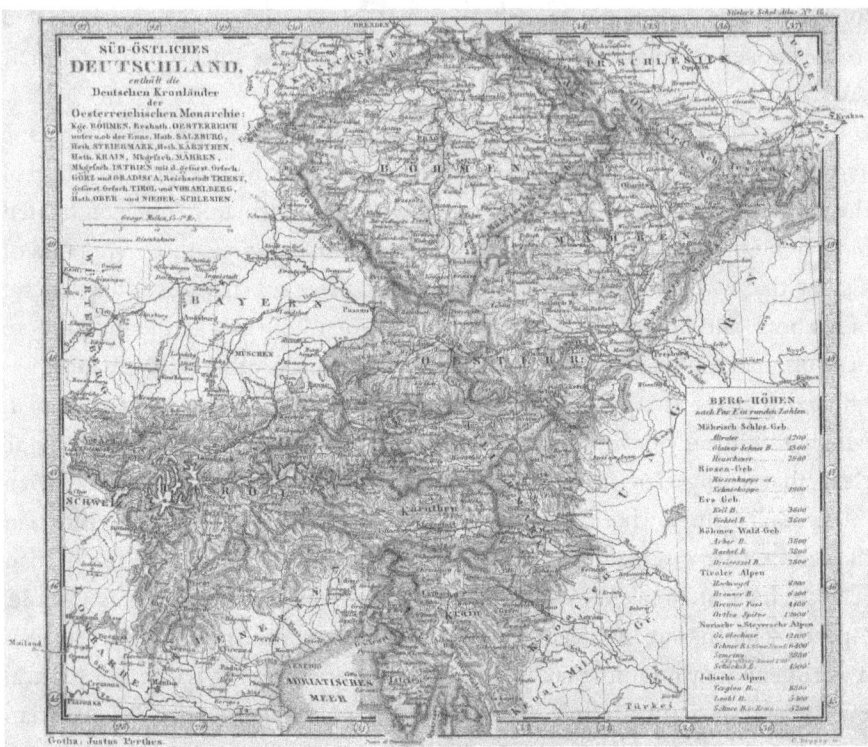

Map 1 Perthes Map of Bohemia and Austria. © Sepia Times/Universal Images Group via Getty Images.

The dominant narrative of modern German intellectual history has largely shaped assumptions about Central European intellectual history down to the present, and it is a view that ignores or obscures the narrative of Austrian intellectual history. During the nineteenth century, the canon in German literature and philosophy was tailored to a very large extent to conform to the story of German unification.[22] From the point of view of Germany, Austrian intellectual history can be difficult to identify and easy to regard as somehow really German. Austrian intellectual history is often implicitly conceived as a part of German intellectual history, although these relationships are usually not spelled out, despite the fact that conventional assumptions about German idealism, romanticism, Hegel, German nationalism, historicism, and the human sciences turn out to be problematic when applied to German-speaking intellectuals in Austria. While Austrian accounts of Austrian and German culture have sometimes been ideological or apologetic, commentators on German history, literature, philosophy, and social science are frequently not even aware of perspectives that open up from the South.²³ Anglo-American perceptions of what is German and Central European have been determined for centuries by our own historical reception of European ideas. The stories of English liberalism, the American Revolution, the French Revolution, the Industrial Revolution, Romanticism, and the First World War have all conditioned what we see as German. Even educated Americans have very little awareness that Germany did not exist before 1871 or that the histories of Prussia, Austria, Württemberg, Bavaria, Hanover, and Hamburg are different from each other, as are the histories of Vienna, Prague, and Salzburg.²⁴

I am arguing for the value of distinguishing an Austrian intellectual tradition within a concept of German intellectual life that emphasizes the German language since the eighteenth century.²⁵ When I speak of modern German culture, I have in mind what most scholars of German literature and philosophy intend: the period after about 1740, with the emergence of a modern literature and the use of German in the universities and in the Enlightenment. My understanding of modern German intellectual life is shaped by the modern German language, by the context of modern German literature and philosophy as they grew out of the Enlightenment, by late modern in the conventions of historians, and by the field of modern European intellectual history as it is commonly understood for England, France, and Germany. The decisive points of departure for my argument are the emergence of the modern German language and the modern Austrian state. I am concerned primarily with an intellectual tradition that took form with modern German in the eighteenth century, especially in the creative work of Goethe, Lessing, and Kant (as well as the German cameralists) and culminated in figures such as Musil, Kafka, Wittgenstein, and Freud, but is still poorly known today.²⁶

For the purposes of intellectual history, I am arguing for a conception of "Austria" that makes explicit the connection to German language and culture and emphasizes the hereditary lands of Austria and Bohemia as the historical core of this intellectual tradition. My account of the Austrian tradition in German intellectual history will concentrate primarily on the geographical region marked by the historical overlap between the Habsburg Monarchy and the German *Reich* (and later the German Confederation) before 1866.²⁷ My argument emphasizes the close ties within Cisleithanian Austria between the Habsburgs' German hereditary lands and the Bohemian hereditary lands, especially after 1749. This conception of Austria is Cisleithanian in the geographical sense (west of the Leitha River), though not in the strictly constitutional sense of the *Ausgleich* or Compromise of 1867, in which Galicia and Bukovina were included. Here we

Map 2 Austrian and Bohemian lands, 1871. © Cartography by Philip Schwartzberg, Meridian Mapping, Minneapolis.

have the core of a German-speaking region that remained under Habsburg rule and within the Holy Roman Empire into the nineteenth century. The Napoleonic era consolidated and clarified these relationships and replaced the Holy Roman Empire with the German Confederation until 1866. This map is intended as a heuristic device to make clear where Austrian intellectual history was between 1740 and 1938/1939. To paraphrase Robert Musil's remark about the word "intuition," this region is a box—someone should open it and see what's inside. My book is an attempt to open this box, to explore this region as a location for German-speaking intellectual life.

The way Americans write European intellectual history today is still predominantly shaped by the original experience of the reception of modern thought, especially the prominence of England and France in the American view of the world since the colonial period and the role of Northern, Protestant German views of Central Europe in the Anglo-American world in the nineteenth century. Modern intellectual history emerged as a field in the United States in the early twentieth century, when European history concentrated on Western Europe and on the national histories of England, France, and Germany. What was not homogeneous in Great Britain, France, and Germany was not ordinarily emphasized; and English, French, and German were the languages most familiar to Western scholars. Even before the First World War, scholars from Western Europe and the United States often assumed teleological visions of nationalism, against which the Habsburg Monarchy seemed puzzling, if not actually "wrong" or immoral. Much of Austria seemed almost German, while still more of it seemed incomprehensibly different and inaccessible, as Neville Chamberlain famously emphasized in 1938.

In many respects, Austria has been lost or obscured in relation to Western Europe.[28] Accounts of modern German intellectual history usually describe a continuous story from Goethe and Kant to Romanticism and Hegel to Dilthey and Weber in a seamless way that hardly knows what to make of major figures such as Bernard Bolzano or Adalbert Stifter or Franz Grillparzer or Friedrich August von Hayek—and it has never quite been clear how to discuss the Germanness of Sigmund Freud or Robert Musil or Franz Kafka or Rainer Maria Rilke.[29] In this way, important figures of modern thought are driven to the periphery in ways that make them more difficult to understand.

Because of the scope and complexity of Austrian intellectual history, it has often been treated collaboratively, in large, even multivolume studies.[30] These comprehensive approaches are usually characterized as studies of literature or philosophy or the human sciences, but they frequently address the full range of issues and authors with which intellectual historians are concerned. The editors of these collections usually set a tone, but leave contributors free to develop their arguments in distinctive ways. Thus, individual essays may adopt quite different points of view, and general questions of overview are often set aside, particularly in light of the *Unübersichtlichkeit* [scope and complexity] of the field. This is understandable, but it means that, in the midst of so many different informing conceptions and perspectives, important questions often remain implicit and unclarified. For a non-Austrian or someone outside the field, it is difficult to gain a coherent overview of the subject. Moreover, since intellectual history touches on so many fields, problems often arise simply from variations of usage in literature, philosophy, and the human sciences. While a number of scholars have written important studies of Austrian philosophy and social science, these fields are not well integrated into accounts of political and literary history.[31] In most cases, historians of Austrian philosophy and social science have emphasized commonalities across the empire as a whole, even when they are concerned primarily with the twentieth century and with work that was written in German.

As a scholarly field, Austrian literature has played an important role in shaping the conventions of Austrian intellectual history, especially for *fin-de-siècle* Vienna,[32] but also more broadly for intellectual history from Grillparzer and

Stifter to Kafka and Musil. In the foreword to his now standard *Literaturgeschichte Österreichs* of 1996, Herbert Zeman explained the usage of the term "Austria" in this multi-authored volume:

> The concepts "Austria" and "Austrian" are related, in the spirit of good old traditions of literary and cultural history since the 18th century, to that political territory and its cultural emanation that has flowed since the Middle Ages through the rule of the Babenbergs and the Habsburgs and finally into Republican Austria.[33]

Thus, Zeman explains that the volume's authors will follow the long-standing convention of allowing "Austria" and "Austrian" to have a variety of meanings over the centuries, beginning with the little Austria of the Babenbergs and the Habsburgs, moving to the crowns of 1526, and finally to little Austria since 1918. This means that "Austria" does not refer to something continuous and specific from a linguistic or social perspective.[34] For a discussion of Austria's relationship to German-speaking intellectual life since the eighteenth century, this definition leaves a great deal to be clarified.[35]

In 1843, an experienced administrator of the Habsburg lands, Victor Andrian-Werburg, pointed out that "Austria is a purely imaginary name, which does not signify an enclosed people or a land or a nation; it is a conventional term for a complex of sharply different nationalities."[36] Between 1804 and 1866, there was literally an Austrian Empire as proclaimed by Kaiser Franz while Napoleon was dismantling the Holy Roman Empire.[37] Using the term "Austria" to refer to the Habsburg Monarchy makes most sense for this period and for diplomatic and military history, but it is not very useful for intellectual history.[38] Indeed, R. J. W. Evans regards the use of the term "Austria" to refer to the Habsburg Monarchy as "incorrect and mischievous" for matters beyond diplomatic history. There have been a great many variations of usage over time, but I am concerned with finding a reasonable usage for intellectual history from the Enlightenment to the middle of the twentieth century, one that makes the Austrian context visible.[39]

The inclusion of Bohemia as part of the Austrian tradition is crucial for understanding the nature of Austrian intellectual life since the eighteenth century, especially the impact of the Enlightenment, but also the wider reception of German culture. This conception of Austria as the lands administered by the Austrian-Bohemian Chancellery is essential for locating and understanding central figures of Austrian intellectual history such as Bolzano, Stifter, and Ernst Mach. Indeed, there is no way to adequately tell the story of Austrian philosophy without Bohemia. Austria's connection to Bohemia was much more fundamental and enduring in intellectual terms than Austria's connection to Hungary or Galicia. There is good reason to think of Hungary and its intellectual history primarily as a separate story, whereas the narrative of Bohemia and Moravia is necessarily a hybrid, an integral part of Austria from 1749 (and really much earlier) until 1918, but the core of a new Czechoslovakian state after 1918.

The story of Hungary has nearly always been clearly distinct from Austria, ranging from Hungary's separation from the rest of the Monarchy during the occupation by the Ottoman Turks between 1526 and the 1680s to its virtually complete political independence under the terms of the Compromise or *Ausgleich* between 1867 and 1918. Twice in the late seventeenth and early eighteenth centuries, the Habsburgs acknowledged the special privileges of the Magyar aristocracy and gentry in return for the recognition of the dynasty.[40] Intellectually, the difference between Hungary and Bohemia is still more dramatic because of the administrative role of Latin in Hungary down to 1848 and the place of Hungarian in politics thereafter. The contrast to Bohemia could hardly be more striking: for Bohemia and Moravia, political independence within the Monarchy was never achieved after 1526, despite the vibrant intellectual life of Bohemia and the blossoming of the Czech language in the fifteenth and sixteenth centuries. What also gave Bohemia a special relationship to Austria and to German culture was its importance for the history of the Holy Roman Empire from the tenth century. From the 1740s to 1848, German was the dominant language in Austria and Bohemia and the basis for intellectual life, while 1848–1918 was a period of bilingual transition that culminated in new Czech and Austrian states after the collapse of the Monarchy at the end of the First World War.[41]

Johann Allmayer-Beck, in his discussion of the extent and variety of the Habsburg lands, emphasized the fundamental "structural distinctions" within the Monarchy, especially "between the German and Bohemian hereditary lands on the one hand and the lands of the Crown of Stephen on the other."[42] This basic distinction is too often overlooked on the assumption that the Monarchy was a coherent unity. The modern state did begin to consolidate the historically quite various Habsburg lands in the 1740s, but absolutism in Austria was only selectively successful, above all in unifying the administration of the German and Bohemian hereditary lands. Gary Cohen and Pieter Judson have drawn attention to the important place of Bohemia in our conception of nineteenth-century Austria, especially for German-speaking liberals. This view of Bohemia's special relationship to Austria in the nineteenth century is implicit (or even explicit) in much recent historical work, but it has for the most part not been integrated into discussions of Austrian literature, philosophy, and social science.[43]

This book aims to locate Austrian intellectual history in a way that will make possible a fuller and more nuanced intellectual history of Europe. What is needed is a better understanding of a German intellectual life that was located not in Berlin, Tübingen, and Weimar, but in Vienna, Prague, and the rest of the Habsburg Monarchy to the west of the Leitha River. Such a clarification would provide a framework that would be helpful to the development of Austrian intellectual history as a field and to European history more broadly. Thinking about Austrian intellectual history is also a way to open up our reading of German intellectual history, to disturb the fixed norms and teleological assumptions of German literary history or the assumption that German idealism was dominant wherever German was spoken in the nineteenth century. This book attempts to open up new relationships and connections that are ordinarily left implicit or ignored entirely because of the conventions of political nationalism, literary history, and the history of philosophy. In relation to assumptions of Austrians about their own cultural and intellectual traditions, my concern is close to Walter Benjamin's when he warned: "In every era the attempt must be made anew to wrest tradition away from a conformism that is about to overpower it."[44]

Chapter 1 introduces the reader to Central Europe, especially to the history of Austria and Bohemia before modern German culture and to the emergence of a modern Austrian state out of the Austrian and Bohemian hereditary lands. Chapter 2 describes the development of modern Austrian intellectual history from the emergence of modern German culture in the mid-eighteenth century to the dissolution and absorption of Austria and Czechoslovakia by the Third Reich in 1938/1939. Chapter 3 addresses the history of philosophy in Austria, emphasizing Bernard Bolzano, Ernst Mach, Franz Brentano, Ludwig Wittgenstein, and the Vienna Circle. Chapter 4 describes the place of Austrian literature within German literature, beginning with Franz Grillparzer and Adalbert Stifter, characterizing the literary and intellectual life of the liberal era, and culminating in the work of Robert Musil, Karl Kraus, Hermann Broch, Hugo von Hofmannsthal, Franz Kafka, and Rainer Maria Rilke. Finally, Chapter 5 considers the less examined subject of the human sciences in the Austrian tradition, emphasizing the contributions of the liberal era and the early twentieth century to economic and social theory and psychoanalysis.[45]

I have tried to begin with the state of the scholarship within the various fields that make up this book—and to build on that. My own book can only be provisional—a beginning, a way to make visible what has not been seen. This is one major reason for the organization of my book, so that Chapters 2, 3, 4, and 5 concentrate in turn on history (though on the history of Austrian history itself only indirectly), philosophy, literature, and social thought.[46] The main exception here is Chapter 1, which sets out from geography and historical context. There is no agreement among historians about how to talk about this region. Here I have presented a new narrative in a synthetic way. Even within the field of history, I have had to work against the grain of at least three fields and conceptions of history—Austrian, German, and Czech—and often even a fourth—European— and its chronological divisions of early modern and medieval.

The theme of this book is the German-speaking intellectual history of Cisleithanian Austria. I am not comparing Austrian intellectual history to the intellectual history of the modern German state, but rather locating this region in relation to the broader realm of German-speaking intellectual life in Central Europe. I do not assume that we know the essence of Imperial German intellectual life,[47] and I am not claiming to identify the essence of Austrian intellectual life. My approach attempts to distinguish Austrian intellectual history from the intellectual history of the Habsburg Monarchy as a whole, but also from Hungarian intellectual history and Polish intellectual history (as well as from German intellectual history in Galicia and Hungary). Implicit in my argument is the view that the intellectual experience of Germans and Czechs in Bohemia and Austria cannot be separated from Austrian intellectual history.[48] I offer this way of thinking as a more constructive approach to the intellectual history of Central Europe, whether in Cisleithanian Austria or in the nation-states of Central Europe.

In 1960 Robert A. Kann pointed out in *A Study in Austrian Intellectual History: From Late Baroque to Romanticism* that "[h]istorians of the future will still have to meet the challenging task of writing the comprehensive German-Austrian intellectual history." The value of the project Kann called for is generally acknowledged, but there is no clear agreement in the field about what a narrative of German-Austrian intellectual history should look like. I want to think from a twenty-first-century perspective about how to configure Austrian intellectual history in relation to national and imperial narratives in Central Europe. The underlying aim for me is to conceive an intellectual history of Austria that is not determined by traditional Habsburg historiography, by the Dual Monarchy, by German nationalism, or by the conventions of Austro-German literature. My book helps us to see relations among many ways of thinking and to see these ways of thinking in relation to an historical and geographical space. I want to move beyond the often-fruitless debates about what is German and what is

Austrian to find an analytically useful way to think about the intellectual history of this region. This book is not about the relationship between Austria and Germany, but about the place of an Austrian intellectual tradition within the German-speaking intellectual world that took form in the eighteenth century. This account of Austrian intellectual life focusses on Cisleithanian Austria from 1740 to 1938/1939. The region began as the Archduchy of Austria and the Kingdom of Bohemia, and in 1918 it divided into the Republic of German-Austria and the Republic of Czechoslovakia. Cisleithanian Austria established peculiar conditions for intellectual life, not just in Vienna but in Prague as well, not just in the Archduchy of Austria but in the Kingdom of Bohemia as well. This book aims to make that intellectual world more visible. This thinking about German-speaking intellectual history in (Cisleithanian) Austria is not intended as a survey but as a new way of thinking about German-speaking intellectual history in Austria. My story begins around 1740 as cosmopolitan German culture began to emerge across Central Europe.

1

Austria and Bohemia before the Austrian State

The long historical connection between Austria and Bohemia since at least the twelfth century is a distinctive aspect of the Austrian tradition, portrayed most beautifully in Adalbert Stifter's historical novel *Witiko: Eine Erzählung*.[1] This connection between Austria and Bohemia was built into the Holy Roman Empire and into the whole history of Austria, especially after Rudolf Habsburg's defeat of Ottokar II of Bohemia in 1278.[2] This relationship continued to intensify with the Reformation and the Counter-Reformation and with the formal legal relationship between these lands, beginning with the personal union of 1526 and escalating to the Battle of White Mountain in 1620 and the administrative union of 1749. Despite the antagonisms of the seventeenth century, which recall in some respects the American Civil War, Austria and Bohemia were closer than ever before.

As a multinational monarchy, the Habsburg Monarchy was never entirely German, and modern German culture did not exist before the middle of the eighteenth century.[3] The intellectual life of the hereditary lands was shaped by the many languages, religions, political territories, and ways of life of its peoples. Its intellectual history after 1740 cannot be adequately described without addressing the complex and confusing past that came together over centuries in ways that are still poorly known and poorly understood.[4] When I speak of "Austrian intellectual history" in this book, I am not referring to an empire or to a dynastic house or to a nation, but to a region of Central Europe with a common past, that is, the region of overlap between the Holy Roman Empire and the Habsburg Monarchy after 1740: what the Austrians called Cisleithanian Austria, that is, Austria to the west of the Leitha River.[5] No coherent historical narrative exists for this region, and for modern eyes its unity is difficult to imagine—although it is the space of Austrian intellectual history, of Bolzano and Wittgenstein, of Musil and Mach, of Rilke and Broch, of Menger and Freud.[6]

The modern Austrian state was created during the eighteenth century out of the Habsburg dynastic lands of Austria and Bohemia, that is, the German hereditary lands of the Archduchy of Austria and the Kingdom of Bohemia (and Moravia).[7] Both the Archduchy and the Kingdom had belonged for centuries to the Holy Roman Empire, and the imperial title had devolved in the late Middle Ages to the princes of these southeastern lands.[8] A distinguished institutional historian of the eighteenth century explains that "the Austrian lands and those of the Bohemian Crown were spoken of as 'the Hereditary Lands' (*die Erbländer*), or, again confusingly, 'the German Hereditary lands.'" Scholars in the field commonly refer to these lands together as "the central lands of the Monarchy,"[9] and they became the basis for the state created by Maria Theresa and Joseph II in the eighteenth century. This state was in turn the basis for German-speaking intellectual life in Austria, and it is the realm of Austrian intellectual history that is described in this book. This chapter aims to make visible this historic core of the Austrian state as it emerged between the high Middle Ages and the eighteenth century. This state also became the basis over the next century and a half for what Jan Křen has called a conflict-community of Germans and Czechs.[10]

Austrian historiography has generally followed either the story of the Habsburg dynasty in Central Europe or the story of the lands along the Danube near Vienna. Other areas accrued to this story over the centuries, from Alpine Austria to the Adriatic, and from Bohemia to Hungary and Galicia. The unity of these stories is usually not clear, and the terminology is frequently contradictory. Generally, it is an imperial narrative that provides the coherence: although this is not the narrative of the Holy Roman Empire, but the narrative of the Habsburg Monarchy between 1526 and 1918.[11] The narrative of this Monarchy grows out of the medieval lands of the Babenbergs and ends with the Austrian republics in the twentieth century. Bohemia and Hungary appear as more or less parallel imperial acquisitions, as do the many lands that belonged to this empire from Italy to the Low Countries to Galicia.

Historians of Central Europe have either subordinated Bohemia to this Habsburg narrative after 1526 or emphasized the history of the Czech nation. The latter narrative is usually written as the prelude to Czechoslovakia and the Czech Republic, emphasizing Bohemia and Moravia but minimizing the roles of Germans, Habsburgs, and Catholics. This national and anti-imperial narrative generally has little interest in what Bohemia shares with Austria, although historians of Bohemia are well aware that the experience of Bohemia was quite different from the experience of Hungary. This situation is not very helpful for Austrian intellectual history. This chapter draws attention to the common political and religious experience of Bohemia and Austria and how this region became the basis for the modern Austrian state—and for my account of the Austrian dimension in modern German intellectual life between 1740 and 1938/1939.[12]

***

The modern Austrian state of the eighteenth century was built on lands that lay to the southeast of what is Germany today. The Austrian lands are close to the Mediterranean and dominated by the Alps, while the region north of the Danube belongs to the Bohemian landmass, which extends to the Carpathians. This terrain is linked by forests that reach to Bavaria in the West, and it is protected by mountains to the North and West. As late as the seventeenth century, the area that became the Austrian lands still had not been unified politically or religiously, although it had been included for some time in the Holy Roman Empire. The territory that became Bohemia and Moravia was more remote from the Mediterranean, at the heart of Europe, and it received the influence of both Eastern and Western Christianity.[13] When the Romans appeared along the Danube in the second century BCE, they established friendly relations with the Celts in what was then known as Noricum and eventually extended their authority into the region around Vindobona, which later became Vienna.[14] Roman soldiers were quartered nearby in Carnuntum, although they were withdrawn from this region by the fifth century. The Roman Emperor Marcus Aurelius (121–180 CE) was engaged in defending the region against German invasions from the North, and he considered establishing a Marcomanian province in the area that is Bohemia and Moravia today. As he accompanied his army along the Danube, he wrote what is usually known as his *Meditations*, and his life and work became key points of reference for modern Austrian intellectuals about their past, as did these Roman origins more generally. In this sense, we might say that the most important early text of Austrian intellectual history is a Roman text, although it was written in Greek.[15]

This region's permeability to the South and the East was apparent throughout its history. It was not only easily accessible to the Romans in the South but also vulnerable to shocks from the East, most dramatically from Attila the Hun in the fourth century and from Ghengis Khan almost a millennium later. From the sixth century to the ninth, the region was dominated by conflicts between German and Slavic tribes. In 799 a military march was established at the edge of Charlemagne's empire; Bavarians, Franconians, and Alemanni migrated to what became the boundary of the Holy Roman Empire, and the Babenberg princes established themselves as the ruling family in this border region.[16] Before the arrival of the Czechs in Bohemia around the sixth century, that region had also been inhabited by a Celtic people. In the ninth century the Byzantine Emperor sent Cyril and Methodius on a mission to the Great Moravian Empire, where they introduced the Slavonic liturgical language. Bohemia and Moravia were later integrated into the Catholic world, and in 955 the advance of the Magyars from the East was stopped at Lechfeld by Otto I to establish the boundaries of the Empire. Meanwhile, the Slovak territory to the east of Moravia had a very different history under the Magyars. The Slovaks were linguistically similar to the people of Bohemia and Moravia, but they were isolated in the very different intellectual and cultural world of Hungary until 1918. The separation of the Slovaks from Bohemia in 1031 defined the border between Moravia and Hungary down to the First World War.

The Přemyslid princes emerged in Bohemia in the ninth century and unified Bohemia and Moravia. In the thirteenth century Bohemia was shaped by increasing German influence and by the immigration of Germans, mainly to the towns. Přemysl Ottokar II's reign (1253–1278) marked a highpoint of German influence in Bohemia, and it included extensive acquisitions in Austria and Inner Austria. After the failure of the Hohenstaufen to centralize the Holy Roman Empire, the Habsburgs in Austria and the Luxemburgs in Bohemia rose to prominence as imperial dynasties in the thirteenth and fourteenth centuries. These families ruled in Austria and Bohemia; and for much of the late medieval and early modern periods, all of these lands were ruled together, whether from Prague or from Vienna.

Rudolf of Habsburg, a Swabian count from the southwestern part of the Holy Roman Empire, was elected German King and Emperor in 1273; in 1278, at the Battle of Marchfeld he defeated the efforts of Ottokar Přemysl II to control the region to the South of Bohemia. In so doing Rudolf brought Austria and Styria into the Habsburg lands and established Habsburg rule in the lands of the Babenbergs.[17] Rudolf made the Austrian provinces along the Danube a hereditary duchy in 1282. The lands to the south of the ducal lands were often ruled separately and were referred to as Inner Austria. Even in the late Middle Ages, the duchies and kingdoms of this region were closely related, whether by elective or hereditary rule or by commonalities of religion or ancestral alliance. The connections within what we think of as Austria today were nearly as loose as the connections of Upper and Lower Austria to Bohemia and Moravia, and the Habsburgs were by no means always the senior partners in the relationships among these principalities. Relationships among these lands varied, but Bohemia and Moravia were generally associated with each other (and often referred to together as Bohemia), as were Lower and Upper Austria.

The Luxemburg family played a major role in this region and in the Holy Roman Empire in the fourteenth century. The medieval glories of Prague were achieved during the reign of Charles IV, who was King of Bohemia and Emperor of the Holy Roman Empire. He made Prague the imperial capital and a cosmopolitan city, as well as the home of the first university in Central Europe.[18] This region was influenced by the cultural currents of Italy and the Renaissance throughout this period, in architecture, music, science, and literature.[19] Charles IV was sympathetic to the Czech language and contributed to the early efforts at reform in the church, but German also played an important role in the intellectual life of Prague along with Latin and Czech.

Perhaps the greatest figure of Czech history, Jan Hus, confronted the papacy at the Council of Basel in 1415,[20] and the enormous impact of his ideas led to Bohemia's near independence from the Holy Roman Empire in the fifteenth century. Hus was influenced by John Wyclif's ideas, and developments in Bohemia were similar in some respects to the English experience in the fourteenth century, but the struggle in Bohemia for an evangelical reform of the Roman Church was quite individual and extraordinary—it was as dramatic and fundamental as Luther's reforms a century later.[21] Out of this grew what came to be known as Hussitism, including both a moderate tradition (the Utraquists), much like Anglicanism, and a more radical movement that was revolutionary (for which the term "Hussite" is often reserved).[22] The Brethren grew out of the Hussite movement after 1450. Frederick Heymann has described the events of the fifteenth century as "by all odds one of the greatest dynamic movements for socio-political and spiritual freedom in all history," and yet Germans and Americans seem to have little awareness of the Bohemian Reformation.[23] The account of the early modern period in terms of Calvinists, Lutherans, and Jesuits does not do justice to the permanent impact of Utraquism (which is Latin for lay communion in both kinds) in Bohemia, even despite the fact that many of the Unity of Brethren emigrated after 1620.[24]

The victory of the Ottoman Empire at the Battle of Mohács in 1526 marked a profound transformation in the history of Central Europe: the defeat and death of the Polish King at Mohács meant the consolidation of the Habsburg line in Austria, Bohemia, and Hungary. Hungary appeared to join Austria and Bohemia at this time, but it did so only in a very partial way because of the invasion of the Ottoman Turks and the very different traditions and conditions in Hungary, which was never part of the Holy Roman Empire. The defeat of Louis II of Poland meant that the Ottoman Empire remained deep in Hungary until a second Siege of Vienna by Suleiman the Magnificent in 1683 and a dramatic reversal in the Second Battle of Mohács in 1687.[25] The Turkish threat created a new situation for early modern Europe, which increased the importance of Atlantic trade routes and strengthened the hand of the Catholic Habsburgs in Bohemia. For a long time, at least until the end of the seventeenth century, Hungary's place in the story of the Habsburg Monarchy was quite marginal, primarily because of the three-way division of Hungary among the Habsburgs, Transylvania, and the Ottoman Empire.

In 1526 Charles V of Habsburg became the Holy Roman Emperor and assumed the Spanish inheritance, while his younger brother Ferdinand received the family inheritance in Central Europe, which included Bohemia and Hungary after 1526, and, after 1556, the imperial title. For this new Central European realm, the decisive crown was the kingdom of Bohemia, which was also an elector in the Holy Roman Empire. In this regard, the Habsburgs succeeded to the legacy of Charles IV and the Luxemburg line in Bohemia, and in 1583 Rudolf II (1576–1612) made Prague rather than Vienna the imperial capital. He also made Prague a center of religious tolerance and heterodoxy, Renaissance humanism, modern science, and the arts.[26] The early sixteenth century was a period of

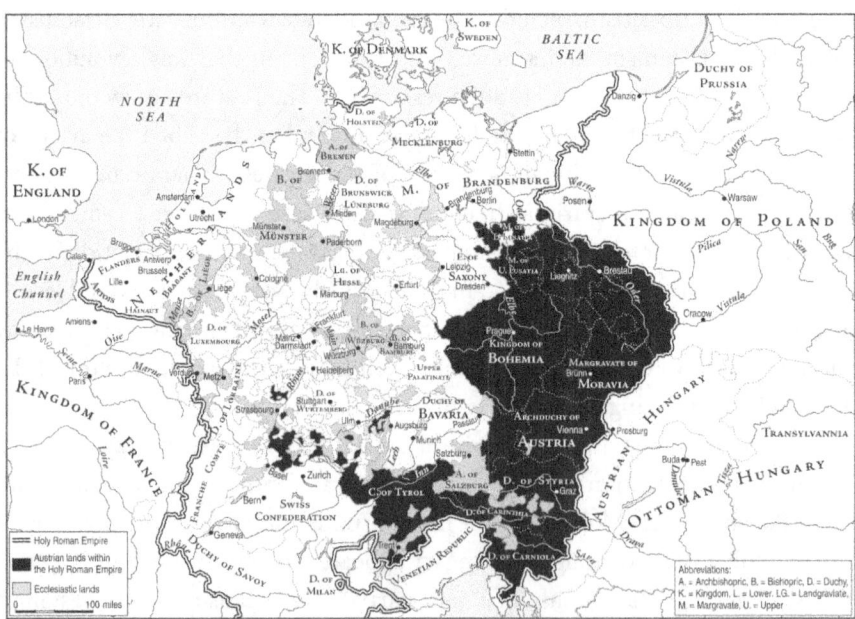

Map 3 Principalities of the Holy Roman Empire, c. 1547. © Cartography by Philip Schwartzberg, Meridian Mapping, Minneapolis.

delicate balance in Bohemia and Austria between Lutherans and Catholics, formalized in the Peace of Augsburg in 1555. Charles V and Ferdinand were both Erasmian reformers of the church, but this humanist middle way did not set the tone after 1555.[27] The Peace of Augsburg in 1555 might have been a good solution for Austria except for the emergence of Calvinism and the Council of Trent.[28] By the early seventeenth century, the Calvinists and the Jesuits mirrored each other as the transformative and polarizing forces in Europe. The Jesuits with their distinctive reform-style had already arrived in Prague by 1555, and they worked closely with the Habsburgs.

The Reformation played an enormous role in Austria, Bohemia, and Moravia and was never entirely driven out. In the sixteenth century Protestantism depended heavily on the German language, and areas such as Bohemia and Silesia had close links to Prussia and Saxony. As the Enlightenment arrived in the Monarchy during the eighteenth century, these links to German and Protestant traditions were important, as were the links to the Low Countries and France. By the early seventeenth century Bohemia had one of the most interesting and varied Protestant cultures in Europe, and, shortly before his deposition, Rudolf II reached an agreement with the Estates, The Letter of Majesty of 1609, which guaranteed religious freedom not only for the Utraquists but also for the Lutherans and the Unity of Brethren.[29] Politics and religion were closely interwoven throughout the early modern period. For politics, religion, and literary culture, Latin was dominant at the beginning of the period, but humanism and the Reformation made both German and Czech more significant, especially through translations of the Bible into the vernacular. The Czech equivalent of the King James Version of the Bible appeared in 1613, and it is a good index of the high literary level of the Czech language at that time. The Kralice Bible was produced by the Bohemian Brethren in the late sixteenth century, and the great cultural achievements of this tiny group culminated in the work of John Amos Comenius (1592–1670) in the early seventeenth century.[30] Currents of conciliation and resistance to Roman power were connected in unstable ways that eventually lost out to polarization. This was a European phenomenon, but Bohemia became the center of the struggle.

After Rudolf II was deposed by his Catholic relatives in 1612, conflicts between Catholicism and Protestantism intensified throughout Europe. When Ferdinand of Styria became emperor in 1619, his quarrel was primarily with aristocrats who feared that Catholicism would be imposed in Bohemia as it had been in Inner Austria.[31] Frederick V, the Calvinist Elector Palatine, was chosen to be King of Bohemia in 1619, and the confrontation between the Bohemian

Estates and the Habsburgs took center stage in the ensuing catastrophe of the Thirty Years' War. Catholicism and loyalty to the Habsburgs were the issues at White Mountain rather than nationalism. Ferdinand II (1619–1637) defeated the attempt of the Bohemian nobility to install a Calvinist prince, first at the Battle of White Mountain in 1620 and then in the imposition of Catholicism. The Calvinist challenge to the Habsburgs was only one response (and not the shrewdest or most diplomatic one) in a prolonged conflict that had begun at least a century before the Lutheran Reformation. These events were only one episode in the story of the polarization between Jesuits and Calvinists, and the European power struggles that kept this war going until 1648 did great damage to Bohemia and Austria—and to the rest of Central Europe.[32] This was an important period for forming the identities of the Habsburg lands as they grew out of the Middle Ages. While England and many of the German states were shaped by Protestant victories, in the Habsburg Monarchy it was Catholicism that triumphed after 1620. The peculiar association of Catholicism with the German language in this context was a crucial factor in the way intellectual life developed in Austria.[33] The destruction of Central Europe furthered the triumph of the Counter-Reformation in Bohemia and Austria, as well as the power of the nobility and the oppression of the peasantry. The seventeenth century was also a period when much of the intellectual vitality of Central Europe was lost, and the events of the Reformation and the Counter-Reformation strengthened the hand of the state in the church and paved the way for the state church in the eighteenth century.

A Catholic, aristocratic Austria, often referred to in retrospect as Baroque, was the product of the Catholic Reformation and of the reassertion of Habsburg leadership.[34] The culmination of the Baroque in the late seventeenth century was an era of glory and prestige, the age of Prince Eugene of Savoy, and it has played a large role in conceptions of what is Austrian—and these are, of course, powerfully stamped by the city of Vienna, at a time when the imperial residence was no longer in Prague.[35] After the military victories against the Turks, the Habsburgs crowned the age of the Baroque with many of the splendid architectural monuments that remain the signature of Austria, Bohemia, and other Habsburg lands down to the present.[36] The Habsburg Monarchy may not have been a great power in the early eighteenth century, but it certainly had the appearance of one, and the extent of its lands and its military achievements against France led Europeans to regard it this way. In the early eighteenth century, Charles VI and Prince Eugene attempted to create a unified state, what Prince Eugene called *ein totum* [a whole], and to persuade Europe to recognize the unity of the Habsburg lands in Central Europe in the probable event of a female heir.[37]

Their failure to achieve a unified Monarchy meant that the Habsburg lands were nearly dismembered when Maria Theresa came to the throne; and a unified state had still not been created by 1740, when Maria Theresa became Archduchess of Austria and Queen of Bohemia and Hungary, but not the Empress of the Holy Roman Empire.

R. J. W. Evans has described the consolidation of the Habsburg Monarchy between 1550 and 1700 as a process by which the Habsburgs mastered the dislocations of the Renaissance and Reformation in a way that allowed them to rule in their many lands that were very different from each other. The Habsburgs achieved this with an imperial and Catholic ideology that was similar in some respects to French absolutism, and yet their Monarchy was "not a 'state' but a mildly centripetal agglutination of bewilderingly heterogeneous elements."[38] In the eighteenth century the Habsburg Monarchy was spread out across Europe from what is now Belgium to Italy and what is now Romania, but the core of this Monarchy and the basis for its standing army were the Austrian and Bohemian lands.

There were many stages in the creation of a centralized Austrian state out of a variety of medieval institutions, but the decisive discontinuity came with the War of Austrian Succession (1740–1748) and the ensuing reforms of the late 1740s.[39] The best estimates indicate that there were about six million people living in Austria and Bohemia at this time.[40] The Kingdom of Bohemia included Bohemia proper, Moravia, and Silesia (most of which was lost to Prussia in the 1740s). Bohemia and Moravia were the principal lands of the Crown of St. Wenceslaus and constituted roughly the area of today's Czech Republic. This centralization of the Austrian and Bohemian lands was largely successful, and it created the basis for a modern state that allowed Austria to survive until 1918. In practice the new arrangements meant a union of Austria and Bohemia in which Bohemian aristocrats played increasingly important, often dominant, roles. This was most dramatically clear in Kaunitz's leadership of the new state under Maria Theresa and Joseph II.

In 1749, the advisors of the Habsburgs began the process of creating the internal conditions for a modern state in Austria, but these efforts focused on Cisleithanian Austria.[41] The reforms of Maria Theresa and Count Haugwitz (1702–1765), including the administrative centralization of Bohemia and Austria, lasted for the duration of the Monarchy. Prince Wenzel Kaunitz-Rietberg (1711–1794) was central to the second phase of reform in the 1760s, and he, like Haugwitz, regarded the Bohemian and Austrian lands as the "heart of the Monarchy."[42] A. J. P. Taylor went so far as to call Maria Theresa "the founder of

Dualism," that is of the separation of Austria from Hungary, because she pursued reform in the hereditary lands but not in Hungary: "Every advance in the hereditary lands made Hungary more of an exception politically and socially."[43] Under Maria Theresa, Joseph II, and Leopold II (1790–1792), the Austrians created a modern, enlightened, absolutist state. The formation of a modern state (including the state-church) also meant the creation of a new bureaucratic stratum. Austria and Bohemia were effectively united under a single chancellery, and an enlightened bureaucracy took over the task of educating their people and bringing them economically and socially into the modern world.[44] Their rule was both authoritarian—in the strictest sense of the word—and modernizing.

The reforms of Maria Theresa and Haugwitz were initially motivated by practical considerations arising from the War of Austrian Succession and the problems of governing the hereditary lands: raising taxes and an army and replacing the old aristocratic regime with a centralized state administration. But the administrators who were charged with accomplishing this, as well as Maria Thersesa's sons, were increasingly influenced by the reception of the ideas of the Enlightenment—of science, education, and human improvement—from Western Europe, especially from France, the Low Countries, and Great Britain. This ideology of understanding and improvement was easy to reconcile with the concerns of the newly emerging modern state.

Maria Theresa and (after 1765) her son worked hard to reform and modernize the Austrian state. Haugwitz and Kaunitz generally had sound ideas about what was needed to improve the lives of the Austrian people and the effectiveness of the Austrian state, and Maria Theresa steadily sustained the work of finding other leadership—from Gerard van Swieten (1700–1772) to Franz Stephan Rautenstrauch (1734–1785).[45] From the start, the process of reform was tied to issues of the church (the central institution of the society) and to the redirection of church wealth (especially monasteries) to education and to priestly work in the parishes.[46] From at least the late 1760s the desperate condition of the peasantry, primarily Czechs in Bohemia and Moravia, was also a major issue. It was understood that economic modernization and productivity would not be possible without reform in the countryside, and Maria Theresa's modest reform of 1775 began to limit the lord with respect to work obligations or *robot* in Bohemia.

The emergence of the Enlightenment in Austria was intimately connected with the creation of a modern state in Austria and Bohemia under the three reform monarchs from 1740 to 1792. Joseph II (like Leopold II) was a child of the Enlightenment as Maria Theresa was not, and yet there was great continuity

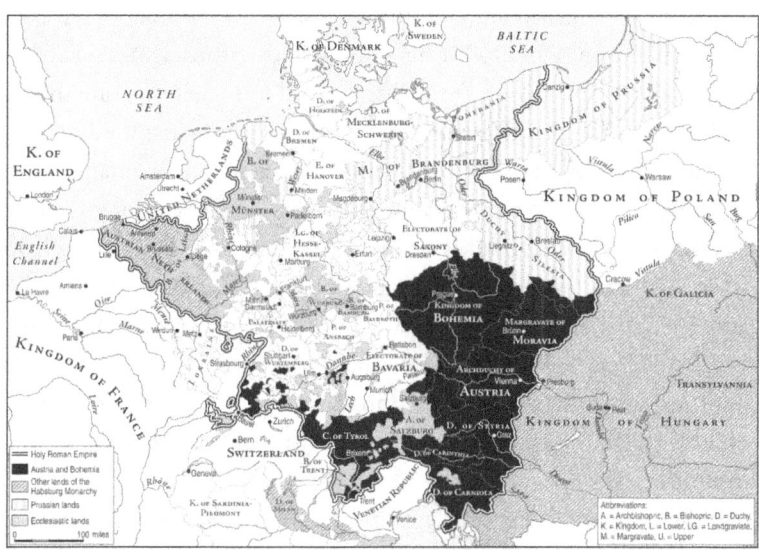

Map 4 Central Europe, 1780. © Cartography by Philip Schwartzberg, Meridian Mapping, Minneapolis.

between Maria Theresia's regime and her son's. Their reigns overlapped for fifteen years, and Joseph inherited Kaunitz, his principal counsellor, from his mother.[47] Another key advisor to Joseph, Gottfried van Swieten (1734–1803), was the son of Maria Theresa's court physician, Gerard van Swieten. Although Joseph II changed the tone and pace of reform between 1780 and 1790, the period from 1740 to 1792 was a single period of enlightened monarchy and reform in which Austria was sufficiently modernized and reformed to endure war and revolution and last into the twentieth century.[48]

The reforms of this period came to be known as Josephinism. Since this term was coined in 1837, it is nearly always anachronistic and it can have a variety of overlapping and surprising applications. "Josephinism" was a term that came to be used in the nineteenth century to refer to the Austrian Enlightenment (including the reforms of Maria Theresa and Joseph II).[49] For some commentators the word referred to the bureaucratic centralism of the new Austrian state, for others, to the reform Catholicism that reshaped the church and education in the hereditary lands. Thus, Josephinism can refer both to the reform bureaucracy and to the reform clergy, that is, to the people who administered the Austrian state, rather than the aristocracy and the Counter-Reformation church. This rationalized Catholicism set the tone for the Austrian church well into the nineteenth century.⁵⁰ Joseph II's rationalist style marked this period of reform, along with his energy and enthusiasm. Josephinism in the church meant a transition from display and spectacle to something more sober and inward, but also from contemplation to pragmatism. Funds from the mediatization of the monasteries became the basis for more practical work by priests and for support to schools and hospitals—and for a long-term impact on Austrian society throughout the nineteenth century. Josephinism helped to shape what William Johnston has characterized as Austria's social capital.⁵¹ This conception was a challenge to aristocratic rule, but by no means a form of liberal or representative government. These changes separated the Austrian church from Baroque Catholicism, but continued the commitment to Catholicism. Intellectually, this meant a tradition of reason and empiricism that became the basis for modern science.

Joseph's achievements, especially immediately after his mother's death, were of undeniable importance: the Patent of Toleration (which granted freedom of worship to Lutherans, Calvinists, Greek Orthodox, and Jews), the Secularization of the Monasteries, and the personal emancipation of the peasantry. These edicts symbolize what might be called the liberal legacy of the Josephinist tradition, the legal basis for the "unbound man" of modern culture.⁵² This period was also marked by the beginnings of tolerance and freedom that laid the basis for the emancipation of the peasants in Bohemian and Moravia and the emergence of a modern, urban society. These reforms were accomplished before the French Revolution, the Prussian Reform Movement, and the achievements of British utilitarianism. At the same time, however, it is misleading to think of Joseph II as liberal. He believed in censorship, which grew more apparent in the later years of his reign, and he was very much an absolutist monarch. Moreover, he died with some of his most important reforms still incomplete. His abolition of personal servitude was a crucial precondition of the liberal era nearly a century later, but the practical aspects of emancipation were still not resolved when Joseph II died in 1790; and the process of peasant emancipation was not completed until 1848, to be sure earlier than in Russia or than the emancipation of the slaves in the United States. These reforms of Cisleithanian Austria established the basis for modern Austrian intellectual life, and Robert Kann emphasizes the ideological and emotional impact of Josephinism, which effected a "profound change in the spiritual climate of civilization in Austria."⁵³

It is sometimes confusing for Americans and West Europeans to have political and religious leadership described with the same term, let alone to have the term refer to the Austrian Enlightenment as a whole. What is most often passed over about Josephinism is that its administrative practices applied primarily to Cisleithanian Austria rather than to the empire as a whole, whether to Hungary or Italy or the Austrian Netherlands. This region (Cisleithanian Austria) was administered by bureaucrats and clergy in German. The term "Josephinism" came to refer both to the enlightened reforms of the eighteenth century and to bureaucrats and priests who continued to work in this spirit into the nineteenth century. Josephinism was not just an approach to state-administration but also a deeply Christian view of the world. Because of the special importance of the efforts at peasant emancipation and education, Josephinism was associated particularly with Bohemia and Moravia, although it applied to all of Austria to the West of the Leitha River.[54] This region and the changes of the late eighteenth century became the basis for the German-speaking Austrian intellectual life.

2

The Developing Context of Austrian Intellectual Life: 1740–1938/1939

This chapter provides a contextual narrative for the development of modern Austrian intellectual life, an historical framework for readings of Austrian philosophy, literature, and the human sciences. The Austrian intellectual tradition presented in this book grew out of the historical experience of Cisleithanian Austria. This tradition, in the sense of a location for German-speaking intellectual life, took form in the middle of the eighteenth century with the creation of a modern bureaucratic state in the hereditary lands, when these lands connected not only with the European Enlightenment but also with the modern German language and culture that emerged in the 1740s and 1750s in the states of Central Europe.[1] Most work in the field of Austrian intellectual history has concentrated on specific periods, although much of it also aims for a characterization of Austrian thought and culture that is broader and more general than the period it addresses. For example, scholars have often emphasized the Baroque roots of Austrian culture—in its architecture and in its social and religious habitus.[2] This is understandable in relation to the reductive criticisms of an ahistorical modernism and the importance of art, music, and architecture in Austrian culture, but this approach does not place enough emphasis on the distinctive qualities of other periods of Austrian culture and intellectual life, especially the Enlightenment, or on the role of language in intellectual life.

In contrast to efforts to generalize Austrian qualities, I want to draw attention to the historicity and variation in Austrian intellectual life and to characterize four distinct periods: (1) the Enlightenment and the emergence of modern German: 1740–1792; (2) the conservative Josephinist era: 1792–1866; (3) the liberal era: 1867–1900; and (4) the transformations of modern intellectual life: 1900–1938/1939. Periodization is the historian's way of deconstructing broad generalizations and coming to more concrete understandings of the past. For the intellectual historian, periodization provides a helpful way to reshape static presentations of the Austrian tradition.³ Instead of thinking in terms of a uniform Austrian essence that expressed itself through the centuries, it is important to bear in mind that there are significant discontinuities in Austrian intellectual history, whether because of wars and revolutions or because of new constitutional arrangements.

The first period, 1740–1792, began with the administrative unification of Austria and Bohemia and included the reigns of the three reform monarchs of the Enlightenment. In this period the Habsburgs and their advisers created and reformed the Austrian state throughout the hereditary lands—and established the basis for modern intellectual life. The second period, the conservative Josephinist era: 1792–1866, was marked by conservative retrenchment, by the increasing vitality of Czech political and intellectual life, and by the emergence of liberalism, nationalism, and the revolutions of 1848 in Vienna and Prague— and in the rest of the Monarchy and Western Europe. German-speaking intellectual life in Bohemia continued to be important for Austrian intellectual life as a whole, first in the work of Bernard Bolzano and later in the reform of the University of Vienna by the leading figures of intellectual life from Prague. In this Josephinist period, distinctive Austrian traditions emerged in both philosophy and literature. The third period, the liberal era: 1867–1900, began with the political separation of Hungary from Austria and the separation of Austria from Germany. This was the age of the dominance of German-speaking upper-middle-class elites, the age of the unbound man and parliamentary (though not democratic) government in the parliament or *Reichsrat*. Many of the aims of Josephinism came to fruition in cooperation with liberal institutions in Cisleithanian Austria. The center of German-speaking intellectual life was the University of Vienna; there was still a German university in Prague, but a second, Czech-speaking university was established in Prague in 1882, even though speakers of Czech continued to play a subordinate role in the politics of the liberal era. The last period, the transformations of modern intellectual life (1900–1938/1939), was marked by dramatic political upheavals: the First World War, the collapse of the administrative union of Austria and Bohemia as the multinational monarchy was dismembered in 1918–1919, the creation of separate Austrian and Czechoslovakian states, the democratic franchise (first as manhood suffrage before the war and then as universal suffrage afterward in both German-Austria and Czechoslovakia), and the assimilation of both German-Austria and the Czech regions of Czechoslovakia into Nazi Germany in 1938 and 1939. Despite the political traumas of these years, the early twentieth century was a period of great intellectual achievement—above all in literature but also in philosophy, psychoanalysis, and the study of modern capitalism.

Underlying these developments in Austrian intellectual history was the long-term, evolving context of a German-speaking bureaucratic, clerical, professional, and economic elite, an elite that was created in the eighteenth century—largely by Maria Theresa and Joseph II. The history of German-speaking intellectual life in Austria was shaped throughout by the evolving relationship between the German and Czech languages in Cisleithanian Austria. This close relationship figured not only in Bohemia and Moravia, but in the Austrian lands as well; not only did German play an enormous role in Prague and elsewhere in Bohemia and Moravia, but Czechs were an important part of the history of Vienna, especially in the nineteenth century.[4] German-speaking intellectuals in this period were conscious of belonging to German intellectual life in a way that had little to do with a German nation-state, and this situation lasted until 1938/1939, even after the break-up of the Monarchy. In this period that we might call the long nineteenth century, philosophy and literature took the lead intellectually. History as a field did not play as great a role in intellectual life as it did in Germany, but psychology and economics were beginning to emerge out of philosophy, the medical school, and cameralism.

Modern German and the Austrian Enlightenment: 1740–1792

The creation of the modern Austrian state under Maria Theresa and Joseph II took place at the same time that the German language reached maturity in Central Europe, and this happened just as the ideas of the Enlightenment were arriving from Western Europe.[5] Reforming absolutism, modernizing German, and the spread of enlightened ideas were closely related processes in late eighteenth-century Austria. These years shaped both church and state and set the terms for German-speaking intellectual life and for the alliance between Catholicism and the Enlightenment that distinguished German-speaking Austria from the familiar conventions of North German thought. Modern German and the Austrian Enlightenment were intertwined in complex ways, since it was the reception of the Enlightenment in German-speaking culture that helped to create the Austrian state, and the Austrian state that established the conditions for modern German and for intellectual life in Austria. The creation of the Austrian state during the period when modern German emerged was decisive for Austrian intellectual history in ways that are rarely appreciated.

In his study of the emergence of modern literary German, Eric Blackall argued that in the early eighteenth century "there was grave concern in many minds about the state of the German language as a vehicle for literary and intellectual expression. Out of this dissatisfaction emerged one of the great literary languages of modern Europe."[6] But before the middle of the eighteenth century, modern German culture did not exist—that is to say, before Johann Christoph Gottsched, Johann Wolfgang von Goethe, Friedrich Schiller, Immanuel Kant, and Gotthold Ephraim Lessing. Modern literary German is understandably sometimes identified with Goethe's genius and creativity, but his achievements were the culmination of a broader process of the maturation of the German language after Martin Luther. Aspects of this process were guided in intentional ways, whether in the transition from Latin to German in university life after 1740 or in the imposition of a literary language in the mid-eighteenth century or in the decisions of chancelleries and state administrations across the Holy Roman Empire.[7] The modern German I refer to here is the symbolic world of German-speaking intellectual and administrative life as it emerged in the lands (or states) of the Holy Roman Empire in the middle of the eighteenth century. These years correspond to what C. J. Wells calls the early modern period in the development of a language, when "a *literary* language is being imposed as a *standard* language."[8] This eighteenth-century creation of a standard language was the basis for the development of an Austrian literature in the nineteenth century and for modern intellectual life throughout Central Europe.[9] By mid-century the leadership in Vienna had decided to follow the reforms advocated by Gottsched and the Saxons.[10]

German was the language of administration and higher education in Cisleithanian Austria in the late eighteenth century. The Austrian state sought to make the Enlightenment and high German available to its citizens, and German became the language of upper-class social life, both aristocratic and upper-middle class. The Austrian understanding of the Enlightenment was connected to service to the state and to the emergence of modern German. As one of the leading figures of the Austrian Enlightenment, Joseph von Sonnenfels, put it in 1761 in announcing the new Society for German Literature: "we provide our fatherland a service, when we contribute to requiring a complete knowledge of the German language in the business of state, of the sciences, in matters concerning all the social strata, yes even in our domestic arrangements."[11] *Aufklärung* [Enlightenment] and the emergence of modern German were not identical, but they were closely interwoven after 1740.[12] These developments preceded modern German nationalism as we understand it today, and they included Cisleithanian Austria and the new Austrian state.

Modern German and the Enlightenment shaped the new Cisleithanian state, and this became the basis for philosophy, literature, and the human sciences in Austria. In the sixteenth century the Protestant Reformation had spread throughout Austria, but because of the Counter-Reformation, Luther's written German did not become standard until the middle of the eighteenth century. One of the leading experts on Austrian German explains:

> The real adoption of the East Middle German of the Meissner stamp that had been established in mid- and north-German regions succeeded in Austria only with the Enlightenment around 1750 under Empress Maria Theresa ... Because people held the view that the progress that was desired was achievable only with the help of a correct language that was adequate to the expression of the new ideas, the written language of East German stamp found speedy acceptance.

It was not only that Maria Theresa adopted Gottsched's new art of the German language for her Academy for young aristocrats in Vienna, but that this style was broadly accepted as the norm for educated elites and for intellectual and administrative life. In his new Viennese weekly, *Die Welt*, Christian Gottlob Klemm announced that "[p]urity of language is particularly close to our hearts." In 1774 Maria Theresia brought Johann Ignaz von Felbinger (1724–1788) from Prussian Silesia to take charge of the new school reform, including intensive instruction in the new German grammar.[13]

Modern German was quite new in the middle of the eighteenth century, especially its centrality as an intellectual and scholarly medium.[14] I am referring here not to a nation-state but to a geographical region with an intellectual life in German, to "a community of speakers" with an acquired skill rather than an ethnic or national identity.[15] This German-speaking world has little to do with *grossdeutsch* [greater German] ideas, but refers simply to the intellectual world of writers and philosophers. There was potential in the German culture of the Enlightenment to be a universal, cosmopolitan culture, beyond the limits of any particular state, and this was how modern German culture began. This world of German-language-speakers was attractive in the nineteenth century both to Jews and to the educated elites of East European minorities, especially in the Habsburg Monarchy. It held the promise of creating a culture beyond anyone's existing culture, whether Bavarian or Jewish or Prussian or Czech. In the nineteenth century, however, it was gradually tailored to the needs of the German nation-state, of the Central European bourgeoisie, and of those in the Habsburg Monarchy who believed that they had a civilizing mission among the Habsburg peoples, but these are all more specific stories within the history of the German language. As German culture became narrowed to these conceptions—whether for Bismarck's state, for Kafka's father, for the bureaucrats, or for the professors in Vienna and Prague—its transformative power as a universalizing modern culture weakened and became assimilated to conventional norms. But all of this was still contested in the eighteenth century; even in the early nineteenth century, it is a mistake to assume a normative German culture to which Jews or Czechs were assimilated.[16] German culture was being created throughout Central Europe, centrally by Goethe and Schiller, but also by Jews in Berlin and bureaucrats in Vienna, and by scholars in Bohemia and Moravia. Goethe did not belong to Bismarck. Indeed, the two were not even from the same country.

There were many sites of the modern German language and the Enlightenment in eighteenth-century Austria: the state bureaucracy; the church and its related institutions (including monasteries and schools), which under Joseph II and Maria Theresa became part of the state and its administration; the places of education from medical schools to technical training colleges, to elementary schools and universities; the aristocracy in the hereditary lands; scientific societies; salons; the world of music; the Masonic lodges (Maria Theresa's husband and their sons were Masons); and, for a time in the 1780s, a new public sphere of pamphlets and brochures,[17] as well as an incipient literary scene. And it is important to bear in mind the close connection between "the great men" in Vienna and less central developments such as the Benedictine Abbeys in Melk or Kremsmünster or scholars in Bohemia and Moravia.[18] At that time, German was an emerging scientific and scholarly language throughout Central Europe, and we can observe the transition from Latin to German even in a field like comparative Slavistics that was still in its infancy. Prague and Vienna were both part of the renewal of the German language in the late eighteenth century, but these were also places where much of the historical and philological work was done that led to the Czech revival or *obrození* in the nineteenth century. Czech was the other main language of Cisleithanian Austria, and it was refined and modernized in this period to establish its own tradition of modern intellectual history.

The Austrian Enlightenment produced important minds such as Joseph von Sonnenfels (the sciences of state), Joseph Dobrovský (the development of modern Czech), and Wolfgang Amadeus Mozart (the great creative figure of the Austrian Enlightenment). But the decisive intellectual development of this period was a political transformation in the structure of the state—which brought fundamental changes in religion and education, as well as the adoption of German rather than Latin or French as the lingua franca of intellectual life. The intellectual achievements of the eighteenth century were primarily practical and institutional—and closely tied to the creation of a modern, bureaucratic state and a reform church by the Habsburgs and their ministers. In that sense, all of the reformers in the Austrian state were also leading intellectual figures of the Enlightenment; Joachim Whaley emphasizes that in the German states "there was no distinction between intellectuals and administrators,"[19] and this certainly holds for the Catholic Enlightenment in Austria. Figures such as Haugwitz, Kaunitz, Sonnenfels, the van Swietens, Joseph II, and Leopold II were the intellectual as well as the political leaders of Austria. And the state was the main engine of improvement in the eighteenth century. For many of the key figures of Austria in the eighteenth century, German was not their native language, but it was the language in which they worked and published. On the whole, people in the Austrian state in this period furthered language reform—most prominently Sonnenfels. At the same time, neither Sonnenfels nor Dobrovský, for example, was a native speaker of German. Gottfried van Swieten, the son of the Dutch-speaking advisor whom Maria Theresa brought from the Austrian Netherlands, "regarded German as his mother tongue and Austria as his fatherland."[20] These men were accommodating to German for practical purposes, indeed to help the society to work better.

Perhaps the greatest achievement of the Austrian Enlightenment was the reform of education, from the universities under Gerard van Swieten to elementary education under Felbinger and Gottfried van Swieten. More than a generation before the Prussian Reform Movement, Austria put education at the center of Enlightened Reform in the hereditary lands. The university system was now to be run for and by the state—to be utilitarian and aimed at state service, a corresponding reform of the school system as a whole followed under Gerard van Swieten.[21] And here it was the clergy who were decisive. David Sorkin has argued that a positive attitude toward religion was the mainstream of the European Enlightenment from the Glorious Revolution to the French Revolution: "influential figures of all the religions not only condoned the Enlightenment but understood it as a means to renew and rearticulate their faith as well as to serve the cause of a common morality and domestic tranquility."[22] This was very much the case in Austria, where there was little opposition between the Enlightenment and religion, whether Catholic or Jewish.

Maria Theresa and Joseph II were both devout Catholics, but Joseph II's church moved away from Baroque Catholicism in a way that sometimes functioned as a quiet reformation. James Van Horn Melton describes the educational and religious reforms of this period in Austria as a "shift away from 'image culture' toward 'word culture,'" away from the Baroque culture of display and processions to a more internal culture of the Bible and education. Pietist inwardness became central to educational reform in Catholic Austria when Felbinger incorporated the Pietist pedagogy of Silesia into reform Catholicism. Melton argues that "in 1774, the Austrian monarchy undertook the most ambitious reform of elementary education on the European continent," and educational reforms brought literate culture, education, and the Bible to Austria.[23] It was not until the 1840s that Count Leo Thun created more independent scholarly and educational institutions for the university. For the men around Van Swieten, Felbinger, and Rautenstrauch, a thorough theological education was crucial to Enlightenment reform. They believed that knowledge of the Bible provided the basis for natural religion. They wanted to move beyond the old dogmatic quarrels of theology to a view that embraced science, morality, and one God who rules and influences human action.

The Josephinist Catholicism of the 1780s emphasized the ethical (and rational) rather than the otherworldly (and miraculous). The new territorial church made the religious and political aspects of Josephinism difficult to distinguish from each other, and the clergy and the monks played important roles in education and in furthering this worldview.[24] This non-dogmatic, ethically oriented Christianity does not fit conventional polarities between Roman Catholicism and the Enlightenment. The most dramatic symbol of this ethos was Joseph II's Patent of Toleration, but it is difficult to say just how far Reform Catholicism or crypto-Protestantism penetrated among intellectual, bureaucratic, and religious elites even before 1781. Under Joseph II, reforms were often directed against common Catholic religious practices but not against Catholicism; the targets of reform included not only the Jesuit order (which was dissolved by the Pope in 1773), but also lay confraternities of all kinds, elaborate burial practices, processions, and saints' days. The reform monarchs raised the level of education and established the basis for a German-speaking intellectual life in Austria, Bohemia, and Moravia. Elementary schools were available now even in the countryside. The lower levels were still in Czech in those areas where the peasantry was largely Czech-speaking.[25] The state attempted to create a middle class—for commerce, industry, military and civil engineering, and agricultural modernization, but also for solidarity with the monarchy and as a balance against the aristocracy. These reforms accomplished a great deal that carried far into the nineteenth century.[26]

Joseph von Sonnenfels (1732–1817) was an adviser to all three of the Habsburg reform monarchs and the leading voice of the Austrian Enlightenment. He was a major figure of the administrative sciences, or cameralism, and a prolific writer. Beginning in 1765, he published a periodical advocating the ideas of the Enlightenment, *Der Mann ohne Vorurtheil* [The Man without Prejudice]; this was the highpoint of his success as a journalist, after which he experimented with several magazines aimed at women.[27] His main influence came under Maria Theresa, despite his Jewish background and her pronounced anti-Semitism. Sonnenfels' grandfather had been chief rabbi of Brandenburg, and Sonnenfels' father had moved from Prussia to Eisenstadt in Western Hungary and then to Nikolsburg in southern Moravia.[28] He converted to Catholicism, became a professor of oriental languages (which dealt mainly with Hebrew and other languages of the Middle East) in Vienna in 1745, and was ennobled the following year.[29] Nonetheless, his son's contemporaries were quite conscious of this Jewish background (they called him "the Nikolsburg Jew").[30] In the nineteenth century, Austrian liberals construed Sonnenfels as an important precursor although he clearly stood for Enlightened absolutism more than liberal individualism, and Sonnenfels was a central figure in the emergence of literary German. "All of his endeavors were directed toward linking Austria to the reform ideas of the Enlightenment on the basis of the common but in Austria still not fully developed possession of the German literary language."[31]

Joseph Dobrovský (1753–1829) was one of the most important figures of the Enlightenment in Bohemia and Moravia, and he was the central theoretical figure in the creation of modern Czech, even though he wrote in German. Dobrovský belonged to German literature and intellectual life, and he saw himself as bringing enlightenment to Bohemia rather than leading a revival of the Czech language. He placed the Czech language in historical and linguistic context with a care and precision that had never been achieved before.[32] He was the decisive advocate of sixteenth-century Czech as the normative standard for the language, even though he saw little prospect in 1791 that Czech would ever be restored to this level for literary life. Dobrovský was one of many eighteenth-century intellectuals who worked on the history of Bohemia, and he could be described as a Bohemian patriot in that sense, which included both Czechs and Germans. Linguists of Dobrovský's generation built on the work of the previous generation of scholars who had gathered in Olomouc, Moravia, in the home of Joseph Freiherr von Petrasch (1714–1772) in the late 1740s and founded a society for historical research (the first learned or scientific society in the Habsburg Monarchy). They called themselves the *Societas incognitorum eruditorum in terris Austriacis* [The Society of Unknown Scholars in Austria], a name with suggestive implications for the Austrian Enlightenment more broadly. By the end of the Enlightenment, modern Czech had taken form, thanks in large part to scholars who spoke and wrote in German. Another major figure of the Enlightenment in Bohemia was Karl Heinrich Seibt, who taught German literature and moral philosophy at Charles-Ferdinand University in Prague.[33] Seibt, the first university chair of German in Austria, played an important role in the intellectual life of Prague in the late eighteenth century, and he was a mentor to Bernard Bolzano.[34] Indeed, modern Czech culture itself was formed and shaped by this modern German culture in a way that Polish culture, for example, was not.

Masonic lodges played a large role in the Austrian Enlightenment, especially in Vienna during the 1780s, but also in Bohemia and Moravia. The principal lodge in Vienna (*Zur wahren Eintract*) was founded by a Bohemian, Ignaz von Born; Born was a key figure in many aspects of the Enlightenment, including scientific societies, and his lodge contained many aristocrats and government officials. Mozart belonged to a smaller lodge in Vienna, *Zur Wohltätigkeit* [To Good Deeds].[35] Ernst Wangermann calls *The Magic Flute* "the culmination of the Austrian achievement in the age of the Enlightenment" and "the most consistent and comprehensive dramatic expression of the political hopes, humanitarian ideals and educational aspirations of the Illuminist Freemasonry."[36] Mozart expressed the values of the Enlightenment, just as Austrian philosophy and literature drew on the powerful artistic and musical currents of the eighteenth century. It is difficult to think of a work in the performance or entertainment repertoire of German culture that could have matched the impact of *The Magic Flute* in 1790.[37] Mozart died in 1791, and Leopold II, the last reform monarch, died in 1792, as the French Revolution intensified, and a long period of European war began.[38] It is easy to forget that during the early stages of the French Revolution, Austrian elites (including Leopold II) were in a position to regard France as simply catching up with the reformist achievements of the Austrian state; on the other hand, Prussia entered its famous period of reform only after a devastating defeat at the hands of Napoleon in 1806.

Josephinism and the Conservative Era: 1792–1866

Between 1792 and 1866 the legacy of the Josephinist tradition remained dominant in church and state, though now in a more conservative, less reformist, form. These years from the accession of Francis II (later Francis I of the Austrian Empire) to the defeat of Austria by Prussia were predominantly years of stabilization and continuity with the past, as well as resistance to nationalism and gradual accommodation to industrialization. This period was by no means homogeneous in political terms, but it was defined by a centralized administrative system, which had replaced the decentralized forms of Baroque, aristocratic power but had not yet given way to the liberal institutions that were established in the *Ausgleich* or Compromise of 1867. Although Francis changed the tone of Habsburg leadership, the period of the Franciscan Era between 1792 and 1835 was largely continuous with the policies of Joseph II "in regard to domestic administration, civil service, economic-military organization, Church-State relations, and even to a point public education."[39] Perhaps most notable about the positive achievements of the early nineteenth century were the codification of civil law and the founding of a Technical University in Prague. The General Civil Law Code of 1811 was an important stage on the path to universal citizenship that laid the foundation for the liberal society of the late nineteenth century, and the Technical University established the basis for Bohemia's major role in industrialization later in the century. Although there were efforts in this period, as there had been in the eighteenth century, to extend the German bureaucratic system of Austria and Bohemia to the rest of the Monarchy, the successes were generally limited and temporary. These were abolished almost entirely in 1848 and then pushed back to a minimum in 1867. In this period, modern Czech culture emerged along with the conflicts between Germans and Czechs that we associate with the late nineteenth century. The impact of the revolutions of 1848 was enormous throughout Central Europe, but the results of these upheavals were not clarified until 1866–1867, and oddly enough it was only between 1849 and 1866 that a serious attempt was made to centralize the Monarchy in the spirit of Joseph II.[40] German continued to be the language of secondary schools and higher education in Cisleithanian Austria, and Graz, Innsbruck, and Olomouc now prepared students for the university.[41] Ernst Hanisch argues that "in Austria an especially strong state bureaucratic tradition had developed" along with "a relatively early development of the social state."[42]

The intellectual fruits of Josephinism and the Austrian Enlightenment were harvested in the first two-thirds of the nineteenth century, not only in philosophy but in literature as well, above all in the work of Bernard Bolzano (1781–1848), Franz Grillparzer (1791–1872), and Adalbert Stifter (1805–1868).[43] These intellectuals represent the unbroken continuity of the Enlightenment in early nineteenth-century Austria and the critique of much of what German idealism and romanticism stood for. These years were marked by a growing awareness of a distinctive intellectual life among Austrian writers and philosophers and by the importance of the Josephinist bureaucracy, the salon, and the theater in this intellectual world. Vienna was the main center of Austrian intellectual life, but many key figures came from Prague as well—and Bohemia was integral to understandings of Austrian identity and intellectual life in these years. The Bohemian philosopher Bolzano was the most important figure for the continuity of Enlightenment ideas in Austria, and he was a powerful influence for both German and Czech intellectuals in the early nineteenth century—primarily in Bohemia but eventually in Vienna as well.[44]

The three great figures of early nineteenth-century Austrian intellectual history (Stifter, Bolzano, and Grillparzer) all had close ties to Bohemia. Stifter was born there and wrote much of his important work about it; Bolzano lived there his entire life, although he had great influence in Vienna after his death; Grillparzer clearly belonged to Vienna, but he located some of his most important dramas in Prague, and his conception of Austria was fundamentally determined by Bohemia—and not by the Monarchy as a whole or by the Archducal Austrian lands alone.[45] Even though the Monarchy was for most of this period technically more unified than at any other time, in a way that included Galicia and all the historic lands of Hungary, the close connection between Austria and Bohemia remained.[46] In this period, Prague was an important center of German-speaking intellectual life, as it had been in the late eighteenth century. There was considerable mobility for the German-speaking upper strata in Cisleithanian Austria—aristocrats, bureaucrats, clergy, students and professors, and teachers—and after 1848 this mobility was increasingly available to lower strata, which included Bohemian peasants who moved to Vienna in large numbers. Vienna and Prague had distinct identities, but they belonged to a shared intellectual world. At least until 1848, German was firmly established as the language of politics and public life in Austria and Bohemia, but Hungary succeeded in resisting this regime to resume the arrangements of the early modern period, including the use of Latin for administration. These were also the years when modern Czech culture developed under the leadership of František Palacký (1798–1876) and Josef Jungmann (1773–1847).[47]

The French Revolution has ordinarily been emphasized in narratives of Austria, but for Austrian intellectual history the decisive event was not so much the immediate impact of the revolution, but rather, as Thomas Nipperdey famously pointed out, Napoleon. As in all of German-speaking Europe, Napoleon's influence was enormous in the nineteenth century: "In the beginning was Napoleon."[48] But the Austrian experience was quite different from the experience of Prussia or of the Confederation of the Rhine in the Southwest. By 1795 Francis II had given up on the reformist approach to the state which his family had adopted since the 1740s, and he was left by Prussia to confront Napoleon more or less alone. It was during the period of peace in Northern Germany between 1795 and 1806 that the distinctive features of North German intellectual life took form: idealism, romanticism, and eventually nationalism.[49] What happened in Prussia in these years but did not happen in Austria was the emergence of the modern university—under the aegis of idealism, romanticism, and historicism. It was then that Prussia assumed a new, modernizing identity, partly modeled on the French Revolution, partly in reaction to Napoleon, which gave Prussia a plausible role as the leader in the process of German unification.[50] Hegel moved from Bavaria to Berlin, where he became a symbol of these transformations, and he represented a style of thought that was strongly criticized by Austrian intellectuals.

As in France, the influence of Romanticism in Austria was weak. The combination of the Enlightenment and Catholicism was not conducive to Romanticism in its English and North German forms, although some of these influences did reach Prague and Vienna. What is perhaps most striking about Austrian intellectual traditions in the early nineteenth century, whether in the theater, the novel, or philosophy, is the lack of emphasis on the romantic self or the heroic ego or the subjectivist understanding of German idealism in its quite different forms from Kant to Fichte to Hegel, including the nationalism that emerged out of radical idealism in Fichte. The relationships among idealism, romanticism, and nationalism in the German tradition are often oversimplified, and certainly more understanding of the Austrian tradition would open up a richer understanding of these issues and the history of Central Europe. Austrian intellectuals generally felt the continuity with eighteenth-century German culture—with Goethe, Schiller, Lessing, and even Kant—but they were mainly skeptical about the leading figures of German idealism and romanticism.[51]

Prince Metternich became the European center of the resistance to Napoleon and nationalism, and he shaped domestic policy for the Monarchy after 1809 and for the new German Confederation after 1815.[52] This period of Austrian intellectual history is ordinarily described in terms of political repression and censorship (especially in the wake of the Carlsbad Decrees of 1819). Metternich and Count Franz Anton von Kolowrat-Liebsteinsky (1778–1861) maintained a regime of police censorship in Austria, although this did not entirely determine what intellectuals thought and said. "Censorship was largely directed against the small domestic intelligentsia, whereas educated Austrians could purchase with ease the works of foreign and especially north and west German authors." During the early nineteenth century, early liberalism began to emerge in the world of the haute bourgeoisie, but in Austria it is difficult to isolate a "pronounced Liberal tradition of any serious, systematic sort before 1848."[53]

During the Napoleonic era, a large number of north German intellectuals, especially Prussians, moved to Vienna. Perhaps most familiar to historians is Friedrich von Gentz, who translated Edmund Burke's *Reflections on the Revolution in France* into German and served as Metternich's advisor.[54] Even more than Burke, Gentz and Metternich were strongly stamped by the Enlightenment, whereas many of those who came from the north were Romantics, often political Romantics such as Adam Müller (1779–1829).[55] Other North Germans arrived later in the century, including Christian Friedrich Hebbel (1813–1863), who was strongly influenced by German idealism and Hegel. Friedrich Schlegel was the most prominent literary figure to move to Vienna in the early nineteenth century; this period of his thought was marked by his dreams of Catholic restoration, but his views were roughly the opposite of the most important Austrian philosopher of this period, Bernard Bolzano, and Schlegel was far less appealing than Gentz to the sober Metternich.

A distinctive social milieu emerged in Vienna in the late eighteenth and early nineteenth centuries. This culture was centered in the upper-middle-class salons of Vienna, where social leadership was often provided by Jewish women—especially from families of wealthy Jews such as the Rothschilds and the Wertheimsteins.[56] These were the leading families of a small, but important minority of tolerated Jews in Vienna before 1848, and Daniel Itzig's daughters brought the spirit of Moses Mendelsohn from Berlin to Vienna.[57] These salons were centers for music, art, and intellectual life, often for those who were involved with the theater. The social groups who frequented these salons came to be known as "second society" or second nobility—which included not only ennobled Jews but also the service elites of the bureaucracy and professional, financial, and commercial elites.[58] These social gatherings were similar to the salons of eighteenth-century Berlin and Paris, and they gained prominence during the assemblage of European elites at the Congress of Vienna in 1814–1815. Salons were important centers of Viennese intellectual life from Grillparzer to Ferdinand von Saar to Hofmannsthal. In addition to the dominant tradition of Josephinism, the Jewish contribution to Austrian intellectual life was already significant in this period, and the influence of Haskalah intensified the Austrian commitment to the Enlightenment.[59] Both Josephinism and Haskallah represented a continuity with the Enlightenment that was less conspicuous north of the Main after 1806.

The reign of Ferdinand I of Austria (1835–1848) was a virtual interregnum because of the emperor's mental incapacity. The bureaucratic state could rule itself, but it could not change and respond to the new challenges of nationalism, industrialization, and population growth. In this period a variety of challenges became more evident, notably in the political writing of intellectuals before the revolution of 1848, including conservatives such as Joseph Freiherr von Helfert, founder of the Institute for Austrian Historical research, liberals such as Anastasius Grün (who was later prime minister under his real name of Count Anton Alexander von Auersperg), imperial administrators such as Viktor von Andrian-Werburg, or democrats such as Charles Sealsfield (Karl Anton Postl). This awakening of political writing included the work of Palacký and Jungmann on Czech history and literature. Liberalism and nationalism often blurred into one another before 1848—as attempts to achieve popular participation in relation to the monarchy. Liberalism was an ideology that emphasized the freedom and dignity of the individual—in political, economic, and religious life. In the early nineteenth century, Austrian liberalism grew out of Josephinism and the Enlightenment without sharp definitions or parties, in resistance to inherited, traditional forms, most dramatically in the revolutions of 1848 and then in a variety of forms in the parliamentary politics of the late nineteenth century. Political liberalism in Austria generally came to mean the freedom of German-speaking men of property and education. Among German-speakers it was difficult to distinguish between liberalism and nationalism before 1848.

The concerns of German nationalism often revolved around models of the unification and modernization of the Holy Roman Empire. The solution most familiar today is the *kleindeutsch* (or small German) model, more or less the Germany of Bismarck but also of the "reunited" Germany of 1990 as well as the proposed German constitution of 1849. A second possibility was the *grossdeutsch* (or great German) model, which was imagined to include Austria, with or without Hungary. A third nineteenth-century possibility, the trias model, imagined a Germany divided along the lines of what became the post-1945 arrangements: Prussia (the German Democratic Republic), Austria, and Southwestern Germany (the largely Catholic region of the Federal Republic in 1949 and of Napoleon's Confederation of the Rhine).[60] Discussions of the Czech national awakening sometimes pass over the substantial number of Germans who lived in Bohemia and Moravia, which meant that in 1848 there were tensions between democracy and nationalism—to complicate other divisions of class, status, and ideology.[61] The bilingualism of Bohemia was sometimes referred to as Bohemian utraquism in the sense of both languages rather than communion in both kinds. Before 1848 German and Czech were relatively balanced in Bohemian life, often in Bolzano's spirit. Bolzano's student Robert Zimmermann wrote a poetic acknowledgment of what Hillel Kieval calls "the liberal bi-ethnic 'Bohemian' consensus of the decade that preceded the revolution of 1848."[62] The term "Habsburg" was sometimes used in the nineteenth century to describe what was not merely Czech national or German national, but which referred to Bohemia in a different sense than it referred to Hungary.[63] And Bohemia's greatest philosopher, Bolzano, argued for an equality of languages (German and Czech) in Bohemia. Tomaš Masaryk points out that the Czechs were bilingual like the Romans, that is, deferring to Greeks or Germans, but proud of their vernaculars as well. Like most Czechs of his generation, Masaryk undertook his advanced education primarily in German, including his study of philosophy in Vienna with Brentano.[64] Czech migration to Vienna became so pronounced after 1848 that the German philosopher Eduard von Hartmann predicted that Vienna would be a Slavic city by 1900.

František Palacký, the Czech Ranke and the political leader of the Czechs in 1848, wrote the first volume of his history of Bohemia in German. He had been planning to translate *Geschichte von Böhmen, grösstentheils nach Urkunden und Handschriften* into Czech after he finished writing it, but the first volume took so long that he decided to translate it as he worked on the German original. The first volume appeared in German in 1836: "To the despair of the Czech-speaking public", his "agreement with the Estates had presupposed this, and he himself had conceded that it was the only way to reach a wide readership in Bohemia and abroad."[65] His translation of the first volume into Czech appeared in March 1848 as *Dějiny národu českého v Čechách a v Moravě*.[66] Palacký was certainly never a German nationalist, but until 1848 he was part of German intellectual life in Austria in the sense I have described here. One way to clarify the significance of the revolution of 1848 for intellectual history is that after 1850 Palacký decided never again to publish in German. This was the end of cosmopolitan German culture as it had been in the Austrian Enlightenment. This change had emerged gradually in the early nineteenth century, but in 1848 the Enlightenment clearly spilled into nationalism. This was the year when the broader Czech population, especially the young people, came to political consciousness: "the Czech national movement was transformed from a cultural (or quasi-political) movement into a full-fledged political one," and the year marked the beginning of increasingly intense conflicts between Germans and Czechs in Bohemia and Moravia.[67]

In 1848 the existence of the Habsburg Monarchy was at stake—and not so much from liberalism as from nationalism: primarily German, Italian, and Hungarian. Slavic nationalism took on a newly public form during the events of 1848, but at this point it was more of a threat to German nationalism than to the Habsburg Monarchy, and it was still entangled with a great many issues from Germany to Russia. Modernization, liberalism, and nationalism (especially in the case of Hungary) were put on new and more powerful courses, and internal migration (in the context of the emancipation of the peasantry in the Kremsier constitution) was perhaps the most important change of all. For intellectual history, the great event of the years after 1848 was the reform of the University of Vienna, as liberals and Josephinists worked together as reformers. It was the conservative Czech, Count Thun (1811–1888), who took the lead in modernizing Habsburg universities, above all the University of Vienna. He was also the leading advocate of Bohemian historical rights and post-Josephinist federalism.[68] Influenced by Bolzano and Dobrovský, Thun represented a genuine spirituality that attempted to build a bridge between the people and the state. Thun's transformation of the University of Vienna became one of the institutional pillars of the liberal era. As Johnston put it in his account of Bohemian philosophy:

> The most enduring monument of Bohemian humanism was the reform of Austrian education executed during the 1850's by Bolzano's friend Count Leo Thun. Sweeping away the confessional bias of Metternich's era, this devout Catholic introduced humanistic and scientific training into both secondary schools and university.[69]

Josephinist institutions and mentalities gave coherence to Cisleithanian Austrian intellectual life down to the liberal era. At the same time, the very un-Josephinist Concordat with the Vatican in 1855 set the tone for conflicts between Catholics and liberals in the late nineteenth century. The Austrian church had begun to move away from Josephinism after 1815, and the Josephinist currents in the church were increasingly suppressed, after 1819 and even more after 1848.

Italian nationalism ushered in the defeat of neo-Josephinism at the Battle of Solferino in 1859 and opened the way to what is known as Old Liberalism and to the prospect of a Great German solution in which the Habsburgs would take the lead.[70] From 1848 to 1866, it was still realistic to think that a workable understanding could emerge with the Czechs (and perhaps with the Slovenes as well).[71] Broader understandings with the South Slavs depended on the outcome of negotiations with the Magyars, and 1867 constituted the explicit decision to allow the Magyars to shape the destiny of the empire east of the Leitha alone. It was often assumed that the Habsburg Monarchy was more or less in the hands of the German-speaking educated strata; the arrangements of 1867 enshrined that view for Austria in the *Ausgleich* just at the point when it had become outdated, and this became the basis for the liberal era. With the deaths of Bolzano, Stifter, and Grillparzer, something new came into being in Cisleithanian Austria: the age of high liberalism and industrial society.

The Liberal Era: 1867–1900

The High Liberal Era in Austria began with the exclusion of Austria from Bismarck's new German state and the creation of arrangements in the Monarchy that separated Hungary even more completely than before from Cisleithanian Austria.[72] After the defeat by Prussia at Königgrätz (Sadowa) in 1866, Franz Joseph was forced to share political power with the Magyars in Hungary and with German-speaking liberals in Austria. According to these agreements, Polish Galicia was now defined constitutionally as part of Cisleithanian Austria; while this mattered for Austrian politics and for the Austrian *Reichsrat* or parliament, the intellectual life of the hereditary lands largely retained its unity, that is, Cisleithania in the geographical sense (west of the Leitha River). The *Ausgleich* or Compromise established the special primacy and near-autonomy of the Magyars in Hungary, while the Czechs found themselves entangled in a long history with the Germans in which the Germans were still dominant. In 1867 and 1871 there were opportunities to make special arrangements for the Czechs within the Austro-Hungarian Compromise. Instead, German liberals were content with a temporary dominance in the West and in the *Reichsrat*, and the Magyars preferred this solution. The franchise for the Austrian *Reichsrat* was not democratic, but favored wealth and education in ways that were common in European constitutions of the nineteenth century. The *Ausgleich* introduced an age of confidence and optimism for the German liberals in Cisleithanian Austria—in politics, in the university, and in the economic life of Austria.

The new constitutional state emerged in the age of European liberalism, just after the appearance of John Stuart Mill's *On Liberty* (1859), and it was stamped by classical liberalism: freedom from the absolute monarch (i.e., representative government), from the church (especially the Catholic Church), and from economic regulation. This ideology of liberation from traditional bonds should be sharply distinguished from what Americans have called "liberalism" since the 1930s. While liberal ideology was problematic politically (in the discomfort of liberals with more popular and democratic movements), it was generally very positive for intellectual life and for the participation of German-speaking upper-middle-class men in high culture in the university, newspapers, theater, musical culture, and the world of books. The *Neue Freie Presse* (founded in 1864) became the most prominent newspaper in Vienna, and it aimed to represent the German liberal elites in the Monarchy as a whole.[73] As in Germany, the liberal era in Cisleithanian Austria began with an explosion of economic activity and growth. The liberal era in politics came to a close by the end of the century with the failure of language reform for the administration of Cisleithanian Austria and with the victory of the Christian Socials in Vienna. In Austria there was a blurring among conceptions of liberalism, German culture, and the social and political dominance of wealth and education. To make matters still more confusing, Jews were welcomed into this upper-middle-class stratum, and they benefitted from the civil rights of the liberal era, which allowed them to participate more fully in intellectual and political life. All of this was closely tied to the way understandings of Austria evolved; Austria was not Germany but still "German"; and, in a way that seemed almost too self-evident to mention, Jews joined in this understanding, while emphasizing not their Jewishness, but only the progress of culture.[74] And, of course, as Pieter Judson has reminded us, it was in these years that liberals became "Germans," as it were.[75]

The year 1866 marked not only the end of the connection to Germany on the level of political institutions, but also the end of Josephinist centralization within the Habsburg Monarchy as a whole. For this period, the word "German" is sometimes taken to mean nationalist and pan-German, and certainly this was one major connotation. But German was not only the language of the Cisleithanian bureaucracy but also the language of choice for many Czechs, Jews, and other minorities who participated in the political and cultural life of Austria and Bohemia. The politics of the liberal era between 1867 and 1900 may be best described as a balance between German liberal and Josephinist leadership;[76] it was also marked by a failure to find a solution to the conflicts between German-speakers and Czech-speakers in Bohemia and Moravia and in the administration of Cisleithanian Austria. The sharp conflicts between political liberalism and conservative Catholicism after the Concordat of 1855 set the terms for hardening the ideological atmosphere of the late nineteenth century and in some ways anticipated the polarization of the 1920s and 1930s between Catholicism and socialism.[77] This period was not only the liberal era, but (after the initial boom of the *Gründerjahren*) the Great Depression of 1873 to 1896 as well—an economic adjustment that stimulated reactions against liberalism, capitalism, industrialization, and Jews.[78] As in Germany, Bohemia and Austria felt the emergence of modern capitalism and the first powerful shocks of industrial society both in the Great Depression and in the movements of populations to the city—although the rest of the Monarchy changed much more slowly. A specifically German (rather than Bohemian) group identity and politics began to develop in Prague during the 1860s.[79]

At the center of the intellectual life of the liberal era was the University of Vienna. Perhaps best known is the Second Vienna Medical School described by Erna Lesky, the center for currents of positivism and scientific materialism in Austrian culture.[80] But it was also in this period that Vienna became a center for modern economics, while art history developed out of the newly created Institute for Austrian Historical Research,[81] above all in the work of Alois Riegl (1858–1905).[82] Philosophy was firmly established at the University of Vienna by Robert Zimmermann, Franz Brentano, and Ernst Mach, although history did not have the same prominence that it had in Berlin.[83] The social and intellectual world of the university was shaped by families such as Gomperzes, the Wertheimsteins, and the Exners.[84] The Austrian commitment to reason and empiricism culminated after 1848 in positivism and the reception of scientific materialism, especially through scientists and physicians arriving from the North.[85]

Viennese social elites were surprisingly homogeneous and dominant in intellectual life—a world built around the university, the *Neue Freie Presse*, the parliament, the *Burgtheater*, the opera, the coffeehouse, and the salon—and guided by upper-middle-class German-speaking men, the elites portrayed by Arthur Schnitzler in *The Road into the Open* (1908). Many of the creative intellectuals of this period were at the University of Vienna: Franz Brentano, Carl Menger, Sigmund Freud, and (after 1895) Ernst Mach, although Mach spent most of his career in Prague. Novelists and realistic storytellers such as Ferdinand von Saar, Marie von Ebner-Eschenbach, Ludwig Anzengruber, and Peter Rosseger expressed the values of this era. Vienna was a magnet for German-speaking intellectuals, but it is easy to forget how many of them came from Bohemia and Moravia. Johnston calls Bohemia and Moravia in the half-century before the First World War "a seedbed of thinkers unsurpassed in Europe" and mentions Sigmund Freud, Edmund Husserl, Karl Kraus, Viktor Adler, Josef Popper-

Lynkeus, Gustav Mahler, Adolf Loos, Hans Kelsen, Robert Zimmermann, Eugen von Böhm-Bawerk, Bertha von Suttner, and Joseph Schumpeter.[86] He might have added Musil and Kafka and Mach, Gustav Meyrink, Alfred Kubin, and Gregor Mendel, the German-speaking monk from Brno in Moravia who opened the way to modern genetics.

After 1879 the move toward combined majorities of Catholic, Czech, and Polish parties in the *Reichsrat* was the clearest sign of the decline of political liberalism. By the 1880s, liberalism seemed to many younger intellectuals to offer no new values, but spent its energies in conflicts with the Catholic Church and in resisting the efforts of the Czechs to be on equal footing with the Germans in Cisleithanian Austria. The German liberal elites had displaced traditional elites, but without creating anything except what Hermann Broch called the museum style of the *Ringstrasse*—the historical eclecticism of an epoch without a style of its own.[87] By 1882 the creative elements of political liberalism were already splitting off to form more democratic political parties, first in the Linz Program of 1882 and then in the three modern mass political parties that grew out of it: the Christian Socials, the Social Democrats (notably at Hainfeld in 1882), and the German Nationalists. A stronger sense of German and Czech nationalism began to emerge in Bohemia and Moravia in the 1860s, but as late as the early twentieth century "national indifference" was still an issue.[88]

William McGrath locates the revolt against the liberal order in the 1870s and 1880s, not in the anti-Semitic parties but in young intellectuals such as Victor Adler, Gustav Mahler, Heinrich Friedjung, Hermann Bahr, and Freud. Some of these figures became prominent in the mass political movements of the late nineteenth century, but McGrath emphasizes the roles of feelings, rebellion, and liberation in Wagner and the young Nietzsche. Schorske argues that this aesthetic culture of feelings (see the Wagner Festival of 1883) was set against the liberal, rational culture of the fathers (see the Schiller Festival of 1859). He emphasizes this new Dionysian culture which he locates mainly in Wagner, yet in a way that was similar to Baroque culture. Freud's thought was shaped by both scientific materialism and philosophical irrationalism, and, like many intellectuals of this generation, he moved away from German nationalism as anti-Semitism increased.[89] Schorske's account of the aesthetic culture of the liberal era culminated in the literary culture of Young Vienna and in the artistic culture of the Secession of 1897. As Schorske points out, his decisive figures in the revolt against liberal Vienna—Schnitzler, Hofmannsthal, Freud—were themselves very much figures of Vienna's liberal ethos. The crisis of the 1890s was primarily a crisis of German liberal elites who had failed to govern successfully in Cisleithanian Austria. Notable among the intellectual elites were crises of male and Jewish identity, particularly noticeable among young Jewish men.[90]

During the liberal era, women became more visible in intellectual and public life, though still in only limited ways. Marie von Ebner-Eschenbach, a Moravian aristocrat and a major figure of the liberal era, received an honorary degree from the University of Vienna in 1900, which provides a helpful point of reference for the increasing recognition of women in the university. Women began to attend classes but did not matriculate at the university in most fields until after 1900, and women were active in secondary school teaching and in the movement for working women.[91] In the 1890s Adelheid Popp addressed the needs of women who worked as servants in well-to-do homes, the majority of whom came from Bohemia.[92] Around this time, public life in Vienna was marked by an explosion of interest and discussion about sexual feelings and behavior. Major factors in this were the development of the women's movement and the increasing social activism of feminists. A sophisticated tradition of Austrian feminism also emerged at this time. These issues appeared in the plays of this period, which often aimed at a critique of social roles, conventions, and mores, and explored the interest in forms of sexuality and sexual orientation. Freud's thought developed in this context, as did the radical critiques of sexuality and gender by Karl Kraus and Otto Weininger, who developed the logic of Schopenhauer and Nietzsche in thinking out the culture's conceptions of femininity and masculinity.[93] We still have more to understand about the preoccupation of men with sexuality and identity and the emergence of the women's emancipation movement. At one time, for example, it was assumed that Otto Weininger was a misogynist and an anti-Semite who was reacting to modern feminism. He seems, in fact, to have been trying to cope with his own sexual identity, and he offered an intense critique of reproductive norms and social conventions surrounding sexuality in his society.

This period was given its most memorable description by Carl Schorske in *Fin de siècle Vienna*, where he emphasized both the dramatic successes of the liberal founders between 1866 and 1879 and the political demoralization of the sons of this generation, which provided the point of departure for the inwardness and creativity of Freud, Schnitzler, Hofmannsthal, and Klimt. The defeat of a narrow liberalism as a political power did not bring an end to the influence of liberal ideas in the intellectual world. Indeed, it was the spread of liberal ideas that made all of the new political groupings possible. By the end of the century, Social Darwinism gave new energy to the blend of liberalism and German nationalism, notably in the work of Houston Stewart Chamberlain (1855–1927), the English admirer of Wagner, who became a key factor in the culture of Vienna 1900 with his *Foundations of the Nineteenth Century*.[94] At the same time, some liberal intellectuals were still active in reform movements and closely connected to Social Democracy, even down to the 1920s.[95] For the most part, however, Austrian liberalism became accommodated to the social and political elites of Vienna, and, in the years before the First World War, writers and journalists who called themselves "liberals" moved increasingly toward German nationalism and imperialism. This was one obvious reason for the complaint in *The Man without Qualities* that there were simply not enough words to go around.

The Transformations of Modern Intellectual Life: 1900–1938/1939

For intellectual history, it is helpful to distinguish the liberal intellectual world of the late nineteenth century from the new impulses of the early twentieth century, which accompanied dramatic changes in social, political, and national life.[96] Between 1900 and 1938/1939 Austria made its greatest contributions to modern intellectual life—whether in literature or philosophy or economics or psychoanalysis—but this was also the period of Austria's demise, first as the core of a multinational monarchy, then as a republic, and finally as a separate state. Austria lost decisively in institutional and political terms, just as it was making its most important intellectual contributions. In the social sciences and in philosophy, the values of the high liberal era and the Enlightenment were carried into the twentieth century.[97] Scholars sometimes forget Schorske's original point about *fin-de-siècle* Vienna in his essay on Schnitzler and Hofmannsthal: that there was a conflict within liberal culture between "the moralistic-scientific and the aesthetic."[98] And the rational element stayed strong in liberal intellectual life—whether in economics or the natural sciences or psychoanalysis—although intellectual life was no longer so centered in the University of Vienna.

The Second Industrial Revolution[99] created a new world, and universal manhood suffrage meant the declining importance of German-speaking upper-middle-class elites in the *Reichsrat* as well as in Vienna and Prague. These changes became a revolution of destruction in the First World War, culminating in the division of Cisleithanian Austria into Czech (now Czechoslovakian) and German-Austrian Republics. Austrian intellectuals then became part of the enormous movement of peoples in the interwar years, which often changed the identity and reception of the Austrian thought in dramatic ways, including emigrations to Switzerland, Turkey, and the Soviet Union, and even to China and the South Pacific, but most significantly to the UK and North America. This period was marked by the internationalism of almost everything, including science, technology, feminism, socialism, communism, and modernism in the arts—and even nationalism, war, and anti-Semitism. Intellectual life was more international than ever before, especially in the natural sciences, but also in philosophy, literature, and the social sciences.[100] Within the realm of German culture there were important links not only between Vienna and Prague, but also between Vienna and Berlin. If many Austrians in this period decided to move to Berlin, as the main center for German-speaking culture, key figures in philosophy, such as Moritz Schlick and Rudolf Carnap, also moved south to create the Vienna Circle. The creative figures of the early twentieth century often carried their ideas into exile, and their fields evolved into new stories in the United States and elsewhere.[101]

With the institution of universal manhood suffrage just after the turn of the century, the new mass political parties were poised to assume the initiative in modern politics.[102] These parties reflected the rise of democracy and the increasing participation of Austrians in political life. In this context, liberalism became less important as a political force and gave way to socialism, Christian Socialism, German nationalism, and the Czech parties. A more diverse and more democratic culture emerged, which meant nationalism but also cosmopolitanism and socialism.[103] Even elite intellectuals were no longer so contained by bourgeois society, and this period was marked increasingly by a sense of the anonymity and isolation of the individual in the mass. Traditional cultures were breaking up and intersecting with each other, especially in cities like Vienna and Prague.[104] The early twentieth century was strongly marked by overwhelming complexity or *Unübersichtlichkeit*, the sheer mass, even chaos, of information that did not lend itself to neat, schematic categories. Robert Musil regarded the fragmentation of culture as the characteristic and positive quality of the twentieth century. The cracking and breaking up of traditional society opened up new spaces for creativity, like flowers growing in the fissures after an earthquake.[105] For many intellectuals, this meant not the decadence and pessimism often associated with the fin-de-siècle but the will to be different, to create a modern culture.

At the center of what was new intellectually was what I call the generation of 1905: those who were born between 1870 and 1890 and grew up in the liberal social world, but moved beyond it, including some of the greatest writers of the twentieth century. In 1905 Europe nearly went to war in the context of a colonial crisis between France and Germany and a revolution in Russia, and for the next decade educated Europeans sensed that war was imminent.[106] In this generation we see a new energy that was not so apparent in the 1890s—an ethical energy that did not always take political form, whether in Musil's understanding of ethics, Kafka's undermining of all ideologies, Broch's critique of Western values, Hofmannsthal's conservative revolution, or Rilke's willingness to set aside most of what the tradition had thought and said. All of this was grounded in the Enlightenment, but moved toward an ungrounded modernism in the spirit of Musil's argument that the Enlightenment had applied its intellectual values in the wrong way in the realm of the ethical. Literary historians often emphasize the end of the Monarchy, but the most important intellectuals of this generation lived beyond the war to continue their creativity into the interwar years, along with younger intellectuals such as Elias Canetti, Heimito von Doderer, Karl Popper, Ferdinand von Hayek, Paul Lazarsfeld, Eric Voegelin, and George Saiko. This younger generation of 1927 was caught up in a period of intense politicization and polarization, from the general strike of 1927 to civil war in 1934.[107]

Austrian intellectuals in the decade before the First World War seem to have reached a point of balance between an embeddedness in the German language and the cultural traditions of Central Europe, on the one hand, and the possibilities for modern technology, intellectual creativity, and rapid social change, on the other. What is sometimes emphasized about this period is the crisis of language, in part because of Hofmannsthal's "Letter of Lord Chandos" or even because of Karl Kraus' critique of language (or Wittgenstein's).[108] But what is actually most striking is the belief in language, the commitment to language. The writers of this generation—Musil, Kafka, Broch, Hofmannsthal, and Rilke, as well as Ludwig Wittgenstein and the idiosyncratic Kraus—believed in language. These writers believed in civilization and modern science as well.

One striking separation in Austrian intellectual life, before and after 1900, was the influence of Schopenhauer and the late Nietzsche.[109] The reception of Nietzsche and Schopenhauer in Austria began in the 1870s, but these philosophers seem to have had relatively little influence on the writers of Young Vienna in the 1890s. Schopenhauer and the later Nietzsche were important after 1900, often by way of Rudolf Kassner. This seems to have been an important key to the transformations of modern culture, especially for younger figures such as Hofmannsthal, for example; even the older Freud seems to have felt the impact of these ways of thinking after his creation of psychoanalysis, as his work moved in the direction of social theory.[110] In literature and in the blurred region between philosophy and literature, there was a new intensity in the exploration of ethics and spirituality that was still continuous in some respects with the Western tradition, although it rejected many of the conventions.

Prague was no longer so important for German-speaking intellectual life in Cisleithanian Austria (although it continued to be important for literature and philosophy), but Vienna and its high liberal culture were also not so central to intellectual life. It was not only that other centers, such as Graz, Innsbruck, and Salzburg, were more significant than before, or that for Czech intellectual life Prague became even more important than it had been in the nineteenth century. But younger German-speaking intellectuals also often moved away from Austria entirely. Even before the First World War, Ludwig Wittgenstein studied in England and Hermann Broch traveled in the United States, while Rilke set out for Paris. A stable world of the Viennese upper-middle class was no longer at the center of intellectual life. For the most part, German-speaking elites felt increasingly embattled in Bohemia and Moravia, although some of them learned Czech. This period was important for both German and Czech literature in Prague. Scott Spector has emphasized the importance of the Prague Circle, to which Kafka belonged, for Bohemian ideology and the blend of German, Czech, and Jewish, which produced a "minor literature" in this generation.[111] This period was marked by the separation of Austria from its roots in Bohemia and of German literature from its connection to Czech. This connection is something we still do not understand or know enough about, except for the powerful evidence of Kafka, Rilke, and Musil.

If Freud has shaped our picture of the liberal era and the 1890s, Karl Kraus has had a similar centrality for discussions of Vienna in the early twentieth century, although the nature of his intellectual contribution has been less clear. He was above all a satirist, a performer, a journalist in revolt against modern journalism (especially against the approach to writing embodied in the Viennese *feuilleton*). Since he came from Bohemia he very much belongs to the themes of this book and to the concern with language that characterized Bohemian intellectuals.[112] And his Jewishness, as well as his commentary on Jewish culture, has been part of his significance for contemporary intellectuals after Auschwitz.[113] But his most important influence was on the turning against *fin-de-siècle* aestheticism in Austrian literature—on Broch, Weininger, Wittgenstein, and the new centrality of ethics.[114] Perhaps most representative of the intellectual excitement of the immediate prewar years in Austria was the provincial journal from Innsbruck: *Der Brenner*, which carried the intense spirituality of these years into the interwar years and even down to the 1950s.[115] The editor, Ludwig von Ficker, was connected to Kraus, Weininger, Wittgenstein, Ferdinand von Ebner, and Georg Trakl. Even the young Georg Lukács, a German-speaking intellectual from Budapest, had an impact on this Expressionist atmosphere and on the revival of Kierkegaard and the critique of Catholicism from within.[116]

One of the most noteworthy signs of modernity after 1900 was the increasing prominence and participation of women in intellectual life. In the early twentieth century a larger number of women emerged who made valuable contributions as intellectuals: Adelheid Popp, Marianne Hainisch, Lisa Meitner, Rosa Mayreder, Bertha von Suttner, and Grete Meisel-Hess.[117] Even with universal manhood suffrage, the franchise for women continued to wait until after the First World War. As elsewhere in Europe, the women's movement intensified in the decade before the war, and the war increased the ways in which women participated in society.[118] Despite the wide interest in feminism in this period, there is still surprisingly little awareness of important intellectuals such as Mayreder.[119] The broad preoccupation of Austrian intellectuals with sexuality and gender went far beyond Freud's interests and contributions. And these issues were often closely related to interest in religion and philosophy. In Harriet Anderson's words, "Being a feminist meant above all cherishing a vision of a new social order which was endowed with clear spiritual components."[120] This society was just beginning to come to terms with conventions and stereotypes about gender and sexuality, and issues cut across each other in complicated ways. It is still not widely understood, for example, that Otto Weininger was drawing attention to just how undigested all these issues were in his society.

The most transformative event of this period was the First World War. The war was a revolution of destruction, as it was throughout most of Europe, which meant the death of the aristocracy, the officer corps, and many of the middle-class and working-class elites. Much of what happened in the interwar years was by no means inevitable before 1914—whether the end of the Monarchy or the separation of Bohemia from Austria. The war opened the way to possibilities that had not been realized before 1914: a Czech nation-state (joined by the Slovaks), Austrian Socialism in Vienna, the Christian Socials in Austria, first in the republic and then in the corporate state, and the great-German nationalism that pulverized Austrian identity from 1914 to 1939.[121] The war accelerated and intensified Czech politics in unforeseeable ways that led to separate Czechoslovakian and German-Austrian Republics by 1918–1919.[122]

It was difficult to live and work in Vienna from the First World War until the *Anschluss*, thanks to the war itself, the revolutions of 1918–1919, the migrations from the Monarchy and Eastern Europe to Vienna, the general strike of 1927, paramilitary conflicts, civil war and the suppression of the socialists, and four years of the Catholic Right in power. But, throughout all of this, most intellectuals remained until Hitler arrived.[123] The political polarization of the German-Austrian Republic moved rapidly in the direction of a failed state by 1927 and 1934. But the other offspring of Cisleithanian Austria (Czechoslovakia) became one of the more liberal and successful states of the early twentieth century in Europe. The Czech state was also multinational (Czech, German, and Slovak) and might have been a state like Belgium, based on two or even three languages. It was in many respects continuous with what was constructive about Cisleithanian Austria, and the political and intellectual life of the young Czech state echoed the experience of the generation of 1905 before the war.[124]

Much of Austrian intellectual life was anti-ideological in ways that emphasized respect for the complexity of the world. Although Friedrich Heer argued that the Austrian principle cannot be grasped, he characterized the resistance to self-righteous ideologies as "the Austrian tradition of the 16th to 20th centuries" (20).[125] This dimension was lost in the interwar years, partly because of the strong sense of German identity, partly because of the weakness of any sense of Austrian identity,[126] and partly because the two main political parties were so deeply polarized in ideological, dogmatic ways. Bismarck's two *Staatsfeinde* in Germany—socialism and Catholicism—actually became the two dominant visions of politics in interwar Austria until the Nazis arrived. Both political movements were defeated by nationalism.[127] The anti-ideological vision was embodied most effectively in Musil—the sense of accepting a variety of ideologies, languages, cultures, worldviews, and personalities.[128] Musil represented the most refined version of an Austrian indifference to dogma and ideology, which began with Josephinism.

Adolf Hitler was the transformative political figure of this period, but it is difficult to say whether he made an intellectual contribution and, if so, what. He seemed at first to respond to the dreams of Germans who were unhappy about modernization and urbanization and resentful about the outcomes of the First World War. His ideas came mainly from others, but he took anti-Semitism to an extreme that few others could have imagined. He also mastered a rhetoric that made Jews into symbols of both Western capitalism and Soviet Communism. Finally, of course, he realized the aims of German nationalism from 1848, but only after dramatic transformations of nationalism and democracy, as well as the Second Industrial Revolution, to create an anti-Marxist state that no one had had in mind in 1848. Despite the anti-Semitism of Lueger and Schönerer before the First World War, Hitler would not have been German Chancellor without the war and the polarization of politics in the 1920s. Certainly, other possibilities can be imagined if Cisleithanian Austria had remained intact. Hitler became Chancellor of Germany in 1933; he annexed Austria five years later and most of Czechoslovakia in the following year.[129] Austrians still debate whether to refer to 1934–1938 as the *Ständestaat* or as fascism, but the decisive fact here is that most of the intellectuals and most of the Jews remained until 1938, when the exit sped up from Prague as well as Vienna.

At least since Neville Chamberlain, Anglo-Americans have had a weak understanding of the place of Bohemia and Moravia in the story of Central Europe, a story that was distorted by both Czech and German nationalism. Karl Popper, writing from New Zealand, provided symbolic representation for the Austrian intellectual tradition with his *Open Society and Its Enemies*, a liberal critique of the fascist era and German philosophy, which he began with a description of his civilization, which Musil or Broch, Freud or Hayek, or the philosophers of the Vienna Circle might have offered as well: "a civilization which might be described as aiming at humaneness and reasonableness, at equality and freedom; a civilization which is still in its infancy."[130] Many Austrian intellectuals died in concentration camps, but even more of them went into exile. Indeed, we may say that National Socialism and the emigration brought an end to what I call the Austrian tradition in German intellectual history. Thanks both to wars and to the disappearance of Cisleithanian Austria as a unity, much of the value of what began around 1900 has still to be recovered and integrated into Western culture and intellectual life. It is perhaps time for an assessment of the impact of the Austrian tradition on German culture, especially in the early twentieth century. It may even be that the consummation of nineteenth-century German intellectual life, especially the exploration of the intellectual and creative possibilities opened up by Schopenhauer and Nietzsche, occurred not in Germany but in Cisleithanian Austria.

The emigration was most pronounced in social science, where Austrians had a big impact in the UK and the United States.[131] This overlapped a bit with philosophy, which also had a great influence in the Anglo-American world. Economics and sociology and even philosophy could migrate relatively easily and find academic homes in England and the United States. Literature was very different. Kafka and Rilke and Hofmannsthal had all died in the 1920s, and Musil died in Switzerland in 1942. The most distinguished exile to North America among the writers was Broch, who made an effort to begin again in the United States.[132] Among the younger writers, Doderer stayed in the *Reich* and in the German air force, while Canetti chose an extended and somewhat exotic exile in the UK. Hilde Spiel spent the war in the UK, but later returned to Vienna. Kafka's work was well received thanks to his literary advocates, but most writers took much longer to find their way into English. Stefan Zweig was perhaps symbolic for the situation of literature when he committed suicide in Brazil in 1942.

3

Philosophy in Austria

There is undoubtedly more logic, care, modesty, and inventiveness in the individual sciences today than among the so-called philosophers.
  —Friedrich Nietzsche, *Schopenhauer as Educator*[1]

Philosophy in Austria displays an astonishing degree of unity and continuity, but it is not the unity of a school. This chapter emphasizes four major philosophers of European or world stature: Bernard Bolzano, Franz Brentano, Ernst Mach, and Ludwig Wittgenstein—and it concludes with a broader movement of the interwar years: the logical empiricism of the Vienna Circle. The contributions of philosophy in Austria have been very great (perhaps greater than those of other more familiar intellectual traditions), and I identify what I take to be the key figures in this tradition without arguing for a single definition of Austrian philosophy.[2] Nonetheless, the commonalities among the philosophers I discuss are considerable. These philosophers are quite different from what has usually been understood to be German philosophy—above all the German idealists after Kant. I characterize this tradition as a "modest positivism"—that is, a philosophy that is marked by a strong affinity for modern science, especially the natural sciences, but without the dogmatic tendencies that are sometimes associated with the Vienna Circle or with French positivism.[3]

Two main philosophical styles have been emphasized in the Austrian tradition: Brentano and his followers, who have been identified by Barry Smith as "Austrian Philosophy," and positivism, which overlaps with both Brentano and the Vienna Circle, as well as Mach. Both of these traditions grew out of the Enlightenment and were committed to science and empiricism. But there still remain the two greatest Austrian philosophers: Bolzano and Wittgenstein. Bolzano is often ignored entirely by intellectual historians,[4] while Wittgenstein is marginalized by the Brentanian tradition as not really Austrian at all and, by those in the scientific tradition, as strangely located between logical positivism and analytic philosophy.[5] Philosophers in Austria made important contributions to semantics, logic, and psychology, as well as modern physics; and both the analytic and the phenomenological traditions had important roots there.[6] When philosophers write about philosophy in Austria, they are often concerned primarily with the origins of a particular philosophical tradition or method— e.g., analytic philosophy or phenomenology—rather than with what is Austrian. For the historian, it is less important to define Austrian philosophy than to describe and understand philosophy in Austria. There was a good deal more variety in this tradition than is sometimes acknowledged. At the same time, anyone who reads Austrian philosophers (and even Austrian writers) with the German idealist tradition in mind is likely to get off on the wrong foot.

Bernard Bolzano (1781–1848)

The first great figure of philosophy in Austria was Bernard Bolzano, who was born near the end of Austrian Enlightenment and became the leading figure in what was known, somewhat confusingly, as the Bohemian Enlightenment. We might reasonably think of him as the first philosophical child of Josephinism.[7] He was an important contributor to the emergence of scientific philosophy and a key figure in the way philosophy developed in Prague and Vienna. Although he wrote in German and largely in response to Immanuel Kant, Bolzano seems to embody the very opposite of what philosophers often mean by German philosophy—this utilitarian, semantic, scientific, and one might even say very "British" philosopher.[8] Peter Simons, one of the contemporary philosophers who has done most to draw attention to Bolzano's significance, argues that he was the most important philosopher of the nineteenth century: "Taken all together Bolzano's achievements mark him in my view as the greatest philosopher of the nineteenth century, bar none. No one else matches his Leibnizian polymathy of such uniformly high quality .... Bolzano has that *balance* and system that constitutes a great synoptic thinker, and his work has a wonderful limpid clarity." It is "a scandal that he and his work are still regularly omitted from university courses teaching nineteenth-century philosophy, that so little of his work is translated into English, and that there is no good introductory textbook in any language, even his own."[9] There is still a great deal of work to be done on such a major thinker; here, I will emphasize his contributions to logic and semantics and touch briefly on his views of religion and politics.

Bolzano was the first great logician after Gottfried Wilhelm Leibniz, and Leibniz was an important figure in Bolzano's intellectual world. For Central

European philosophers, Leibniz was a major alternative to Spinoza and Descartes, and he framed the issues of modern science in a distinctive way. He represented the reconciliation of Christianity and science in the Enlightenment and an anti-ideological reconciliation of Catholicism and Protestantism. Because of the pace of publication of his work and the variety of receptions, it is usually difficult to say just which Leibniz was being received in a given context, especially after Christian Wolff (1679–1754) had developed a more popularized version of his thought. By the twentieth century, philosophers were interested in what Leibniz had to say about propositions, while people in psychology and literature were intrigued by his view of apperception and unconscious ideas.[10] Bolzano's views were influenced by, but by no means identical with, Leibniz's view, and Bolzano worked to develop his own ideas in the direction of objectivity and universality rather than a personalized philosophy. Although his ideas grew out of this tradition, he distinguished himself, especially in his ethics, from his Austrian contemporaries "in the precision and persistence with which he thought through their common principles to their ultimate consequences." The distinctive notion in his philosophy was the "truth in itself," and logic is the point from which to understand all his thought. Truth is objective and to be discovered—like counting the number of petals on a particular rose. God thinks these truths because they are true; they are not true because God thinks them. Yet Bolzano did not believe in the stabilized harmony of Leibniz but "in a developing world, which is capable of and continually striving to, perfect itself." His ethics aimed to realize the justified wish of all human beings for happiness.[11]

Bolzano was a Catholic priest and professor of religion, and even in the early nineteenth century he was still shaped intellectually by the Enlightenment to a degree that was no longer acceptable to Church authorities in Vienna. His father was an art dealer whose family came from Italy, although Bernard grew up in Prague; his mother was devoted to her many children despite her poor health, and his parents seem to have been wonderful people,[12] who persuaded their son of the emptiness of honors and vanity. He attended a Piarist gymnasium, and, after studies that included physics and mathematics, Bolzano was appointed professor of religious instruction at Prague.[13] Bolzano served in this capacity between 1805 and 1819, and his teachings and sermons flowed from the rational Catholicism in which he had been brought up. Paul Rusnock and Rolf George put it this way: "He was educated both at home and in school in the spirit of the Bohemian Catholic Enlightenment, with its emphasis on clarity of thought, the cultivation of useful knowledge, and promotion of the common good."[14] Around the time that Hegel was moving to Berlin to shape the worldviews of a generation of German intellectuals, Bolzano was being removed from his university position in Prague for his unconventional religious and political views.[15] In just fifteen years as a professor in Prague, Bolzano became the leading figure of intellectual life in Bohemia, and his ideas continued to be influential through his students such as Joseph Fesl, who advocated many of Bolzano's political ideas, and Franz Exner, who played a leading role in the reform of the University of Vienna. Bolzano's influence on German and Czech elites in the early nineteenth century was wide and deep. George and Rusnock argue that "it would be difficult to find an example of a philosopher who had a greater impact on the political culture of his country."[16] And he wrote an entire book on his thoughtful views of political and social reform, although he did not imagine that his conception of the best state could or should be implemented quickly and easily.[17] Like most Josephinists, Bolzano was not attracted to revolutionary violence, but he was very much an advocate of progressive reform, and the suffering and cruelty of the 1840s made him curse both absolutist monarchies and constitutional states.[18] Roger Bauer locates Bolzano as part of a broader ideological tradition of South German Catholic philosophy that was directed against Kant's *Critique of Pure Reason*.[19] Catholic philosophy emphasized the objective reality of God's world in a way that was often very close to the commitments of modern science. Bolzano did everything he could to sustain the Enlightenment in this context, and we might characterize him as the opposite of Anton Günther, Bolzano's former student and the leading Catholic romantic of this period in Austria. Bolzano called Günther a dreamer, whose success "makes you want to tear your head off."[20]

Bolzano defined religion as "the sum of such doctrines or opinions which have either detrimental or beneficial influence upon the virtue and happiness of a human being."[21] His style of utilitarianism was very much continuous with eighteenth-century Josephinism, and his lectures on religion displayed the same qualities of mind that informed his work on logic and his theory of science.[22] Bolzano contrasted happiness to the preoccupation with selfishness or purely sensuous well-being, and he found his well-being in serving the greatest good. Many historians would be surprised to learn about this Catholic priest who advocated the complete equality of mankind, including the equality of women. His removal from his position of religious instruction allowed him to write his *Theory of Science* and many other important works.[23] After he was forced to step down from his position at the University of Prague, he lived with Josef and Anna Hoffmann from 1823 to 1841 in Těchobuz, a tiny town in central Bohemia.[24] He then returned to Prague, where he received support from Count Thun and continued his relationships with the high nobility and their sons.

For those who are not professional philosophers, Bolzano's lectures on the relationship between the two peoples of Bohemia constitute perhaps his most important and accessible work.[25] In these public lectures designed for religious edification, Bolzano argued that Christ's intention was not simply heavenly but earthly happiness as well, and that here on earth Christ was concerned "not only with the inner condition of human beings but also with their external condition."[26] He argued that the problem with politics in the early nineteenth century was not patriotism or love of country, but the evil of the upper classes, especially the indifference of the ruling classes toward the lower classes. His view of nationalism was striking in a period we normally refer to matter-of-factly as the age of nationalism, and it puts in perspective the usual assumption that Austrian opposition to nationalism was simply reactionary: "Bohemians [i.e. Czechs] and Germans! You must become one people; you can only be strong when you are united in a friendly way; you learn each other's language only to achieve a fuller equality; to share each other's concepts and knowledge in a brotherly way and without reservation." Bolzano regarded himself as a "Bohemian of the German tongue" who came to the defense of "Bohemians of the Slavic tongue."[27] This was of course not the view of language and nationality that was victorious in the nineteenth century. As Bolzano grew older, it became increasingly clear to him (writing of himself in the third person) that

> the perverse arrangements we still find more or less in all civic constitutions are, if not the only, certainly the most powerful obstacle to the improvement of things on earth. From this time on, he dedicated many of the hours he devotes to solitary reflection to the investigation of *how a state must be organized in order to accord with the most perfect advancement of the general well being.*

He believed that the aim of the state must be "the greatest possible promotion of the virtue and happiness of the whole." And he imagined a time when the entire human race will consider itself a single whole and then will constitute "*one single state*," which will include smaller societies and communities within it.[28]

Bolzano believed in reason and empiricism very much in the spirit of the Enlightenment. He shared a great deal of common ground with Kant, and it is a mistake in this sense to dwell too much on his rejection of Kant, but he did not accept the possibility of a priori synthetic propositions. He did not believe that human reason can know anything other than empirical truths except for definitions (analytic truths).[29] Bolzano (like Kant and the Enlightenment as a whole) was interested in the foundations of the natural sciences and mathematics, whereas Hegel, the most influential figure of German philosophy in the early nineteenth century, was centrally concerned with history and the human sciences. Some commentators argue that it was as if Austria had skipped the Kantian influence. It would be truer to say that Austria had skipped post-Kantian idealism and that Bolzano could be described as the Austrian Kant, in the sense that he was the philosophical culmination of the Enlightenment. Bolzano was a serious, though critical, student of Kant's works. His decisive contribution to a critique of Kant was his emphasis on the importance of making a sharp distinction between the subjective and the objective, that is, between subjective ideas or representations and objective thoughts in themselves. But this criticism of Kant had little to do with Bolzano's dislike for Hegel's method and for post-Kantian idealism in general. Indeed, Kant was a very clear thinker, and Bolzano quarreled with him only over very specific issues such as the possibility of a priori synthetic truths.

Far from being harshly polemical toward Kant, Bolzano may have taken Kant more seriously than any philosopher of his generation.[30] He referred to Kant as "our philosopher" and never engaged in sweeping polemics against idealism, although Bolzano's influence in Vienna certainly encouraged a broad resistance to German idealism.[31] In *The Critique of Pure Reason*, Kant was interested in how knowledge is possible, in understanding what was involved in perception and in any experience. For Bolzano, this approach was a matter of exploring the subjective grounds for truth rather than the objective grounds. Kant wanted to show how knowledge is possible (and he drew on the notion of pure intuition to do this), whereas Bolzano wanted to show what makes knowledge objective and communicable (thus anticipating twentieth-century concerns about private languages). Bolzano did not aim for a distinctive, personal philosophy, but rather for a sound basis for science and for any kind of thinking, and his thought captured the way in which science was crucial to the Enlightenment. This was the subject of his most important philosophical work : the *Wissenschaftslehre* or *Theory of Science* of 1837, which appeared in English more than a century later, when two translations were published almost simultaneously in 1972 and 1973.[32]

Bolzano intended his book as a theory of science, which he calls "logic" in the sense of establishing the conditions of knowledge.[33] Logic, for Bolzano, is concerned with the rules that hold for truth in general, what he called "propositions in themselves"; a proposition in Bolzano's sense is an "abstract non-linguistic *proposition (Satz an sich)*."[34] As John T. Blackmore, the distinguished biographer of Ernst Mach, put it when the translations of Bolzano's principal work appeared: "for those historians and translators who seek a major intellectual opportunity and challenge: here it is. A great man is waiting for you."[35] And he still is. And yet, as great as Bolzano's work was, it was frustratingly modest. *The*

Theory of Science is really a book about how to write a textbook [*Lehrbuch*], how to present some part of the body of knowledge. In that sense it is not quite what we mean today by a book on logic. He aims instead to show what belongs to knowledge, and how to explain it and clarify it. His notion of truth is propositional rather than an event in the mind, and he is concerned with what kinds of propositions belong in a textbook as part of the body of knowledge. He wanted to circumscribe what knowledge is objective and public rather than subjective and private, to present the objective grounds for a science.

For Bolzano, philosophy is concerned with how things are said, how propositions are formulated, and in this he is the founder of the modern semantic tradition.[36] He also invented a form of logic that emphasizes not the subject, predicate, and copula, but whole propositions; he is thus the founder of propositional logic, who pointed the way to Frege, Brentano, Russell, Wittgenstein, and twentieth-century British analytic philosophy. One recent commentator argues that his *Theory of Science* lays out "completely new semantico-logical foundations for the sciences."[37] Bolzano rather than Gottlob Frege is now acknowledged as the founder of modern analytic philosophy. He was a crucial figure in the nineteenth-century tendency to separate logic from mental processes, a view that is generally associated today with Frege and Edmund Husserl. As Frege put it, thoughts are "not contents of the mind."[38] Logic for Bolzano is not about thinking, not "psychologistic" in the sense of a process in the mind, as other logicians thought about it in the nineteenth century; Dummett characterizes the decisive issue here as "the extrusion of thoughts from the mind."[39]

Frege's distinction between ideas and senses coincides with Bolzano's distinction between ideas possessed (subjective ideas) and ideas in themselves (objective ideas). Frege seems not to have been aware of Bolzano's work, although Husserl was, and yet the folklore of analytic philosophy has preserved Frege in memory as the great founder. In the twentieth century, language came to provide the replacement for a mythological Platonic realm. Dummett argues that Frege and Husserl, two contemporaries writing in Germany around 1900, were like the Rhine and the Danube, rising nearby each other but flowing in quite different directions.[40] The analytic tradition argued that there was no meaning apart from language, but someone else appeared before Husserl and took philosophy in a different direction. Brentano was doing something very different; he was centrally concerned with psychology and the inner world and with *Vorstellungen* (usually translated as "presentations" rather than "representations," as in Kant).

Propositions in themselves are simply truths, true propositions, entities that are known. Propositions are composed of ideas, just as sentences are composed of words. For Bolzano, "ideas and propositions in themselves are objective" but not actual or real; that is, they do not exist. In an implicit clarification that he was not a Platonist, Bolzano explained to his friend Exner that objective truths have only the being of "being true."[41] Jan Berg characterizes what Bolzano means by "logic" as "a kind of metatheory, the objects of which are the several sciences and their linguistic representations," that is to say that what he means by logic is a theory of science.[42] Bolzano believed in "a fixed order among all true propositions" and "that our life on earth will be better and happier if more people gain insight into the world of scientific truth."[43] His book is an epitome of clear thinking and expression, which the Swedish philosopher Anders Wedberg describes this way: "To read the *Wissenschaftslehre* is also to receive a lesson in intellectual morality."[44]

Bernard Bolzano was a great mind in many regards, but the reason he is important to philosophers is that he was the first major philosopher in the analytic tradition, even though the modern analytic tradition is usually understood as a British tradition, growing out of the work of Moore and Russell, though indebted to Frege and Wittgenstein.[45] Thanks to Count Thun and Franz Exner, Bolzano's approach to philosophy arrived in the University of Vienna with Robert Zimmermann. Zimmermann was the son of one of Bolzano's friends, but he proved not to be the kind of mind Bolzano had hoped he would be. He represented Bolzano's ideas as his own and combined them with Johann Friedrich Herbart's, since, even after 1848, Bolzano's ideas were not politically and ideologically acceptable.[46] Indeed, Zimmermann brought Herbart into the mainstream of the University of Vienna.[47] Zimmermann never produced a Bolzano edition, but he did write a textbook for Austrian Gymnasia that was in Bolzano's spirit, which proved to be a "highly significant plagiarism."[48] In this indirect way, Bolzano' logic became the basis for teaching philosophy in Austria, especially after Zimmermann assumed the chair of philosophy in Vienna in 1861. Zimmermann was a familiar figure of the liberal era, and he knew writers such as Ferdinand von Saar, Robert Hamerling, and Marie von Ebner-Eschenbach. After 1848 Bolzano, Herbart, Zimmermann, and Exner emerged as the leading figures in Austrian philosophy.

Franz Brentano (1838–1917)

Franz Brentano was a mainstream European philosopher of the 1860s and 1870s, more or less continuous with Auguste Comte, J. S. Mill, and the positivist tradition.[49] He represents a distinctive combination of deep (and contemplative) religiosity with a strictly empirical, anti-speculative approach to philosophy. He is a peculiar case for Austrian philosophy because he was born and educated outside of Austria in what later became Imperial Germany, but his impact as a professor in Vienna was so great that it is probably right to regard him as the central figure of philosophy in Austria. Perhaps even more strangely, some philosophers regard his work as typically Austrian in the philosophical sense, quite apart from his connection to Austria.[50] He was born in Cologne and studied philosophy in Germany, submitting his Habilitation in 1865 at Würzburg, where he taught philosophy until he went to Vienna. The young Brentano took Aristotle rather than German idealism as his guide, and he set out from the correspondence theory of truth, "in which 'true' is interpreted as a relation between a judgment and a state of affairs."[51] He was ordained a priest in 1864 and resigned from the priesthood in 1873 over the issue of papal infallibility, but *Betrachtung* [contemplation or meditation] continued to be central to his life. He told Carl Stumpf that he would rather die than give up daily contemplation, and Edmund Husserl recalled him as "an image from a higher world." Brentano accepted a chair in philosophy in Vienna in 1874, but in order to marry in 1880 became a citizen of Saxony and stepped down from his professorship, which was never restored; he continued to teach in Vienna for fifteen years as an unsalaried lecturer, retiring in 1895 and moving to Italy.[52]

Brentano is somewhat better known than Bolzano, mainly because of his influence on two philosophers who are usually associated with Germany: Husserl and Martin Heidegger. They both taught in Germany, but Husserl was born in Moravia and studied with Brentano, while Heidegger spent his life in Germany.[53] Brentano's work seems likely to have less permanent philosophical significance than Bolzano's, but his influence was enormous in the late nineteenth century, including Robert Musil's teacher Carl Stumpf, Husserl (the main figure of phenomenology), Alexius Meinong (the founder of object-theory), Thomas Masaryk (the first president of Czechoslovakia),[54] Anton Marty, and Sigmund Freud, as well as Georg von Hertling, who was briefly chancellor of Imperial Germany at the end of the First World War. Since Brentano did not publish much in his lifetime, we know him primarily through his *Psychology from an Empirical Standpoint* of 1874, but he was one of the greatest teachers of philosophy who ever lived. It is evident that Brentano attracted the best students at the University of Vienna, whether from mathematics or medicine, and those who decided to continue with him in philosophy often made major contributions in their own right. Indeed, we may say that Brentano's significance as a philosopher disappeared into the achievements of his students in phenomenology and existentialism, philosophy of mind, Gestalt psychology, object-theory, and psychoanalysis.[55] Brentano emphasized scientific method in philosophy as well as a passion for empiricism. As he put it when he joined the faculty at Würzburg in 1866: "The true method of philosophy is none other than that of the natural sciences."

Brentano belonged to the intellectual world of William James, when philosophy and psychology were close together; we may think of him as part of the emerging field of psychology, including aspects of it that still seem difficult to quantify. Historians of philosophy ordinarily emphasize Brentano's contributions to the philosophy of mind. The great historian of psychology, Edwin Boring, located Brentano as part of "a humanistic trend in psychology" in contrast to Wilhelm Wundt's experimental psychology, although Brentano was apparently not at odds with Wundt on this subject, and some of Brentano's students did pursue laboratory research.[56] Brentano did not have a lab in Vienna, but his intentions were certainly scientific. Indeed, Simons emphasizes "the uncanny sense of direction with which he made psychology into a respectable empirical science."[57] Poli emphasizes Brentano's commitment to work in philosophy that is "rigorous, exact, and clear" and the broad influence of this approach in twentieth-century philosophy, but he also contends that Brentano's view of science as "an enrichment of our conceptions of the world" rather than an impoverishment was not successful in the twentieth century.[58]

Brentano wanted to give an account of consciousness or subjectivity. In this sense, he was a positivist, describing empirical phenomena, although subjectivity had not ordinarily been emphasized in this tradition. He contributed to the development of modern psychology and to the philosophy of mind at a time when these fields were difficult to distinguish. Brentano established his students as professors in Berlin (Stumpf and Husserl), Graz (Meinong),[59] and Prague (Ehrenfels, Marty, and Kraus). Twardowski, the founder of the Polish School of Logic, did much of his important work in Vienna under the influence of Brentano and Zimmermann.[60] Christian von Ehrenfels was a student of Brentano who opened the way to Gestalt psychology, which was later developed in Berlin by Stumpf, Max Wertheimer, and Wolfgang Köhler.[61] Karl Schuhmann calls Meinong's theory of objects "an ontological application of the principles of Brentano's psychology" and John Searle "the true revival of Brentano's idea of a descriptive psychology."[62]

Brentano argued for the importance of psychology by reminding us that "our mental phenomena are the things which are most our own," much as our solar system interests us more than other solar systems do. And he emphasized the importance of psychology for society, even calling it "the science of the future."[63] His philosophy is primarily a "descriptive psychology," and his aim was to find clear ways to describe mental experience. The English text of *Psychology from an Empirical Standpoint* is volume one of a projected, but never completed, three volumes; in this volume, Brentano is concerned mainly with method and with circumscribing the subject matter of psychology.[64] The book is beautifully written, thoughtful, clear, and grounded in the best of nineteenth-century science and empiricism. It is also the basis for the later development of psychoanalysis and phenomenology, which seem so different from the positivism of the late nineteenth century. Brentano carefully considered the importance of physiology for psychology, but he concluded (much as Freud did later) that physiology (brain physiology for example) could not do much to be useful to psychology at that stage. Thus, he attempted to identify what could be achieved by psychological rather than physiological means. Brentano argued that it was best in 1874 to concentrate on understanding normal, healthy relationships in the mind. We can see in his approach many of Freud's assumptions about the mental life of the self and others, but it is also clear that the framework he lays out contributed to modern psychology and psychiatry more broadly.

Brentano's definition of the field of psychology follows Aristotle's understanding of "the science of the soul," which Brentano formulates as "the science which studies the properties and laws of the soul, which we discover within ourselves directly by means of inner perception, and which we infer by analogy, to exist in others."[65] Brentano's other formulation—the "science of mental phenomena"—sounds more scientific to modern ears and is close to Ernst Mach's view that there are no wholes such as bodies and souls, but simply physical and mental phenomena or sensations.[66] If we think in terms of the tradition of empiricism or positivism in the nineteenth century, let us say of Comte or Mill, it is possible to have mental events as objects of knowledge only from a subjective or first-person point of view, that is as phenomena: whether by inner perception or by inner observation.

"Psychology, like the natural sciences," Brentano explains, "has its basis in perception and experience."

> Above all, however, its source is to be found in the *inner perception* of our own mental phenomena. We would never know what a thought is, or a judgement, pleasure or pain, desires or aversions, hopes or fears, courage or despair, decisions and voluntary intentions if we did not learn what they are through

> inner perception of our own phenomena. Note, however, that we said that inner *perception* [*Wahrnehmung*] and not introspection, i.e. inner *observation* [*Beobachtung*], constitutes this primary and essential source of psychology.⁶⁷

Brentano believed that we can never focus our attention on an "object of inner perception," which means that inner observation is possible only through memory.

For Brentano, the mind is always intentional. Its acts always point beyond it to something else or to a thought or judgment or feeling that is being presented.⁶⁸ Physical things are simply what they are. They do not point to anything, although we can use them as signs. The point, for Brentano, is that the mind is always aiming itself at something; that is, this is what human consciousness is like. Brentano used the word "intentional" but not the word "intentionality." Nonetheless, he did point in the direction of Husserl's later arguments, and the ideas of Jean-Paul Sartre and Emmanuel Lévinas grew out of Husserl's approach to intentionality.⁶⁹ As early as chapter two of *The Psychology* Brentano introduces the concept of "intentional inexistence," which is a medieval term: it means that when I think I am always pointing to an object, although the literal thing is not in my mind.⁷⁰ This became important in Brentano's later work, where he took a different view, and to his students such as Meinong and Twardowski. The term helps us to understand Freud's thinking about mental objects. Brentano's way of approaching these questions, which underscored the relationship between empiricism and the subject of knowledge, raised the issue for his students of distinguishing objects from mental states. In philosophy, Brentano was central for the work of Husserl, Twardowski, and Meinong. Meinong was brought to the attention of the English-speaking world by Russell, who emphasized Meinong's logical realism, while Twardowski shared Meinong's interests in the relation between "content" and "object."⁷¹ Meinong and his students have generally not emphasized his relationship to Brentano, but Brentano and Meinong were both "trying to work out a clear way of speaking of our inner experiences, of their various connections with each other and with their objects."⁷²

Brentano's most important book established the intellectual framework for Freud's work, although Brentano did not argue for unconscious mental processes. He did, however, undertake a careful discussion of views of the unconscious as they stood in the 1870s, when Freud was listening to his lectures. Brentano discusses in great detail the question of whether there are "unconscious mental acts." A lot depends here on definitions, of course, but Brentano takes the history of such ideas back to Aquinas, Leibniz, and even to Kant and John Stuart Mill's father, although the serious advocates of unconscious mental processes in 1874 were Henry Maudsley and Eduard von Hartmann, as well as Herbart, Wundt, and Gustav Fechner.[73] Particularly interesting on the question of Brentano's influence on Freud is William J. McGrath, who points out that Freud took five courses with Brentano; McGrath emphasizes Freud's debt to Brentano's efforts to balance physiological and psychological research: "a scientific working back and forth between evidence of the inner 'subjective' world and the outer 'objective world.'"[74]

The crucial issue for Brentano was that it seems impossible by definition to have consciousness of unconscious activities, since unconscious thoughts never appear as phenomena. He does point out that this problem could be avoided by arguing either "that certain facts given in experience demand the hypothesis of an unconscious mental phenomenon as their *cause*" or "that a fact given in experience must bring about an unconscious mental phenomenon as its *effect*, even though none appears in consciousness."[75] And these are, of course, approaches Freud later explored. Freud worked very much in Brentano's frame of reference: moving away from experimental psychology, working for a science of mental life and the soul, studying inner perception, emphasizing the importance of memory for psychological method, and searching for the laws of mental life. Brentano's was a descriptive psychology, however, whereas Freud attempted a causal, or what Brentano called a "genetic," psychology; this is meant to distinguish between describing phenomena and explaining them. Moreover Freud attempted to explain mental events that were not phenomena or inner perceptions. It is, oddly, Brentano's strict commitment to empiricism that makes him seem peculiar today. His aim was to describe mental events, which is to say events of consciousness, but this did not allow him to describe the mental events of others or to offer causal explanations. Freud did not adopt all of Brentano's ideas, but Brentano seems to have cleared the ground methodologically for the approach Freud decided to adopt, including his use of the word *Seele* or soul.[76] An understanding of Brentano's conception of psychology in his class on Psychology from an Empirical Standpoint would help to clarify the degree to which Freud's work did not appear simply by surprise, and not only in relation to Josef Breuer, Wilhelm Fliess, Friedrich Nietzsche, and Arthur Schopenhauer. Indeed Freud's work was directly connected to the mainstream of scientific developments in psychology in ways that are rarely appreciated.

Brentano's work and influence constituted an extraordinarily fruitful moment in the history of philosophy, when the field was close to psychology and all avenues of psychological research seemed to be open. This moment was also fruitful for analytic philosophy and phenomenology. Jacquette calls Brentano "the most notable bridge figure between the traditions of analytic and continental philosophy."[77] On the other hand, Jacquette argues "that what has come to be known as the scientific community in the study of cognitive psychology is firmly in the grip of a narrow conception of empirical science advocated by logical positivism, engaged exclusively in the work of what Brentano would call 'genetic' or causally reductive neurophysiological, behavioristic, or computational psychology."[78]

Ernst Mach (1838–1916)

Ernst Mach was an experimental physicist, who is best known as a philosopher of science. He was born in Moravia and spent most of his academic career in Prague (1867–1895), although he studied at the University of Vienna and moved again to Vienna near the end of his career. He was perhaps the most anti-ideological figure of modern positivism, and he moved away from the French tradition of Saint-Simon and Comte—later so forcefully criticized by F. A. von Hayek—to what Mach regarded as the strictly anti-metaphysical ground of the exact natural sciences. He came from a family of German-speaking peasants from Northern Bohemia. His father, Johann Mach, had studied philosophy (in the 1820s) at Charles-Ferdinand University in Prague and for a time had considered becoming a Piarist.[79] He was German-speaking but not drawn to either German or Czech nationalism. His thinking was very much continuous with Joseph II and Bolzano, and his son seems to have shared his political views.

Ernst Mach spent his childhood in Moravia near Brno and in a small town about twenty miles from Vienna, where his father was a teacher and tutor. It is clear that even as a child Mach had an instinct for the natural sciences, although he never had much training in mathematics. It was also as a child that he became intrigued and puzzled by questions of perception and perspective, which laid the groundwork for a lifetime of exploring these questions. He attended secondary school in Kremsier, the Moravian town where the constitution of 1848–1849 had been written and ratified. He studied at the University of Vienna, receiving his doctorate in physics in 1860. In 1862, while he was teaching in Vienna, Mach met Josef Popper-Lynkeus (one of the most unconventional minds of the nineteenth century), who became his closest friend.[80] Mach taught in Graz between 1864 and 1867, when he began to develop his ideas for *Contributions to the Analysis of Sensations*. His early work in Graz and in Prague after 1867 was mainly experimental, but he also wrote a history of mechanics in 1883.[81] He was rector of the university in Prague in 1879–1880 and, after the university divided, rector of the German university in 1883–1884, but he stepped down because of the politics and because he wanted to finish his book on sensations. His work belonged to a stage in the development of science, when a number of fundamental questions were open but moving toward resolution. As with many Austrian scientists, Darwin's *Origins of Species* was a defining moment.[82] Yet Mach was not a biologist but a physicist with a strong experimentalist orientation, and he was influenced by Gustav Fechner and the discussion around psycho-physics. All of this coincided with the early development of atomic physics. Mach's genius as a scientist was his sensitivity to perception, which drew him to experimental work on acoustics, *Gestalt* qualities, and what were later known as Mach bands. His interests were close to psychology as well as to physics and philosophy, and he aimed for a way of doing modern science that stayed free of metaphysical implications, especially free from ideas of substance or ego. Religion seems to have played almost no role in his thinking, at least not Christianity. His experimental orientation and his commitment to the unity of scientific knowledge led him to develop the view that was central to his most important work.

In writing *Contributions to the Analysis of Sensations* (1886) Mach set out from the great achievements of physics since the seventeenth century, but also from the danger that the perspective of physics would dominate the other sciences in an unfruitful way. His aim in this book was the unity of knowledge, and he grounded all knowledge in ordinary sensations. We build up our picture of the world from our sensations, and we distinguish other unities, such as the ego or the body, for practical purposes. But "the primary fact is not the *I*, the ego, but the elements (sensations). The elements *constitute* the *I*."[83] He observed that "the complex of memories, moods, feelings, joined to a particular body (the human body), which is denominated the 'I' or 'Ego,'" appears to be relatively permanent. "Of course the ego also is only of relative permanency."[84] Like Brentano around the same time, Mach was concerned with distinguishing between the psychical and the physical. Like Musil and Freud, he was interested in understanding more about emotions, including unconscious processes in the mind. Here Mach was concerned with emphasizing the way we take up different perspectives and regard the same sensations first as physical objects and then as physiological sensations. He emphasized that everything we know about reality is relational, and at times he sounds like a biological Kant and seems close to Kant's critique of metaphysics, arguing that the human being is a psycho-physical animal studying physical phenomena. In 1900 Mach published a revised edition of this argument, in which he moved a statement about the ego from a footnote to the main text and gave it even more emphatic formulation:

> The ego must be given up. It is partly the perception of this fact, partly the fear of it, that has given rise to the many extravagances of pessimism and optimism, and to numerous religious, ascetic, and philosophical absurdities.[85]

Here Mach seems to have been concerned primarily with the assumptions in his culture, which of course shaped science as well, rather than with responding to Descartes or some other specific philosopher. He was close to Nietzsche's views around the same time, and Georg Lichtenberg seems to have led him to the view that there was no ego or self, that is, no unity or reality that was not present in sensations. "No point of view has absolute, *permanent* validity. Each has importance only for some given end."[86]

Like Brentano, Mach was a phenomenologist; that is, he emphasized the role of sensations and experimental relationships in knowledge rather than some more fundamental, unknown reality. Mach argued that the basis of all knowledge is sensations (i.e., phenomena), and he saw no need to postulate a thing-in-itself or noumenon in Kant's sense. He was a presentationalist "in identifying the physical world with what could be immediately sensed" and a phenomenalist "in rejecting causes as agents or forces in favor of describing conscious referents in terms of mathematical functions or equations."[87] We have only the immanent world of our sensations as the basis for our knowledge; sensations are all we have to work with when we try to understand what reality is. He also argued that no one set of sensations (no single field of knowledge) was more fundamental than others, that no one bundle of sensations, whether matter or the self, is more fundamental than any other; in this respect, he was challenging the special prominence of physics and the physical understanding of the world. He regarded science as a way for the human being to master his experience and the practical demands of existence. This was a worldview only in the sense that this was the way he viewed the world, but not in the sense that he claimed to know the truth about reality. For Mach, knowledge was always relative and practical. Mach used the word "sensation" only to emphasize what is connected to the subject, but he grew to prefer the term "element," which emphasized the objective connections.[88] In Erwin Hiebert's words, Mach was not attracted to "large syntheses and over-arching reductive world views." In a late edition of *Analysis of Sensations*, Mach teased some who had commented on the original edition: "Thus, first and foremost," he mocked, "you have to choose a system; then within the walls of that system you may think and speak."[89] And Philipp Frank adds: "If physics is to become a church, Mach cries out, I would rather not be a physicist."[90]

Mach and Brentano were exactly the same age, and their ideas grew out of nineteenth-century positivism rather than German idealism; in somewhat different ways, they both influenced the sympathy for scientific thought among Austrian intellectuals at the turn of the century, although Brentano was close to psychology while Mach was a physicist. Mach brought physics close to psychology, and he did much to refine and develop the empirical and positivist traditions. Although Mach's views were similar to Brentano's, he was not a priest or a Catholic; his approach was secular, and, unlike Brentano, he was not interested in ontology. William James recalled the impact Mach made on him as a person: "I don't think anyone ever gave me so strong an impression of pure intellectual genius. He apparently has read everything and thought about everything, and he has an absolute simplicity of manner and winningness of smile."[91] Partly thanks to the efforts of Heinrich Gomperz, Mach was offered and accepted an invitation to Vienna to fill one of the vacant chairs in philosophy, which was sometimes referred to as Brentano's chair.[92] Mach's position was tailored to his concern with the "history and theory of the inductive sciences." He had a great impact in Vienna and abroad when he first arrived, and he found more appreciation and recognition in Vienna than he had in Prague.

Mach's ideas contributed to the intellectual atmosphere of the 1890s in Vienna, and this was the view that Otto Weininger was reacting against in his critique of modern science. Mach, Nietzsche, and Musil all moved away from the ego, and together they constitute an important critique of conventional nineteenth-century liberalism.[93] Certainly the notion (if not the practice) that the ego must be given up is one prominent tendency from Mach that was strongly influential in the 1890s. This was a peculiar culmination for the liberal era, which was continuous with the assumptions of late nineteenth-century liberalism, Mill, science, and progress, but challenged the central assumption of most nineteenth-century liberal thought: the free individual. Austrians often emphasize the contrast to Kant's notion of the thing in itself; Mach did indeed point to the superfluity of this concept, but the word describes exactly what Lenin and most physicists had in mind. Scientists who find Mach's anti-atomism annoying or amusing are rarely thinking of the peculiar views and metaphysical monstrosities that had been believed by scientists in the nineteenth century or of Freud. Mach certainly was not Kantian in the sense of "the thing in itself," although in this regard he was sometimes thinking of popular conceptions of reality (the belief in a real object apart from the one we observe) rather than Kant's text, and he mocked distinctions between appearance and reality that were common in the literature of the time. He wanted to emphasize that all appearances simply represent different perspectives. In the later edition, he added an example of a pencil in the air and in the water: "In both cases we have to do with facts which present us with different combinations of the elements, combinations which in the two cases are differently conditioned."[94]

Mach was influential for important physicists such as Einstein and Planck, but they also moved away from Mach's phenomenalism in physics. Mach and Ludwig Boltzmann are often paired in controversies about atomic theory around 1900, and much of Mach's late career was submerged in these debates about atomic particles. This is still how Mach is remembered by many historians of science. For many scientists, Planck's harsh critique of Mach has been influential, while Mach had difficulty taking Planck seriously as a philosopher. Notable here are Mach's relativism and irony and Planck's seriousness and absolutism. It was not clear until about 1910 that Mach's view of physics had been defeated, and Planck's suicide apparently had little or nothing to do with his controversy with Mach. Mach preferred to avoid theory (of which there were a number at the time that are no longer accepted) and to emphasize describing experiences. He thought in terms of describing experimental regularities in an economical way, but not trying to divine a deeper reality beneath. Mach had always been intrigued by the experimental basis of knowledge, and, in that sense, it seems obvious that he would have had reservations about atomic theory as a kind of scientific metaphysics.

Although Mach is often associated with the Vienna Circle, his most important work appeared nearly fifty years before logical positivism, and he generally resisted the dogmatic style associated with some figures of the Vienna Circle. Mach dedicated *Knowledge and Error* in 1905 to the memory of David Hume, Richard Avenarius, and Wilhelm Schuppe (whose philosophy of immanence united subject and object); these names make clear his own sense of location in the philosophical tradition. Mach's ideas contributed to the emerging ideal of a unified science,[95] but the ideological temperature of positivism in Vienna was raised by Monism (a widespread but often not very clearly defined movement),[96] Marxism, and the polarization of politics after the First World War. The Monist Society might be called a scientific religion, and Mach was not comfortable with this new movement despite its similarities to his own views.

Mach was interested in a sensible approach to scientific knowledge, and in this way all his work connects with the Vienna Circle. He had a strong sense of the provisionality (or tentativeness) of scientific knowledge, along with a good deal of respect for the normal worldview of the average man. But he believed that the aim of science must be "a freer, fresher view, conforming to developed experience, and reaching out beyond the requirements of practical life." It "never occurs to [the plain man] to regard the whole world as the creation of his senses."[97] Although Mach was not a worldview philosopher, his followers (including some in the Vienna Circle) often were.[98] Mach exercised an enormous impact on philosophers, writers, and scientists in Austria, but also in Germany and elsewhere in Europe.[99] Both Mach and Wittgenstein were interested in how scientists describe the world, and it is not surprising that these ways of thinking culminated in the Vienna Circle.

Ludwig Wittgenstein (1889–1951)

Like Freud, Ludwig Wittgenstein lived in Austria and wrote in German. As *Wittgenstein's Vienna* and the responses to it made clear in the 1970s, what this means for philosophy is complicated.[100] Wittgenstein was, of course, influenced by British and European philosophy, especially by Bertrand Russell, G. E. Moore, Alfred North Whitehead, and Gottlob Frege. But he wrote in German, grew up in Vienna, and published his first philosophical work after serving in the Habsburg army during the First World War. In the last two decades of his life, he lived and worked for the most part in Cambridge, England, and here I will distinguish between the early Wittgenstein and the later Wittgenstein, whose work is properly understood in an English context.[101] There is certainly a break in his activity as a creative philosopher in the 1920s and in his biography; his philosophical work resumed only after his departure for Cambridge.

Wittgenstein was born just outside of Vienna to a family of industrialists and creative people. His father was a German who came to Austria in the late nineteenth century. The Wittgenstein family on the paternal side was Protestant, but the earnest, ethical style of the family seems to have borne a Jewish stamp, although the members of the family did not regard themselves as Jewish. The family had emigrated from Southern Germany in the late nineteenth century, and their Jewish background is often emphasized. The maternal side of the family had assimilated to Catholicism, so that Ludwig and his siblings were brought up Catholic; Ludwig's mother's family was very Viennese and very musical, and the Wittgenstein home became a salon in the best Austrian tradition, so that the children were exposed to leading social and cultural figures of Vienna.[102] Karl Kraus and Otto Weininger were both important influences on Wittgenstein's thought as a young man, especially on his thinking about sexuality and what it meant to be Jewish, and Arthur Schopenhauer seems to have been a powerful philosophical influence at this time as well. That three of his brothers committed suicide speaks volumes about the family, the culture, and what Wittgenstein himself was dealing with as a young man—and why Schopenhauer's *The World as Will and Representation* (1819) resonated so powerfully with him. Wittgenstein decided to become an engineer, and he was studying in a *Realschule* in Linz at the time of Weininger's notorious suicide. In 1908 he went to Manchester to study aeronautics, and he seems to have brought this problem-solving approach to philosophy. Wittgenstein began his academic career as an engineer and a mathematician, and he developed an idiosyncratic but practical and logical approach to philosophical problems.[103] An important factor in his life seems to have been the strong sense of social isolation he felt because of his sexual orientation, which apparently motivated his admiration for Weininger's struggles with his own sexuality.[104] Wittgenstein's years of solitary intensity in Norway before the war were followed by his religious experience while he was at the front during the war. Throughout these years he worked on his ideas about logic. After the war he gave up his large inheritance and went to Kirchberg in southern Austria to teach.

Wittgenstein was interested in what it is like to describe the world, to make a picture of it, and he was influenced in this approach by Heinrich Hertz's *The Principles of Mechanics*.[105] Wittgenstein's concern (in comparison to Schopenhauer, for example) was especially with the structure of these representations and what this tells us about the structure of the world. He was not a physicist, but a logician, and he was interested in "the logico-ontological character of the world," which "precedes any theories or scientific formulations about facts."[106] Thus, he was interested in the structure of the world and the way this is represented in propositions. For Wittgenstein "the whole of reality is a picture" (2.063), and John Koethe has pointed to the continuity throughout his philosophical work of "the ocular metaphor of the pictorial character of language and thought."[107] What makes this view distinctive is that every picture has a logical form, the form of reality.

Unlike Brentano and Mach, Wittgenstein did not belong to the empiricist tradition in philosophy—the tradition of Berkeley and Hume—nor was he a German idealist as this term is ordinarily understood. (He was also interested in propositions rather than phenomena.) Aside from modern science and music, he seems to have been influenced primarily by Arthur Schopenhauer and Gottlob Frege. Wittgenstein himself emphasized the link to Frege, and for those who are interested in the development of modern logic and semantic philosophy, this was the connection that was easy to follow. Less familiar was the reference to Schopenhauer, and this connection underlay much of the argument of *Wittgenstein's Vienna*, although Schopenhauer was of course no more Austrian than Kant, and he was not a German idealist. Schopenhauer was, however, crucial for the leading figures of the generation of 1905 in Austria.[108] What distinguishes the young Wittgenstein from nineteenth-century positivism is his emphasis on linguistic definitions rather than empiricism, although it was in the name of a refined empiricism that Wittgenstein wrote his book. In all of these regards he pointed the direction for the Vienna Circle, even if their emphasis proved to be different from his own. In this regard he was closer to Bolzano than to Brentano or Mach.[109]

Before he was thirty, Wittgenstein had written his first important work of philosophy, the *Tractatus-Logico Philosophicus*, an account of how language pictures reality.[110] The world is such that it can be pictured in logical space—and thus show the order of the world. Wittgenstein's account focuses on language, but the problem it deals with is the nature of reality. It is important to emphasize the beauty of Wittgenstein's writing—both the elegance and economy of the design and the care and precision of each sentence. Wittgenstein's "writing is extraordinarily compressed, and it is necessary to ponder each word in order to understand his sentences."[111] Wittgenstein advocated restraint in matters of meaning, a cleaner way of talking about the world that makes clear the limits of language, and he was very like Bolzano in these respects. The elegance with which he did this is all his own, but his sobriety and irony resonate with the Austrian tradition in philosophy and literature from Bolzano and Grillparzer to Musil. His own summary of his argument is that "what can be said at all can be said clearly, and what we cannot talk about we must pass over in silence" (3). The concluding formulation of the book repeats this theme: "What we cannot speak about we must pass over in silence."[112] His view that what is beyond the limits of language is nonsense is indeed close to the Vienna Circle, but Wittgenstein's tone and emphasis are different.

Wittgenstein elaborates on Schopenhauer's view that the world is my representation of it, although Wittgenstein's language is somewhat different. His picturing of reality focuses on the form of representation, which he discusses in terms of *abbilden* (making a picture or a model) rather than *vorstellen* (representing). I have always regarded "picture" as an adequate translation of Schopenhauer's *Vorstellung* for the purposes of understanding, even if there may be some technical difficulties with this word, which has been used in a variety of philosophies. Thus, we might say that "the world is my picture of it" (my translation of Schopenhauer's German). We know that Wittgenstein was influenced by Schopenhauer, but Wittgenstein used the word *Bild* and discussed this term in some detail with his translator, C. K. Ogden. Wittgenstein's view of a picture of the world is more atomistic than Schopenhauer's, in the sense of propositional: i.e., my picture of the world is built up out of propositions. But it seems likely that Wittgenstein's impulse to approach his project in these terms came from his reading of Schopenhauer—and, before that, from his reading of Kant. He introduced a distinction between *Vorstellung* (something in the mind) and *Darstellung* (propositions), which corresponds to Bolzano's move away from Kant. The real key is the move to language and propositions, that is, the linguistic turn. This was an important philosophical move for Wittgenstein, but it grew out of his deep interest in Schopenhauer as a young man.

What is exciting about Wittgenstein's argument is that he argues that logical form is the form of reality.[113] That is, logic is not simply a self-contained set of abstractions, but the logic of reality. Thus, logic is the common ground between the world (or the whole of reality, 2.063) and the models that we make to picture this reality (2.18).[114] This allows him to proceed simply by defining and clarifying his terms, which he takes to be the task of philosophy, a task that was important in this tradition from Bolzano to the Vienna Circle. What the *Tractatus* does is to give an account of what language and logic can do to describe the world. It also thereby dispenses with most metaphysical problems. Wittgenstein's solution validates the scientific project without being ideological. As Wittgenstein put it in his *Notebooks* while he was writing the *Tractatus*: "The great problem round which everything that I write turns is: Is there an order in the world a priori, and if so what does it consist in?"[115] His book attempts to show what sort of language can do this, since a colloquial language cannot.

Wittgenstein makes clear what words mean in order to eliminate confusions. For example, the world is everything that is the case; that is, the world is the sum of meaningful propositions, and this is what "the world" means. This is not what most people mean when they say "world." But it is close to what Schopenhauer meant by the world as representation, except that Wittgenstein thought of the world in propositional terms: "The totality of true propositions is the whole of natural science (or the whole corpus of the natural sciences)." (4.11) Wittgenstein's ideas in this period were closely related to Russell's, and their somewhat different approaches at this time are often brought together with the term "logical atomism," which holds "that the reasons we have for believing in the atoms come not from physics or psychology but from logic."[116] In the *Tractatus*, Wittgenstein simply wants to say what philosophy can do, what it can say. His clarifications are impressive and illuminating in a way that helps us to understand what we have been saying. "Philosophy does not result in 'philosophical propositions,' but rather in the clarification of propositions" (4.112). What the *Tractatus* does is to give an account of what language and logic can do to describe the world. Once this is done, Wittgenstein argued, there are no philosophical questions left. What the logical positivists were less attuned to and less inclined to emphasize was that, at that point, the problems of life have not been addressed at all.

Proposition 6.53, near the end of the *Tractatus*, seems to say two different things at the same time. "The correct method in philosophy would really be the following: to say nothing except what can be said, i.e. propositions of natural science—i.e. something that has nothing to do with philosophy—and then, whenever someone else wanted to say something metaphysical, to demonstrate that he had failed to give a meaning to certain signs in his propositions." This became the guiding principle of the Vienna Circle, but what these philosophers were less concerned with was Wittgenstein's understanding of what cannot be said. Wittgenstein is sometimes closely associated with logical positivism, though he seems to have been more interested than the Vienna Circle in what cannot be said: "We feel that even when all possible scientific questions have been answered, the problems of life remain completely untouched. Of course there are then no questions left, and this itself is the answer" (6.52).[117]

The Vienna Circle

In the broadest, most ecumenical sense, the Vienna Circle was a group of philosophers and scientists who were interested in scientific knowledge and in ways of extending and furthering it.[118] In this sense the connection to the early Wittgenstein is not difficult to understand—that is to say, the task of philosophy is science, that is, clarifying the propositions of science.[119] Even in its programmatic forms, especially when it became a public movement in 1929, the aim of the Vienna Circle was a unified science, and it was resistant to systematic philosophy or to any philosophy that was not scientific, public, and verifiable. There was considerable variety among the individuals associated with the Circle, but these formulations sometimes took on a dogmatic, exclusive tone. At the same time, it is important to bear in mind the ideological context of the 1930s, when the alternative seemed to be frankly anti-scientific and metaphysical.

The Vienna Circle began to take shape in the 1920s, most notably with the arrival of Moritz Schlick in Vienna in 1922 to assume the chair for the philosophy of the inductive sciences. Schlick was German and a physicist, but he knew philosophy, and he became the center of a group of mainly younger philosophers and scientists who were interested in the unity of sciences.[120] The philosophers of the Vienna Circle first presented themselves as a distinct group at the meetings of the German Physical Society and the German Mathematical Association in Prague in 1929. The group was under threat in the 1930s, and Schlick was actually assassinated on the university steps in Vienna in 1936. After 1938 the Vienna Circle dispersed, especially to the United States and England, where the group had great influence. Karl Popper never attended the meetings but he was in touch with Rudolf Carnap, Herbert Feigl, and Viktor Kraft.

The broader context for the Vienna Circle was the Ernst Mach Society, which was founded in 1928 by Schlick and others; this association was devoted to scientific education and popular understanding of modern science: "The history of the Ernst Mach Society cannot be understood apart from the 'late enlightenment currents' of the Ethical Movement, Monists, and Free thinkers in the context of the Social Democratic cultural movement and related streams of liberalism."[121] A number of conflicting ideas and tendencies and organizations came together in the 1920s—the Ernst Mach Society, especially the commitment to adult education, the long empiricist tradition in Austria, and the preoccupations of physicists and mathematicians. The manifesto took much of its language and tone from Otto Neurath. It was written to announce the Vienna Circle and to honor Schlick and keep him from taking a position in Bonn, although Schlick was not entirely comfortable with their language.

> The Vienna Circle does not confine itself to collective work as a closed group. It is also trying to make contact with the living movements of the present, so far as they are well disposed toward the scientific world-conception and turn away from metaphysics and theology. The Ernst Mach Society is today the place from which the Circle speaks to a wider public. This society, as stated in its program, wishes to "further and disseminate the scientific world-conception. It will organize lectures and publications about the present position of the scientific world-conception, in order to demonstrate the significance of exact research for the social sciences and the natural sciences. In this way intellectual tools should

be formed for modern empiricism, tools that are also needed in forming public and private life."[122]

The Vienna Circle was neither as distinctively Viennese nor as dogmatic as it has sometimes been reputed to have been. Victor Kraft emphasizes that the members of the Circle were mainly concerned not with the traditional problems of philosophy but very narrowly with scientific knowledge.[123] And most of them were physicists or concerned with logic and mathematics. Many of them were young and enthusiastic in the interwar years and launching an international mission.[124] The central concern of the Circle was a unified philosophy of the sciences, and its characteristic feature was to add a more sophisticated approach to mathematics, concepts, and symbols to the earlier position of Ernst Mach. Their aim was to bridge the divide between concepts and intuitions, between mathematics and sensations, that was present from Bolzano to Mach.[125] But the circle did have a strong ideological component—the scientific worldview—which can be formulated dogmatically or in a more modest, softer way.[126] The more dogmatic formulations of the scientific worldview seemed sometimes to exclude anything but science from thoughtful discussion. As Edmund Husserl, perhaps the greatest philosopher of the early twentieth century, put it, "[p]ositivism, in a manner of speaking, decapitates philosophy."[127] But many members of the circle resisted this ideological tendency that Mach had warned about.[128] In its less dogmatic forms, positivism advocated modern science and aimed to keep the connection to experience; in the latter regard, they believed that the principal obstacle was language, which was crucial to the efforts of logical positivism.

Conclusion

This chapter does not, of course, discuss all philosophers or all philosophies in Austria, and my aim is not to define the essence of Austrian philosophy. These are simply the philosophers who worked in Austria who have been especially important for modern philosophy. They are meant to give points of orientation to readers who are not already familiar with the field, and there were of course other philosophers in Austria from Rudolf Steiner or Max Adler to Eric Voegelin. Georg Lukács might be considered here or as part of German-speaking intellectual history, but I see him as part of German-speaking intellectual life in Hungary.[129]

I am not arguing that Kant, Hegel, and Marx exercised no influence in Austria, but they were not Austrian philosophers in the sense of living and working in Austria. It is true that Kant had nothing like the same impact in Austria as he had elsewhere in cosmopolitan German culture, and Metternich eventually did a good deal to limit his influence. Hegel was criticized by Austrian philosophers throughout the nineteenth century, but Marx had much the same impact on Austrian Socialism as he did elsewhere. All of German-speaking philosophy was read by Austrians, and Austrians were read in Germany. Husserl and Mauthner and Stumpf spent their academic careers in Germany, and Brentano, of course, left Germany as a young man to become the most influential philosopher in Austria. Gestalt psychology began in Austria, but became famous in Berlin, while Haeckel and Monism were influential in Austria.

Bolzano, Brentano, Mach, and Wittgenstein represent quite distinct approaches to philosophy, but they also share a strong affinity for modern science and its methods, as well as a desire to clarify these methods, though without arguing for world-views or belief-systems. These philosophers were advocates of science and scientific method in philosophy but not of the "scientific worldview" in the sense of the Vienna Circle or nineteenth-century French positivism. But from Bolzano to the Vienna Circle we see the concern with how to communicate knowledge or, we may say, how to write a textbook. Despite their common commitment to modern science, Brentano and Bolzano had different intentions in their philosophical work. While Bolzano aimed for the precision of a scientific language and thus contributed to logic and to the semantic tradition, Brentano's work was grounded in empiricism, experience, and everyday life, especially the phenomena of consciousness. Bolzano's greatest influence has been in the field of logic, establishing a secure basis for valid truth, whereas Brentano's interest in mental phenomena tended to emphasize ordinary language rather than the strict mathematical language of science. But common to both philosophers was what we might characterize as an Austrian tendency to turn away from speculative philosophy and to emphasize a slow, patient style of philosophical work. Philosophers have not been as interested in Mach as in Brentano and Bolzano. But Mach is important for the history and philosophy of science. Wittgenstein was so important for analytic philosophy that he nearly blots out the contributions of Bolzano, Brentano, and the Vienna Circle for many analytic philosophers, while the influence of Husserl and Heidegger in Germany frequently obscures the contributions of Brentano. At the same time, the continuity from Mach to the Vienna Circle tended to assimilate and obscure Brentano's significance, even within Austria.

Formulating a single definition of Austrian philosophy seems to me less important than understanding where Austria was in the nineteenth century and how important this region was in intellectual terms. For Bolzano and Brentano, what is most evident is the common commitment to modern science and to matters of method and style that accompany it; and the third major Austrian philosopher of the nineteenth century, Ernst Mach, clearly fits such a conception. Certainly, the contrast to post-Kantian idealism is clear enough, at least for these nineteenth-century figures. At the same time, it is important to realize that there were other kinds of philosophy in Austria and that even the scientific philosophers (including Wittgenstein) could be scientific and still be different from the Vienna Circle. For the historian, it is less important to define Austrian philosophy than to understand philosophy in Austria.

The Austrian tradition in philosophy resisted philosophy in big slices, that is, anything like a worldview philosophy. Indeed, this is what most separates the Vienna Circle from the four main philosophers I have described. Philosophy in Austria and the broader tradition of thought were inclined to an ironic, modest style that was strongly influenced by modern science, empiricism, and the Enlightenment, but resisted dogmatism even in the name of science. Walter Weiss, one of the most thoughtful scholars of Austrian intellectual history, put it this way:

> In relation to pre-idealistic philosophy, for example Leibniz, there developed from the 19th into the 20th century, from Bolzano to Brentano, Husserl to the Vienna Circle of analytic philosophy, down to Carnap and Popper, a specific tradition of what began as a religiously grounded ethical, logical, methodological objectivism or realism, which set itself against the idealistic-dialectical as well as the later materialistic-dialectical totalitarian construction of the world. Robert Musil stands close to this philosophical direction and created the most impressive literary equivalent.[130]

Ulrich, the protagonist of Musil's *The Man without Qualities*, "took a somewhat ironic view of philosophy," and the narrator emphasizes that he "was no philosopher":

> Philosophers are despots who have no armies to command, so they subject the world to their tyranny by locking it up in a system of thought.[131] This apparently also accounts for the presence of great philosophers in times of great tyrants, while epochs of progressive civilization and democracy fail to bring forth a convincing philosophy, at least to judge by the disappointment one hears so widely expressed on the subject. Hence today we have a terrifying amount of

philosophizing in brief bursts, so that the shops are the only places where one can still get something without Weltanschauung.[132]

Between the Enlightenment and the Second World War, Austrian philosophers made important contributions to our understanding of objectivity and knowledge. Bolzano set the terms for the modern understanding of truth and logic, while Wittgenstein summarized the advances of nineteenth-century science and realism, and introduced the twentieth-century's preoccupation with language. In the work of these philosophers, notably Brentano and Mach, these efforts moved in the direction of understanding the mind, ethics, and psychology, but by the twentieth-century Wittgenstein's clarifications emphasized the limits of what can be said and the incommunicability of the concerns of ethics and aesthetics. For the most part, however, Austrian philosophers, especially in the Vienna Circle (but in Popper as well), stopped with defining the limits of possible knowledge and what can be said. Austrian literature, too, began with the Enlightenment—with nature, reason, and social reality—but it moved by the end of the nineteenth century to the realm of ethics and imagination.

For the most part Austrian philosophy may be characterized as "nominalistic," a term developed to describe the medieval ways of thinking that eventually led to John Locke.[133] Its characteristic quality is the view that human beings are not able to know the nature of reality in the universalistic way that the scholastics had hoped for. This point of view came to characterize economic theory in Austria in the liberal era, but it also helps to distinguish two kinds of positivism, one dogmatic and one more modest. The mainstream of Austrian philosophy is this more modest strand. This way of thinking cannot claim to know the universal nature of reality and is not in a position to impose its view on others. It is content to accept the wisdom of Musil's protagonist that the world is not obliged to conform to our conceptions of it.

4

German Literature in Austria

If Austrian philosophers have often been ignored by those with an interest in German philosophy, scholars of German literature have been more inclined to absorb Austrian literature into German literature without making much effort to distinguish writers who are not from Germany. As Ulrich Greiner playfully put it, twentieth-century critics in Germany periodically rediscovered that their favorite German writers actually came from another country.¹ And Franz Blei made a similar remark in the early twentieth century about Robert Musil and Hermann Broch: "Strange, that it should be two Viennese writers who have written the fundamentally different novels, from which we will date a new epoch of the German novel."² This pattern continued after the Second World War and even into the twenty-first century. In his recent history of Austrian literature since 1945, Klaus Zeyringer wonders how it is that Fischer Verlag can publish titles such as *Deutschland erzählt—Von Rainer Maria Rilke bis Peter Handke*.³ And this title is by no means an anomaly. The impulse to treat Austrian intellectuals as if they lived in Germany is common in discussions of German literature in a way that we do not find in German philosophy. As with philosophy, I will concentrate here on major texts, but again in this chapter I am concerned primarily with how scholars frame Austrian texts and writers—and concerned to present Austrian literature to the field of European intellectual history.

Consciousness of Austrian literature as a field began to emerge in the nineteenth century, especially in relation to Franz Grillparzer, Adalbert Stifter, and Viennese theater, and key figures such as Hugo von Hofmannsthal and Josef Nadler shaped these arguments further in the early twentieth century.⁴ There surely has been a German literature in Austria, but it is not necessary to present it as an ideology, as a single, coherent set of values, or as a polemic against what is "German"—or to identify it with the Habsburgs or with the Monarchy as a whole.⁵ What is too rarely brought out in accounts of Austrian literature is the place of Bohemia and Moravia in this literature. At times critics have conceded that their fundamental motive for writing about Austrian literature and tradition is to make sense of the significance of a handful of great writers from the early twentieth century, such as Robert Musil, Hermann Broch, Hugo von Hofmannsthal, Franz Kafka, and Rainer Maria Rilke.[6] Although Grillparzer and theater were enormously important for Austrian culture and identity, I am particularly concerned here with the prose tradition, which reached a first great height in Stifter, matured in new ways (especially adjusting to the urban world and modern economic life) through the short stories and essays of the late nineteenth century, and culminated in the generation of 1905 in the early twentieth century. I want to emphasize a few major writers—Grillparzer, Stifter, Musil, Hofmannsthal, Broch, Kafka, and Rilke—rather than the counter-narratives that Austrians have told about themselves and their literature in response to the literary conventions, master narratives, and ideologies of Germany. As with Austrian philosophy, there is a significant body of scholarly work on Austrian literature. This literature is enormous and, here again, it is often concerned with questions of essence and defining what Austrian literature is—often in contrast to German literature.[7] Some of these generalizations seem valid and helpful, although these commentaries are always about a literature in German. Many scholars prefer a more extensive, imperial definition of Austria, but the center of gravity of Austrian literature is always the German hereditary lands of Austria and Bohemia, mainly Vienna and Prague, although other provincial cities and towns west of the Leitha play their parts. The selections in this chapter are representative rather than exhaustive. I might have said more about writers such as Johann Nestroy or Karl Kraus, but these figures and traditions are difficult to convey in translation or as a presentation of ideas.

Grillparzer and Theater in Vienna

The impulse to distinguish a specifically Austrian literature crystallized in relation to the work of Franz Grillparzer (1791–1872) and in the context of theater in Vienna. In the late eighteenth and early nineteenth centuries, Vienna produced the most vital theater culture in the German-speaking world, a culture that included not only Grillparzer, but also Johann Nestroy (1801–1862), Ferdinand von Raimund (1790–1836), and all the other talents required for a major center of theater.[8] Theater was part of popular culture and public life, close to the worlds of music and the salons, and perhaps best known for its comic tradition from Hans Wurst to Raimund and the farces of Nestroy. For many Viennese, theater has been at the heart of their literary tradition. Here many factors contributed: the sense of spectacle, beauty, drama, and costume from the Catholic Church (especially during the Baroque period); the influence of opera and Italian culture and music more broadly; and a style of satire, wit, and popular entertainment that developed in the eighteenth century. This was a public, social art that drew on an oral tradition in which comedy was prominent.[9] But the great intellectual figure of this world was Franz Grillparzer, a serious dramatist who ranks with Lessing and Kleist, and represents what was most thoughtful and significant in Austrian intellectual life.[10]

Theater in Vienna was more than just a literary form. Like all theater, it aimed at performance—that is, at an audience in a theater, whether the *Burgtheater* (court theater) or the more middle-class venues of the suburban theaters. This theater tradition arose out of groups of traveling players, many of whom were in the Italian tradition of the *commedia del arte*, and, even into the nineteenth century, much of it was extemporaneous, along the lines of vaudeville, stand-up comedy, or sketches. At times this theater relied on mask, mime, and physical comedy—and on linguistic plays between high speech and local dialect. This took place in a very local theater, although in a large, imperial city. It resisted much of the high seriousness and formalism of German classicism and stayed close to the lived situations of people and language in Vienna.[11] This tradition of comedy, farce, and satire continued down to the interwar years in Austria in the work of Hofmannsthal, Musil, Kraus, and the cabaret, but for tragedy and serious drama Grillparzer remains an isolated pinnacle in the nineteenth century. Grillparzer's genius was for a kind of dramatic poetry that is difficult to convey to an English-speaking reader. It is a portrayal of action and gesture, of lived situations for a living audience, although he left highly literary texts as firm points of reference. "For him theater was a play to be comprehended with all the senses, not a dreamed poem or a book that is read."[12]

Grillparzer was a child of the Enlightenment, and he came from a family of jurists and bureaucrats, including his father and three generations of men on his mother's side. His mother's family (the Sonnleithners) was close to the world of theater, music, and literature. Franz was born in 1791, and his childhood in the inner city seems to have been solitary and depressing, though secure. He achieved his greatest public impact in his mid-twenties when he was still living with his mother.[13] His first major success, *Die Ahnfrau* (*The Ancestor*, 1817), was in some ways an opaque story that drew on the contemporary interest in Spanish Baroque theater, including the theme of fate.[14] A few years later his brother and his mother both committed suicide, revealing the tensions in his family, if not in his culture. Grillparzer was not happy in life, but he was tremendously creative and productive, able to fill the prime stage of Austria for twenty years until he began to recede from public view. He published no plays after 1838, but continued in the civil service until 1856, when he retired as a Hofrat. He instinctively represented the Josephinist tradition of serving the state and holding it together, and, despite his gradual retreat from the theater and public life, he was honored as one of the great figures of Austria and named to the House of Lords near the end of his life. Grillparzer was very much in the mainstream of the tradition established by Maria Theresa and Joseph II. Whatever his misgivings about the state in which he lived, he portrayed the central themes of Austrian history with wisdom and perceptiveness. His gift was for seeing and reflection.

Grillparzer wrote about a dozen important plays, about half of which were historical dramas about the hereditary lands, while the other half were set in ancient Greece. Hofmannsthal points out that Grillparzer's plays concentrated on the Austrian and Bohemian lands, except for the plays about classical Greece, which took place in nowhere and portrayed his own subjectivity.[15] His second important play, *Sappho* (1818), brought him the wide recognition that established him as the leading figure of the theater in Vienna.[16] Here he addressed sexual and psychological themes in a classical setting, and he chose a surprising subject for a young man—the portrayal of an aging ruler, a woman torn between love and art. This was followed by another classical theme between 1818 and 1820, a trilogy about Jason and the Voyage of the Argonauts. Like Freud, Grillparzer was drawn to classical models that were grounded in Greek myths and stories, and his exploration of the mother-child relationship as a model for the relationship between lovers in his play about Hero and Leander gives nothing away to Freud in its complexity and intensity.[17] Most of Grillparzer's work aims at the creation of figures on the stage, characters in the imagination, who could be historical or mythological.

At twenty-five Grillparzer wrote *König Ottokar*, a play which anticipated many of the qualities of his mature theater and focused on the historical relationship between Bohemia and Austria. Grillparzer has often been regarded an apologist for the Habsburgs, but this play is not built around Rudolf, the founder of the dynasty, but around Ottokar, the Přemyslid prince who united the Bohemian and Austrian lands in the thirteenth century. Birthe Hoffmann rightly points to the similarities between Ottokar and Napoleon, these heroic figures against whom the more prosaic Habsburgs have been measured (in this play, the unheroic Rudolf).[18] A year later in *Ein treuer Diener seines Herrn* (A Loyal Servant of his Lord, 1826), Grillparzer portrayed the limits of bureaucratic leadership and his own ambivalent relationship with the state both as a bureaucrat and as a playwright. His was sensitive to the tensions between loyalty and subservience in Austrian culture and personally inclined toward resignation to life's limits. Sometimes lost in critical controversies about his attitudes toward the Habsburgs are his wisdom and greatness as a student of human nature, his ability to see through ideologies to accept the complexity of reality.

Three of his greatest plays were never performed during his lifetime: *Libussa, Ein Bruderzwist in Habsburg*, and *Die Jüdin von Toledo*. Libussa was the mythical founder of the Přemyslid dynasty; that Grillparzer wrote a play about her is perhaps even more striking than his portrayal of Ottokar. In another play about Bohemia, *Ein Bruderzwist in Habsburg* (Family Strife in Habsburg), Rudolf II opposes the selfishness and self-promotion of those in his family (Mathias and his allies) who want a new order, which will eventually lead to the Thirty Years' War. Ivar Ivask calls this play "perhaps his greatest dramatic achievement."[19] One striking fact about Grillparzer's dramas is the prominence of female characters, beginning with the *Ancestress*. And women continued to play leading roles in his plays, including Sappho, Medea, Hero, Libussa, Rahel, and Esther. Moreover, Grillparzer often concentrated his own experience as a creative person in these women. Seen together, his plays raise important questions regarding our assumptions about the way men portrayed women in the nineteenth century.[20]

Grillparzer suffers from being presented as the Austrian national poet. The musicality of his poetry and its theatricality are both difficult for modern English-speaking audiences to appreciate (although these issues arise in somewhat different ways with Goethe, to say nothing of Nestroy).[21] Nonetheless, certain themes still attract the attention of contemporary critics: the prominence of women in his plays, his explorations of politics, his psychological subtlety, his unconventional approach to freedom and fate, and his anticipations of postmodernism.[22] Grillparzer's characters are often driven by irrationality or conditioned by external powers that they are unable to control, and his mature dramas present protagonists who are marked by humility, wisdom, and a realistic sense of limitations. Hofmannsthal regarded Grillparzer as "next to Goethe and Kleist the most political mind among the newer writers of the German language."[23] By comparison with the ideological style of most early nineteenth-century writers, Grillparzer had a very Austrian sense of *Realpolitik*. "While the others were drawn to what was general, he saw the particular ...."[24] Grillparzer is important for his wisdom about power and those who rule and for his understanding of human relationships, regardless of social status or gender.

Although many Austrians regarded Vienna as the center of German theater, this was difficult for North Germans to reconcile with the German they heard in Viennese coffee shops. Moreover, Grillparzer seemed to North German critics to embody a pessimistic, fatalistic, and unmanly view of the world.[25] While Grillparzer conceded the silliness of making tiny distinctions between Swabian and Austrian literature and the like, he did think that certain qualities of Austrian literature stood out: modesty, healthy common sense, and authentic feeling.[26] And his work challenged North German assumptions and perspectives of the early nineteenth century such as idealism, romanticism, and subjectivity. Although Grillparzer's work grew out of the literary achievements of Goethe and Schiller, he was not part of German romanticism and the Protestant idealism of the Prussian Reform Era, and he was decidedly opposed to nationalism. Like Bolzano, he was a product of the Austrian Enlightenment. He was powerfully drawn to classical Greece as a foundation for exploring his own subjectivity, but also to Shakespeare and to the Baroque theater of the Spanish Renaissance. Benno von Wiese has suggested that Grillparzer's Catholic view "saw divinity in a very objective way and could not subsume it within an idealistic view of history as in romantic theory."[27] We need not regard Grillparzer as pious to recognize that a Josephinist Catholicism was a fundamental shaping feature of his world, a significant dimension of his cultural location, whatever his religious convictions may have been. Although Wiese's account is generally sympathetic and perceptive, this remark recalls how much the modern conception of German intellectual history has been shaped by a Protestant perspective.

Writing in 1877, Ferdinand Kürnberger, one of the most expert commentators on nineteenth-century Austria, argued that "[i]n the history of culture [Grillparzer] stands for the separation of Austria from Germany."[28] And Grillparzer's importance for shaping an Austrian tradition was by no means merely literary. His delightful remark about Hegel set the terms for the Austrian reception of German idealism: "What is it that I like best about your system? That it is as incomprehensible as the world."[29] One could hardly imagine a view more distant from the standard German intellectual histories of the early nineteenth century. At the same time, Grillparzer has a tendency simply to fall out of the German narrative about the nineteenth century as insufficiently national and not part of the teleological account, even though modern Germany did not exist until the year before he died. Ideologically, Grillparzer challenged the liberal and nationalist values of the early nineteenth century that seemed obvious to many German and French intellectuals. Later in the century Friedrich Nietzsche expressed his admiration for "honest Grillparzer" and his critique of the ideology of progress.[30] Grillparzer's well-known epigram on nationalism is hardly a remark that would have occurred to most West European intellectuals in 1849: "The path of modern education goes from humanity through nationalism to bestiality."[31]

Grillparzer was thoughtfully critical of most public figures and political parties, but he clearly represents a distaste for the consequences of liberal and national revolution after 1848. He was even more impatient than Bolzano with linguistic nationalism; he was a Josephinist and very far from German nationalism. This associates him with an Austrian political tradition that was alert to what went wrong with the French Revolution. One of Grillparzer's poems, "The Language War," is a devastating critique of linguistic nationalism after Herder:

> In Aesop's times the animals spoke; in this way they became educated like human beings. But then it suddenly occurred to them that the tribal tongue should be the highest. "I want to growl once again," said the bear, and the wolf wanted to howl. "I want to bleat," said the sheep, and only someone who barks seemed virtuous to the dog. Then they became again like animals, and the culture of the beasts became their own.[32]

It was generally difficult for liberals and Marxists and nationalists in the nineteenth century to take conservatism, monarchy, and Christianity very seriously.

Among Grillparzer's most important creations, Hofmannsthal counted "his still unknown diaries" and *The Poor Fiddler*; his diaries are well worth the attention of historians, and *The Poor Fiddler* (1847) has become surprisingly popular in English.[33] *The Poor Fiddler* is a novella[34] about a man who lived for his music, not because he had talent but because playing the violin was the meaning of his life. Oddly enough, this story may be the most wonderful work of art by Austria's greatest dramatist because of the subtle communication of inner life through the events of the external world. Ivask emphasizes the place of this story in an Austrian prose tradition, especially the connection to Kafka.[35] It would be difficult to surpass J. P. Stern's account of this novella:

> The annihilating conclusion toward which this quiet, unadorned story takes us is no less than the intimation of a deep and consistent distrust of the substantial world, which appears as a place radically incapable of yielding form and substance to the good will. The pure heart, in this vision, remains disembodied. The value of everything in the world, of art even—its "objective value"—is as nothing to the purity and goodness and devotion that resides in the heart, mutely, unexpressed, perhaps inexpressible. The rift between being and doing, the severing of intention and realization, of spirit from matter—even the all but tangible "matter" of music—is complete.[36]

Grillparzer devoted more than a decade to writing this story, beginning in the 1830s. If we may say that Goethe was Faust, then Grillparzer was the poor fiddler.[37]

Adalbert Stifter and the Novel

Between Goethe and Thomas Mann, there were only a few German novelists of great stature: the Swiss Keller, the Prussian Fontane, but above all Adalbert Stifter. His late stories are like cut stones, and his early stories were already well-known when he expressed his admiration for Grillparzer's *The Poor Fiddler* in 1847.[38] Grillparzer's novella and Stifter's stories show the common ethical and aesthetic ground of the two writers who more or less invented what has come to be known as the Austrian tradition in literature: an unpretentious view of the artist and an emphasis on modesty, simplicity, and the celebration of human kindness. As a mature man, Stifter wrote three enormous epic works: *Der Nachsommer*, *Witiko*, and *Die Mappe meines Urgrossvaters*, two of which are among the great European novels of the nineteenth century, although his biographer argues that Stifter always remained a storyteller in his own mind.[39]

Stifter (1805–1868) grew up in Bohemia in Oberplan near Český Krumlov and lived much of his adult life nearby in Upper Austria. Almost all of his work deals with Bohemia or with the region on the border between Bohemia and Austria—and it touches on Vienna much as it does on Prague, as the great urban centers of this region. This is the same Austria that Grillparzer circumscribed in his plays as the German and Bohemian crown lands. After Stifter's father died, his grandfather arranged for him to study at the Benedictine Abbey in Kremsmünster, where he received an excellent education and developed his love for literature to a high level between 1818 and 1826 (an extended period of study somewhere between boarding school and college).[40] His reading acquainted him with every sort of European literature and established the basis for his creativity as an adult.[41] The next fifteen years were a difficult part of his life. He lived for the most part in Vienna, never completed his legal studies, and worked as a tutor, sometimes for quite noble families, including Metternich's. Stifter never married the woman he loved (Fanny Greipl), and he was not happy in his marriage to Amalia Mohaupt (1847–1868). The intensity of Stifter's struggles as a young man with love and marriage recall the experiences of Soren Kierkegaard and Kafka, and he struggled with feelings of unhappiness for most of his adult life. But these emotionally difficult resolutions did allow him to devote his life to literature, again much like Kafka (and Grillparzer).

He was a painter for a time and quite a good one, roughly a contemporary of Baudelaire and living in Vienna in the 1840s, thinking about painting and criticism.[42] His stories from this period are often very modern or take place in Vienna, with an emphasis on the urban atmosphere. He was briefly involved with ideas of reform in 1848, but his discouragement with the revolution led him to retreat to Linz in Upper Austria, where he worked as an educator in the schools and continued to write for the remainder of his life. Like Kafka and Grillparzer, he was both an administrator and a writer for much of his adult life. Like Grillparzer, he retired as a Hofrat. His life was not happy, but he continued to mature as a writer. The influence of Herder was strong after 1848, especially in Stifter's commitment to education, but Matz argues that Stifter moved beyond even this, not only to pessimism but to a deep respect for each human being. Suffering from cirrhosis of the liver, Stifter died by his own hand in 1868, cutting his throat with a razor.

Stifter is important for his stories and novels rather than for theoretical arguments about art and politics, but much of his fiction is well-described by his notion of *das sanfte Gesetz*, "the gentle law," first presented in the preface to *Bunte Steine* in 1852, in response to Friedrich Hebbel's criticism that he wrote only about unimportant things. Stifter conceived "the gentle law" to describe his stories of the 1840s, but it applies as well to the epic narratives of his mature work. It is, to be sure, an image and not a mathematical formula or a sharply defined philosophical concept. "The blowing of the wind, the rippling of the water, the growing of the grain, the waves in the ocean, the greening of the earth, the shining of the heavens, the shimmer of the stars I regard as great …." Among less great phenomena he thought of thunder and lightning, earthquakes, and other temporary disturbances.[43] And roughly this is his view of what is great and less great in the human world. As Wolfgang Matz put it: "Think like the forest—that is Stifter's central idea. Nature as our mentor, as aesthetic model, as he formulated it in his 'gentle law.'"[44] His stories did include lightning bolts and terrible storms, but the slow growth of the forest dominates much of his work. Helena Ragg-Kirby emphasizes the tension throughout Stifter's writing between the willed calm of the literary surface and the threats of natural catastrophe and chaotic depths: "Beneath the surface of Biedermeier solidity is a vision of fracture, emptiness, meaninglessness not only more radical than that of any other nineteenth-century author, but more radical than the vision of any twentieth-century author, precisely because there is such a disjuncture between text and sub-text."[45] In the 1960s Walter Weiss characterized Hegel as "the most powerful opponent of Stifter, today more than ever," arguing that Hegel lay behind even

Hebbel's familiar critique—all part of a historical-sociological critique that goes through Marx and down to the late twentieth century.[46]

Stifter began as a fashionable storyteller in 1840—at the forefront of modern science and literary sensibility (see "The Condor"). This was a period of great creativity for Stifter, in which the original versions of many of his stories were written—but also some of the carefully considered revisions. In this early period, Stifter became a storyteller; and he had good stories to tell, but he was still very much a painter, even as a writer. The story was often the frame he hung his painting on, but his painting in words is extraordinary for its patience and richness. Hermann Broch called him "perhaps the greatest landscape portrayer in all of German literature."[47] He portrayed not only the world of forests and nature, but the world of traveling, of walking and coaches, of road-side inns, of solitary men and beautiful young women (mostly at a distance). The mature Stifter was writing the epic of nature, of the forest, of the community, but this tendency was apparent in the early stories as well. In "Der Hochwald" [The Alpine Forest], Stifter already emerged as a master of the epic in a story that reaches back to the Thirty Years' War and the early eighteenth century as well as the Middle Ages. This powerful epic impulse appeared again in "Briefe meines Urgrossvaters" [Papers of my Great-Grandfather], a novella which he continued to revise throughout his entire creative life. The novel brings home Stifter's close connection to Bohemia, but the manuscript of *Die Mappe* remained unfinished when he died.[48]

Many of his stories were about children, but for the most part he wrote about men, from sweet young men to wise old men, but rarely about villains or fools. The impact of romanticism is apparent in his early stories, in his writing about feelings. He was interested in feelings of exaltation but also in the beautiful women who inspired these states. As in Grillparzer, powerful female figures stand out in Stifter's work, especially Ditha, Brigitta, and the dark-skinned girl. "Brigitta" is the rare story by Stifter that takes place in Hungary (he went there briefly), and it is also one of his most striking portrayals of women. Another early novella, "Abdias" (1842), is an intensely sympathetic portrayal of a Jew and his suffering, but a less sympathetic portrayal of Europe. "Abdias" culminates in the story of Abdias' daughter Ditha, who had a special relationship to thunder and lightning and electricity. At one point, Abdias reflects on his experience in Europe after coming from North Africa:

> Europe had disappointed him bitterly … [the people] here did not seem to him like human beings, but like manufactured creatures, one like another, who know

what they will say throughout their entire life, and act, as if they were machines, which he also hated, daily doing the same actions and bringing forth wonderful things and in the end are only gruesome wood.

It is difficult to think of anything more devastating from the arsenal of modernism than the idea that Europeans "know what they will say throughout their entire life."[49] His daughter, Ditha, dies from her intense relationship with nature, from her connection to the lightning.

In the 1850s, Stifter refined the classical voice of his later years, not only in his stories but in his great prose works: *Der Nachsommer* and *Witiko*; each has a sustained beauty that is extraordinary in works of such length, what Grillparzer might have described as classical in the sense of flawless. Sebald calls Stifter's *Nachsommer* "the vision of a secularized heaven."[50] It is a novel about the relation of the human being to the world, things, nature, and other people. It is grounded in stillness and respect for things. The right comportment toward things is the state of reading Stifter, and this set the tone for much of what is best in Austrian literature.[51] We learn the name of the first-person narrator, Heinrich Drendorf, only near the end of the novel. He finds his way quite by accident to the Rose House, the home of Baron Risach, who is central to the novel along with his gardens and fields and the world in which he lives.[52] He is a second father to Heinrich, and he builds on the values of Heinrich's first father in his attention to gardening and order, his respect for books and things. In *Indian Summer* the great love is a point of reference for the rest of the narrative, but the novel is focused on the reality of things—not only on nature, but often on collections and rooms and the order human beings give to the world.[53] But it is also a recovery of things past in the account of the Baron's relationship with Mathilde and his experiences in Vienna (before and during 1848).

Nature is Stifter's model even in writing history, as in *Witiko*, Stifter's account of the origins of the Rosenberg family in the region on the upper Moldau (Vltava) in Southern Bohemia. Here Stifter established the objective reality of nature in a way that anticipated much of today's environmental movement, but also emphasized the objective reality of history. The book rivals Stifter's more famous *Indian Summer*—because of the elegance of the prose and because of the imaginative representation of the world of Germans and Czechs in the twelfth century. The German literary critic Ulrich Greiner calls *Witiko* "one of the least known and most astonishing novels of world literature."[54] Although Witiko is a great warrior in an age of heroic knights, he sees himself and behaves as part of a cooperative community. His characteristic expression is *"ich füge mich*"—roughly, I conform myself or follow or fit in. This is the voice on almost every page of this long novel, whether Witiko is walking through the forest, caring for his horse, leading in battle, or providing counsel for the duke or king.

In this historical novel, Stifter achieved what he had aimed at: "The novel has a scholarly side, which before the fact lies in no human soul, but which it must achieve: the historical. This must be so faithfully approximated that author and reader breathe in the air of those bygone times, and the present no longer exists. This alone gives truth. But, for that, historical knowledge alone is not enough."[55] Stifter's emphasis on the powerful forces of nature and the objective world is quite striking by comparison with North German writers of the early nineteenth century. The emphasis in Grillparzer and Stifter on respect for the objectivity of the world recalls the identification of God with reality in Leibniz, and one critical study speaks of "that typical interplay of scientific and religious vocabulary in Stifter."[56] Nietzsche's model of an ideal history could have been describing Stifter by drawing on Grillparzer:

> A historiography could be imagined which had in it not a drop of common empirical truth and yet could lay claim to the highest degree of objectivity. Indeed Grillparzer ventures to declare: "What is history but the way in which the spirit of man apprehends events impenetrable to him; unites things when God alone knows whether they belong together; substitutes something comprehensible for what is incomprehensible."[57]

This passage almost seems to invoke Stifter's *Witiko*. His way of writing evokes a state of being, of calm, of presence, of awareness of the world, appreciation for the world.

The Writers of the Liberal Era

The literature of the high liberal era was a moral, serious art—a realistic art of representation and social concern. It was close to the broad stream of European realism and modern science, although, in the generation after Adalbert Stifter, liberal Austria did not produce a major novelist who stands comparison with Dostoevsky or Flaubert or Eliot or Zola.[58] The second generation of writers in liberal Austria in the 1890s[59] was notable not for its emulation of realism, but for its resistance to it, although Arthur Schnitzler was as much a continuation of liberal realism as a revolt against it. Schnitzler continued his commitment to science and social issues, and his progressive politics continued for the remainder of his life. It was other figures of Young Vienna, especially those from the lower nobility, such as Hofmannsthal and Andrian, who made the sharp turn toward modernism, following the lead of the French symbolists and aesthetes. Common to all of the writers of Young Vienna were interests in psychological themes, sexuality, and the concerns of young Jewish men, and a large scholarly literature has developed in a variety of fields to address these themes.[60] In 1951 Hermann Broch provided a fascinating argument about the liberal era as a whole that emphasized the aestheticism that accompanied the realism of the liberal era and expressed itself in the literary revolt of Young Vienna and Hugo von Hofmannsthal.[61] Since Schorske, the literary achievements of the high liberal era have seemed less compelling by comparison with the work of the rebellious liberal sons in the 1890s. In this section I want to emphasize the unity of the liberal era across both generations (especially its belief in the individual) and to identify both the considerable achievements of the writers of high liberalism and the distinctive contributions to literary modernism by Young Vienna. The liberal era is important for the history of literature in two ways: the steady refinement of modern prose, which established the basis for the great age of the novel, and the development from workmanlike realism to modernism.

The liberal era brought to literary prominence the realities of social change in the nineteenth century and the value of social realism as a literary form. As with the Enlightenment, the rationalism of this period was not always conducive to the literary and artistic imagination, but it is easy a century and a half later to overlook the value of what we may call a bourgeois literature and the significance of stories that now seem old-fashioned or sentimental. Ferdinand von Saar (1833–1906) and Marie von Ebner-Eschenbach (1830–1916) especially deserve to be remembered, and their elevated social status draws attention to the important role of the lower nobility as traditional society changed in the nineteenth century. Ebner-Eschenbach's success as a woman was an anomaly before 1900,[62] whereas Saar's status as a former officer in the Habsburg army was more representative of the age.[63] Two other writers deserve to be mentioned from the high liberal era: Ludwig Anzengruber (1839–1899) and Peter Rosegger (1843–1918).[64] Most of these writers were born in the 1830s and correspond to Schorske's generation of the fathers (as well as the mothers) who continued the culture of the salon and second society.[65]

Saar was a wise and quiet storyteller, who usually wrote about men (often officers in the Habsburg army) who were sensitive to relationships with women. The women were often from the upper classes or the nobility, but they were sometimes poor, even very poor, or off the social map almost entirely. Even though Saar lived in Vienna during the liberal era, Bohemia and Moravia—the castles in Prague and the towns of Bohemia and Moravia—bulked large in his imagination as did the war in Italy in 1859. Saar's narrators consistently express great awe for women, and his stories sometimes recall the opening line of *Beyond Good and Evil* from around this time: "Supposing truth is a woman, what then?" The recurring theme of nearly all Saar's stories and novellas is the fascination of the mystery of the woman—and male tolerance for this mystery. The woman is very much the "other," part of the story of male and female gender identity that unfolded in the late nineteenth century.[66]

Marie von Ebner-Eschcnbach was an extraordinary woman, who became a wonderful writer, particularly after she was about sixty. She lived at the heart of the liberal order—but as an aristocrat and as a woman—and both identities set limits to her place in that world. She came from a liberal Catholic, Josephinist family in Moravia for whom the revolutions and other upheavals of the mid-century were confusing and ambiguous, but she did not idealize the order in which she lived. Her life shows how difficult it was for a woman to be a full participant in the intellectual world of the liberal era, and yet, as she matured as a writer and as a person, she won the respect of the intellectual world in Austria and Germany. She was surrounded all her life by conventions about what women could and could not do and by familial reminders that she should not withdraw from the social world to write. She belonged to a generation of European intellectuals that was strongly influenced by Arthur Schopenhauer, although she read him in a Catholic, empathic way. *Das Gemeindekind*, one of her best-known works, portrays the social dynamics of village life with skill and wisdom, addressing issues of class, status, and gender. One recent biographer characterizes her novellas as "exemplary for a literature of genuine pathos."[67]

A younger generation of writers emerged in the 1890s; these writers drew attention to the limitations of liberal rationalism and to the hypocrisy of bourgeois society, and they developed a stylized aestheticism that echoed French aestheticism and Oscar Wilde. In figures such as Schnitzler the concerns of these writers overlapped with the psychological and sexual themes of the young Freud, while Leopold von Andrian and Hugo von Hofmannsthal began to move away from realism to symbolism, aestheticism, and modernism. These writers also epitomized the values of liberalism in their preoccupation with the individual, and many of these names remind us of the presence of both upper-middle-class intellectuals and lower nobility in the social world of these writers. *Jung Wien* was a distinctive collective phenomenon of the 1890s that has contributed a great deal to our picture of the *fin de siècle* and Viennese decadence. Much of the scholarship has emphasized what separated the Austrian literary scene from German literary life in the 1890s, but Viennese writers in this period were very much emulating Paris and French literary life as were Czech writers in Prague. Much like the Viennese Secession or the music of Schoenberg, Austrian poets and other writers in the 1890s belonged to the broadest currents of an artistic modernism that had begun to emerge at least as early as Baudelaire. These writers were very much part of the liberal era, in Vienna as in Europe, even as they began to transform understandings of representation and expression. Broch's book on Hofmannsthal is still one of the most important interpretations of European modernism as it emerged in the second half of the nineteenth century, and he located the center of the liberal value vacuum in Vienna. The inability of liberalism in the late nineteenth century to offer new values was later portrayed as the negative formulation of liberal freedom in Ulrich, the protagonist of *The Man without Qualities*. This understanding of the origins of modernism in the crisis of nineteenth-century liberalism was also crucial to Carl Schorske's interpretation of *fin de siècle* Vienna.

The two literary figures at the heart of Schorske's argument, Arthur Schnitzler and Hugo von Hofmannsthal, were sons of high liberal culture. Schnitzler, like Freud, was trained in medicine at the University of Vienna; Hofmannsthal was the finest flower of liberal wealth and second society in Vienna. Both were major figures of the theater.[68] Schorske's argument underscored the crisis of liberal culture and the impact of political decline on the retreat from public life and the exploration of irrationality and feelings in these writers—as well as the other writers of Young Vienna and Freud and Klimt. Schorske emphasized the connection between the crisis of public culture in this generation and a preoccupation with a private, erotic, emotional world of fantasy. He did not emphasize the Jewishness of liberal culture, although other commentators have, especially the Jewishness of Young Vienna.[69] Schorske saw the 1890s as the culmination of the crisis of liberal politics and a liberal culture of reason and morality, and he was interested in Hofmannsthal's later exploration of a more conservative political style. He was not very concerned, however, with the strong continuity of liberal values in Schnitzler's work for the rest of his life or with the way Hofmannsthal's ideas developed as he moved away from modernist poetry.[70]

Leopold von Andrian's *Der Garten der Erkenntnis*[71] was the epitome of the culture of aestheticism in the 1890s. Andrian was a friend of Hofmannsthal and a kind of Oscar Wilde figure; his portrayal of Erwin's feeling of connection to things, to experience, and to strangers he meets foreshadows the Prince in Musil's *Young Törless*. Andrian's writing expressed the preoccupation with sexuality and gender, with beauty, impressionism, style, and the life of the senses; and Erwin was the epitome of individuality and aristocratic style. A change took place in language at this point that is apparent in Hofmannsthal as well. Saar found that he could not fully understand Andrian's book, although he admired it and its description of "moods and feelings, of colors."[72] Andrian's book set a new signal for modernism, but in the atmosphere of the *fin de siècle* and aristocratic decline.[73] This was a literary turning point in the midst of the most elite culture. Even before Schorske's book, the reality of studies in Austrian literature was the enormous amount of scholarly attention given to Young Vienna, perhaps most of all because of Arthur Schnitzler but also because of Hermann Bahr.[74] The notion of decadence was introduced into the literary world by Bahr, whose articles from the 1890s have shaped the way scholars talk about modernism, especially in Vienna.[75] Bahr was a crucial figure in the interactions among philosophy, psychology, literature, and the arts in Vienna after 1890. The writers of the 1890s opened the door on modernism in a still stable and traditional social world in which German-speaking liberalism was dominant.

The Generation of 1905: Ethics and the Novel

"Modernism" is the most common way to refer to innovations in ways of writing in the early twentieth century.[76] It is a vague and circumstantial term, a convenient simplifier and a term that is often narrowly tied to national traditions that do little to integrate a broader, more international definition of the term. The keys to modernism seem to have been the impact of the Second Industrial Revolution, the First World War, and the decline of traditional ideologies and literary forms. This phenomenon is usually associated with the social isolation of the writer and the individual and with the move away from social realism to a more inner, psychological, symbolic world. In the generation of 1905 in Austria, there was a sharp move away from aestheticism, especially in Otto Weininger and Karl Kraus, but there was also a broader return to reason and objectivity in Musil and Broch and Hofmannsthal. This included a turn to the novel and to an ungrounded approach to ethics that was characteristic of Austrian modernism. Musil, in particular, found creative ways to balance the ill-reconciled moralistic-scientific and aesthetic components of liberal culture.

I will discuss six writers of this generation: Karl Kraus, Robert Musil, Hugo von Hofmannsthal, Hermann Broch, Rainer Maria Rilke, and Franz Kafka. Except for Kraus, they were all novelists. Although they were men, they were by no means advocates of the male idea—and, in this regard, Musil and Rilke were especially interesting. These novelists made dramatic contributions to the extraordinary renaissance of the German novel in the early twentieth century, although none of them was from Germany. They represent the ironic move beyond tradition to come to terms with the realities of modern life, and for most of them the war was the ultimate ironic event, which dissolved much of what had been taken for granted.[77] The ethical fearlessness of this generation of intellectuals allowed them to advance into "the value vacuum" of the late nineteenth century described by Broch. But these possibilities were largely diverted by the war and the fascist era, and Musil believed that the generation after the Second World War would have to begin anew where his generation had left off—trying to balance thinking and feeling, the ethical and the aesthetic, inwardness and social reality.

After a century in which the German contribution to the history of the novel had been modest, the novel seemed to this generation well suited to think out the situation of the individual in modern society. And it was just this isolation of the solitary individual that became the hallmark for the understanding of ethics in the generation of 1905; for them, the novel was the freest form in which to portray the situation of the individual in modern society. And many of these novels recall Schopenhauer's view from the middle of the nineteenth century: "A novel will be of a high and noble order, the more it represents of inner, and the less it represents of outer, life; and the ratio between the two will supply a means of judging any novel, of whatever kind, from *Tristram Shandy* down to the crudest and most sensational tale of knight or robber."[78] Rudolf Kassner (1873–1959) was a key figure in introducing Schopenhauer and Nietzsche to the generation of 1905, as I emphasized in my essay on Schopenhauer[79]: "Hofmannsthal's first reaction to reading Kassner was that 'never before were continuous thoughts of Schopenhauer, or Nietzsche or the like, capable of giving me such inner happiness ... such understanding of why one writes poetry ... and what it has to do with existence.'" Rilke, Kafka, Musil, Broch, and Hofmannsthal were all deeply and powerfully inspired by Nietzsche, who took the lead in exploring the heart of Western spirituality.[80] None of these writers took Nietzsche to be decadent—or even nihilistic.[81]

The power of Nietzsche's way of thinking is apparent in his summary of Schopenhauer's significance in 1874. "*The Schopenhauerian man voluntarily takes the pain of truthfulness upon himself*, and his suffering serves to kill his individual will to prepare that complete revolution and reversal of his being, the attainment of which is the actual meaning of life." As Nietzsche put it in the same essay, the late nineteenth century had lived "on the inherited capital of morality which our forefathers accumulated, and which we only squander instead of increasing."[82] Schopenhauer and the early Nietzsche began to have some influence on Freud's generation in the 1870s, but they seem to have had little significance for the poets of Young Vienna twenty years later. It was only after 1900 that Schopenhauer and Nietzsche became important for Austrian intellectuals such as Kassner, Hofmannsthal, Musil, Wittgenstein, Kraus, and Weininger. In this generation we no longer find the classical liberal indifference to religion (what Nietzsche called not knowing what religions were good for) or even its anti-Catholicism. In such matters this generation was very different from the mainstream of liberalism, which was focused on clearing away the debris of religious convention and authoritarian control. But there was also in the best of these writers no attempt to synthesize a new religion of their own. Their efforts concentrated especially on inner experience, although many of them acknowledged the validity of the real, the external, even the surfaces, and the complex dynamic between inner and outer. Musil, Kafka, Rilke, and Broch were ready for the novel when the society created the solitary individual described by Lukács in *The Theory of the Novel* (*Die Theorie des Romans*, 1914–1915). Karl Kraus's response to the war was more dramatic.

Karl Kraus (1874–1936)

The great newspaper of Vienna in the late nineteenth century was *Die Neue Freie Presse*, and its journalists and editors were liberal and often Jewish. Karl Kraus made this great metropolitan newspaper the object of his verbal attacks; rather than being an editor for *Die Neue Freie Presse*, he chose to write a one-person newspaper, *Die Fackel* [The Torch], which set the tone for much of Viennese intellectual life in the early twentieth century.[83] No one in this generation was more devoted to language than Kraus. And no one was more representative of the moral intensity of the generation. No one in Austria contributed more than Kraus to the turn away from aestheticism and the writers of Young Vienna and to sharpening the distinction between the *fin de siècle* and the early twentieth century, most dramatically in his essay on *Die demolierte Literatur* [The Demolished Literature] in 1896.

Kraus was the self-appointed critic of his age. He was a journalist, and he chose journalism, especially yellow journalism, as the central object of his attack. He was Jewish, and he struggled with his Jewish identity all his life. He wrote for the *Neue Freie Presse* and then became the leading critic of the liberal elites who read it. As the virtually sole author of a satirical magazine that appeared irregularly from 1903 to 1936, he was known to everyone in the German-speaking elites of Austria. He set the tone for moral purity in the generation of 1905, and he had a broad impact on Austrian culture and intellectual life. He was important for his rejection of the world he lived in—whether we characterize that world as liberal Vienna or Austria-Hungary or the First World War. He is a difficult writer to appreciate through media other than the German language to which he was devoted in a way that made him savagely critical of nearly all speaking and writing in his world. For many intellectuals he became an incarnation of morality and the right way to live—and this was what he intended to be. His moral judgments—on the war or the elites of Vienna—were what was most important to him, but he produced a literature that was oblique and idiosyncratic. He meant a great deal to Viennese intellectuals from the 1890s to the 1930s—and since then.[84] The political significance of his satire became more apparent during the First World War, especially in *The Last Days of Mankind*, where he wrote out of the satirist's confidence that he need only portray the ordinary people who allowed this war to happen. More than any other writer he formulated the apocalyptic significance of the war. Edward Timms' translation of *Die letzten Tagen der Menschheit* brings home the importance of the war in Kraus' identity and significance.[85]

Jonathan Franzen has recently published an unconventional and accessible introduction to Kraus, entitled *The Kraus Project*. Franzen shows the centrality of anger in Kraus's work and some of the reasons for its untranslatability to his own culture and ours. Kraus worked hard on his writing to make it inaccessible to the elite intellectuals he was mocking, and Franzen makes explicit why Kraus does not fit the parameters of this intellectual history:

> He was known not for his novels (he didn't write any) or his drama (his plays were never much produced) or his thinking (it was deliberately unsystematic) but for his lyric poetry and for the characteristic wit and irony of his reportage and travel writing and polemics.[86]

Nonetheless, I address his contributions here because he spoke so powerfully to his generation of intellectuals. Kraus was himself inspired as a young man by another peculiar writer, Otto Weininger, who played an important role in Ludwig Wittgenstein's life as well. Weininger also came from a Jewish family, and his work was even less suited to success in the world. Like Weininger, Kraus was not a novelist, but a hybrid figure. It might be right to say that Weininger said the opposite of Kraus, but meant the same thing, that is, the rejection of the world in which he lived. He was as devoted to the German language as Kafka, and he used German to stand in moral judgment of his age. Kraus and Weininger were moral absolutists, which for Kraus meant the condemnation of the liberal era in the name of the feminine, for Weininger the celebration of the masculine.[87] They make clear in very different ways from Wittgenstein that what is most important cannot be said.

The distinction between "morality" and "ethics" is not firm and clear for these writers, and even Musil did not always emphasize the distinction. But what usually separated "morality" from "ethics" for Musil was self-righteousness—absolutism, judgment, and taking the ego literally and seriously. Musil and others in this generation moved in a strongly ethical direction but they were not so opposed as Kraus to Young Vienna or its aestheticism. In Musil, and even in Wittgenstein, we see the assertion of the ethical, but in combination with the aesthetic. Musil's choice of a quotation from Maurice Maeterlinck to introduce his first novel underscores the limits of language in this generation.

> In some strange way we devalue things as soon as we give utterance to them. We believe we have dived into the uttermost depths of the abyss, and yet when we return to the surface the drop of water on our pallid finger-tips no longer resembles the sea from which it came. We think we have discovered a hoard of wonderful treasure-trove, yet when we emerge again into the light of day we see that all we have brought back with us is false stones and chips of glass. But for all this, the treasure goes on glimmering in the darkness unchanged.[88]

A level of the German language was achieved in this period—in Hofmannsthal, Musil, Rilke, Kafka, and Broch—that invites comparison with German classicism and romanticism and seems unlikely ever to be surpassed. The prose of these writers constituted a dramatic moment in the history of literature and the German language. In this generation, Austrian literature was no longer so concentrated on the world of Vienna and Viennese elites. There were many other fine writers in Germany and Austria and elsewhere in Central Europe in this period, but we still do not really understand why this extraordinary level was achieved in Cisleithanian Austria.[89] The early twentieth century in Austria represents something quite different from the themes we often associate with *fin de siècle* Vienna: not decline, but an effort to create a new culture or the possibilities for a new culture. It is a story of renewal, of the recovery and exploration of the ethical imagination. The emphasis was not on decadence and loss, but on an exploration of human life and spirituality that had nothing to do with Franz Joseph and very little to do with what was local to the Habsburg Monarchy.

Robert Musil (1880-1942)

Robert Musil was concerned in *The Man without Qualities* not with the details of a declining monarchy, but with a particularly clear case of the modern world. What interested him about the setting of this novel, the imperial and royal Monarchy, is that the modern situation had become so apparent to the ordinary person:

> In so far as this can at all become apparent to every eye, it had done so in Kakania, and in this Kakania was, without the world's knowing it, the most progressive State of all; it was the state that was by now only just, as it were, acquiescing in its own existence. In it one was negatively free, constantly aware of the inadequate grounds for one's own existence and lapped by the great fantasy of all that had not happened, or at least had not yet irrevocably happened, as by the foam of the oceans from which mankind arose.[90]

And much later in the novel Musil returns to the situation of Kakania with a different metaphor that echoes Nietzsche's essay on Schopenhauer:

> For Kakania was the first country in our present historical phase from which God withdrew His credit: the love of life, faith in itself, and the ability of all civilized nations to disseminate the useful illusion that they have a mission to fulfill [….] Although men are not normally aware of it, they must believe that they are something more than they are in order to be capable of being what they are; they need to feel this something more above and around them, and there are times when they suddenly miss it. What is missing is something imaginary … this nothing had become as disturbing as getting no sleep or seeing no sense in anything.[91]

Robert Musil believed in science, reason, and liberalism as much as any figure of the nineteenth century, but he did not believe that the investigation of highly individualized "ethical experiences" of the kind he portrayed in *Young Törless* and *Vereinigungen* was incompatible with the values of science and empiricism.[92] His commitments to democracy and science were accompanied by a sense of adventure about the possibilities that were being opened up by the cracks in the old social and ideological order. He was conscious of the inadequacy of all the political parties in Austria before the First World War, and it was clear to him that most scientists were quite unaware of the problems human beings were having with modernity. The scientists "bore in with their heads at the place in science where they have landed; continuing frugally, differently from one another, and in ignorance of any other culture, the life of the spiritual hamlet from which they happen to have come." Musil wanted to set out from "the social chaos and moral contradictions of modern life to consciously become even bolder." His impulse was to turn the apparently negative into the basis for new possibilities: "For what is more precious in art today … than the freedom of movement of the feelings, which we owe to a loosening of moral prohibitions and aesthetic uniformity, in the last analysis here also to the too-great number of human beings?"[93] Musil was able to bring home in a more effective way the issues that Nietzsche was concerned about and to bring these themes into relation with modern science.

Musil argued that these problems with modernity were part of a broadly European and German phenomenon that was only poorly characterized in terms of the *fin de siècle*. As he put it after the war: Around 1900 "people believed in the future. In a social future. In a new art. The fin de siècle gave the period a veneer of morbidity and decadence: but both these definitions were only contingent expressions for the will to be different, to do things differently from the way people had done them in the past."[94] In the 1920s Musil wondered "how so much genuine ability and accomplishment could be concealed for so long beneath the illusion of decadence."[95] Even before the war Musil argued for a reason "that would strive to discover and systematize truths giving new and bold directions to the feelings …. a rationality, in other words, for which thinking would exist only to give an intellectual armature to some still problematic way of being human: such a rationality is incomprehensible today even as a need."[96] For Musil, literature was an experimental laboratory for exploring new possibilities for being human. The themes of gender, ego, the male idea, traditional ideologies and religions, and inherited social conventions of all kinds offered countless opportunities for irony and new possibilities, and Musil came to see 1914 as a symptom of the breakdown of all ideologies. He wanted to make clear the openness of this new historical situation in an atmosphere not of discouragement but of excitement and adventure. Indeed, Musil aimed at the recovery of the genuine sources of the ethical imagination.

Musil believed there was "a profound connection between the civilizing character of morality and of the scientific spirit," whereas "the truly ethical experience, such as love, introspection, or humility, is, even where it is of a social nature, something difficult to transmit, something quite personal and almost anti-social." Musil emphasized the contrast between a morality that depended on social convention and a more positive sense of the word, which he called ethics. "But morality [here in the more positive sense of 'ethics'] actually begins only in the solitude that separates each person from every other. That which is incommunicable, the encapsulation in the self, is what makes people need good and evil."[97] Musil's way of understanding his own values and intellectual concerns often comes close to describing intellectuals from Nietzsche and Emerson to Rilke and Kafka, Kassner and Hofmannsthal, as when Musil defines the essayists in *The Man without Qualities*: "Their domain lies between religion and knowledge, between example and doctrine, between *amor intellectualis* and poetry; they are saints with and without religion, and sometimes they are also simply men on an adventure who have gone astray."[98] Musil frequently contrasted such ethical figures with a usage of "morality" that is rigidified and disconnected from living human experience: "Ulrich regarded morality as it is commonly understood as nothing more than the senile form of a system of energies that cannot be confused with what it originally was without losing ethical force."[99]

Musil's approach to ethics was often close to Ludwig Wittgenstein's formulations in *The Tractatus*: "that ethics cannot be put into words .... [and that] (Ethics and aesthetics are one and the same.)"[100] According to Musil, his preoccupation with ethics was quite compatible with modern science, and he refused to describe the concerns of ethics in ways that were at odds with knowledge or rationality: "The significant person is the one who commands the greatest factual knowledge and the greatest degree of rationality in connecting the facts: in the one area as in the other. But one person finds the facts outside himself and another within himself; one meets with coherent sequences of experience and another doesn't."[101] Indeed, "the pointless battle in contemporary civilization between scientific thinking and the claims of the soul can be solved only by adding something, a plan, a direction to work in, a different valuing of science as well as literature!"[102] Musil was looking for "experimental intellectual principles for forming the inner life"[103] but also for "that condition of awakening that all mystics have prized as entering into a new existence."[104] Musil's understanding of modern science was distinctive. He was concerned with the relationship between science and our personal lives and feelings, and he brought with him a satiric genius for portraying people in his culture: an ironic wisdom, an ability to turn his satire back on himself (this ironic capacity is a form of objectivity and a form of love); an ability to apply intellect to individual experiences of feeling; an understanding of the relationship between metaphor and modern historical change; a sensitivity to the relationship between ideology and feelings; and a new understanding of religious experience.

Hermann Broch (1886–1951) and Hugo von Hofmannsthal (1874–1929)

The locus classicus for a distinction between the aestheticism of the late nineteenth century and a more ethical turn in the early twentieth is Hermann Broch's essay from 1951: *Hofmannsthal and His Time: The European Imagination, 1860–1920*. This was a seminal work about the late nineteenth century in Vienna, but it was also more broadly a book about European art and style. Broch's aim was to explain Hofmannsthal's move away from aestheticism in a more ethical direction. Here Broch made an argument about aestheticism after 1880, but also an argument about ethics in his own generation. Hofmannsthal was only ten years older than Broch, but Hofmannsthal is often associated with the older generation because of his precocity as a poet in the 1890s, when he was a central figure of Young Vienna.[105] Broch described Vienna as a city of decoration at the heart of the liberal value vacuum. For Broch, the value vacuum of the late nineteenth century was the basis for aestheticism, hedonism, and cynicism. He emphasized "the Austrian love for spectacle and decoration" and "the celebration of beauty that marked" Hofmannsthal's youth, but he also pointed to Hofmannsthal's "ethical earnestness" in the 1890s.[106] Even in his first years as part of Young Vienna, Hofmannsthal had moved in an ethical direction: "The sequence of Hofmannsthal's 'ethical' pieces begins with *Death and the Fool* (1893), in which the aesthetic is first condemned," which is to say that Hofmannsthal was already working to overcome aestheticism even as a very young man.[107] Even then, poetry for Hofmannsthal was "the ritual of ethicality."[108] Like Hofmannsthal, Broch wanted to break out of this aestheticism to an ethical art. As he put it: "I am concerned with the processes which lead the human being to the loss and regaining of his *vérités fondamentales*, in short, his religious attitudes."[109]

Much like Musil and Broch, Hofmannsthal saw himself as part of the broader experience of German literature and culture since the Enlightenment (beyond the political borders of Bismarck's Empire). As with many intellectuals of this generation, Hofmannsthal believed that Nietzsche played a special role in the history of German intellectual life; he saw Nietzsche as a "taut soul" who challenged the false way of living of modern Germans and aimed at something higher than literature: "the spiritual life of the nation." He believed that the "whole concept of an intellectual-spiritual tradition" was recognized in German culture "only in a highly conditional way." With the word "Schrifttum" Hofmannsthal referred to a conception of the spiritual-intellectual life of the nation that went beyond a narrow and conventional understanding of literature.[110] The leading writers of his generation were conscious of their identities as German writers, as Austrians, and as part of a broader European experience. They did not advocate for a parochial Austria, but for a cosmopolitan vision of German literature and intellectual life that was very different from Hitler's fascist transcendence of the German nation to achieve European hegemony.[111]

Broch is best known for *The Sleepwalkers* (1932), one of the most ambitious novels of modern literature and in many respects comparable to *The Man without Qualities* or to Thomas Mann's *The Magic Mountain*.[112] But, although Broch was a major novelist in his own right, Hannah Arendt argues that he was a "writer against his will" because of his preoccupation with ethics and his theory of values,[113] and in that sense his essay on Hofmannsthal is both a major work of his maturity and an essay on himself, much like Nietzsche's essay on Schopenhauer.[114] Broch was preoccupied with "the dissolution of the European system of values," and he made this theme central to *The Sleepwalkers* as well as to his book on Hofmannsthal.[115] But Broch's decision to invoke Hofmannsthal for his argument about the move from aestheticism to ethics is the crucial point here.[116] Hofmannsthal never finished *Andreas*, his most serious effort at the novel, but his play from 1921, *Der Schwierige* [The Difficult Man], belongs to Musil's world of irony and people without qualities. Hannah Arendt and Michael Steinberg have invited us to see Broch and Hofmannsthal together. As Steinberg puts it: "As critics of the world that produced them, both Hofmannsthal and Broch strove for an ethical response to the demands of that world through varying modes of expression: the philosophical essay, the political essay and tract, and a great variety of stories, novels, and plays."[117]

Rainer Maria Rilke (1875–1926)

Perhaps the most spiritual figure of this generation was Rainer Maria Rilke. Hofmannsthal has often been compared to Stefan George, his German friend from the 1890s, but his most important connection to lyric poetry in this generation was to Rilke. Musil characterized Rilke's poetry "as pure process and shaping of spiritual powers, which in him, for the first time, find name and voice."[118] Musil argued that Rilke "saw differently: in a new more inward way," and he characterized Rilke's poetry as a "jewellike stillness within a movement that never pauses." He called Rilke "the greatest lyric poet the Germans have had since the late Middle Ages," but Rilke was also an important prose stylist, above all in his novel, *The Notebooks of Malte Laurids Brigge*, of 1910.[119] If lyric poetry is the wellspring of literature, as Musil argued, we may say that the wellspring of German literature in the twentieth century was in Bohemia. Rilke was no more from Vienna than he was from Germany, but he was also broadly cosmopolitan, as much from Paris as he was from Prague—much as a Czech poet in his generation might have been.

Rilke began his career as a writer with his explorations of a new spirituality, at least partly under the influence of his powerful relationship with Lou Andreas-Salomé and her understanding of Nietzsche's ideas. A lovely line from *The Book of Hours*, a volume of poems written in the late 1890s and the early years of the twentieth century, set the tone for the themes he wanted to explore. In a poem to God, he wrote: "We will not be herded into churches, for you are not made by the crowd, you who meet us in our solitude."[120] Rilke had a deeply personal sense of God, as he did of his own individuality and his own death,[121] and his words to God at the turn of the century hardly sound like decadence: "I am living just as the century ends …. We see the brightness of a new page where everything yet can happen." Rilke felt the loss of tradition, but he was definitely setting out on something new. He wanted to strip "bare of all inessentials," to find "new modes of feeling and creating" (20–1)[122]—and this was the task of his poetry. He wanted to say what had never been spoken: "No forcing and no holding back, The way it is with children."[123] Rilke's *Notebooks* speak on behalf of his poetry. As he puts it there: "For the sake of a line of poetry one must see many cities, people, and things, one must know animals, must feel how the birds fly, and know the gestures with which small flowers open in the morning."[124]

Rilke produced one of the distinctive novels of modernism even as he was learning to see in the streets of Paris.[125] His first-person protagonist, Brigge, begins to think at the age of twenty-eight on a gray Paris afternoon:

> Is it possible … that one has not yet seen, recognized, and said anything real and important? Is it possible that one has had thousands of years of time to look, reflect, and write down, and that one has let millennia pass away like a school recess in which one eats one's sandwich and apple?
>
> Yes, it is possible.
>
> Is it possible that in spite of inventions and progress, in spite of culture, religion,

and worldly wisdom, that one has remained on the surface of life? ...

Yes, it is possible.

Is it possible that the whole history of the world has been misunderstood? ...

Yes it is possible.

Later in this passage is one of Rilke's most creative insights:

> Is it possible that there are people who say "God" and think that it is something they have in common? Just look at two schoolboys: one buys himself a knife, and the same day his neighbor buys one just like it. And after a week they show each other their knives and it turns out that they bear only the remotest resemblance to each other—so differently have they developed in different hands .... Ah, so: is it possible to believe that one could have a God without using him?
>
> Yes, it is possible.[126]

Brigge concedes that he "would so gladly remain among the meanings that have become dear to [him] ...." but the task of the *Notebooks* is more adventurous: "Is it possible that one believed one had to make up for everything that happened before one was born?"[127] One dimension of his adventure was close to Musil's project of understanding gender and the relations between men and women as a key to rethinking ethics. It was also close to Musil's sense of possibility.

> For centuries women have accomplished the totality of love, they have always played the whole dialog, both roles. For the man has only repeated after them, and badly .... his jealousy that was also a kind of negligence. But women nevertheless persevered day and night, and grew in love and misery. (99)

And again:

> But now, when so much is changing, is it not up to us to change ourselves? Could we not try to develop ourselves a little, and slowly, gradually, take upon ourselves our share of the work in love? .... what if we were to begin from the very beginning to learn the work of love that has always been done for us? (100–1)

Franz Kafka (1883–1924) and the Modern Imagination

Perhaps the most important writer of this generation was Franz Kafka, who has come to epitomize the voice of the modern imagination. Kafka never finished his three major novels (*Amerika* or *Der Verschollene*, *The Trial*, and *The Castle*), and he asked that they not be published, like Virgil burning the *Aenead* in

Broch's novel. Moreover, one can make a case that, just as Rilke was a lyric poet, Kafka was above all a writer of short stories and short pieces.[128] But it is certainly true that for the last thirteen years of his life, Kafka was engaged in a creative adventure that was enormously important for German literature, especially for German prose, and critics have found it convenient to characterize him as a novelist. No writer was more intense or interior or more the embodiment of the ethical imagination in his generation. As Broch put it, "a genius like Kafka is born once a century."[129] Especially apparent in Kafka is the writer's relationship to the breakdown of ideologies and conventional ways of thinking and living. Wilhelm Emrich argues that Kafka wrote out of "the complete absence in the twentieth century of all security-giving earthly and metaphysical conceptions and systems," adding that, because of this, the story Kafka wants to tell is "the antithesis of every delimited individual story."[130] Benno Wagner emphasizes in Kafka "the resistance of an oeuvre that cannot be colonized by any of the dominant ideologies of the twentieth century."[131]

It is astonishing to see what Kafka's stories and short pieces from before the war can accomplish in just a few pages. A simple description of a passenger on a tram can give the essence of what Kafka has to say, including his puzzlement at being in the world at all.

> I stand at the end of the platform of the tram and am completely unsure of my footing in the world, in this town, in my family. Not even casually could I indicate any claims that I might rightly advance in any direction. I have not even any defense to offer for standing on this platform, holding on to this strap.[132]

In these words, he expressed a very different sensibility from the typical citizen on a trolley in the years before the war. In "Clothes" Kafka portrays the faces which have been "seen by too many people" so that they are "hardly wearable any longer."[133] The single page of "The Sudden Walk" is a powerful portrayal of the dissatisfactions of European family life in the years before the First World War.[134]

1912 was the year when Kafka met Felice Bauer, and it was also the year when he discovered himself as a writer.[135] In Peter Gay's book on modernism, he argues that "Kafka's last word in all its forms was 'No.'"[136] But to the most important question Kafka discovered in this year of inspiration, the answer was "Yes!" He learned "How everything can be said, how for everything, for the strangest fancies, there waits a great fire in which they perish and rise up again."[137] For more than a decade Kafka was able to write out of this fire. Kafka's engagement break-up occurred in 1914, leading up to his intense writing in

August, and Heinz Politzer emphasizes the years between 1914 and 1917 as "the peak of his literary mastery" (83), thus including *The Trial* with the earlier short prose pieces.[138]

A passage in Kafka's *Diaries* from 1910 captures what he was trying to do: "If until now our whole person had been oriented upon the work of our hands, upon that which was seen by our eyes, heard by our ears, upon the steps made by our feet, now we suddenly turn ourselves entirely in the opposite direction, like a weather vane in the mountains."[139] Kafka's *Metamorphosis* is perhaps his best-known work and arguably the most representative creation of the decisive years of his emergence as a writer. Particularly appealing about this story of a traveling salesman who wakes up one morning as an insect is that no one has any preconceptions about the inner life of *Ungeziefer* or vermin, which liberates Kafka from convention and cliché from the outset. Kafka was learning to see around the same time as Rilke, and Kafka's writing was his effort to "raise the world into purity, truth, immutability."

***

The ethical energies of this generation of intellectuals seem to have been most apparent before the First World War, and by the end of the war much of the creativity had been spent. But this did not prevent the writing of *The Man without Qualities*, *The Sleepwalkers*, *The Castle*, the *Duino Elegies*, and the *Sonnets of Orpheus*, as well as some of Hofmannsthal's finest prose and *Der Schwierige*, a play that is focused on a character very like Ulrich. These writers—Musil, Hofmannsthal, Broch, Rilke, and Kafka—did not come from Germany but from Cisleithanian Austria, and they represent the culmination of an intellectual tradition since the Enlightenment.

5

The Human Sciences in Austria

In the human sciences, more than in philosophy and literature, the terminology is problematic, even arbitrary or anachronistic.¹ The human or social sciences developed fairly recently in Austria, mainly since the 1860s.² Austria was slow to develop social science fields as we think of them today, and the connections of the human sciences to history and philosophy were less marked in Cisleithanian Austria than in Imperial Germany.³ Sociology and the *Geisteswissenschaften* (the human or mental sciences) were less prominent in Austrian universities than in other German-speaking states, and even political theory did not develop in a pronounced way in nineteenth-century Austria.⁴ Instead we find psychology (in close connection to philosophy and medicine) and economics (mainly in the law schools), while the origins of political science in Austria lie in cameralism—the eighteenth-century name for the sciences of governing in the German states. Although there are considerable scholarly literatures on both philosophy and literature in Austria, there is nothing comparable on the human sciences or on the history of social thought, which is one reason why Austrian intellectual history has been outside the mainstream of European intellectual history. Even within this broadly conceived subject, this is not a large field, and I will concentrate primarily on the significance of economics and psychoanalysis for social thought.⁵ I begin with understandings of the state and then consider the importance for modern social thought of the Austrian school of economics and of psychoanalysis, both of which developed out of the thinking of the liberal era and the newly reformed university.

The modern social sciences emerged in the twentieth century as products of the decomposition of the world I describe in this book.⁶ As Keith Tribe points out, it is important to be aware of the temptation to fall into "anachronistic retrospective histories," to apply "a twentieth-century theoretical apparatus to the writings of previous centuries."⁷ Cameralism was central to the development of the human sciences in Austria, as it was in the German states across central

Europe, but cameralism was very different from political science, economics, and sociology as we think about them today. At the same time, the sciences of the state were not strongly shaped by Hegel as they were to the North, and these fields were not influenced by broad theorizing about society and the nation.[8] In Central Europe, political theory and economics were both taught in the law schools and they were closely related to each other, as is apparent in the work of Othmar Spann, who wrote both an economic history and a theory of the ideal state. What did emerge in the late nineteenth century was a powerful tradition of work on modern economics, which set the tone for much that was distinctive about Austrian social theory. Psychoanalysis, on the other hand, did not grow out of cameralism or the theory of the state, but out of the medical school, yet it was a major—and very different—approach to the human sciences.

In the Shadow of the State: From Cameralism to the Authoritarian State

The modern social sciences in Austria began as the sciences of the state or cameralism, which included what we would call political science, economics, and even sociology today. This intellectual tradition began in the German states during the early modern period as the science of managing the responsibilities of the prince (as a foreman or caretaker would manage a property), as a way of giving formality and system to knowledge gleaned from experience in the state.[9] This way of thinking was grounded in turn in the broad tradition of Western social thought since Plato and Aristotle and in efforts to address the needs of man as a social animal.[10] The authors who developed the field were mainly German-speakers from Central Europe. They were concerned not only with major eighteenth-century states such as Austria, Prussia, and Saxony, but also with the many smaller states that dotted the map of Central Europe. It is not surprising that one of the most prominent administrators of the new Austrian state, Joseph von Sonnenfels, was a major figure of cameralism. Albion Small, author of one of the classic studies of cameralism, presents Sonnenfels as the culminating figure of the field.[11] Although cameralism became a university-field in the late eighteenth century, its orientation was decidedly practical, and this practical sense of the administrator left a powerful stamp on the intellectual life of the Enlightenment and the Austrian tradition.[12] From the Enlightened monarchs to Austrian Socialism and Christian Socialism, the state was a given in Austrian politics. In the eighteenth century this approach did not distinguish economics as a separate field or emphasize the agency of citizens. It was only later that what we think of as economics emerged in the context of a modern liberal economic order that was independent of the state. Indeed, the title of one of the most important books on twentieth-century Austria is *Der lange Schatten des Staates*.[13] For nearly two hundred years Austrian social theory developed in the shadow of the state, strongly influenced both by the practical needs of the state and by the theoretical assumption that the state was the basis for any social order.

A great deal of thought went into understanding the tasks of governing in the nineteenth century—in the many German-speaking states of Central Europe—including welfare and social and economic change. Most German-speaking universities were shaped by the cameralist tradition in the fields of law and economics, and this tradition in turn influenced Marx and Weber, as well as Menger and modern economics.[14] Theories of the state, let alone utopias, were something quite different from the pragmatism of cameralism, but both reflected shared assumptions about the centrality of the state to social life. In the early nineteenth century Bernard Bolzano wrote an entire book on his thoughtful views of political and social reform, although his book did not appear during his lifetime, and he did not imagine that his conception of the best state could or should be implemented quickly and easily.[15] New work in the sciences of the state developed in the early nineteenth-century, in the wake of the Prussian reform movement and the Napoleonic reorganization of the smaller German states, primarily in Northern and Southwestern Germany.[16] What came to be known as the German historical school included Marx and Engels, Lorenz von Stein, Wilhelm Roscher, Karl Rau, and Karl Knies.[17] Their work was characterized primarily by an interest in historical stages of economic and political development.

After Sonnenfels, the Austrians contributed very little to this discussion until the 1850s, when Lorenz von Stein assumed a chair in Vienna as part of the reform and modernization of the faculty. Stein was one of the leading figures of German social sciences in the mid-nineteenth century, and he spent the major part of his career as a professor of political economy at the University of Vienna from 1855 to 1885.[18] His approach to the analysis of social and political developments in France was similar to the work of Marx and Tocqueville; the similarities to Marx were apparent in Stein's approaches to class, to the proletariat in particular, and to the relationship between the state and society. Marx appreciated Stein's work, although the degree of influence is uncertain and both of them were influenced by Saint-Simon and the French socialists of the 1840s. Stein did not advocate for the proletariat, and he was by no means a revolutionary, but he represented a new awareness of social issues, and he added an awareness of Hegel and Comte to the sciences of state, which later attracted the critique of liberal economists. By 1866 "the notion of the sciences of state as a coherent field was becoming less and less meaningful."[19] In Austria, the state and its bureaucracy continued to play important roles, but these were increasingly balanced by the developing parliamentary system, first in 1861 and then more strongly after 1867. The rise of new mass parties in the late nineteenth century and the emergence of democratic institutions in the twentieth century shifted the emphasis to the ideological conflict among the parties.

Karl Knies, one of the leading figures of the German historical school, contributed to the methodological discussion of the sciences in a way that was later developed by Rickert and Weber. Knies contrasted the natural sciences to the human sciences, which emphasized "the inward mental life of individuals and groups (e.g. in philosophy, theology, and literature)." Knies regarded the political and social sciences as a third category, which was shaped both "by nature and by internal human motives."[20] It was Knies who first introduced the distinction later developed by the Baden neo-Kantians "between the so-called idiographic interpretation of social science and the 'nomothetic' one, that is, between the presentation of concrete particulars and of general laws."[21] This was the same distinction that Menger later developed in relation to the field of economics in the 1870s and 1880s. But in the middle of the nineteenth century the Germans were still committed to a strongly historical approach.

In the 1870s Gustav Schmoller became the central figure of the younger German historical school, bringing together many of the ways of thinking of both socialism and nationalism. What this school did not do was to explore the possibilities for the application of the methods of the natural sciences in the realm of economics. Schmoller wanted to study economic phenomena in historical context, and he was also concerned to work closely with the new German state. This was the world as the young Max Weber found it, and it became the basis for his view of understanding, ideal types, comparative cultures, and the rationalization of modern life. Weber's view was sensitive to the role of the state and to the importance of social issues in modern society, and it was powerfully stamped by the centrality of German nationalism. He benefited from the insights of Ranke into historical method, especially the history of institutions, the legal views of Karl von Savigny (which were close to Burke's), and the emphasis of Hegel on the role of the state. In Austrian historical studies, we see a strictly empirical approach that stayed close to the positivism of the natural sciences. Günther Fellner has emphasized "the empiricist, atheoretical bent" of the historical profession in Austria and its resistance to German debates about historicism. This was one reason that historical studies in Austria, however scholarly or even in the spirit of Ranke, did not have more impact outside of Austria.

The war with Prussia was an important turning point for social thought in Austria. Austria was no longer so closely connected to developments in what now became Germany. Moreover, the emergence of modern capitalism and a liberal political order lent new and independent significance to economics as a field. Political science and economics, however, were slow to develop distinct profiles in the law school. Government remained a practical science, and, in Austria, liberalism and Josephinism worked closely together down to the First World War. As late as the 1920s, the leading political theorist of the Catholic Right in Austria, Othmar Spann, also taught economics at the University of Vienna.[22] At the end of the First World War, Hans Kelsen emerged as the leading theorist of the liberal state in Austria, which provided a framework in which Social Democrats seemed to be at home.[23] Neither the Catholics nor the German nationalists were comfortable with the liberal order, and by the 1930s these parties moved toward the right and toward each other.[24] New intellectual impulses for the importance of the state emerged with the successes of Austrian Socialism under Victor Adler and the next generation of leaders who shaped the Second and a Half International in the 1920s: Otto Bauer, Karl Renner, and Max Adler.[25] In this period, however, Austrian Socialism remained close to the local level and unable to take over the state or genuinely threaten it.[26]

One aspect of democracy that raised difficult questions in the nineteenth century for both the Austrian state and Austrian Social Democracy was the nation. It was in Austria that it became most apparent that the age of nationalism did not quite know what the nation was, but also that there were special challenges and opportunities for Austrian Socialism. These issues crystalized in the early twentieth century with universal manhood suffrage in 1907 and with the split in Austrian Socialism between the Germans and the Czechs. The most important intellectual contributions of Austromarxism came here, not with a theory of Marxist revolution but with a new understanding of the nation and its relationship to socialism. The decisive figure was Otto Bauer (1881–1938), the leader of the Austro-Marxist left, who published a major study on this subject in 1906 and a new edition in 1924. Bauer worked toward a more historical understanding of national character that was grounded neither in a fixed concept of race or ethnicity nor in language alone, but in a combination of national character and common fate.²⁷ The successes of Austrian Socialism came in the reform and modernization of the urban world in Vienna during the 1920s. On the other hand, the uprising of February 12, 1934, was a defense of socialist institutions by the workers against the consolidation of power by the right.²⁸ The theoretical problems of Austro-Marxism were on the whole similar to those in German Social Democracy, and there was never a planned effort by the Austrian Socialists to seize the state. In retrospect Austrian Socialism was not as distinctive as it had been thought to be, but it did play a mediating role in international socialism, and Bauer and Renner held the party together while accomplishing important practical work in Vienna.²⁹

After 1900 Christian Socialism and Austrian Socialism became more significant in addressing the problems of the modern city and mass society, and the First World War brought an end to an international economic world and encouraged a state that played a powerful role in the modern economy.³⁰ After the war the modern state played a mainly local role in postwar reconstruction in Red Vienna. The state under the Christian Socialists became even more dominant in the *Ständestaat* [corporate state], which aimed at the Catholic regulation of the economy and society, and in the assimilation of Austria and Czechoslovakia to the new German state. Karl Lueger, the leading figure of Christian Socialism before the war, was too pragmatic to take much interest in Romantic ideas, and it was not until the 1920s that the Christian Socials under Ignaz Seipel began to take the lead in the state.³¹ Spann's corporatist ideas helped to shape the state between 1934 and 1938, when Eric Voegelin wrote his analysis of the authoritarian state.³² In the early twentieth century, both war and socialism drew attention to the role of the state in the economy, and the Austrian economists generally emphasized that the limits of knowledge determined the limits of the state in allocating resources.

The 1930s also brought more modern approaches in the field of sociology, which were prominent after the Second World War. Sociology emerged as a significant academic field in the interwar years, first with Karl and Charlotte Bühler, who brought their work on psychology and sociology from Germany in 1922, and later in the work of Paul Lazarsfeld and Marie Jahoda; and this approach has been developed more recently by Christian Fleck.³³ Lazarsfeld was a pioneer of sociology in the 1930s, and he was an inspiration for the social sciences in Vienna after 1945. In some ways sociology grew out of motivations similar to cameralism, but it had moved from the center of policy in the state to studying the experience of ordinary people and the agency of non-state actors, consumers, and citizens.³⁴ Lazarsfeld was himself an example of a pattern he identified in his presidential address at the American Sociological Association in 1962: the origins of empirical social research in Europe, especially around 1930, and its migration to the United States.[35] Lazersfeld's experience was one of the many ways in which Austrian intellectual life migrated to the United States, although in his case the migration happened very early in his career, so that his impact in Austria mainly came after the war. The field that did develop strongly between 1871 and the First Republic was economics. The German historical school left the application of the methods of the natural sciences in the realm of economics to the Austrians and to the mathematically oriented economists in France and England. The irony here is that the Austrians took the lead in applying the methods of the natural sciences to the human world, but increasingly emphasized the limits of this kind of knowledge and the extent to which the methods of the natural sciences should not be extended to the human world.

Austrian Economics and Social Thought: From Menger to Hayek

Austrian economics was an important departure from the German historical school and from political economy as it had been understood in the nineteenth century. I want to draw attention to the significance of this approach for social thought. Carl Menger and Friedrich August von Hayek are the two central figures in my story—but I am concerned not so much with the history of economics as with the way economics shaped social thought in Austria, in ways that were quite different from social theory in Germany and France, although they resonated in England and the United States. This tradition emphasized what we do not know and what we cannot control: the unanticipated consequences of human action and conscious intention. Bruce Caldwell has done a great deal to integrate the Austrian economists into modern intellectual history and to clarify Hayek's contribution to modern social thought: "a thoroughly modernist critique of the scientistic pretensions of his age," which also pointed toward "some surprising (some might even label them *postmodern*) new directions."[36]

Carl Menger (1840–1921) was one of the founders of modern economics. He wanted to persuade German-speaking economists to be more open to what we think of today as economics. He succeeded in this regard in Vienna, where he and his students developed the Austrian School of Economics. His *Grundsätze der Volkswirtschaftslehre* (1871)[37] was one of several major contributions to the theory of marginal utility (satisfaction) during the 1870s.[38] In 1883 he published a second major work that concentrated on method and led to the famous *Methodenstreit* [Battle over Method] with Gustav Schmoller and the German Historical School.[39] Menger was born on his parents' new estate in Galicia, but the family was German-speaking and from Bohemia. Although he studied at Vienna and Prague, Menger completed his Habilitation at Krakow, by then part of Cisleithanian Austria in the constitutional sense of 1867; but his entire career and influence belong to the University of Vienna and to the intellectual world of Cisleithanian Austria. He represents a critique of the view that there is a privileged point of view informed enough to undertake planning for an entire economy, although he did not think of this as a moral issue. Hayek later thought out the methodological implications of this view.

Although Menger did not use the term marginal theory, his *Gründsätze* or *Principles* of 1871 was one of the founding works of neoclassical economics and the marginal theory of value (as opposed to the labor theory of value, which had developed from Smith and Ricardo to Marx). His contribution to social theory was immense in a way that is too rarely appreciated. Much more familiar to intellectual historians are the developments in German sociology in the late nineteenth and early twentieth centuries, whereas it has been primarily economists who have been interested in Menger. Between the Austrian *Ausgleich* in 1867 and the disappearance of Austria from the map in 1938, concern with the social question in the form of socialism came to be contrasted not simply to capitalism but to the science of economics. This meant that Austrian economists from Menger to Hayek were sensitive to methodological themes that people in other fields were not, but they were also drawn into the debate about socialism.[40]

The Austrian School of Economics is in many respects an artificial, imposed terminology, which means roughly: economics in Austria after Menger; this was the stream in which Austrian social thought took shape. The term arose, as labels often do, as an attempt to disparage—on the part of the German historical school against their colleagues to the south. The term is often identified with the theory of marginal utility, although Menger did not think in these terms. Menger emphasized themes for social theory that were influential in this tradition: the unintended consequences of social action and the difficulty of prediction and controlled intervention in the social sciences. What Menger pointed to in an entirely sober way was an empirical mystery that was already present in the German historical school: How do social phenomena like money emerge without conscious intention or control? Still more, how is it that such phenomena can serve the common good without any general intention to create them? Such questions derived from Edmund Burke and Friedrich Karl von Savigny, but they became the methodological basis for liberal approaches to modern capitalism. Menger emphasized that some institutions, which emerged without conscious intention, served the common welfare nonetheless, but he did not accept the conservative view that wanted to preserve ancient institutions for their own sake and to avoid reform.[41] Although Menger is ordinarily regarded as a marginalist, his subjectivism also led him to emphasize "the importance of knowledge, time, human perception, and the possibility of error in individual decisionmaking, and all of these created problems for the clean application of the marginalist calculus."[42]

For Menger's view of method, the central text is *Untersuchungen*, often translated as *Investigations*, which gives the sense of the German title.[43] Menger begins by challenging conventional German distinctions between the natural and the human sciences. He is a very bad writer, so that it is extremely painful to read his argument, but he is aiming at something very like Musil's later distinction between ratioid and non-ratioid.[44] The point is that the emphasis on the distinction between the natural sciences and the human sciences obscures key issues of method. Menger wants to understand how any science can begin with individual phenomena in the world and then find its way to what he calls "exact laws" (theoretical) as opposed to individual phenomena (empirical). Menger's point is roughly in the spirit of "how can chemistry be a science if oxygen does not exist in the phenomenal world?" What process of selection and abstraction must empirical phenomena undergo in order to allow investigators to speak in terms of laws?

The issue that Menger raised was whether and to what extent it was useful or desirable to abstract from specific historical contexts to develop arguments in the form of laws. At issue was the question of the relative autonomy of economic variables in relation to social, cultural, and institutional realities. Everything that is important to the fields of history and legal history was on the side of the German historical school, and we may think of Marx as an attempt to combine these methods of historical context with abstract, hypothetical reason on the model of the natural sciences. The issue for Menger was what could be known and to what extent it was possible to abstract from specific historical situations as we would in physics. The reception of the Austrian School of Economics is a reminder of Nietzsche's view that we can only hear what we already know. The marginalists saw only themselves in Menger, so that much of what he had to say was lost for two generations until events seem to have encouraged a different emphasis. Then some of Menger's ideas became easier to see. Menger's two most famous students, Friedrich von Wieser (1851–1926) and Eugen von Böhm-Bawerk (1851–1914), were civil servants in Vienna who did not take Menger's classes but read his book. They were not interested in issues of social theory but in substantive economics, and they contributed to the development of the field and to the concerns of marginalist economics with maximizing utility.[45] They emphasized "aspects of the Austrian message that were more in line with marginalist thinking elsewhere .... It was not until subsequent generations rediscovered them that Menger's writings on the evolution of social institutions were recognized as a valuable contribution to social theory."[46]

Aspects of Menger that were not highlighted in the next generation were his emphasis on the complexity and unpredictability of human beings, their creativity in response to life, subjectivity and taking the individual into account.[47] Allan Oakley has emphasized the importance of "debunking" the myth that Menger was primarily one of the three great theorists of marginal economics, along with Léon Walras and William Stanley Jevons, the founders of neoclassical orthodoxy. Like many other commentators in recent years, Oakley wants to emphasize what set Menger apart from the other marginalists, arguing that it was not simply that he did not rely as much on mathematics, but that he actually had a different view of the world: "his ontology of subjectivist and individualist human agency ... cannot be confined within mechanistic neoclassical principles."[48] Streissler and Oakley conclude as follows:

> [Menger] wrote a completely subjective theory; and that meant that he eschewed deriving concrete results. He was content to show all the manifold dimensions of causation in the economic field. In his view the final outcome of all these forces at work could not be fully described. And that is the basic failure of his theory: he ended in doubt and not in positive theorems.[49]

The leading figures of the next generation after Wieser and Böhm-Bawerk were Ludwig von Mises (1881–1973) and Joseph Schumpeter (1883–1950). Von Mises' *Privatseminar* met every two weeks at the Chamber of Commerce, and it was the institutional equivalent in economics of the Vienna Circle.[50]

F. A. Hayek's thought grew out of the Austrian School of Economics. He was trained in Böhm-Bawerk's seminar in Vienna and published in the field of economics; he went to England to work in the 1930s. By 1936, Hayek had moved away from writing primarily about economics to more methodological and philosophical concerns. Caldwell emphasizes the impact of living and working in England and writing in English, but Hayek's distinctive ideas also grew out of his education and experience in Austria, that is, both his liberalism and the emphases of the Austrian School of economics.[51] Many think of Hayek in terms of monetary theory or political ideology, but I am concerned here with his ideas about the possibility of knowledge about society, methodological concerns that crystalized during his time at the London School of Economics, but were very much continuous with Menger and the Austrian School of Economics.

In 1952 Hayek published a collection of his essays on social theory under the title *The Counter-Revolution of Science*. The book has rarely received the attention it deserves. It is a strange book, but it is an important critique of the mainstream of Western political thought over the past two centuries. Hayek puts French positivism at the heart of his discussion and emphasizes that the methods of the natural sciences should not be casually extended to the social sciences as if this kind of objectivity were possible in the human sciences. The subtitle, "Studies on the Abuse of Reason," points in the direction of his more familiar ideological concerns in *The Road to Serfdom* (1944), but in this book he is concerned above all with method in the social sciences.[52] The central questions are laid out in the first two essays; these were written in London just as the Second World War began and published separately in the journal *Economica*. His arguments are grounded in convictions about individualism and socialism, but he is concerned here with something different: the relationship between the methods of the natural sciences and what is possible in human studies. At the core of his argument is a critique of nineteenth-century French positivism, and he describes the close historical relationship between the rise of state socialism and the advocacy of social science on the model of the natural sciences.

Hayek begins his argument in *The Counter-Revolution of Science* with a time before the term "*science*" had assumed "the special narrow meaning it has today."[53] He argues that in the early nineteenth-century the term "science" was increasingly identified with physics and chemistry, and it was offered as a methodological model for the human sciences as well. This tendency in the social sciences, which is often referred to as positivism, was rejected by Hayek, but he repeatedly makes clear that his argument is not directed against the natural sciences: "It scarcely needs to be emphasized that nothing we shall have to say is aimed against the methods of Science in their proper sphere or intended to throw the slightest doubt on their value."[54] His critique is aimed at scientism in the human studies and at the related tendency toward social engineering. His point of reference was the French experience in the nineteenth century: the excitement of the French about modern science, the advocacy of positivism by Saint-Simon and Comte, and the efforts of the French at social engineering and state socialism.[55] Hayek emphasized the broad impact of these ideas in the nineteenth century—in Germany as well as France—and he argued that Marx and Hegel were part of this broader enthusiasm for a scientistic approach to the problems of society.

Hayek's view of method focuses on "the systematic subjectivity and individualism of the social sciences."[56] One might study the social sciences for a lifetime without having this thought. Moreover, Hayek challenges a common assumption of social and cultural theorists: that society and culture are man-made and distinct from natural objects because of that. He argues that society is not like a text or an artifact that has been created by a single conscious agent. For Hayek, society is like language. It was created inadvertently and without conscious intention. For Hayek, the goal of the social sciences is to understand how society came into being without conscious intention. His argument is directed against all forms of social theory that proceed abstractly and ab novo, including Freud.[57] The abstract method, in the sense of Rousseau or Kant, may be a way to establish a moral model, but it does not explain how to institute such a model in the world, how to engineer it. The key implication of all this is a counsel of modesty and restraint in matters of social action. For Hayek, approaches that emphasize design and intention are theological vestiges. His arguments are largely nineteenth-century liberalism's response to positivism, and, in that respect, they have a strong nineteenth-century flavor. But Hayek also wants to show the enormous influence positivism had on modern sociology. His central point was virtually unchanged from Menger's insight seventy years earlier. The social studies are "concerned with men's actions, and their aim is to explain the unintended or undesigned results of the actions of many men."[58]

Hayek's *Counter-Revolution of Science* is the best summary we have of the Austrian critique of positivism in the social sciences. It is roughly the opposite of the views of another contemporary, Herbert Marcuse, who made his way in the United States at the same time, although Hayek does not refer to Marcuse here, and he wrote before Marcuse was influential. Hayek's account of scientific method set out from the assumption that science had been on the defensive for a long time; for him, positivism (or scientism) was an exaggerated response to these real dangers, especially in the nineteenth century. He believed that by his own period the danger was "the opposite one of the predominance of scientism impeding the progress of the understanding of society."[59] He was certainly not writing an attack on science or even on positivism in Mach's sense. Hayek's understanding of liberal economics challenged the assumption that there is any objective, rational position that can assume its truth and scientific basis in relation to other views. The issue here is not the competition of values in the political arena, but whether an objective science is possible that would guide the state and all individuals in the society to a good world. A crucial theme of the resistance to socialism is skepticism about the possibility of achieving the rational overview of a society that is required for planning. Hayek believed that society depends on unintended outcomes in ways that French positivism never appreciated.

Psychoanalysis and Intellectual History

Sigmund Freud and the literature on him have strongly shaped our perceptions of the intellectual history of Vienna, especially in the 1890s. *The Interpretation of Dreams* (1900), Freud's letters to Wilhelm Fliess, and Freud's relationship with Joseph Breuer have all become important dimensions of our perception of this period, along with the themes of sexuality, gender, anti-Semitism, and psychoanalysis. It is difficult today to give a disinterested account of the history of the idea of the unconscious since this whole subject has been so successfully colonized by psychoanalysis.[60] The question of Freud's influence on the twentieth century has also been shaped by the literature on psychoanalysis itself. And it is impossible to say how much Freud's ideas were influenced by the concerns of literary modernism with inwardness and the unconscious, although most students of Austrian literature are aware of these issues in some way, whether via Young Vienna or Robert Musil.[61] The large and often excellent literature on Freud comes from many perspectives and should not be regarded as a unified field. It is a literature that does not always agree with itself, which can be stimulating. Freud's reputation is certainly far less settled and undisputed than it was fifty years ago—especially in the United States, where there have been dramatic changes in perceptions of Freud since the 1950s. One reason for this is the sheer number of fields for which his ideas have been important; another is that, as with most influential intellectuals, strikingly different accounts have been given of his ideas, making it difficult to know what each commentator is assuming. The poles of the debate since the 1970s have been the advocates of psychoanalysis, who see themselves as deeply identified with the founder of their tradition, and a variety of unsympathetic views of both psychoanalysis and its origins.[62]

Freud is unlike most of the other intellectuals discussed in this book in that he is well known to educated people.[63] Indeed, we may say that he has been the most influential social thinker to come out of Austria. The biographical details of his life have been recounted many times,[64] but there is also a surprising degree of ignorance about his ideas. More or less as with Nietzsche, or even Marx, many of those who dislike his ideas have never read him. I ask the reader to bear this problem of audience in mind—whether he or she is a Freud scholar, a psychoanalyst, a scientist of the natural world or the social world, a literary critic or a historian, an Austrian or someone who has never much cared about Freud—or even someone who is quite sure that Freud was wrong.

Freud is very much a symbol of the liberal era in Austria, a secularized Jew who celebrated Christmas and Easter in his home. Like so many Austrian Jews, he was born in Moravia (not far from Vienna); his father moved to Vienna, hoping that his son could one day enjoy success in the emerging liberal society. Freud studied at the University of Vienna, mainly at the medical school, and he grew from being a German nationalist and an avid reader of Schopenhauer and Nietzsche to being a scientist in Ernst Wilhelm Brücke's lab, where he took a good deal of distance from the political world.[65] The most distinctively Austrian dimension of the origins of Freud's thought was the high quality of the Vienna medical school (where Darwin was warmly received) combined with the powerful impact of Schopenhauer and Nietzsche at the University of Vienna at that time.[66] Some of the peculiarities of Freud's psychology and his social thought can be understood from the fact that he was deeply imbued in the natural sciences and medicine and he had another way of thinking about human nature that was not available to the English and the French: that is, the thought of Schopenhauer and Nietzsche. He also had a strong point of departure for his work in the teachings of Franz Brentano.[67] As he reached maturity and founded the psychoanalytic movement, he turned to new issues of social theory; he also showed the influence of the late Nietzsche as he undertook his revision of the theory of instincts, especially during the First World War.[68] His personal commitment to civilization compelled him to try to understand the problems of civilization in the twentieth century.

Freud was a crucial figure in the development of modern European intellectual history as a field in the United States, and he was central to the interest in Austrian history in American culture. He was the principal figure of H. Stuart Hughes' *Consciousness and Society* (1958), but also of Carl E. Schorske's *Fin-de-Siècle Vienna* (1980). Although Peter Gay began as a historian of the French Enlightenment and then wrote *Weimar Culture: Outsider as Insider* (1968), by far the central preoccupation of his published work was Sigmund Freud. Dominick La Capra, Gerald Izenberg, William McGrath, and Paul Robinson were all centrally preoccupied with Freud's work and ideas, and the connection to Freud was important for many other intellectual historians of this generation. Freud's significance for intellectual history has been his vision of human experience rather than the technicalities of psychoanalytic practice. Much of the field of intellectual history has adopted aspects of Freud's understanding of the roles of guilt, repression, neurosis, projection, transference, the power of the life and death instincts, and the search for authority and scapegoats.[69]

In the 1890s, especially during his creative illness from 1894 to 1899, Freud built on his work with Breuer (*Studies in Hysteria*, 1895) and moved away from his own work in *Scientific Psychology* (1895) to create his distinctive view of the centrality of the unconscious minds of children to his understanding of human beings: the view that the emotional and sexual experiences in the mind of the child determine the neurotic life of the adult.[70] His *Interpretation of Dreams* of 1900 brought together insights from his work with patients and his self-analysis to develop the model of psychoanalysis, which became the basis for all his later work. The postulation of an unconscious mind became the underlying assumption for his understanding of human sexuality, child development, and adult neurosis. He emphasized the dynamic in the child's mind that focused on the triangular relationships among father, mother, and child. He concluded that the decisive event in the mind of the young boy was aggression toward the father and the resulting guilt that became the basis for the moral sense of the adult. He found the evidence for his view in dreams, which led to his distinctive understanding of gender identity and object relations, beginning with the Oedipus Complex.[71] Shortly after he published *Interpretation of Dreams*, Freud became an associate professor at the University of Vienna and founded the International Psychoanalytic Movement. In his *Three Essays on the Theory of Sexuality* (1905), he elaborated his understanding of human sexuality and the links among childhood sexuality, homosexuality, and the heterosexuality of neurotic (or normal) adults.[72] In 1909 he was received by William James at the Clark lectures in Massachusetts as the great psychologist of the century. Throughout these years Freud developed his sensitivity to the unreal life of the mind, to the ambivalence of human beings, and to the mysterious dynamics of transference and projection in the therapeutic relationship, matters that were much less visible to physicians concerned with the body or to laboratory psychologists.

The notion of an unconscious was primary in all of Freud's models of the human mind. In the 1890s Freud assumed that this unconscious energy was divided between drives (or instincts) of self-preservation and sexuality (or libido). Although this was a new way to think about human nature, it was grounded in the assumptions of nineteenth-century positivism. It was only during the First World War that Freud developed the familiar dramatis personae of the self: the id (representing all of the mind's unconscious energy), the ego (or executive, the conscious self), and the super-ego (the source of guilt and repression, which takes its energy from the id). Bruno Bettelheim suggests that the best translations for Freud's German terminology, usually translated as ego, id, and superego, would be "the I, the it, and the above-I."[73] The adult individual or ego is caught between the constant infantile demands of the id and the guilt, judgment, and repression of the super-ego. The task of the adult ego and of psychoanalysis is to teach the adult to negotiate a mature resolution of the conflicting demands of the id and the super-ego. This description of the mind was closely connected to Freud's revision of his theory of the instincts during the First World War. The decisive change came in *Beyond the Pleasure Principle* (1920), where Freud postulated a death instinct (or Thanatos)—that is, not fear of death but a desire for it, an instinct for aggression against the self and others. He also postulated a life instinct (or Eros), which included sexuality but aimed more broadly at erotic connections among human beings.

This revision of the theory of the instincts also meant a quite different view of human suffering and the development of the child. The early theory had assumed a child motivated by pleasure, particularly a male child caught between his desire to possess the mother and his fear of the father; love and anger toward the father created the fear of castration, which Freud regarded as the basis for repression in the adult male. This dynamic assumed that the primary energy in the child was erotic; here aggression and guilt grew out of the conflict with the father in the mind of the child. The later theory was very different. It assumed that the original instincts or drives were not only sexual but aggressive, indeed destructive. The human being was not simply in search of erotic gratification, but motivated by an instinct to destroy, which could be directed both at the self and at the other. This model established the assumptions for his later work after the war. Freud developed these ideas in relation to politics, religion, and the prospects for civilization.

In *Totem and Taboo* (1912–1913) Freud applied psychoanalysis to the problem of the state of nature.[74] What would social thought look like if Freud were right about human nature, that is, about the nature of the individual human being? In his most important books from 1912 to the end of his life, we see his very Austrian commitment to liberal civilization and to the sublimation of powerful energies in the name of human beings working together. In *Totem and Taboo* Freud drew on the analogy of the Oedipus Complex to argue from theory rather than from anthropological research that there had been an analogous act of violence at the beginning of civilization. At the dawn of civilization, the infantile wish had been real: the psychic violence in the child's mind was not repressed but enacted in the killing of the father by the primal horde, whether by the hero or by the brother clan. This revolt against the dominant father's monopoly of sexual objects—the mothers and the sisters—led to the same dynamic of ambivalence and internalized guilt, except that at the beginning of civilization this violent event had actually taken place. The repression of violence and desire led to guilt as the murdered father became the basis for religion and later for civilization.

The First World War intensified Freud's thinking about social life in a variety of ways. The war and madness of modern civilization seemed to him like a revolt against civilization (as Musil put it) and anticipated the anxiety of the intellectual in relation to the repressed needs of the masses. In *Group Psychology and the Analysis of the Ego* (1921) Freud reduced politics to the psychological relation of the hero to the repressed needs of the masses in the crowd or in the modern state. Here Freud presented history as a psychic drama in which politics became the dual search for the authority figure and the scapegoat. These powerful unconscious drives unleashed the pain of living in civilization. *Beyond the Pleasure Principle* (1920) made the problem of finding happiness in civilization far more difficult than it had been in Freud's original version of psychoanalysis.[75] Here and in *Civilization and Its Discontents* (1929/1930), Freud argued that civilization operated by repressing not only sexual desire but also innate hostility and aggression. This repression worked through guilt, but it also raised the possibility that the death instinct might ultimately destroy civilization. In *The Future of an Illusion* (1927) Freud emphasized the role of religion in coping with life in civilization.[76] He posed the question of whether the ordinary person could be moral without a God. He hoped that civilization and science would successfully replace God, but he was doubtful, and he emphasized human dependence on religion, what he called "the universal obsessional neurosis of humanity."[77]

Freud addressed the basic question of the human being's discomfort in culture in *Civilization and Its Discontents* [*Das Unbehagen in der Kultur*]. There he set out from the assumption that all civilization is achieved at the expense of the psychic needs of the individual. Freud raised the possibility that repression might actually lead to the weakening of Eros (libido) and the strengthening of the energies available to Thanatos (the death instinct). He feared that too much civilization and goodness (repressed guilt) might lead to an outburst of aggression that would destroy civilization. Freud's early thought had suggested the possibility of a progressive minimizing of unnecessary repression that might lead from religion to sexuality, from authority to democracy, but this also raised the possibility of generating more responsibility and repression than the average individual could endure. Another avenue in Freud's thought was that repression (the refusal to listen to the unconscious and its demands) might be transformed into sublimation: the translation of instinctual energies into messages that are acceptable to consciousness and civilization. Finally, Freud's late theory was not only pessimistic but radical, and it raised the possibility that the death instinct might be weakened by strengthening Eros. In the decades after Freud's death, Herbert Marcuse and Norman O. Brown explored these theoretical possibilities while human civilization explored the possibilities of total destruction from concentration camps to nuclear war. Freud's theory of civilization was far more global and theoretical than any economist would have ventured, far more a worldview than most Austrian philosophers would have expressed. The death instinct seemed to be most prominent in politics and religion, in the need for a coherent illusion that protected the individual from reality even at the cost of embracing a death instinct. Freud doubted the capacity of civilization to replace religion, and he was concerned about the power of the dual dynamic of the search for an authority figure and the need for a scapegoat. It was not just that civilization could not meet the individual's need for pleasure, but that death might be a more powerful aim than life. If the Freud of the 1890s invented a distinctive view of human development and sexuality, his ideas were still largely continuous with positivism and utilitarianism. He addressed the needs of the individual for pleasure and explored the ways in which dreams and therapy can help to uncover unconscious needs and conflicts. The revision of the instincts refined the account of the self to elaborate the role of guilt-feelings and their relation to a destructive need (a death instinct) that now competed with eros for the energies of the individual.

Freud helped to move modern therapy and medicine, as well as Western culture as a whole, in a more psychological direction.[78] But this fundamental achievement is often obscured by quarrels about specific issues such as developmental stages in childhood or the Oedipus Complex or by ahistorical critiques of Freud's views on gender or even by ad hominem arguments that concentrate on these issues or on incest or on the peculiar views of his friend Fliess. Nonetheless, the talking cure has won the day across the Western world, even if little of this is described today as psychoanalytic. Freud left Austria with his daughter Anna in March 1938, shortly after the annexation of Austria by the Third Reich, and died in London a year later as Hitler occupied the remainder of

Czechoslovakia.[79] Although Freud died in 1939, his ideas had enormous impact after the Second World War, not in Austria, but in the United States, and his broad influence contributed to the interest in the intellectual migration of the 1930s and to the interest of American scholars in Austria.[80]

Freud's commitments to science, civilization, and nineteenth-century liberalism were the points of departure for all his work, and he, much like Musil, seems never really to have doubted these values even in his darkest explorations of human sexuality and aggression. Philosophers have emphasized the speculative dimensions of his ideas, but this testing in relation to scientific models may not be the most fruitful way to see his work.[81] He had a vision of human nature that grew out of his commitment to science, but also from his insights into human sexuality and aggression. These discussions in English rarely emphasize that *Wissenschaft* simply does not mean what science means in English. There is indeed some reason to see Freud more as a writer [or *Dichter*] than as a scientist, which also helps to explain his enormous influence on the fields of literature and intellectual history, and on people in the helping sciences in the postwar era who wanted to find better ways to address human feelings and aspects of medicine that were not simply physical or mechanical. His work is an argument for the value of self-knowledge, and it provides important ideas about how to gain such knowledge, although self-knowledge does not always coincide with contemporary expectations about happiness. Feminist arguments have drawn attention to the limitations of Freud's approach to gender, even though these limitations were very characteristic of the period in which he lived.[82] Freud's ideas have been important for modern social thought and for the understanding of social relationships. I hesitate to describe them as social science, both because of his methodological individualism and because his methods were often problematic from a scientific point of view. Nonetheless, his ideas had enormous influence on understandings of human nature in society over the next half-century quite apart from their place in psychoanalysis or psychology.

***

There is not much point in trying to generalize about the Austrian tradition in human studies. Whatever unity we can see in it now is retrospective (especially if we include psychoanalysis). Work in social science in Austria did not differ much from the other German states and universities before 1871. These ways of thinking developed in close connection to cameralism, the German historical school, and the law. Austrian economics emerged and went its own way in part because of German unification, but mainly because of the strong emergence of modern capitalism and a liberal order. And finally, in a completely different intellectual context, Freud developed psychoanalysis, which has very little in common methodologically with either cameralism or Austrian economics.

After Cisleithanian Austria

In *The Phenomenology of Mind*, Hegel famously remarked that the Owl of Minerva flies only at dusk; that is, we are able to understand a historical phenomenon only after it has completed its work in the world. Cisleithanian Austria from the Enlightenment to Anschluss, from the 1740s to 1938/1939, constituted an institutional and linguistic framework for intellectual life.[1] It was, very like Victorian England, a particular constellation of society and culture in the long nineteenth century. In that sense it was as much a period as a region. During this period Austria and Bohemia were joined together in a way that recalls a term that Otto Bauer used somewhat differently: "a community of fate."[2] Vienna after 1945 was no longer the intellectually electric place it had been in 1900, but Prague was also no longer a major center of German language, literature, and philosophy. Many intellectuals had already left Austria and Czechoslovakia by 1938, and others left soon afterward. For the most part, philosophy, sociology, and psychoanalysis emigrated during the interwar years, especially to the UK and the United States, and in all these fields the interruption of intellectual life continued beyond 1945. The Vienna opera house and the operatic tradition were restored, but not the intellectual life.

The configuration of the Second Austrian Republic followed for the most part the geographical and demographic contours of the First Republic. The Cisleithania of the Empire before 1918 had been lost from memory, and there was no longer much awareness of a deep connection between Austria and Bohemia. Austria was simply assumed to mean the lands of the Austrian Archduchy (including the Alpine lands). But the centers of intellectual life were also mainly gone, not only the large Jewish population of Vienna, but also the broader infrastructure of intellectual life that had shaped the years from 1740 to 1938/1939, including the connection to Prague. The First Republic, from 1918 to 1938–1939, belonged to this world in a way that the Second Republic did not; it belongs to my story as part of the process of decomposition, but also because

German-speaking intellectual life had continued without much break into the interwar years.[3]

The Holocaust was a radical divide in Austrian intellectual history because of the loss of most of the Jewish population of Vienna—and because many of the most prominent intellectuals of the interwar years chose to go into exile (including many non-Jews). On the other hand, the nature of the Jewish contribution to Austrian culture is difficult to formulate precisely because it had been so integrated into Austria in both Prague and Vienna since the Enlightenment. Dagmar Lorenz makes a perceptive observation about the assumptions that often underlie discussions of the Jewish contribution to Austrian culture. She points out that this term "suggests that the role of the Jews in Austria was an extraneous one, or that it was nothing more than a matter of a Jewish influence on Austrian culture. Nothing could be further from the truth: for the last two hundred years, since the beginning of emancipation, Jews and Gentiles together created Austrian literature, fine arts, and music."[4] In the 1940s Vienna became the city without Jews that Hugo Bettauer had written about in the 1920s.[5]

The introduction and the first chapter of this book clarify where Austria was and how the hereditary lands of Austria and Bohemia came to be the basis for the modern Austrian state in the 1740s. It was around this time that the modern German language and the Enlightenment arrived in Central Europe. Chapter 2 describes the evolution of this new situation between 1740 and the absorption of the Austrian and Czech Republics into Nazi Germany in 1938 and 1939. I emphasize the stages in the development of this intellectual world as the context for understanding German-speaking literature, philosophy, and the human sciences to the west of the Leitha River. I have tried to show where this region was and why it functioned as a unity. I also looked inside this region and this period to see what was there. I did not aim to generalize about Austrian thought, but to make more visible an overview of what Austrian thought looks like. For some readers in the Anglo-Saxon world or in Germany, this may be an introduction to unfamiliar thinkers and writers, while for those who are interested in Austrian history and culture my approach may contest assumptions they have about this intellectual world. My account is not meant to be exclusive or definitive, but exploratory of ways we might think about the field. I have tried to give some sense of the intellectual world in which these figures lived and worked. This is what I would like the reader to know about Austrian intellectual history, despite the fact that what I say is inevitably selective. I hope to encourage a frame of reference for Central European intellectual life that will enhance our understanding of Czech and Slovenian, Hungarian and Polish intellectual history. I hope that my account (which is meant to be heuristic rather than encyclopedic) will allow intellectual historians to see developments in Central Europe more clearly. This ought not to impair Czech intellectual history, but to allow us to see it more clearly, and to sort out the various roles of the German language in Bohemia and Moravia. Similarly, Hungary and Galicia can be treated separately in ways that take German-speaking intellectuals into account.

The Austrian tradition in German intellectual history was fundamentally sympathetic to the Enlightenment. This was most apparent in philosophy, from Bolzano and Brentano to Mach, Wittgenstein, and the Vienna Circle. But it was clear as well in literature—from Grillparzer and Stifter to Musil and Kafka. There were at times sharp oppositions between science and religion—as in high liberalism, Freud, and the Vienna Circle. But, especially thanks to the influence of Josephinism and the weaker influence of the German revolution of the mind as it developed after Kant, the contrasts between ideologies were not as sharp as in France or as in Northern German states after 1848. Perhaps most striking in the leading figures of the Austrian tradition were the efforts to explore ethics and religion without either rejecting the modern sciences or reducing these fields to simplistic formulations. This tradition looked for ways to emphasize what human beings share with each other, while exploring the individuality of human experience and new ways of thinking and feeling and being in the world. My aim is not to establish the internal coherence of Austrian thought or to identify the comparative significance of a way of thinking in relation to German or European thought. I point to comparative aspects, but I am concerned primarily to identify Austrian thought and describe it. Still, it is true that Austrian intellectuals tend to be good at sober, objective tasks like science, linguistic analysis, economics, and the novel. The unifying themes of this tradition are a positive attitude toward the Enlightenment and modern science, combined with a resistance to reductionism and ideological polarization, the emphasis on ethics and inner experience, and respect for unconscious energies and what we cannot control. This was a tradition that ended not with the decadence and decline of the old century, but with the creativity and imagination of the new century and the generation of 1905.

Notes

Introduction

1. See David S. Luft, "Austrian Intellectual History and Bohemia," *The Austrian History Yearbook*, Vol. 38 (2007), 108–21.
2. See David S. Luft, "Austria as a Region of German Culture: 1900–1938/1945," *Austrian History Yearbook*, Vol. XXIII, 1992, 135–48.
3. One of the classic commentaries on the relationship between Germany and Austria was written by Hugo von Hofmannsthal during the First World War. Even in the midst of the war, Hofmannsthal contended that "among the countries of the world Austria is for Germans one of the least known or most poorly understood." But he also argued that "Austria's entire existence is revealed if … we comprehend the whole of German history as present." See "We Austrians and Germany," in *Hugo von Hofmannsthal and the Austrian Idea: Selected Essays and Addresses, 1906–1927*, trans. and ed. David S. Luft, Purdue University Press, West Lafayette, Indiana, 2011, 67 and 69.
4. Eric Hobsbawm, "Has History Made Progress?" in *On History*, The New Press, New York, 1997, 69.
5. If England and Scotland provide the obvious linguistic analogy to Germany and Austria, the political analogy to England and Scotland is Austria and Bohemia.
6. Marc Bloch, "Toward a Comparative History of European Societies," in *Enterprise and Secular Change: Readings in Economic History*, ed. Frederic C. Lane and Jelle C. Riemersma, Richard D. Irwin, Inc., Homewood, IL, 1953, 498. Bloch points out that even adjacent and apparently quite similar societies such as England and France can be very different from one another, concealing striking differences from historians who study only one of them.
7. There are other German-speaking traditions within the German culture of Central and Eastern Europe: in Hungary, Russia, the Baltic states, Poland, and Switzerland (which began to distinguish itself from German culture as early as the eighteenth century), and elsewhere.
8. For a recent presentation of these arguments see Gerald Stieg, *Sein oder Schein: Die Österreichische Idee von Maria Theresia bis zum Anschluss*, trans. from *L'Autriche: Une nation chimérique?* Böhlau Verlag, Vienna, 2016.
9. For an example of an explicitly German-Austrian literary history of the Dual Monarchy, see *Deutsch-Österreichiche Literaturgeschichte: Ein Handbuch zur*

Geschichte der deutschen Dichtung in Österreich-Ungarn, ed. Johann Willibald, Jakob Zeidler, and Eduard Castle, 4 volumes, Carl Fromme, Vienna, 1937.

10 In "The meanings of 'Austria' and 'Austrian' in the eighteenth century" (*Royal and Republican Sovereignty in Early Modern Europe*, ed. Robert Oresko et al., Cambridge University Press, Cambridge, 1997, 423–78), Grete Klingenstein contrasts a variety of older usages of the word "Austrian" with our contemporary meanings.

11 Robert A. Kann, *The Multinational Empire: Nationalism and Reform in the Habsburg Monarchy 1848–1918*, Columbia University Press, New York, 1950, Vol. I, 28.

12 Robert A. Kann, *A History of the Habsburg Empire, 1526–1918*, University of California Press, Berkeley, 1980.

13 Pieter M. Judson, *The Habsburg Empire: A New History*, Harvard University Press, Cambridge, MA, 2016.

14 My approach emphasizes a region as in a book like Perry Miller, *The New England Mind: From Colony to Province*, Harvard University Press, Cambridge, 1953, but also a period as in Raymond Williams, *Culture and Society, 1780–1950*, Columbia University Press, New York, 1958.

15 Ralf Dahrendorf, *Society and Democracy in Germany*, Anchor Books, Garden City, New York, 1969, 267. My use of the term "intellectual history" is not meant to discount other forms of human creativity, whether art or music or science, but rather to concentrate on the history of those who work primarily with words. On the broader social history of intellectuals, see Helmut Rumpler, "Die Intellektuellen in Cisleithanien," in *Die Habsburgermonarchie: 1848–1918*, Vol. IX/part 2, ed. Helmut Rumpler and Peter Urbanitsch, Österreichischen Akademie der Wissenschaften, Vienna, 2010, 1119–55.

16 In *Political Man: The Social Bases of Politics*, Seymour Lipset (Doubleday and Company, Inc, Garden City, NY, 1960, 311) defines intellectuals more broadly as "those who create, distribute, and apply culture, that is, the symbolic world of man, including art, science, and religion."

17 One recent book on Austrian thought is devoted entirely to Austrian economics: Jürgen G. Backhaus, ed., *Modern Applications of Austrian Thought*, Routledge, New York, 2005.

18 For recent views of the development of modern European intellectual history as a field, see *Rethinking Modern European Intellectual History*, ed. Darrin M. McMahon and Samuel Moyn, Oxford University Press, New York, 2014.

19 William M. Johnston, *The Austrian Mind: An Intellectual and Social History, 1848–1938*, University of California Press, Berkeley, 1972, 269. Johnston's book is still the most comprehensive effort to come to terms with the intellectual history of the Habsburg Monarchy, and it is broadly representative of much of the work on the cultural and intellectual history of the empire.

20 See the telling remark by Walter Weiss, the great postwar historian of Austrian literature. "It is more than a joke when I have claimed that really only the Germanists in the other successor states can work on Austrian literature in the full sense." Walter Weiss, "Ausblick auf eine Geschichte österreichischer Literatur," in *Was heist Österreich? Inhalt und Umfang des Österreichbegriffs vom 10. Jahrhundert bis heute*, ed. Richard G. Platschka, Gerald Stourzh, and Jan Paul Niederkorn, Verlag der österreichischen Akademie der Wissenschaften, Vienna, 1995, 319.
One of the first attempts at an intellectual history along these lines was originally published in Hungarian, although it follows the contours of the earlier literature in German: see Endre Kiss, *Der Tod der K.u.k. Weltordmung in Wien: Ideengeschichte Österreichs um die Jahrhundertwende*, Böhlau, Vienna, 1986.

21 William M. Johnston, *Zur Kulturgeschichte Österreichs und Ungarns 1890–1938: Auf der Suche nach verborgenen Gemeinsamkeiten*, trans. Otmar Binder, Böhlau Verlag, Vienna, 2015.

22 On the invention of a national literary culture, see Peter Uwe Hohendahl, *Building National Literature: The Case of Germany, 1830–1870*, trans. Renate Baron Franciscono, Cornell University Press, Ithaca, 1989.

23 The intellectual history of Germany has had a primacy in the study of the intellectual history of Central Europe that is neither necessary nor desirable for understanding modern thought. My point here is not that idealism, romanticism, and nationalism were not present in Austrian intellectual life, but that this is poor point of departure for understanding Austrian thought.

24 On where Germany was in the nineteenth century, see James J. Sheehan, *German History 1770–1866*, Clarendon Press, Oxford, 1989. For a recent account of where Germany was in the modern period, see Helmut Walser Smith, *Germany: A Nation in Its Time: Before, during, and after Nationalism, 1500–2000*, W. W. Norton, New York, 2020. "Its primary argument is that across five centuries, there were radically different ways of knowing, representing, and experiencing the German nation" [p. xi].

25 One might do something similar for Switzerland or Hungary or Galicia or as well.

26 I am exploring a question that has rarely been asked: Why did an intellectual tradition that has been assumed to point toward the modern German state culminate to such a degree in the intellectuals of Austria?

27 Barbara Stollberg-Rilinger points to the tendency among Austrian historians to blur terminology for the German *Reich* and the Habsburg lands, while largely ignoring Austria's relationship to the *Reich* or simply assimilating it to the Austrian story. See Barbara Stollberg-Rilinger, *Maria Theresia: Die Kaiserin in Ihre Zeit: Eine Biographie*, C.H. Beck, Munich, 2017, 157–60.

28 Jerrold Seigel's *The Idea of the Self: Thought and Experience in Western Europe since the Seventeenth Century*, Cambridge University Press, Cambridge, 2005 is

a revealing example of the marginalization of Austria in accounts of European intellectual history, and it brings out especially clearly the broader conventions of the field of European intellectual history.

29 See, for example, *Freud, Jews, and Other Germans*, Oxford University Press, New York, 1978.

30 See, for example, Herbert Zeman, ed., *Literaturgeschichte Österreichs*, Akademische Druck- u. Verlagsanstalt, Graz, 1996; Michael Benedikt et al., ed., *Verdrängte Humanismus—verzögerte Aufklärung: Philosophie in Österreich*, Turia and Kant, Vienna, 1992, 4 volumes; Karl Acham, ed., *Geschichte der österreichischen Humanwissenschaften*, Passagen Verlag, Vienna, 1999, 6 volumes.

31 See, for example, Barry Smith, *Austrian Philosophy: The Legacy of Franz Brentano*, Open Court, Chicago, 1996; Rudolf Haller, *Studien zur österreichischen Philosophie: Variationen über ein Thema*, Rodopi N.V., Amsterdam, 1979 and *Questions on Wittgenstein*, Routledge, London, 1988; J. Nyíri, *Am Rande Europas: Studien zur österreich-ungarischen Philosophiegeschichte*, Böhlau Verlag, Vienna, 1988; and *Austrian Economics: Historical and Philosophical Background*, ed. Wolfgang Grassl and Barry Smith, Croom Helm, London, 1986. David F. Lindenfeld's *The Transformation of Positivism: Alexius Meinong and European Thought*, University of California Press, Berkeley, 1980, is an example of a careful situating in intellectual history.

32 See Carl E. Schorske, *Fin-de-siècle Vienna: Politics and Culture*, Alfred A Knopf, New York, 1980.

33 Zeman, "Vorwort" to *Literaturgeschichte Österreichs*. Zeman characterizes this collaborative volume as the fourth attempt at a comprehensive literary history of Austria—and as the first since Nadler. See Josef Nadler's *Literaturgeschichte Österreichs*, Österreichischer Verlag für Belletristik und Wissenschaft, Linz, 1948. For the history of Austrian Germanistik from 1848 to 1914, see Werner Michler and Wendelin Schmidt-Dengler, "Germanistik in Österreich: Neuere deutsche und österreichische Literatur," in *Geschichte der österreichischen Humanwissenschaften*, Passagen Verlag, Vienna, 1999, Vol. 193–228.

34 One can imagine, for example, an Austrian literature that ranges from Karel Čapek to Italo Svevo, but this possibility is rarely discussed in the scholarly literature, presumably because of the great range of languages.

35 In relation to the medieval duchy of Austria, Weiss points out (314) that "das wichtige Merkmal der Kontinuität" from the Middle Ages to the present is missing, and this is more broadly true for the whole of Austrian history and literature. Weiss, "Ausblick auf eine Geschichte österreichischer Literatur," in *Was heist Österreich?* 313–24.

36 Anonymous [Victor Andrian-Werburg], *Oesterreich und dessen Zukunft*, Hoffmann and Campe, Hamburg, 1843, 6–7. Cited in Robert A. Kann, *The Multinational*

Empire: Nationalism and Reform in the Habsburg Monarchy 1848–1918, Columbia University Press, New York, 1950, Vol. I, 28.

37 "Austria" is sometimes used to refer to the House of Austria and thus to all the lands of the Habsburgs. See Adam Wandruszka, *The House of Habsburg: Six Hundred Years of a European Dynasty*, trans. Cathleen and Hans Epstein, Sidgwick and Jackson, London, 1964. In her account of the lands Maria Theresa inherited in 1740, including Tuscany, Stollberg-Rilinger emphasizes that "this conglomerate of lands as a whole did not have a name." Stollberg-Rilinger, *Maria Theresia*, 87.

38 It seems best in these matters for intellectual historians to distinguish clearly between "Habsburg" and "Austrian," and at the same time to take some distance from the Habsburg ideology of state creation.

39 See R. J. W. Evans, *The Making of the Habsburg Monarchy: 1550–1700: An Interpretation*, Oxford, 1979, xiii: Writing about the emergence of the Habsburg Monarchy in the sixteenth and seventeenth centuries, Evans argues that "[n]o proper nomenclature exists for the political entity whose consolidation is the subject of this book."

40 See István Deák, *The Lawful Revolution: Louis Kossuth and the Hungarians 1848–1849*, Phoenix Press, London, 2001, 1. Original edition: Columbia University Press, 1979.

41 The peoples of the Archduchy of Austria were Italian and Slovene as well as German, just as the people of Bohemia and Moravia were both Czech and German. In these two centuries, it was the Czechs who were most important for the German-speaking culture of Cisleithanian Austria.

42 Johann Christoph Allmayer-Beck, *Der Konservatismus in Österreich*, Isar Verlag, Munich, 1959, 13. As part of the partition of Poland by Russia, Prussia, and Austria in 1772, the Habsburgs adopted the name "Galicia" for their new imperial acquisition. See Larry Wolff, *The Idea of Galicia: History and Fantasy in Habsburg Political Culture*, Stanford University Press, Stanford, 2010. On the structural differences referred to by Allmayer-Beck, see John Deak, *Forging a Multinational State: State Making in Imperial Austria from the Enlightenment to the First World War*, Stanford University Press, Stanford, 2015.

43 See Gary Cohen, *The Politics of Ethnic Survival: Germans in Prague, 1861–1914*, Princeton University Press, Princeton, 1981; Pieter Judson, *Exclusive Revolutionaries: Liberal Politics, Social Experience, and National Identity in the Austrian Empire*, The University of Michigan Press, Ann Arbor, 1996. Galicia is a more problematic periphery, but it was geographically, institutionally, and historically more separate from the Austrian lands than Bohemia was—and much closer to the context of Polish culture than to German or Austrian culture. See, for example, Gary Cohen, *Education and Middle-Class Society in Imperial Austria: 1848–1918*, Purdue University Press, West Lafayette, 1996, 8. Cohen's argument

about education distinguishes Hungary and Galicia in terms of the social and economic basis for intellectual life in the late nineteenth century. "In analyzing the social functions of advanced education and the recruitment of the educated elites during the second half of the nineteenth century, there are good reasons to treat the Austrian half of the Habsburg Monarchy separately from Hungary and, within Austria, to focus primarily on the Alpine and Bohemian lands."

44 Walter Benjamin, "Theses on the Philosophy of History," *Illuminations*, ed. Hannah Arendt, trans. Harry Zohn, Schocken Books, New York, 1969, 255.

45 Chapter 1 identifies the region of Cisleithanian Austria, while Chapters 2 to 5 open this box to see what's in it.

46 The organization of my chapters in terms of philosophy, literature, and the human sciences draws attention to the prominent features of intellectual life in this period, but also to the dominant position of men in Austrian intellectual life before the Second World War.

47 Our conception of German thought has been centrally defined by philosophy. This rarely means Leibniz, and even Kant has often been poorly understood in the English-speaking world. Our conceptions for the most part begin after Kant, especially with Hegel, and they are deeply influenced by a feeling of difference, most strongly defined by the experience of the French Revolution and the sense that the German response was nationalist and reactionary. An afterthought to this model has been "German Romanticism," a term that has often been used to describe everything obscure and anti-industrial about German thought. Our understandings of German literature have followed in this train, although the sense of difference has been softened by affinities with English Romanticism and American Transcendentalism.

48 The other side of this is that Czech intellectual history cannot be written adequately apart from its relationship to German-speaking intellectual life in Austria, although that is not the theme of this book.

Chapter 1

1 Adalbert Stifter, *Witiko: Roman*, afterword by Fritz Krökel, Deutscher Taschenbuch Verlag, Munich, 2001. This edition of Stifter's historical epic about the twelfth century follows the first edition of 1865–1867 with notes by Karl Pörnbacher. In 1158, the Duke of Bohemia and Moravia was crowned King by Frederick I, Barbarossa, Emperor of the Holy Roman Empire. *Witiko*, 798–9.

2 As Robert Bartlett emphasizes in his account of medieval colonization, "Bohemia, although maintaining a high degree of autonomy and distinctiveness within the Holy Roman Empire, was always tied to that body in a way that Poland and

Hungary were not." Robert Bartlett, *The Making of Europe: Conquest, Colonization and Cultural Change 950–1350*, Princeton University Press, Princeton, 1993, 8.

3   For a discussion of the eleven languages of the Monarchy, see R. J. W. Evans, "Language and State Building: The Case of the Habsburg Monarchy," *Austrian History Yearbook*, Vol. 35 (2004), 1–17. Evans also points to the negative impact of "linguistic tunnel vision" on historical work on East Central Europe: "Historical traditions have been defined and often hermetically sealed off by language, to yield narrow and exclusive interpretations, typically resting on some type of ethnic assumption or prejudice. Not that linguistic factors are alone guilty of this, as the neglect of Austria by so many of those writing—within a single Sprachgemeinschaft—about the pre-1866 'German' past demonstrates. But language proved a fundamental determinant …. Altogether, the constraints of linguistic particularity have done much to establish the parameters of this or that national heritage, casting a shadow over supranational investigation as over polyglot discourse. For that reason too, to serve means as well as ends, it is surely time for a greater sensitivity to the role of language in its own right within Habsburg studies" (24).

4   There are many histories of Austria and the Habsburg Monarchy. See, for example, Hugo Hantsch, *Die Geschichte Österreichs*, 2 volumes, Styria, Vienna, 1937–1950; C. A. Macartney, *The Habsburg Empire, 1790–1918*, The Macmillan Company, New York, 1969; Barbara Jelavich, *Modern Austria: Empire and Republic 1815–1986*, Cambridge University Press, New York, 1987; Erich Zöllner, *Geschichte Österreichs: Von den Anfängen bis zur Gegenwart*, 8th edition, Verlag für Geschichte und Politik, Vienna, 1990; Gordon Brook Shepherd, *The Austrians: A Thousand-Year Odyssey*, Carroll & Graf Publishers Inc., New York, 1996. Paula Sutter Fichtner, *The Habsburg Monarchy, 1490–1848: The Attributes of Empire*, Palgrave Macmillan, New York, 2003; Steven Beller, *A Concise History of Austria*, Cambridge University Press, Cambridge, 2006; Gerald Stieg, *Sein oder Schein: Die Österreichische Idee von Maria Theresia bis zum Anschluss*, trans. from *L'Autriche: Une nation chimérique?* Böhlau Verlag, Vienna, 2016; Pieter M. Judson, *The Habsburg Empire: A New History*, Harvard University Press, Cambridge, MA, 2016.

5   As Evans points out, when Joseph claimed German as the *Universalsprache meines Reichs*, this was a linguistic, not a national, assertion; but he was also referring to his German empire, not to his "Austrian monarchy, though historians have regularly misconstrued this." Evans, "Language and State Building," 7–8.

6   See Karl Vocelka, *Geschichte Österreichs: Kultur—Gesellschaft—Politik*, Verlag Styria, Graz, 2000. Vocelka finds thoughtful solutions to some of the problems I have referred to, and he consistently points to ambiguities and confusions, including conceding that "for the modern period the German-speaking parts of the Danube Monarchy stand at the center of interest for the Austrian historian" (10). This issue is central for intellectual history, and it is too rarely treated directly.

Indeed, the history of these German-speaking parts is sometimes presented as if this *were* the Habsburg Monarchy.
7   See Thomas Fellner and Heinrich Kretschmayr, ed., *Die österreichische Zentralverwaltung*, Institut für Österreichische Geschichtsforschung, Mitteilungen, Vienna. This gigantic work began to appear in 1907. The volumes reached to 1867 in 1971, completing the record of the central administration.
8   Geoffrey Barraclough, *The Origins of Modern Germany*, Basil Blackwell, London, 1988.
9   See P. G. M. Dickson, *Finance and Government under Maria Theresia 1740–1780*, Oxford University Press, Oxford, 1987, Vol. I, 20–2.
10 See Jan Křen's discussion of German-speaking Central Europe in this period in his *Die Konfliktgemeinschaft: Tschech und Deutsche 1780–1918*, trans. Peter Heumos, Oldenbourg, Munich, 1996, 43.
11 Three overlapping but distinct ways of talking about empire need to be carefully distinguished: the Holy Roman Empire, the German Empire, and the Austrian (or Habsburg) Empire. The Holy Roman Empire was a complex set of institutions that existed from Otto I in 962 to Napoleon; political relationships and practices within these institutions varied enormously over this period. The German Empire (or the Holy Roman Empire of the German Nation) is a term sometimes used in retrospect to refer to periods of German hegemony in this empire, especially under the Hohenstaufen family in the High Middle Ages. The Austrian Empire did not exist at all until the nineteenth century, and it referred, again mainly in retrospect, to the Habsburg lands in Central Europe; these Habsburg lands constituted what I will refer to as the Monarchy. After 1526, the Habsburg lands were nearly always more unified and effective as a political actor than the Holy Roman Empire. The Habsburg Monarchy overlapped with the Holy Roman Empire, and its head was often the Holy Roman Emperor (although Maria Theresa had to delegate this title to her husband and her son). Unfortunately, these three ways of speaking (the Holy Roman Empire, the German nation, and the Habsburg Monarchy or the Austrian Empire) have often been used too casually and interchangeably, either from lack of clarity or for ideological and rhetorical purposes. "The German Empire" took on a new sense, of course, with Bismarck's empire of 1871. These distinctions can be confusing, but they are important and need to be taken into account. None of these empires is the subject of this book.
12 My aim is not to write a new master narrative but to identify where Austrian intellectual history took place. I want to locate geographically and historically where Austrian intellectual life emerged between 1740 and 1938/1939: where and when was Austrian intellectual history?
13 Franz Palacký, *Geschichte von Böhmen* Vols. 4–5, F. Tempsky, Prague, 1857–1867 [republication of earlier volumes by Kronberger und Řiwnač, 1944–1954]. In English, see Derek Sayer, *The Coasts of Bohemia*, Princeton University Press,

Princeton, 1998; Hugh Le Caine Agnew, *The Czechs and the Lands of the Bohemian Crown*, Hoover Institution Press, Stanford, 2004; Franz von Lützow, *Bohemia: An Historical Sketch*, Dent and Sons, London, 1939; Vladimir Nosek, *The Spirit of Bohemia: A Survey of Czechoslovak History, Music, and Literature*, Brentano, New York, 1927; R. W. Seton-Watson, *A History of the Czechs and Slovaks*, Archon Books, Hamden, Conn., 1965; S. Harris Thomson, *Czechoslovakia in European History*, Princeton University Press, Princeton, 1943; and A. H. Hermann, *A History of the Czechs*, Allen Lane, London, 1975.

14 See Géza Alföldy, *Noricum*, trans. Anthony Birley, Routledge & Kegan Paul, London, 1974. See also Erich Swoboda, *Carnuntum: Seine Geschichte und seine Denkmäler*, 3rd edition, Hermann Böhlau, Vienna, 1958.

15 Marcus Aurelius, *The Emperor's Handbook: A New Translation of the Meditations*, trans. C. Scot Hicks and David V. Hicks, Scribner, New York, 2002. Our first record of his manuscript comes from a Byzantine source in the tenth century. The *Meditations* announced themes that proved attractive to Austrian elites centuries later—Stoic precepts and the acceptance of the world, of nature, and of human beings as they are.

16 Eric Zöllner gives 996 for the first use of the word *Österreich* or *Ostarrichi* to describe the area on the Danube that was ruled by the Babenberg family. See Zöllner, *Geschichte Österreichs*, 63.

17 See Oswald Redlich, *Rudolf von Habsburg: Das deutsche Reich nach dem Untergang des alten Kaisertums*, Neudruck der Ausgabe, Innsbruck, 1903, Scientia Verlag Aalen, 1965.

18 See Alfred Thomas, ed., *Anne's Bohemia*. University of Minnesota Press, Minneapolis, 1998: when Charles IV's daughter married Richard II in 1382, London was a step down from Prague and "Bohemia was a byword for chic" (1).

19 Emil Skála, "Zum Prager Deutsch des 16. Jahrhunderts," in *Festschrift für Hans Eggers: Zum 65. Geburtstag*, ed. Herbert Bakes, Max Niemeyer, Tübingen, 1972, 283–305.

20 On the dramatic events of the Hussite Revolution, see Frederick G. Heymann, *John Žižka and the Hussite Revolution*, Princeton University Press, Princeton, 1955, reissued by Russell & Russell, 1969 and Frederick G. Heymann, *George of Bohemia: King of Heretics*, Princeton University Press, Princeton, 1965.

21 See the thoughtful discussions in Howard Kaminsky, *A History of the Hussite Revolution*, University of California Press, Berkeley, 1967. See also Ernest Denis, *Georges de Podiébrad*, Vol. 1 of *Fin De L'indépendance Bohème*. Armand Colin et Cie, Paris, 1890.

22 The emphasis on the failure of aristocrat Protestant leadership (Calvinist but also Lutheran) often overlooks the presence of a plebian/urban tradition that was not revolutionary, but moderate, liberal, even conservative. This tradition helped to shape liberal Catholicism or reform Catholicism in the eighteenth century.

See Zdeněk David's *Finding the Middle Way: The Utraquists' Liberal Challenge to Rome and Luther*, Woodrow Wilson Center Press, The Johns Hopkins University Press, Baltimore, 2003. R. J. W. Evans called this book "one of the most original and suggestive books on the age of the Reformation for many years." *European History Quarterly*, Jan 2005, Vol. 35 (1), 136. For a comprehensive account of the long process of the Reformation in Europe, see Euan Cameron, *The European Reformation*, Oxford University Press, Oxford, 1991.

23 Heymann, *George of Bohemia*, 600. It hardly seems adequate to explain Western ignorance about this extraordinary century by observing that the printing press was invented toward the end of this upheaval.

24 Utraquism was quite different from both Roman Catholicism and Lutheranism. It resisted the legal authority of the Pope and differed from the Roman church on a few important issues, but it regarded itself as part of the universal church in a sense that Lutheranism did not. We might translate the peculiar Latin term as both-ism, both the bread and the wine.

25 Daniel Goffman, *The Ottoman Empire and Early Modern Europe*, Cambridge University Press, Cambridge, 2002.

26 R. J. W. Evans, *Rudolf II and His World: A Study in Intellectual History: 1576–1612*, Thames and Hudson, 2nd edition, Oxford, 1997. Evans' book on Rudolf II is a reminder of an astonishingly cosmopolitan age with a vital intellectual life. This was one of the most exciting moments in the intellectual and cultural life of the Habsburg lands.

27 A tradition of tolerance and pluralism existed in Bohemia and Moravia throughout the sixteenth century, and it was often associated with Erasmus and Christian humanism, functioning as a Middle Way much like Utraquism. Recently historians have argued that the boundaries between religious confessions may have been much more fluid than previously assumed. See, for example, Petr Maťa, "Constructing and Crossing Confessional Boundaries: The High Nobility and the Reformation of Bohemia," in *Diversity and Dissent: Negotiating Religious Difference in Central Europe, 1500–1800*, ed. Howard Louthan, Gary B. Cohen, and Franz A. J. Szabo, Berghahn Books, New York, 2011, 1–29.

28 Tridentine is a liturgical way of referring to the Catholic Reformation, as based on the Council of Trent in the sixteenth century.

29 Thomas A. Brady Jr, *German Histories in the Age of Reformations, 1400–1650*, Cambridge University Press, New York, 2009, 372.

30 See Thomas Winkelbauer, *Ständefreiheit und Fürstenmacht: Länder und Untertanen des Hauses Habsburg im Kofessionellen Zeitalter*, Teil 2, Carl Ueberreuter, Vienna, 2003.

31 In the sixteenth century, the duchies of Styria, Carinthia, and Carniola, and other southern lands including Trieste were ruled by secondary lines of the family; it was in this mainly independent Inner Austrian territory that the reconversion

from Protestantism to Catholicism began. Catholicism was extended to the rest of Austria and Bohemia in the seventeenth century against the vigorous resistance of the estates, most notably in Prague. Inner Austria included Italians and Slovenes.

32 John G. Gagliardo, *Germany under the Old Regime: 1600–1790*, Longman, New York, 1991 and Geoffrey Parker et al., *The Thirty Years War*, 2nd edition, Routledge, New York, 1997. The exodus of Protestants took place not only from Bohemia but also from Upper and Lower Austria, Styria, and Carinthia.

33 See Howard Louthan, *Converting Bohemia: Force and Persuasion in the Catholic Reformation*, Cambridge University Press, Cambridge, 2009. Traditional accounts of reconversion and the imposition of Catholicism are accurate in that the sources available to us concentrate on the externals of religious life. We seem to have little to go on about the thoughts and feelings of Utraquists and Lutherans who decided to become Catholic. But this also meant that the experiences of people in Austria and Bohemia were strongly marked by private religious lives withdrawn from public perception.

34 See Wilhelm Kühlmann, *Gelehrtenrepublik und Fürstenstaat*, Max Niemeyer Verlag, Tübingen, 1982. See also Eduard Winter, *Frühhumanismus: Seine Entwicklung in Böhmen und deren europäische Bedeutung für die Kirchenreformbestrebungen im 14. Jahrhundert*, Akademie-Verlag, Berlin, 1964.

35 It was only after the second siege of Vienna in 1683 that Joseph I and Prince Eugene reasserted Habsburg control in Hungary.

36 See Fichtner, *The Habsburg Monarchy, 1490–1848*.

37 Erich Zöllner, *Der Österreichbegriff: Formen und Wandlungen in der Geschichte*, Verlag für Geschichte und Politik, Vienna, 1988, 56.

38 R. J. W. Evans, *The Making of the Habsburg Monarchy 1550–1700: An Interpretation*, Oxford University Press, Oxford, 1979, 447.

39 It is easy to forget in the context of the successes of the second half of the eighteenth century that 1740 was nearly an even more dramatic catastrophe for the Monarchy than 1848 later was. Before 1740, despite all the efforts of Charles VI, Austria was not a unified state: there was no central administration, and the monarchy was dependent on the nobility.

40 On the population of the hereditary lands, see P. M. G. Dickson, *Finance and Government und Maria Theresia, 1740–1780*, Oxford University Press, New York, 1987, 2 volumes, Vol. I, 22–3 and Charles W. Ingrao, *The Habsburg Monarchy 1618–1815*, 2nd edition, Cambridge University Press, Cambridge, 2000, chapter 5.

41 Haugwitz was empowered to draw together all aspects of the administration in the name of the monarch: the chancelleries of Bohemia and Austria were abolished, although there were no changes to the chancelleries for Hungary, Italy, and the Netherlands. See Barbara Stollberg-Rilinger, *Maria Theresia: Die Kaiserin in Ihre Zeit: Eine Biographie*, C.H. Beck, Munich, 2017, 204–6. Historians now emphasize this cesura (the creation of a modern state) less dramatically than they did in the

nineteenth century, when the temptation was to argue for the creation of a national state. Ibid., 243–5.

42 Karl Vocelka, *Glanz und Untergang der höfischen Welt: Repräsentation, Reform, und Reaktion im Habsburgischen Vielvölkerstaat*, 2001, 53. See R. J. W. Evans, *Austria, Hungary, and the Habsburgs: Essays on Central Europe, c.1683–1867*, Oxford University Press, New York, 2006, 93. "Bohemia and Moravia thus became the twin heartlands—distinct but developing in parallel."

43 A. J. P. Taylor, *The Habsburg Monarchy 1809–1918*, new edition, Hamish Hamilton, London, 1948, 17. This relationship was dramatized both by Joseph II's successes and by his failures.

44 Waltraud Heindl argues that by 1780 the high, primarily juridically trained officials constituted an intensification of the development and reshaping of the bureaucracy as a modern institution. She argues (17) that there were no changes down to 1848 and in many respects even down to the present. Waltraud Heindl, *Gehorsame Rebellen: Bürokratie und Beamte in Österreich, 1780 bis 1848*, Böhlau Verlag, Wien, 1991, 16–17.

45 Franz Anton von Blanc characterized the true purpose of the state in terms that inspired Maria Theresia in 1769: "the lasting bonds of society and the potential perfection of the whole." See Karl Gruenberg, "Franz Anton Blanc: Ein Sozialpolitiker der theresianisch-josephinischen Zeit," *Schmollers Jahrbuch für Gesetzgebung*, 1911, 133–42. Cited in Ernst Wangermann, "An Eighteenth-Century Engine of Reform," *Austrian History Yearbook*, Vol. 37, 2006, 60.

46 On the clergy in Austria see William D. Bowman, *Priest and Parish in Vienna, 1780–1880*, Humanities Press, Boston, 1999.

47 On reforms under Maria Theresa and Joseph II, see Franz A. J. Szabo, *Kaunitz and Enlightened Absolutism, 1753–1780*, Cambridge University Press, New York, 1994. Szabo emphasizes the importance of Kaunitz in the development of the Austrian state and what came to be known as Josephinism. Szabo especially emphasizes the role of neo-stoicism in Kaunitz's thought, especially "his eudemonism and stress on the common good." See Szabo, *Kaunitz*, 23.

48 Ernst Wangermann, *The Austrian Achievement 1700–1800*, Harcourt Brace Jovanovich, London, 1973.

49 Karl Eder calls Josephinism "the Austrian form of the Enlightenment." Karl Eder, *Der Liberalismus in Altösterreich: Geisteshaltung, Politik und Kultur*, Verlag Herold, Vienna, 1955, 27. In Chapter 1 Eder emphasizes the role of Kaunitz in Josephinism and the contributions of Ferdinand Maass to understanding these developments in the Austrian church. John Robertson defines the Enlightenment as "the commitment to understanding, and hence to advancing, the causes and conditions of human betterment in this world." See John Robertson, *The Case for the Enlightenment: Scotland and Naples, 1680–1760*, Cambridge University Press, Cambridge, 2005, 28.

50 To appreciate this blurring of definitions in the conception of Josephinism, it helps to consider Joseph's "pastoral letter" of 1783. As John Deak puts it: "For Joseph, officials had their own pastoral mission: bringing the state to the people." This understanding of service applied to the clergy as well to the bureaucrats. See John Deak, *Forging a Multinational State: State Making in Imperial Austria from the Enlightenment to the First World War*, Stanford University Press, Stanford, 2015, 27.

51 William M. Johnston, *Der österreichische Mensch: Kulturgeschichte der Eigenart Österreichs*, Böhlau Verlag, Vienna, 2010, 287–96. Hugo von Hofmannsthal drew attention to the decisive contribution of Maria Theresa in founding modern Austria, qualifying somewhat the conventional emphasis on Josephinism and its masculine style: "What we call Josephinism is sharper in outline and easier to understand; the Theresian is by far stronger, more mysterious and more fateful. In it was a summary of the essence of Austrian society, which has remained essential for what followed." Hofmannsthal, *Reden und Aufsätze* II, *Gesammelte Werke*, ed. Bernd Schoeller and Rudolf Hirsch et al., Fischer Taschenbuch, Frankfurt am Main, 1979–1980, 452.

52 Georg Franz, *Liberalismus: Die deutschliberale Bewegung in der Habsburgischen Monarchie*, Verlag Georg D.W. Callwey, Munich, 1955. Franz emphasizes the roots of the German liberal movement in Josephinism, but the intellectual strands of this tradition were even more dispersed.

53 Robert A. Kann, *A Study in Austrian Intellectual History: From Late Baroque to Romanticism*, Frederick A. Praeger, New York, 1960, 137.

54 On the special meaning of Joseph II and Josephinism for Bohemia and Moravia, see Nancy M. Wingfield, *Flag Wars and Stone Saints: How the Bohemian Lands Became Czech*, Harvard University Press, Cambridge, 2007. See also Larry Wolff's recent and comprehensive definition of Josephinism: "the encouragement of administrative centralization from Vienna, the imposition of state control over religious life, the concession of religious toleration, the relaxation of censorship, the partial abolition of serfdom, and an assault on noble privileges." Larry Wolff, *The Idea of Galicia: History and Fantasy in Habsburg Political Culture*, Stanford University Press, Stanford, 2010, 20.

Chapter 2

1 Although Vienna and Prague were the most important cities of Cisleithanian Austria, Graz, Brno, and other smaller cities were also important urban centers. Northern Bohemia, a region that was open to North German and Protestant influence, contained a concentration of population that stretched well into Moravia.

2   The enduring significance of the Baroque for Austrian cultural life has sometimes been exaggerated by literary historians in ways that diminish the significance of the Enlightenment and modern German. Herbert Zeman speaks of the "no longer sustainable scholarly legend of a continuing 'Baroque' tradition." Herbert Zeman, "Die österreichisher Literatur im ausgehenden 18. und im 19. Jahrhundert," in Herbert Zeman, ed., *Literaturgeschichte Österreichs*, Akademische Druck- u. Verlagsanstalt, Graz, 1996, 303.

3   See Ernst Schönwiese, *Nachwort to Das zeitlose Wort*, ed. Joseph Strelka, Stiasny Verlag, Vienna, 1964, 229–36. Schönwiese's afterword concentrates on lyric poetry and on the twentieth century, but it is also a good example of the impulse to generalize Austrian qualities. Schönwiese cites familiar commentators on this theme, including Oskar A. H. Schmitz, Oskar Benda, and Hugo von Hofmannsthal.

4   See Monika Glettner, *Die Wiener Tschechen um 1900: Strukturanalyse einer nationalen Minderheit in der Grossstadt*, R. Oldenbourg Verlag, Munich, 1972. For a time, Vienna was actually the largest Czech city.

5   It is hardly surprising that Joseph II chose to underscore the role of German in the 1780s; he was the first Habsburg monarch to be tutored in proper German as a child, but, even before that, the German language had been connected to the spread of the Enlightenment and good government in the Austrian and Bohemian lands. See also Pieter Judson on Joseph II's relationship to German: "A century after his death German nationalists in Austria misinterpreted his effort to make German the administrative language for the entire monarchy as a nationalist act and memorialized him with countless statues." Judson, *The Habsburg Empire: A New History*, 55.

6   Eric A. Blackall, *The Emergence of German as a Literary Language 1700–1775*, Cambridge University Press, Cambridge, 1959.

7   Sometimes Luther's Bible is referred to as the basis of modern German culture; my usage is somewhat different here, but it is also important to bear in mind that Luther's Bible penetrated most of Cisleithanian Austria in the sixteenth century.

8   This was a broad phenomenon of church, state, and intellectual life in the eighteenth century throughout Central Europe. See C. J. Wells, *German: A Linguistic History to 1945*, Clarendon Press, Oxford, 1985, 306. See also Ulrich Ammon, *Die deutsche Sprache in Deutschland, Österreich und der Schweiz: Das Problem der nationalen Varietäten*, W. de Gruyter, New York, 1995 and R. E. Keller, *The German Language*, Humanities Press, New Jersey, 1978.

9   See Herbert Seidler, "Die österreichische Literatur als Problem der Forschung, *Österreich in Geschichte und Literatur*, 14. Jahrgang, 1970, Heft 7, 354–68 and R. J. W. Evans, "Language and State-Building: The Case of the Habsburg Monarchy," Robert A. Kann Memorial Lecture (2003), *Austrian History Yearbook*, 2004, Vol. 35, 1–24.

10 The formation of modern written German was a process in which Saxony came to play an important role and in which Austrian writers and grammarians figured significantly and cooperatively, as the Swiss philologists, for example, did not. See Pieter Wiesinger, "Die deutsche Sprache in Österreich: Eine Einführung," in *Das österreichische Deutsch*, ed. Peter Wiesinger, Böhlau Verlag, Vienna, 1988, 14–15; Wiesinger, "Die sprachlichen Verhältnisse und der Weg zur allgemeinen deutschen Schriftssprache in Österreich im 18. und frühen 19. Jahrhundert," in *Sprachgeschichte des Neuhochdeutschen: Gegenstände, Methode, Theorien*, 319–67; and Walter Weiss, "Zum Deutschen in der österreichischen Literatur," in *Tradition und Entwicklung: Festschrift Eugen Thurnher zum 60. Geburtstag*, ed. Werner M. Bauer et al., Innsbrucker Beiträge, Innsbruck, 1982, 47–58.

11 Cited in Dolf Lindner, *Der Mann ohne Vorurteile, Joseph von Sonnenfels 1733–1817*, Österreichischer Bundesverlag, Vienna, 1983, 30.

12 The influence of the Enlightenment in Austria was broadly European—from England, France, Italy, the Low Countries, and the German *Aufklärung*, including the Haskalah or Jewish Enlightenment.

13 See Wiesinger, "Die deutsche Sprache in Österreich," in *Das österreichische Deutsch*, 14–15.

14 Indeed, this was very much like the emergence of modern, literary Czech a generation later.

15 See M. H. Abrams, "How to Do Things with Texts," *Partisan Review*, Vol. 46 (1979), 586. This literary context not only provides elegant definitions for key terms but also draws attention to what matters for an intellectual historian.

16 Judson emphasizes his reluctance to use "normative terms like 'Czechs,' 'Germans,' 'Poles' or 'Slovenes,' preferring instead descriptive terms like 'Czech speakers.'" Judson, *The Habsburg Empire*, ix.

17 For an excellent account of the intellectual life of the 1780s, see Leslie Bodi, *Tauwetter in Wien: Zur Prosa der österreichischen Aufklärung: 1781–1795*, S. Fischer, Frankfurt am Main, 1977. The relaxation of censorship in the 1780s under Joseph II opened the way to a flood of brochures and exciting public discussion, primarily in Vienna. Many aspects of this new freedom of the press represented an independence that foreshadowed nineteenth-century liberalism; the anti-clericalism expressed a broader intellectual liberation and an opposition to the Church that came to characterize political liberalism.

18 Benedictines played a large role in the Austrian Enlightenment as they did in German Reform Catholicism more broadly. See Ulrich Lehner, *Enlightened Monks: The German Benedictines, 1740–1803*, Oxford University Press, Oxford, 2011. The Benedictine monasteries, especially Melk and Kremsmünster, were an important dimension of Austrian intellectual life in the Enlightenment. Benedictine monasteries were among the most highly intellectual institutions in Europe and, by the second half of the eighteenth century, one of the most modern. Their

libraries often functioned as research institutes, and they contributed a great deal to education in Austria.
19 Joachim Whaley, "The Transformation of the *Aufklärung*: From the Idea of Power to the Power of Ideas," in *The Culture of Power in Europe during the Long Eighteenth Century*, ed. Hamish Scott and Brendan Simms, Cambridge University Press, Cambridge, 2007, 158. Here Whaley is summarizing T. C. W. Blanning's arguments.
20 Ernst Wangermann, *Aufklärung und staatsbürgerliche Erziehung: Gottfried van Swieten als Reformator des österreichischen Unterrichtswesens 1781–1791*, Verlag für Geschichte und Politik, Vienna, 1978.
21 Richard Meister, *Entwicklung und Reformen des Österreichischen Studienwesens*, Teil I; Abhandlung. Hermann Böhlaus Nachf., Vienna, 1963.
22 David Sorkin, "Reform Catholicism and Religious Enlightenment," in *The Austrian History Yearbook*, Center for Austrian Studies, Minneapolis, MN, Vol. 30, 1999, 188. See also David Sorkin, *A Wise, Enlightened, and Reliable Piety: The Religious Enlightenment in Central and Western Europe, 1689–1789*, Oakes Institute Pamphlet, No. 1, University of Southampton, 2002, 8 and Sorkin, *The Religious Enlightenment: Protestants, Jews, and Catholics from London to Vienna*, Princeton University Press, Princeton, 2008.
23 James Van Horn Melton emphasized the internal side of Enlightenment rule in his *Absolutism and the Eighteenth-Century Origins of Compulsory Education in Prussia and Austria*, Cambridge University Press, New York, 1988, 60–6. He calls Felbinger "the foremost Catholic pedadogue in eighteenth-century Central Europe" (105). See also James Van Horn Melton, *The Rise of the Public in Enlightenment Europe*, Cambridge University Press, Cambridge, 2001.
24 See Fritz Valjavec, *Der Josephinismus: Zur geistigen Entwicklung Österreichs im achtzehnten und neunzehnten Jahhundert*, 2nd edition, R. Oldenbourg, Munich, 1945.
25 It is difficult to define who was German and who was Czech in the early modern period since there are no systematic surveys, and language itself was the principal way to distinguish German from Czech culture.
26 See Kann's sobering reservation in *A Study*, 134: "the elementary-school and medical-training-school reform and the systematic indoctrination of the new bureaucracy with the ideas of political science of the day are practically isolated islands of enlightened progress in a vast sea of ignorance." But these were also the foundations of intellectual life in Cisleithanian Austria in the nineteenth century. See also Wangermann, *Aufklärung und staatsbürgerliche Erziehung*, 37–41.
27 Lindner, *Der Mann ohne Vorurteil*, 71 and 89.
28 Kann, *A Study*, 147.
29 Orientalism and the study of languages were at the heart of intellectual life in the Enlightenment, as both Sonnenfels and Dobrovský exemplify.
30 Kann, *A Study*, 161. Jews were prominent contributors to intellectual life in Austria (as they were elsewhere in Europe in this period). Just what it meant to be a Jew

was contested then and now, but clearly many of the best minds in Austria came from Jewish families—in Vienna and Prague and elsewhere. This was already apparent with Sonnenfels, who was reared a Catholic.

31 Ibid., 152.
32 In 1791, Dobrovský published *Die Geschichte der böhmischen Sprache und Literatur*, a landmark in the study of the Czech language.
33 Ivo Cerman, "Secular Moral Philosophy: Karl Heinrich Seibt," in *The Enlightenment in Bohemia: Religion, Morality and Multiculturalism*, ed. Ivo Cerman, Rita Krueger, and Susan Reynolds, Voltaire Foundation, Oxford, 2011, 147–68.
34 More than a century later, Tomaš Masaryk emphasized the close connection between the Czech people and the Enlightenment. See Tomaš Masaryk, *The Meaning of Czech History*, ed. René Wellek, trans. Peter Kussi, The University of North Carolina Press, Chapel Hill, 1974, 20: "The Czech movement that began in the latter part of eighteenth century ... was basically progressive, enlightened, and free-thinking .... Josephinism was the official expression for this ideology in the Austrian lands."
35 See H. C. Robbins Landoon, *1791: Mozart's Last Year*, Schirmer books, New York, 1988, 58. See Andreas Önnerfors, "Freemasonry and Civil Society: Reform of Manners and the *Journal für Freymauer* (1784–1786)" in Cerman, *The Enlightenment*, 111–28. Mozart was actually from Salzburg, which became part of Austria only later, but he went to Vienna as a child and spent his creative career in Cisleithanian Austria.
36 Wangermann, *The Austrian Achievement 1700–1800*, 153–5. See also Margaret C. Jacob, *Living the Enlightenment: Freemasonry and Politics in Eighteenth-Century Europe*, Oxford University Press, New York, 1991, especially on the "rich masonic symbolism" in *The Magic Flute* (135).
37 The Czech historian Jan Křen argues that Austria saw itself in the eighteenth century (and was seen by others) as the center of Germany. See Křen, *Die Konfliktgemeinschaft*, 30. This view is most plausible in the realm of music, which included opera and the world of performance and theater. Certainly, Joseph II had hopes of providing both political and cultural leadership for Germany, although this did not come to be while he was emperor, in part because of his pointless military adventures in the East. The possibility of uniting the German Empire—the Holy Roman Empire but not the Austrian Empire—under Austrian leadership was not very strong at this time. The live issues in the eighteenth century were cultural leadership and prestige.
38 By this point the Estates of the Monarchy, especially in Hungary and the Austrian Netherlands, had lost patience with the reform and rapid modernization of Joseph II, and Austria was faced with the radicalization of the French Revolution and the prospect of a modern European war. On eighteenth-century attempts to preserve order in European states, see Marc Raeff, *The Well-Ordered Police State: Social and*

Institutional Change through Law in the Germanies and Russia 1600–1800, Yale University Press, New Haven, 1983.
39 Kann, *A Study*, 261 and passim.
40 See John W. Boyer, *Political Radicalism in Late Imperial Vienna: Origins of the Christian Social Movement 1848–1897*, The University of Chicago Press, Chicago, 1981 and John Deak, *Forging a Multinational State: State Making in Imperial Austria from the Enlightenment to the First World War*, Stanford University Press, Stanford, 2015.
41 Kann, *A Study*, 274.
42 Ernst Hanisch, *Der lange Schatten des Staates: Österreichische Gesellschaftsgeschichte im 20. Jahrhundert*, Ueberreuter, Vienna, 1994, 15.
43 For more on philosophy and literature in Austria, see Chapters 3 and 4.
44 Hanisch, *Der lange Schatten*, 28–9. See Zdeněk V. David, *Realism, Tolerance, and Liberalism in the Czech National Awakening: Legacies of the Bohemian Reformation*, Johns Hopkins University Press, Baltimore, 2010, 17, on "the continuing sway of the Catholic Enlightenment, personified by the stellar triumvirate of Karl H. Seibt, Bernard Bolzano, and Franz Exner."
45 Hugo von Hofmannsthal emphasized the gentle culture of the Middle Ages that shaped Grillparzer's sense of Austria: "his Austrianness had nothing problematic. The Slavic Bohemians and Moravians stood as close to his innermost temperament, to the life of his life, to his imagination, as did the Styrians or the Tyroleans .... That Bohemia belongs to us, the sublime and indestructible unity: Bohemia and the hereditary lands, that, to him, was a divinely ordained given, not only to him but to the genius in him." Hugo von Hofmannsthal, "Grillparzer's Political Legacy," in *Hofmannsthal and the Austrian Idea*, trans. and ed. David S. Luft, Purdue University Press, West Lafayette, Indiana, 2011, 76.
46 Historians who accept Francis I's claim to have created a new empire in 1804 generally do so with many important reservations, primarily about Hungary and Galicia. Although Pieter Judson emphasizes the imperial dimensions of Habsburg Empire, his arguments often apply in only limited ways to Hungary or Galicia. He does not emphasize the sheer scale of Transleithanian Austria or the degree to which arguments about economic backwardness apply there. See Judson, *The Habsburg Empire*. The Polish partitions of the late eighteenth century had added a substantial area to the Monarchy (Galicia and Bukovina), which continued in its somewhat anomalous position until the First World War. The Austrian Empire of the early nineteenth century was not a new empire, as literary histories sometimes argue, pointing to the cosmetic changes by Francis, but a diminished version of the Reform Monarchy, which had been unable to centralize the Monarchy as a whole.
47 For a thoughtful introduction to Czech literature and intellectual history, see "The Two Traditions of Czech Literature," in *Essays on Czech Literature*, ed. René Wellek, Mouton & Co., The Hague, 1963, 17–31.

48 Thomas Nipperdey, *Deutsche Geschichte 1800–1866: Bürgerwelt und starker Staat*, C. H. Beck, Munich, 1994. These words have special meaning for the Habsburgs, since they played major roles in the coalitions against Napoleon. On Austria's impressive military accomplishments against Napoleon, see Gunther E. Rothenberg, *Napoleon's Great Adversaries: The Archduke Charles and the Austrian Army 1792–1814*, B.T. Batsford, London, 1986.
49 See Friedrich Meinecke, *The Age of German Liberation, 1795–1815*, trans. Peter Paret and Helmuth Fischer, University of California Press, Berkeley, 1977.
50 Heinrich Ritter von Srbik, *Metternich: Der Staatsmann und der Mensch*, 3rd edition, Bruckmann, Munich, 1957. On the struggle for German leadership in the nineteenth century, see John Breuilly, *Austria, Prussia and Germany, 1806–1871*, Pearson Education Limited, London, 2002. See also Helmut Rumpler, *Eine Chance für Mitteleuropa: Bürgerliche Emancipation und Staatsverfall in der Habsburgermonarchie*, Verlag Carl Ueberreuter, Vienna, 2005. Throughout this period—from 1792 to 1866—the Habsburg Monarchy played a major role in European diplomacy, attempting to balance both France and Prussia. On the Congress of Vienna, see Henry Kissinger, *A World Restored*, Houghton Mifflin, Boston, 1957 and Harald Nicolson, *The Congress of Vienna; A Study in Allied Unity, 1812–1822*, Constable & Co., London, 1946.
51 Romanticism, whether in philosophy or literature or social thought, was not a prominent feature of Austrian intellectual life in the early nineteenth century. The notable figures in this regard, Friedrich von Schlegel and Adam von Müller, were both from Northern Germany and were not strongly influenced by the Austrian Enlightenment and Josephinism.
52 The Habsburg Monarchy shared with England in this period the project of resisting the new forces of nationalism and democracy and the victorious marches of Napoleon's armies across Europe.
53 Boyer, *Political Radicalism*, 5–8.
54 Friedrich Gentz, *Betrachtungen über die französische Revolutuion: nach dem Englischen des Herrn Burkes*, bei Friedrich Vieweg der älteren, Berlin, 1794.
55 See Adam Müller, *Die Elemente der Staatskunst: Sechsunddreisig Vorlesungen*, Haude & Spenersche, Berlin, 1936 [original edition: 1806–1809].
56 The influence of Jews became even more dramatic after 1848 as Jews migrated to Vienna from all parts of Austria and Hungary. This theme has always received a great deal of attention, but it has often been treated in a mechanical way. Many intellectuals of Jewish heritage came to regard themselves as Catholic or Protestant or unaffiliated with any church. For a long time, these conversions were assumed to be motivated by concerns about assimilation or by the state's requirements for marriage. But such interpretations are inadequate for Wittgenstein or Weininger or Hofmannsthal or Kraus.

57 What is known as the Jewish Enlightenment or Haskalah grew out of the friendship between Moses Mendelsohn and Gotthold Ephraim Lessing in Berlin.
58 See *Briefe an und von Josephine von Wertheimstein*, selected by Heinrich Gomperz and edited by Robert A. Kann, Verlag der Österreichische Akademie der Wissenschaften, Vienna, 1981 and Hanns Jäger-Sunstenau, "Die adelte Judenfamilien im vormärzlichen Wien," Diss., Vienna 1950.
59 On the role of Jews in the intellectual life of nineteenth-century Vienna and Berlin, especially in the culture of the salons, see Hilde Spiel, *Vienna's Golden Autumn: From the Watershed Year 1866 to Hitler's Anschluss, 1938*, Weidenfeld and Nicolson, New York, 1987 and Spiel, *Fanny von Arnstein: Daughter of the Enlightenment 1758–1818*, trans. Christine Shuttleworth, Berg, New York, 1991. See also Deborah Hertz, *Jewish High Society in Old Regime Berlin*, Yale University Press, New Haven, 1988.
60 In the nineteenth century, many observers expected this region to assume the form of three Germanies; an interesting presentation of this perspective is Karl Dietrich Erdmann, *Die Spur Österreichs in der deutschen Geschichte: Drei Staaten zwei Nationen ein Volk*? Manesse Verlag, Zurich, 1989.
61 Friedrich Prinz, *Prag und Wien 1848: Probleme der nationalen und sozialen Revolution in Spiegel der Wiener Ministerratsprotokole*, Verlag Robert Lerche, Munich, 1968. On the close connections between liberalism and nationalism in the formation of the German nation-state, see Brian E. Vick, *Defining Germany: The 1848 Frankfurt Parliamentarians and National Identity*, Harvard University Press, Cambridge, MA, 2002.
62 See David Brodbeck, *Defining Deutschtum: Political Ideology, German Identity, and Music-Critical Discourse in Liberal Vienna*, Oxford University Press, New York, 2014, 30–8, especially 30. Eduard Hanslick, a music critic and later a characteristic figure of liberal Vienna, shared the pre-1848 bilingualism of his friend Zimmermann. On the role of Jews in defining *Deuschtum*, see Hillel J. Kieval, *The Making of Czech Jewry: National Conflict and Jewish Society in Bohemia, 1870–1918*, Oxford University Press, New York, 1988, 8: "Particularly in the cities and towns of Bohemia, Jews remained committed devotees of German language and education, loyal servants of the Habsburg kind, and ardent supporters of the (German) Progressive party." See also Kieval, "The Social Vision of Bohemian Jews," in *Assimilation and Community: The Jew in Nineteenth-Century Europe*, ed. John Frankel and Steven J. Zipperstein, Cambridge University Press, Cambridge, 1992, 253 and Sayer, *The Coasts of Bohemia*, 107–8.
63 See Jeremy King, *Budweisers into Czechs and Germans: A Local History of Bohemian Politics, 1848–1948*, Princeton University Press, Princeton, 2002. The citizens of Budweiser actually called their politics "Austrian."
64 He regarded Brno as a suburb of Vienna. See Karel Čapek, *Talks with T. G. Masaryk*, trans. Michael Henry Heim, The University of North Carolina Press,

Chapel Hill, 2014. Masaryk was not a Czech nationalist, but he had read most of Czech and Slovak literature, and he was the first president of Czechoslovakia. He came from the Slovakian region of Hungary. Zdeněk David includes Jungmann along with Seibt and Dobrovský in the Enlightenment tradition in Bohemia. David refers to this tradition as realistic-empirical and liberal. See Zdeněk David, "Johann Gottfried Herder and the Czech National Awakening: A Reassessment," The Center for Russian and East European Studies, Pittsburgh, 2007.

65 Joseph Frederick Začek, *Palacký: The Historian as Scholar and Nationalist*, Mouton, The Hague, 1970, 55–6. Jiří Kořalka, *František Palacký (1798–1876): Der Historiker der Tschechen in österreichischer Vielvölkerstaat*, trans. the author with Helmut Rumpler and Peter Urbanitsch, Verlag der Österreichischen Akademie der Wissenschaften, Vienna, 2007.

66 See Franz Palacký, *Geschichte von Böhmen: grösstentheils nach Urkunden und Handschriften*, Kronberger und Weber, Prague, 1844–1867, 5 volumes.

67 Stanley Z. Pech, *The Czech Revolution of 1848*, The University of North Carolina Press, Chapel Hill, 1969, 336. Judson estimates that of the roughly one hundred newspapers and journals that were registered in Bohemia in 1848, slightly more than half were in German, while the remainder were in Czech. See Judson, *The Habsburg Empire*, 186. On the dramatic change in the situation of the Czech language in the early nineteenth century, see Jan Neruda's formulation about Joseph Jungmann: "When Jungmann appeared on the scene, it was the dark of night, when he left [he died in 1848] it was already completely daylight." Cited in Robert Sak, *Josef Jungmann: Život obrozence*, Vyšehrad, Prague, 2007, 7. The translation is mine.

68 See Christoph Thienen-Adlerflycht, Graf Leo Thun im Vormärz: Grundlagen des böhmischen Konservatismus im Kaisertum Österreich, Hermann Böhlaus Nachf, Vienna, 1967 and Hans Lentze, *Die Universitätsreformen des Ministers Graf Leo Thun-Hohenstein*, Hermann Böhlaus Nachf, Vienna, 1962.

69 Johnston, *The Austrian Mind*, 279. Johnston emphasizes "the Leibnizian premise that religion and science cannot contradict each other."

70 The Habsburgs' Italian possessions were very different from the German and Hungarian lands; the Italian possessions had grown out of the European balance of power over centuries—including the nineteenth century. There were obviously important cultural influences in both directions as well. Regarding Old Liberalism, see Karl Eder, *Der Liberalismus in Alösterreich: Geisteshaltung, Politik und Kultur*, Verlag Herold, Vienna, 1955 and Georg Franz, *Liberalismus: die deutschliberale Bewegung in der habsburgische Monarchie*, G. D. W. Calwey, Munich, 1955.

71 During this period Slovenian was emerging in southern Austria as an interregional language. See Judson, *The Habsburg Empire*, 150 and Joachim Hösler, *Von Krain zu Slowenien. Die Anfänge der nationalen Differenzierungs-prozesse in Krain und der

Untersteiermark von der Aufklärung bis zur Revolution 1768 bis 1848, R. Oldenbourg Verlag, Munich, 2006.

72 Although Austria and Hungary were independent in their domestic political arrangements, they shared a common monarch and common ministries of foreign affairs, military affairs, and finance. Austria and Hungary belonged to the same economic community, and, despite their political separation, the economic and technological interactions between Austria and Hungarian steadily increased throughout this period. See David F. Good, *The Economic Rise of the Habsburg Empire, 1750-1914*, UC Press, Berkeley, 1984. On the other hand, industrialization took place primarily in Cisleithania—in Bohemia, Moravia, Lower Austria, and Styria—underscoring the distinction between Cisleithanian and Transleithanian Austria. On the importance of regional industrialization for the development of socialism, see Vincent J. Knapp, *Austrian Social Democracy, 1889-1914*, University Press of America, Washington, DC, 1980.

73 See Adam Wandruszka, *Geschichte einer Zeitung: das Schicksal der "Presse" und der "Neue Freie Presse" von 1848 zur Zweiten Republik*, Neue Wiener Presse, Vienna, 1958.

74 See Steven Beller, *Vienna and the Jews 1867-1938: A Cultural History*, Cambridge University Press, Cambridge, 1989. Beller adopts a very broad definition of what was "Jewish."

75 Judson, *Exclusive Revolutionaries*.

76 See Boyer, *Political Radicalism*, chapter 1.

77 See Hanisch, *Der lange Schatten des Staates*, 30: "Between 1850 and 1950 the Church was ruled by the anti-revolutionary, counter-Enlightenment spirit."

78 See P. G. J, Pulzer, *The Rise of Political Anti-Semitism in Germany and Austria*, John Wiley and Sons, New York, 1964.

79 Gary B. Cohen, *The Politics of Ethnic Survival: Germans in Prague, 1861-1914*, 2nd edition, Revised, Purdue University Press, West Lafayette, 2006.

80 Erna Lesky, *The Vienna Medical School of the 19th Century*, Johns Hopkins University Press, Baltimore, 1976.

81 See Alphons Lhotsky, *Geschichte des Instituts für österreichische Geschichtsforschung 1854-1954*, Hermann Böhlaus Nachf, Graz, 1954. Evident here are the close connection to the official bureaucracy (and the central state) and the resistance to theory and grand narrative. The slow development of Austrian history as a field offers little to compare with developments during the golden age of historical writing in France and Prussia in the early nineteenth century. See Hayden White, *Metahistory: The Historical Imagination in Nineteenth-Century Europe*, Johns Hopkins University Press, Baltimore, 1973.

82 See Michael Gubser, *Time's Visible Surface: Alois Riegl and the Discourse on Historicity and Temporality in Fin-de-siècle Vienna*, Wayne State University Press,

Detroit, 2004 and Diana Reynolds Cordileone, *Alois Riegl in Vienna 1875–1905: An Institutional Biography*, Ashgate, Burlington, VT, 2014.

83 See *Theodor Gomperz: Ein Gelehrtenleben im Bürgertum der Franz-Josefs-Zeit*, ed. Robert A. Kann, Verlag der österreichischen Akademie der Wissenschaften, Vienna, 1974.

84 See Deborah R. Coen, *Vienna in the Age of Uncertainty: Science, Liberalism, and Private Life*, Chicago University Press, Chicago, 2007.

85 On the broad impact of Darwinism in liberal Vienna, see Werner Michler, *Darwinismus und Literatur: Naturwissenschftliche und literarische Intelligenz in Österreich, 1859–1914*, Böhlau Verlag, Vienna, 1999.

86 Johnston, *The Austrian Mind*, 269. Johnston points out that most of them settled in Vienna. On the adjustments of Bohemian Jews to German-speaking culture in the nineteenth century, see Hillel J. Kieval, *Languages of Community: The Jewish Experience in the Czech Lands*, University of California Press, Berkeley, 2000.

87 Hermann Broch, *Hugo von Hofmannsthal and His Time: The European Imagination, 1860–1920*, trans. Michael P. Steinberg, The University of Chicago Press, Chicago, 1984.

88 See Tara Zahra, *Kidnapped Souls: National Indifference and the Battle for Children in the Bohemian Lands, 1900–1948*, Cornell University Press, Ithaca, 2008, Chapter 1. Czech activists worked to overcome national indifference.

89 See David S. Luft, "Science and Irrationalism," *Modern Austrian Literature*, Vol. 23, No. 2 (1990), 89–97, Luft, "Schopenhauer, Austria, and the Generation of 1905," in *Central European History*, March 1983, 53–75, and John Toews' 1980 presentation at the Pacific Coast Branch of the American Historical Association on Freud.

90 Jacques Le Rider, *Modernity and Crises of Identity: Culture and Society in Fin-de-Siècle Vienna*, trans. Rosemary Morris, Continuum, New York, 1993.

91 See Harriet Anderson, *Utopian Feminism: Women's Movements in fin-de-siècle Vienna*, Yale University Press, New Haven, 1992.

92 On the reaction of Viennese liberals like Freud to Mill's *The Subjection of Women* (1869), see David S. Luft, *Eros and Inwardness: Weininger, Musil, Doderer*, The University of Chicago Press, Chicago, 2003, 39–40.

93 On the question of why and when women became visible as historical agents, see Joan Wallach Scott, *Gender and the Politics of History Gender and the Politics of History*, revised edition, Columbia University Press, New York, 1999. On the peculiarities of thinking about gender in Vienna, see Luft, *Eros and Inwardness in Vienna*. On the preoccupation of men with these issues, see Le Rider, *Modernity and Crises of Identity*. See also Otto Weininger, *Geschlecht und Charakter: Eine prinzipielle Untersuchung*, Matthes & Seitz Verlag, Munich, 1980 [reprint of the first edition, Vienna, 1903]. In the arguments of Weininger, the usual term for sex [*Geschlecht*] became problematic in ways that began to anticipate the later recasting of the word "gender" in both English and German.

94 Houston Stewart Chamberlain, *Foundations of the Nineteenth Century*, trans. John Lees, John Lane Company, New York, 1914, 2 volumes.

95 Liberal reform energies carried into the twentieth century in figures such as Josef Popper-Lynkeus, a Jew from Bohemia who was an inventor, reformer, and writer—and a friend of Ernst Mach and Sigmund Freud. See Ingrid Belke, *Die Sozialreformerischen Ideen von Josef Popper-Lynkeus* (1838–1921), J. C. B. Mohr, Tübingen, 1978. The transformative elements of liberalism continued to inspire and shape democratic and popular movements.

96 Helmut Rumpler emphasizes how little influence intellectuals had on politics during the liberal era (and the fin-de-siècle) but also how much things had changed after 1900. See Helmut Rumpler, "Die Intellektuellen in Cisleithanien," in *Die Habsburgermonarchie: 1848–1918*, Vol. IX/part 2, ed. Helmut Rumpler and Peter Urbanitsch, Österreichischen Akademie der Wissenschaften, Vienna, 2010, especially 1142–55.

97 In the fields of philosophy and political economy, this period of intellectual history is largely a story of continuity with the values of liberalism and the nineteenth century.

98 Carl E. Schorske, "Politics and the Psyche: Schnitzler and Hofmannsthal," *Fin-de-siècle Vienna: Politics and Culture*, Alfred A. Knopf, New York, 1980. Schorske emphasized the "ill-reconciled moralistic and aesthetic components" (5) of Austrian liberal culture, but his point on the next page is often set aside: that the "moral and scientific culture of Vienna's haute bourgeoisie can scarcely be distinguished from garden-variety Victorianism elsewhere in Europe" (6).

99 David S. Landes, *Unbound Prometheus: Technological Change and Industrial Development in Western Europe from 1750*, Cambridge University Press, Cambridge, 1969, especially chapters 3–4. The Second Industrial Revolution came into being with cars and airplanes, sewing machines, bicycles, film, steel and electricity, cartels, and assembly lines.

100 On the internationalism of scientific knowledge in the decades before the First World War, see Robert Fox, *Science without Frontiers: Cosmopolitanism and National Interests in the World of Learning: 1870–1940*, Oregon State University Press, Corvallis, 2016.

101 See *The Intellectual Migration: Europe and America, 1930–1960*, ed. Bernard Bailyn and Donald Fleming, Harvard University Press, Cambridge, MA, 1969 and H. Stuart Hughes, *Sea Change: The Migration of Social Thought, 1930–1965*, Harper and Row, New York, 1975.

102 John W. Boyer, "Power, Partisanship, and the Grid of Democratic Politics: 1907 as the Pivot Point of Modern Austrian History," *Austrian History Yearbook*, Vol, 44 (2013), 148–74.

103 On Austria's connections to international and Pan-European movements, see Katherine Sorrels, *Cosmopolitan Outsiders: Imperial Inclusion, National Exclusion,*

and the Pan-European Idea, 1900–1930*, Palgrave Macmillan, New York, 2016. For the roots of these traditions in the Bohemian nobility, see Count Coudenhove-Kalergi, *An Idea Conquers the World*, Hutchinson & Co., London, 1953.
104 Hermann Broch wrote an important novel, *The Sleepwalkers*, on this theme, although it was set in Imperial Germany.
105 Robert Musil, "Politics in Austria," in *Precision and Soul: Essays and Addresses*, trans. and ed. Burton Pike and David S. Luft, University of Chicago Press, Chicago, 1990, 19. Musil put it slightly differently: "a nonintellectual but cracked soil in whose fissures, despite its barren inauspiciousness, culture is now settling better than ever on what are, for it, barely suitable surfaces."
106 See David S. Luft, *Robert Musil and the Crisis of European Culture: 1880–1942*, University of California Press, Berkeley, 1980. See also H. Stuart Hughes, *Consciousness and Society*, Robert Wohl, *The Generation of 1914*, Harvard University Press, Cambridge, 1979, and Thomas Harrison, *1910: The Emancipation of Dissonance*, California University Press, Berkeley, 1996. One of the most famous accounts of this generation in the prewar years in Austria is Stefan Zweig, *The World of Yesterday*, intro. Harry Zohn, University of Nebraska Press, Lincoln, 1943/1964.
107 In the words of Ernst Robert Curtius, "[t]he youth of 1905 wanted to be aesthetic; the youth of 1925 want to be political." Ernst Robert Curtius, "Zu Hofmannsthals Gedächtnis," in *Kritische Essays zur europäischen Literatur*, Francke Verlag, Bern, 1963, 117.
108 Fritz Mauthner is sometimes introduced into accounts of language skepticism in Vienna. He came from Prague and spent most of his career in Germany. On his relationship to the German Empire, see Katherine Arens, *Empire in Decline: Fritz Mauthner's Critique of Wilhelminian Germany*, Peter Lang, New York, 2001.
109 Luft, "Schopenhauer, Austria, and the Generation of 1905," in *Central European History*, March 1983.
110 Even Freud, oddly enough, increasingly moved away from his concerns in the 1890s to explore the impact of his understanding of the individual, not only on sexual life but on politics, war, and the whole of human culture and civilization. And in this his ideas were shaped by Schopenhauer and Nietzsche, much like those of the younger writers of the generation of 1905.
111 See Scott Spector, *Prague Territories: National Conflict and Cultural Innovation in Franz Kafka's Fin de Siècle*, University of California Press, Berkeley, 2000. Spector's argument about a minor literature draws on Gilles Deleuze and Félix Guattari, *Kafka: Toward a Minor Literature*, trans. Dana Polan, University of Minnesota Press, Minneapolis, 1986. We might argue that Austrian literature was itself a minor literature. See Cohen, *The Politics of Ethnic Survival*, 95: "A Czech group which normally gathered in the Café Union and included the Čapek brothers, František Langer, and C. V. Štek met with Max Brod, Franz Kafka, Egon

Kisch, Paul Leppin, and Franz Werfel at the Café Arco or in various 'bilingual' establishments."

112 Allan Janik and Stephen Toulmin, *Wittgenstein's Vienna*, Simon & Schuster, New York, 1973. See also J. P. Stern, "Karl Kraus's Vision of Language," *The Modern Language Review*, Vol. 61, No. 1 (January 1966), 71–84.

113 See Paul Reitter, *The Anti-Journalist: Karl Kraus and Jewish Self-Fashioning in Fin-de-siècle Europe*, University of Chicago Press, Chicago, 2008 and Paul Reitter, "Karl Kraus and the Jewish Self-Hatred Question," *Jewish Social Studies*, New Series, Vol. 10, No. 1 (Autumn 2003), 78–116.

114 Elias Canetti regarded him as "an intellectual tyrant." See Reitter, *The Anti-Journalist*, 78.

115 See Walter Methlagl and Allan Janik, "The Brenner," in *Major Figures of Austrian Literature: The Interwar Years 1918–1938*, ed. Donald G. Daviau, Ariadne Press, Riverside, 1995, 83–106 and Albert Fuchs, *Geistige Strömungen in Österreich 1867–1918*, reprint with an intro. by Friedrich Heer, Löcker Verlag, Vienna, 1949/1984, 81.

116 See Endre Kiss, "Über Wiens Bedeutung für die essayistische Periode des jungen Georg Lukács," in *Die Östereichische Literatur: ihr Profil von der Jahrhundertwende bis zur Gegenwart (1880–1980)*, ed. Herbert Zeman, Akademische Druck, Graz, 1989, part 1, 371–83. Kiss points out (372 and passim), in the context of *Die Seele und die Formen* and the existentialist moment in Lukács' own development, just how unclear it was for the young Lukács what aspects of his world were Hungarian or Austrian or even Viennese or European. Kiss emphasizes the powerful influence of Kierkegaard and Nietzsche on the young Lukács. Musil's work often emphasized the intellectual excitement of this prewar period. See Luft, Introduction, *Robert Musil and the Crisis of European Culture*.

117 The importance of women in intellectual life became even more apparent after 1945, especially with the impact on Austrian literature of women born in the first quarter of the century.

118 See Adelheid Popp, *The Autobiography of a Working Woman*, trans. E. C. Harvey, F. G. Browne and Co., Chicago, 1913 and Agatha Schwartz and Helga Thorson, *Shaking the Empire, Shaking Patriarchy: The Growth of a Feminist Consciousness across the Austro-Hungarian Monarchy*, Adriane Press, Riverside, 2014.

119 Between 1740 and 1938/1939 there were many more men than women who were educated and active in public intellectual life. My organization in terms of the three disciplines of philosophy, literature, and the human sciences may tend to underscore this.

120 Anderson, *Utopian Feminism*, xi.

121 See Rudolf Pannwitz (1881–1969), *Der Geist der Tschechen*, Verlag "Der Friede," Vienna, 1919, 125: "The danger existed for Czech culture that it would become a province of German culture." But this did not happen.

122 See Paul Molisch, *Vom Kampf der Tschechen um ihren Staat*, Wilhelm Braumüller, Vienna, 1929. See V: "The prehistory of the founding of the Czechoslovakian state contains … a good part of the political history of the Austrian Germans." And 1: "From Palacký's well-known remark from 1848 down to the declarations of the Czech Association of Deputies during the war, which demanded to be sure, a reordering, but not a destruction of Austria, … the most outstanding Czech leaders have at least outwardly expressed support for the state and the dynasty."

123 See Helmut Gruber, *Red Vienna: Experiment in Working-Class Culture 1919-1934*, Oxford University Press, New York, 1991, Anson Rabinbach, *The Crisis of Austrian Socialism: From Red Vienna to Civil War 1927-1934*, The University of Chicago, Chicago, 1983, and Janek Wasserman, *Black Vienna: The Radical Right in the Red City, 1918-1938*, Cornell University Press, Ithaca, 2014.

124 See Thomas Ort, *Art and Life in Modernist Prague: Karel Capek and His Generation, 1911-1938* (Palgrave Macmillan, 2013). "… a pragmatic and relativist vision that combined elements of reason and intuition alike" (3). Ort calls Czechoslovakia "perhaps the empire's truest successor state," something that is often lost in emphases on nationalism (7). A large portion of the population continued to be German, even with the addition of the Slovakians from Hungary.

125 Friedrich Heer, *Land im Strom der Zeit*, Herold, Vienna, 1958, 14–20.

126 For the very different development of Austrian identity after the Second World War, see Peter Thaler, *The Ambivalence of Identity: The Austrian Experience of Nation-Building in a Modern Society*, Purdue University Press, West Lafayette, 2001.

127 See Erin Hochman, *Imagining a Greater Germany: Republican Nationalism and the Idea of Anschluss*, Cornell University Press, Ithaca, 2016.

128 As Heimito von Doderer moved away from National Socialism, he was sensitive to his debt to Marcus Aurelius.

129 The Second Republic is still close to the experiences of the 1930s in ways that are not always expressed in public (see Elfriede Jelinek). Hitler was, of course, Austrian himself, and his party had been founded in the Sudetenland before the war. It was thus an Austrian who realized the dreams of *Grossdeutschland*, which is of course one reason many Austrians emphasize that Austria has nothing to do with Germany or is really not German in any sense.

130 K. R. Popper, *The Open Society and Its Enemies*, Princeton University Press, Princeton, 1963, Vol. I, 1. The first edition appeared in 1943 at the height of the Second World War.

131 See Hughes, *The Sea Change* and *The Intellectual Migration*, ed. Fleming and Bailyn.

132 Donald L. Wallace, *Embracing Democracy: Hermann Broch, Politics and Exile, 1918-1951*, Peter Lang, Oxford, 2014.

Chapter 3

1. Friedrich Nietzsche, "Schopenhauer als Erzieher, Unzeitgemässe Betrachtungen III," *Nietzsche Werke: Kritische Ausgabe*, Walter de Gruyter, Berlin, 1972, Vol. 1, 416. The translation is mine.
2. See Barry Smith, *Austrian Philosophy: The Legacy of Franz Brentano*, Open Court, Chicago, 1994. In his Introduction, Smith points to the tension between a geographical definition of Austrian philosophy (for him, within the borders of the Habsburg Monarchy) and "a certain *way of doing philosophy*" (2). See Mark Textor, *The Austrian Contribution to Analytic Philosophy*, Routledge, New York, 2006, Introduction, 15–16: "Wittgenstein is a philosopher *from* Austria, but not an *Austrian* Philosopher. Brentano, in contrast, is from Germany, but is an Austrian Philosopher." See Johannes L. Brandl's review of Smith's book in *Philosophy and Phenomenological Research*, Vol. 57, No. 3 (September 1997), 697–782.
3. Exemplary for the modest positivism I have in mind are Robert Musil and Richard von Mises. See Richard von Mises, *Positivism: A Study in Human Understanding*, Dover Publications, New York, 1951 (1968), trans. Jerry Bernstein and Roger G. Newton with von Mises; based on *Kleines Lehrbuch des Positivismus: Einführung in die empiristische Wissenschaftsauffassung*, Van Stockum and Zoon, The Hague, 1939.
4. The classic and comprehensive account of nineteenth-century European thought, which emphasizes philosophy almost exclusively, is Maurice Mandelbaum's *History, Man, & Reason*, The Johns Hopkins Press, Baltimore, 1971. Mandelbaum discusses virtually every European philosopher from Lotze to Fiske, but he does not mention either Bolzano or Brentano. Similarly, Bertrand Russell makes no reference to Bolzano or Brentano in Bertrand Russell, *A History of Western Philosophy*, Simon and Schuster, New York, 1945, although he certainly knew who they were.
5. Rudolf Haller and Barry Smith have been two of the most prominent commentators on Austrian philosophy. See, for example, Rudolf Haller, *Studien zur österreichischen Philosophie: Variationen über ein Thema*, Rodopi N.V., Amsterdam, 1979 and *Questions on Wittgenstein*, Routledge, London, 1988; and Smith, *Austrian Philosophy*. See Simon's summary of the Neurath-Haller thesis as "an emphasis on psychological and linguistic analysis," although even these are rather different approaches: Peter Simons, "Bolzano, Brentano and Meinong: Three Austrian Realists," in *German Philosophy since Kant*, ed. Anthony O'Hear, Cambridge UP, Cambridge, 1991, 109.
6. See J. Alberto Coffa, *The Semantic Tradition from Kant to Carnap: To the Vienna Station*, ed. Linda Wessels, Cambridge UP, Cambridge, 1991. The story of what was continental, let alone "German," was far more complicated than is ordinarily assumed. Both of the main currents of twentieth-century philosophy had important

origins in Austria: both the so-called continental tradition (phenomenology) and the Anglo-American tradition (analytic philosophy).

7   In *The Austrian Mind* William Johnston drew attention to the importance of Bohemian philosophy and reform Catholicism, and his commentary is often valuable on philosophers who were connected in some way to Austria. Johnston underscores the importance of Gottfried Wilhelm Leibniz (1646–1716) for Bohemian philosophy and the emphasis on the good of the whole throughout this tradition.

8   One of the oddities of the Austrian tradition in philosophy is that it is close to the British tradition in spirit but written in German, which can seem to contradict our common assumptions about German philosophy, much like discovering that Austrians drove on the left side of the road until 1938. See http://www.worldstandards.eu/cars/driving-on-the-left/

9   See Peter Simons, "Bolzano, Brentano and Meinong," in O'Hear, *German Philosophy*, 115. The situation has improved somewhat since Simons wrote this. Sandra Lapointe, Anders Wedberg, Edgar Morscher, and others have also emphasized Bolzano's enormous importance for contemporary analytic philosophy.

10 See Bertrand Russell, *A Critical Exposition of the Philosophy of Leibniz*, Longwood Academic, George Allen & Unwin Ltd, Wolfeboro, N. H., 1964 [first published in 1900] and Nicholas Jolley, *Leibniz*, Routledge, New York, 2005. See also Donald Rutherford, *Leibniz and the Rational Order of Nature*, Cambridge UP, Cambridge, 1995, 2: Rutherford points out that "the absurd apologies of Pangloss have at most a tenuous connection to Leibniz's doctrine of the best of all possible worlds."

11 Roger Bauer, *Idealismus und seine Gegner in Österreich*, Carl Winter, Heidelberg, 1966, 50–60. The quotation on the developing world is from Bauer, 56.

12 His father founded an orphanage.

13 On the role of physics in Catholic thought in the early modern period, see Marcus Hellyer, *Catholic Physics: Jesuit Natural Philosophy in Early Modern Germany*, University of Notre Dame Press, Notre Dame, 2005.

14 Bernard Bolzano, *Selected Writings on Ethics and Politics*, trans. Paul Rusnock and Rolf George, Rodopi, New York, 2007. Introduction, 2.

15 Both Hegel and Bolzano were powerfully stamped by the Enlightenment, but Hegel's way of thinking was distinctively historical, while Bolzano's thought concentrated on the natural sciences. The intellectual traditions that grew out of their work generally continued these emphases: historical change and scientific truth.

16 Rolf George and Paul Rusnock, "Bolzano's Political Philosophy," in *The Austrian Contribution*, 265 and passim.

17 *Vom besten Staate* has now been translated into English. Bolzano outlines his understanding of reform and social change at the outset. Bernard Bolzano, "On the

Best State," in *Selected Writings on Ethics and Politics*, trans. Paul Rusnock and Rolf George, Rodopi, New York, 2007, 233–357.

18 Bauer, *Idealismus*, 40.
19 Ibid., Chapter I, especially 12–14.
20 Ernst Winter, *Der Böhmische Vormärz in Briefen B. Bolzanos an F. Přihonský (1824–1848)*, Akademie Verlag, Berlin, 146.
21 Bernard Bolzano, From his Religious Teaching, in *Selbstbiographie*, Wilhelm Braumüller, Vienna, 1875, 199. See also Rusnock and George, From *The Concept of Religion*, in *Selected Writings*, 192: "I call a person's religion the collection of all his beliefs that have either a beneficial or a detrimental influence on his virtue or his happiness."
22 Edgar Morscher, *Das logische An-sich bei Bernard Bolzano*, Verlag Anton Pustet, Salzburg, 1973.
23 An excellent introduction to Bolzano is now available: Edgar Morscher, *Bernard Bolzano's Life and Work*, Akademia Verlag, Vienna, 2008. See also Bernard Bolzano, "Lebensbeschreibung," *Selbstbiographie*, 1–88.
24 See the appreciation of Bolzano by Peter Demetz: *Auf den Spur Bernard Bolzanos: Essays*, Arco Wissenschaft, Vienna, 2013, especially "Sprachphilosophie im Nationalitätenkonflikt. Nocheinmal: Patočka, Jungmann, Bolzano," 43–62.
25 Bernard Bolzano, *Über das Verhältnis der beiden Volksstämme in Böhmen: drei Vorträge*, Wilhelm Braumüller, Vienna, 1849. Lectures from the University of Prague in 1816; forword by Joseph Fesl. See Eduard Winter, *Die Sozial- und Ethnoethik Bernard Bolzanos*, Verlag der österreichischen Akademie der Wissenschaften, Vienna, 1977.
26 Bolzano, *Über das Verhältnis der beiden Volkstämme*, 16.
27 Bernard Bolzano, "Was ist Vaterland und Vaterlandsliebe?" *Erbauungschriften an die Jugend 1810* (Ausgabe 1850), 111.
28 Bolzano, "On the Best State," in *Selected Writings on Ethics and Politics*, 237, 245, and 248.
29 See J. P. Stern, "Bolzano, Language and Nationalism," *Journal of European Studies*, Vol. 19, Part 3 (1989), 169–89. This is an interesting essay on the relationship between Bolzano's philosophy and his approach to religion.
30 The contrast between Bolzano and Kant, especially on the subject of synthetic-a priori judgments, is often emphasized for polemical reasons, even though quite different positions are often at stake, for example, Bolzano and Carnap. See Edgar Morscher's "The Great Divide within Austrian Philosophy: The Synthetic a Priori," in Textor, *The Austrian Contribution*, especially 261: Morscher concludes that Bolzano was not only not an anti-Kant but actually "more Kantian than Kant himself, i.e. a Super-Kant."
31 See Sandra Lapointe, *Bolzano's Theoretical Philosophy: An Introduction*, Palgrave Macmillan, New York, 2011, especially 59–61. Bolzano took everything Kant

said about analyticity very seriously. For a valuable account of Bolzano's critique of Kant, see František Přihonsky, *New Anti-Kant or Examination of the Critique of Pure Reason*, according to concepts laid down in Bolzano's *Theory of Science*, Bautzen, 1850 in *New Anti-Kant*, ed. and trans. Sandra Lapointe and Clinton Tolley, Palgrave Macmillan, 2014. Although Přihonsky rather than Bolzano is the author, the volume was written in collaboration between the two in the last decade of Bolzano's life. The book appeared after Bolzano's death and after the revolutions of 1848.

32 Bernard Bolzano, *The Theory of Science: Attempt at a Detailed and in the Main Novel Exposition of LOGIC: With Constant Attention to Earlier Authors*, ed. and trans. Rolf George, University of California Press, Berkeley, 1972. Bernard Bolzano, *Theory of Science*, ed. and intro. Jan Berg, trans. Burnham Terrell, D. Reidel Publishing, Boston, 1973. Neither edition is complete. I rely primarily on George's translation, but I also recommend Berg's introduction to the Terrell edition.

33 In his development of a pure logic, Husserl relied heavily on Bolzano, especially on his distinction between a theory of science and pure logic, which is about propositions in themselves or ideas in themselves. See Lapointe, *Bolzano's Theoretical Philosophy*, especially chapter 11.

34 Jan Berg, Introduction to *Theory of Science*, 3.

35 See review by John T. Blackmore in *Isis*, Vol. 67, No. 2 (1976), 319–21.

36 See Coffa, *The Semantic Tradition*. The origins of the semantic tradition were both continental and Catholic. Perhaps most surprising is the impact of the Catholic Enlightenment on modern science and philosophy.

37 See Dagfin Føllesdal, "Bolzano's Legacy," in *Bolzano and Analytic Philosophy*, ed. Wolfgang Künne, Mark Seibel, Mark Textor, Rodopi, Amsterdam-Atlanta, 1997, 2.

38 Michael Dummett, *Origins of Analytic Philosophy*, Harvard UP, Cambridge, 1994, chapter 4. See also Gilbert Ryle, *The Concept of Mind*, Barnes and Noble, New York, 1969 [1949]. Ryle's book is a critique of what he regarded as the official doctrine of a ghost in the machine since Descartes, the mind of the mind/body problem (15ff.).

39 Ibid.

40 Dummett, *Origins*, 26.

41 *Der Briefwechsel B. Bolzano's mit F. Exner*, ed. Eduard Winter, Königliche Böhmische Gesellschaft der Wissenschaften, Prague, 1935, 29.

42 Jan Berg, "Editor's Introduction to Bernard Bolzano," in *Theory of Science*, trans. Burnham Terrell, D. Reidel Publishing Company, Boston, 1973, 1–2.

43 Ibid.

44 Føllesdal, "Bolzano's Legacy," in *Bolzano and Analytic Philosophy*, 10, quoting Anders Wedburg. Anders Wedberg's *History of Philosophy*, Vol. 3 is entitled *Bolzano to Wittgenstein*, Clarendon Press, Oxford, 1984, and the second chapter is devoted entirely to Bolzano.

45 See *The Analytic Turn: Analysis in Early Analytic Philosophy and Phenomenology*, ed. Michael Beaney, Routledge, New York, 2007.
46 See Eduard Winter, Einleitung, in *Robert Zimmermanns philosophische Propädeutik und die Vorlagen aus der Wissenschaftslehre Bernard Bolzanos*, Verlag der Österreichischen Akademie der Wissenschaften, Vienna, 1975, 7–35, especially 9. Winter explains the conflicts within Austrian philosophy during the nineteenth century and the ways in which Bolzano's ideas from Prague entered the University system in Vienna through the influence of Zimmermann, Exner, Fesl, and Thun. On Johann Friedrich Herbart (1776–1841) and Robert Zimmermann (1824–1898), see Johnston, *The Austrian Mind*, 281–6 and 286–9. Zimmermann helped to move Austrian philosophy toward empiricism and away from German idealism.
47 Winter generally uses the term "Danube Monarchy" to include the universities of Bohemia and Moravia. See Harold B. Dunkel, *Herbart and Education*, Random House, New York, 1969. Herbart espoused a peculiar form of philosophical realism, quite unlike the German idealists, but not what most Americans would think of as a realism. Although Herbart studied with Fichte at Jena, he held Kant's chair at Königsberg (1808–1833). He was in some respects similar to Kant, and he was a contemporary of Bolzano, but his real interest was pedagogy. He lectured on Johann Heinrich Pestalozzi, whom he met during his time in Switzerland as a young man.
48 Winter, "Einleitung," *Robert Zimmermanns philosophische Propädeutik*, 22.
49 For Brentano's own understanding of his philosophical context, see Franz Brentano, "Die vier Phasen der Philosophie und ihr augenblicklicher Stand" (1895) in *Vier Phasen der Philosophie*, ed. Oskar Kraus, Verlag von Felix Meiner, Hamburg, 1968, 3–34.
50 The intellectual atmosphere of the University of Vienna was congenial to Brentano's approach to philosophy, but it seems extravagant to argue that only his style of philosophy is Austrian.
51 Kurt Rudolf Fischer, "Franz Brentano's Philosophy of *Evidenz*," diss. University of California, Berkeley, 1964, 70.
52 See Oskar Kraus, *Franz Brentano; zur kenntnis seines lebens und seiner lehre*, Mit Beiträgen von Carl Stumpf und Edmund Husserl, Oskar Beck, Munich, 1919, 93–4 and 167. Kraus, a student of Brentano who taught at Prague, emphasized the late Brentano and his unpublished work. A helpful point of reference for English readers on liberal Catholicism and the debate in the 1860s about papal infallibility is Gertrude Himmelfarb, *Lord Acton: A Study in Conscience*, University of Chicago Press, Chicago, 1952. This was very much Brentano's world.
53 Heidegger grew up in the area of Freiburg, which had been part of the Austrian educational system in the eighteenth century before Napoleon made it part of Baden.

54 On the importance of Bolzano and Brentano for Czech realism and political history, see Zdeněk David, "Masaryk a rakouská filosofická tradice: Bolzano a Brentano," *Filosoficky cašopis*, Vol. 56 (2008), 345–61 and Eva Schmidt-Hartmann, *Thomas G. Masaryk's Realism: Origins of a Czech Political Concept*, R. Oldenbourg, Munich, 1984. On Brentano's influence in Prague not only before the First World War (in the work of Anton Marty, Alfred Kastil, Oskar Kraus, and Christian von Ehrenfels) but in the Republic of Czechoslovakia as well, see Rudolf Haller, "Brentanos Spuren im Werke Masaryks," in *T.G. Masaryk und die Brentano-Schule*, ed. Josef Zumr and Thomas Binder, Filozofický ústav Československé akademie věd, Prague, 1992, 10–20. Brentano's student and the first president of the republic, Thomas Masaryk, founded the Brentano Society in Prague.

55 See Robert Poli, "The Brentano Puzzle: An Introduction," in *The Brentano Puzzle*, Ashgate, Brookfield, USA, 1998, 1–13. The successes of the students obscured the significance of the teacher. Poli mentions Husserl, Twardowski, and Meinong. See Fischer's thoughtful account of Brentano's influence in Fischer, "Franz Brentano's Philosophy," 21–44. On Brentano's influence, see *The School of Franz Brentano*, ed. Liliana Albertazzi, Massimo Libardi, and Roberto Poli, Kluwer Academic Publishers, Boston, 1996.

56 Edwin G. Boring, "Foreword" to Antos C. Rancurello, *A Study of Franz Brentano: His Psychological Standpoint and His Significance in the History of Psychology*, Academic Press, New York, 1968, viii.

57 Dale Jacquette, "Introduction: Brentano's Philosophy," in *The Cambridge Companion to Brentano*, ed. Dale Jacquette, Cambridge UP, Cambridge, 2004, 18. For a thoughtful account both of Brentano's broad influence in the twentieth century and of the philosophical links among these ways of thinking, see Karl Schuhmann, "Brentano's Impact on Twentieth-Century Philosophy," *The Cambridge Companion to Brentano*, ed. Dale Jacquette, Cambridge UP, Cambridge, 2004, 277–97.

58 Poli, "The Brentano Puzzle," in *The Brentano Puzzle*, 7 and 12. See Biagio G. Tassop1ne, *From Psychology to Phenomenology: Franz Brentano's "Psychology from an Empirical Standpoint" and Contemporary Philosophy of Mind*, Palgrave Macmillan, New York, 2012, 1. "Brentano's philosophical psychology still forms one of the overlooked alternatives in contemporary philosophy of mind." His view in his most important work "is almost never examined in itself as a whole and within its historical context."

59 See Lindenfeld, *The Transformation of Positivism*.

60 Brentano's approach to *Vorstellungen* is similar to Schopenhauer's, but he discusses feelings in a way that emphasizes intentionality, as Schopenhauer did not.

61 See Mitchell G. Ash, *Gestalt Psychology in German Culture 1890–1967: Holism and the Quest for Objectivity*, Cambridge UP, Cambridge, 1995.

62 Schuhmann, "Brentano's Impact," in *Cambridge Companion*, 280.
63 Brentano, *Psychology from an Empirical Standpoint*, ed. Oskar Kraus, Linda L. McAlister, intro. Peter Simons, trans. Antos C. Rancurello, D. B. Terrell, and Linda L. McAlister, Routledge, London, 1973, 1995, 20, 25.
64 See Peter Simons, "Bolzano, Brentano and Meinong: Three Austrian Realists," O'Hear, *German Philosophy since Kant*, 109–36.
65 Brentano, *Psychology*, 5.
66 Ibid., 9.
67 Ibid., 29. In English it can be easy to confuse presentations, ideas, and perceptions, as well as perceptions and observations.
68 Jacquette summarizes this in terms of the "object-directedness of the psychological." See Jacquette, "Introduction," *Cambridge Companion*, 5. In *Brentano's Mind* (Oxford Scholarship Online, 2017), Mark Textor argues against Brentano's view of intentionality and mental phenomena.
69 See plato.stanford.edu/entries/intentionality.
70 See Linda L. McAlister, "Brentano's Epistemology," in *The Cambridge Companion to Brentano*, 149–67.
71 See Lindenfeld, *The Transformation of Positivism*, 138.
72 J. N. Findley, cited in Fischer, "Franz Brentano's Philosophy of *Evidenz*," 31 and passim. See Lindenfeld, *The Transformation of Positivism* on the theory of objects: the problems that arose out of Brentano's thought about distinguishing between mental acts and the objects to which these acts refer.
73 Brentano, *Psychology*, 30–4.
74 Brentano recommended Freud to Theodor Gomperz as a translator for Mill. See William J. McGrath, *Freud's Discovery of Psychoanalysis: The Politics of Hysteria*, Cornell UP, Ithaca, 1986, 137. See also *The Letters of Sigmund Freud to Eduard Silberstein 1871–1881*, ed. Walter Boehlich, trans. Arnold J. Pomerans, Harvard UP, Cambridge, MA, 1990 and James R. Barclay, "Franz Brentano and Sigmund Freud. A Comparative Study in the Evolution of Psychological Thought," diss., University of Michigan, 1959. Freud seems to have believed that following Brentano in believing in God would require anti-scientific views that Brentano himself never advocated (McGrath, 116–19).
75 Brentano, *Psychology*, 105.
76 See Bruno Bettelheim, *Freud and Man's Soul*, Alfred A. Knopf, New York, 1983.
77 Jacquette, "Introduction," *Cambridge Companion*, 6.
78 Ibid., 18–19.
79 See John T. Blackmore, *Ernst Mach: His Work, Life, and Influence*, University of California Press, Berkeley, 1972, 3–5.
80 On Popper-Lynkeus, see Belke, *Die Sozialreformerischen Ideen von Josef Popper-Lynkeus* (1838–1921).

81 See Ernst Mach, *The Science of Mechanics: A Critical and Historical Account of Its Development*, trans. Thomas J. McCormack, Open Court, London, 1942. Here in 1883 he introduced the view that he developed more fully three years later. Mach published seven editions of his history of mechanics in his lifetime, the last of these in 1912.

82 His views seem to have taken mature form around 1860 (at the age of twenty-two), including his acceptance of Darwin's understanding of human beings and his resistance to atomic theory. See Blackmore, *Ernst Mach*, chapter 3.

83 Ernst Mach, *Contributions to the Analysis of Sensations*, trans. C. M. Williams, Open Court, Chicago, 1897, 19.

84 Ibid., 3. In a footnote (3–4), Mach explained this in a way that pointed ahead to the views of Freud a decade later: "in dreams the ego can be very distinct, doubled, or entirely wanting," while "the little habits that are unconsciously and involuntarily kept up for long periods of time … constitute the groundwork of the ego."

85 Ernst Mach, *The Analysis of Sensations and the Relation of the Physical to the Psychical*, trans. C. M. Williams, revision Sydney Waterlow, Dover, New York, 1959, 24–5. See Judith Ryan, *The Vanishing Subject: Early Psychology and Literary Modernism*, The University of Chicago Press, Chicago, 1991.

86 Mach, *Contributions*, 26. In the later edition, Mach includes a wording that Nietzsche would have enjoyed: "Personally, people know themselves very poorly." [Mach, *Analysis*, 4].

87 Blackmore, *Ernst Mach*, 164.

88 See Erik C. Banks, *Ernst Mach's World Elements: A Study in Natural Philosophy*, Kluwer Academic Publishers, London, 2003.

89 Thomas Szasz, Introduction to Mach, in Mach, *Analysis*, xi.

90 Ibid. Thomas S. Szasz was citing Philipp Frank.

91 See Erwin N. Hiebert, introduction, in Ernst Mach, *Knowledge and Error: Sketches on the Psychology of Inquiry*, ed. Erwin N. Hiebert, D. Riedel Publishing, Dordrecht, 1976, xiii.

92 Mach ended his career as a professor of philosophy at the University of Vienna (1895–1901), but it is sometimes forgotten that he developed his ideas while teaching in Prague and Graz.

93 Otto Weininger thought of this as the Jewish view, although none of these writers was Jewish. Weininger held out for an eighteenth-century view of the ego, as Freud did in a somewhat different way for the purposes of psychoanalysis. Both views are what I mean when I refer to the male ego. See Luft, *Eros and Inwardness* and Weininger's *Geschlecht und Charakter*, which was largely a rejection of Mach's view.

94 Mach, *Analysis*, 10.

95 The most continuous theme from Mach to the Vienna Circle was the effort to unify the sciences, especially the natural sciences.

96 See Tracie Matysik, *Reforming the Moral Subject*, Cornell UP, Ithaca, 2008.
97 Mach, *Analysis of Sensations*, 31 and 34.
98 On the various forms of Mach's influence, especially in the United States, see Gerald Holton, *Science and Anti-Science*, Harvard UP, Cambridge, 1993. See chapter 1, "Ernst Mach and the Fortunes of Positivism," 1–55.
99 Mach's work was enormously influential for Robert Musil, both in his approach to science and in his ironic attitude toward ideologies and the self. Musil wrote his dissertation on Mach as a student in philosophy and psychology (Robert Musil, *Beitrag zur Beurteilung der Lehren Machs*, diss., Berlin, 1908), but he was also studying at the time with one of Brentano's most influential students, Carl Stumpf, who was an experimentalist, as was Musil. See Luft, *Robert Musil and the Crisis of European Culture 1880–1942*, 78–88.
100 Janik and Toulmin, *Wittgenstein's Vienna* and Dominick LaCapra, "Reading Exemplars: *Wittgenstein's Vienna* and Wittgenstein's *Tractatus*," in *Rethinking Intellectual History: Texts Contexts Language*, Cornell UP, Ithaca, 1983, 84–117.
101 The late Wittgenstein of *The Philosophical Investigations* thought and wrote in new ways after he moved to England in 1929. See James C. Klagge, *Wittgenstein in Exile*, MIT Press, Cambridge, MA, 2011. Some philosophers have raised questions about the extent to which the contrast between early and late Wittgenstein should be emphasized: see Alice Crary and Rupert Read, *The New Wittgenstein*, Routledge, New York, 2000. I will not address issues of the late Wittgenstein here.
102 See Ray Monk, *The Duty of Genius*, The Free Press, New York, 1990. On the Wittgenstein family, see Alexander Waugh, *The House of Wittgenstein: A Family at War*, Doubleday, New York, 2008.
103 Janik and Toulmin were right to correct the parochial vision of Wittgenstein as a product of Cambridge and more or less the same as Russell, but off the mark in the way they tried to construct a single Viennese context with Kraus at the center—while bringing in European science and philosophy that would have been just as available to an Englishman as to an Austrian. Their emphasis on the importance of Schopenhauer was right. See Brian McGuinness, *Young Ludwig: Wittgenstein's Life, 1880–1921*, Clarendon Press, Oxford, 2005 (1988).
104 See W. W. Bartley, III, *Wittgenstein*, J.B. Lippincott Company, Philadelphia, 1973.
105 Henry Leroy Finch, *Wittgenstein—The Early Philosophy: An Exposition of the Tractatus*, Humanities Press, New York, 1971, 13–15. See Heinrich Hertz, *The Principles of Mechanics Presented in a New Form* (original English edition 1900), reprinted NY, 1956.
106 Finch, *Wittgenstein*, 17.
107 John Koethe, *The Continuity of Wittgenstein's Thought*, Cornell UP, Ithaca, 1996, x.
108 See David S. Luft, "Schopenhauer, Austria, and the Generation of 1905," in *Central European History*, in *Central European History*, March 1983, 53–75.

109 Wittgenstein does not seem to have read Bolzano when he wrote the *Tractatus*. See Michael Cohen, "Was Wittgenstein a Plagiarist?" *Philosophy,* Vol. 76, No. 297 (July 2001), 451–9. Cohen seriously entertains the claim that Wittgenstein plagiarized from Bolzano and rejects this idea.
110 Ludwig Wittgenstein, *Tractatus Logico-Philosophicus*, trans. C. K. Ogden, intro. Bertrand Russell, Routledge and Kegan Paul, New York, 1978 [original: 1922].
111 G. E. M. Anscombe, *An Introduction to Wittgenstein's Tractatus*, Harper and Row, New York, 1959, 19.
112 Wittgenstein, *Tractatus*, proposition 7.
113 See Finch, *Wittgenstein*, 15, citing Wittgenstein: "everything that we find out [about how the world may be represented] tells us something about the essence of the world."
114 See Wittgenstein, *Tractatus*, propositions 2.063–2.15.
115 Max Black, *A Companion to Wittgenstein's 'Tractatus,'* Cornell UP, Ithaca, 1964, 5. See Ludwig Wittgenstein, *Notebooks 1914–1916*, trans. G. E. M. Anscombe, Basil Blackwell, Oxford, 1961 (1969). Black's book is a wonderful introduction to reading the *Tractatus*.
116 Peter Simons, "Logical Atomism," in *The Cambridge History of Philosophy 1870–1945*, ed. Thomas Baldwin, Cambridge UP, Cambridge, 2003, 384.
117 On the interpretive issues raised by Wittgenstein's later work at Cambridge, see *The Textual Genesis of Wittgenstein's Philosophical Investigations*, ed. Nuno Venturinha, Routledge, New York, 2013. For other approaches to these questions, see Stanley Cavell, *Must We Mean What We Say? A Book of Essays*, Charles Scribner's Sons, New York, 1969.
118 The state of the art on this subject is Friedrich Stadler, *Studien zum Wiener Kreis: Ursprung, Entwicklung und Wirkung des Logischen Empiricismus im Kontext*, Suhrkamp Verlag, Frankfurt am Main, 1997.
119 On the relationship between Wiitgenstein and the ideas of the Vienna Circle, see Ludwig Wittgenstein and Friedrich Waismann, *The Voices of Wittgenstein: The Vienna Circle*, ed. Gordon Baker, trans. Gordon Baker et al., Routledge, London, 2003.
120 This group included Rudolf Carnap (the natural sciences), Philipp Frank (physics), and Herbert Feigl (philosophy). Other familiar figures were Kurt Gödel, Hans Hahn, Richard von Mises, Otto von Neurath, Friedrich Waismann, and Edgar Zilsel.
121 Friedrich Stadler, *Vom Positivismus zur "Wissenschaftlichen Weltauffassung": am Beispiel der Wirkungsgeschichte von Ernst Mach in Österreich von 1895 bis 1934*, Löcker Verlag, Munich, 1982, 135.
122 "The Manifesto of the Vienna Circle: The Scientific Conception of the World" (*Wissenschaftliche Weltauffasssung*), in Otto Neurath, *Empiricism and Sociology*,

ed. Marie Neurath and Robert S. Cohen, D. Reidel Publishing, Boston, 1973, 305. See Friedrich Stadler, *The Vienna Circle Studies in the Origins, Development, and Influence of Logical Empirical*, trans. Camilla Nielsen et al., Springer Verlag, Vienna, 2001.

123 Victor Kraft, *The Vienna Circle: The Origin of Neo-Positivism*, trans. Arthur Pap, Philosophical Library, New York, 11.

124 See Nancy Cartwright, Jordi Cat, Lola Fleck, and Thomas Uebel, *Otto Neurath: Philosophy between Science and Politics*, Cambridge UP, New York, 1996.

125 The Vienna Circle is sometimes associated with its more dogmatic figures such as Neurath and A. J. Ayer, whereas Stadler makes the group part of a broad tradition of sympathy for science.

126 See Richard von Mises, *Positivism*. Von Mises was part of the Vienna Circle and taught philosophy at both Prague and Harvard. He emphasized the centrality of language in science, and for him positivism is simply the extension of what we would regard as "a reasonable or judicious attitude in most situations of life" (1).

127 Edmund Husserl, "The Crisis of the Sciences," in *The Crisis of European Sciences and Transcendental Phenomenology: An Introduction to Phenomenological Philosophy*, trans. and intro. David Carr, Northwestern University Press, Evanston, 1970, 9.

128 Karl Popper's *Logik der Forschung* appeared at the end of 1934, and he developed his distinctive views largely in response to the Vienna Circle. Popper was one way the English-speaking world learned about the Vienna Circle, but his views were different from the logical positivists, especially from Neurath. His primary commitments were to science and philosophy, and he was resistant to dogmatism, close to the broad tradition of philosophy in Austria, but not really part of the Vienna Circle. See Malachi Haim Hacohen, *Karl Popper—The Formative Years, 1902–1945: Politics and Philosophy in Interwar Vienna*, Cambridge University Press, 2000.

129 In a similar though somewhat different way, I believe that Joseph Roth should be seen in the context of Galicia and thus as part of the story of German-speaking intellectual life in Poland.

130 Walter Weiss, "Thematisierung der 'Ordnung' in der österreichischen Literatur," in *Dauer im Wandel: Aspekte Österreichischer Kulturentwicklung*, ed. Walter Strolz, Herder &. Co., Vienna, 1975, 39.

131 Musil's notion of ethics is the opposite of this.

132 Musil, *The Man without Qualities*, 272–3. Walter Weiss argued that Ulrich, the protagonist of *The Man without Qualities*, represents in contrast to Arnheim "on the one hand the tradition of empirical as well as theological Austrian realism and, on the other hand, he points ahead to Wittgenstein, to anti-dogmatic scientific theory and the concept of an open society of Karl Popper." Weiss, "Zum deutschen in der österreichischen Literatur," 53–4.

133 See Karl Přibram, a social theorist from Bohemia, in *Conflicting Patterns of Thought*, Public Affairs Press, Washington, DC, 1949. See also Johnston's discussion of Přibram's use of this term and Přibram, 3: Of the leading patterns of thought in the West, only the nominalistic pattern has rejected the principle of the identity of thinking and being; "its adherents have insisted that human reasoning is governed by rules of its own and that, consequently, any attempt to grasp the order of the universe must proceed by way of assumptions and purely hypothetical concepts—whose validity cannot be postulated but whose usefulness must be demonstrated."

Chapter 4

1 See Ulrich Greiner, *Der Tod des Nachsommers*, Carl Hanser Verlag, Munich, 1979, 11.
2 Franz Blei, "Hermann Broch und seine Romantrilogie 'Die Schlafwandler,'" in *Zwischen Orpheus und Don Juan*, ed. Ernst Schönwiese, Stiasny Verlag, Graz, 1965, 88. See Ernst Schönwiese, *Literatur in Wien zwischen 1930 and 1980*, Amalthea Verlag, Vienna, 1980, 20, where Schönwiese cites Blei.
3 Klaus Zeyringer, *Österreichische Literatur seit 1945*, Haymon Verlag, Innsbruck, 2001, 27. The English translation is awkward but still very funny: *Germany Narrates: From Rainer Maria Rilke to Peter Handke*. Neither Rilke nor Handke was from Germany.
4 See Josef Nadler's *Literaturgeschichte Österreichs* of 1948 (Österreichischer Verlag für Belletristik und Wissenschaft, Linz) and Herbert Zeman, ed., *Literaturgeschichte Österreichs*, Akademische Druck- u. Verlagsanstalt, Graz, 1996. Zeman regards his collaborative volume as the fourth attempt at a comprehensive literary history of Austria—and as the first since Nadler. There is also a more recent history of Austrian literature: Klaus Zeyringer/Helmut Gollner, *Eine Literaturgeschichte Österreich seit 1650*, Studien Verlag, Vienna, 2012. For the history of Austrian Germanistik from 1848 to 1914, see Werner Michler, Wendelin Schmidt-Dengler, "Germanistik in Österreich: Neuere deutsche und österreichische Literatur," in *Geschichte der österreichischen Humanwissenschaften*, ed. Karl Acham, Passagen Verlag, Vienna, 2003, Vol. 5, 193–228.
5 I am not primarily concerned to distinguish what is Austrian from what is German, but to describe the intellectual tradition that depended on German within this space.
6 In "Das grosse Erbe: Die übernationale Struktur der österreichischen Dichtung," Ivar Ivask argued that Vienna was central to Austrian literature, but he did not return to this point when he characterized Kafka, Rilke, and Musil as the most

important Austrian writers of the twentieth century. See Otto Basil, Herbert Eisenreich, and Ivar Ivask, *Das Grosse Erbe: Aufsätze zur österreichischen Literatur*, Stiasny-Verlag, Graz, 1962, 5–59.

7   See David S. Luft, "Cultural Memory and Intellectual History: Locating Austrian Literature," *Studies in Twentieth and Twenty First Century Literature*, Vol. 31, No. 1 (Winter 2007), 30–51.

8   There was also a German theater in Prague.

9   Reinhard Urbach has emphasized the untranslatability of Austrian comedy and the degree to which it was aimed at a very specific audience. See Reinhard Urbach, *Die Wiener Komödie und Ihr Publikum: Stranitzky und die Folgen*, Jugend und Volk, Vienna, 1973. See also Katherine Arens, *Vienna's Dreams of Europe: Culture and Identity Beyond the Nation-State*, Bloomsbury, New York, 2015.

10 See Roger Bauer, *La réalité royaume de Dieu: Études sur l'originalté du théâtre viennois dans le première moitié du IXe siècle*, Max Hueber Verlag, Munich, 1965.

11 Johann Nestroy was the great extemporaneous genius in this comic tradition. His wit and comedy are difficult to reproduce—even for another actor, to say nothing of another language. And his work was not primarily literary, but often based on other writers and aimed at entertainment and at attacking a very specific suburban audience in Vienna.

12 Hugo von Hofmannsthal, "Address on Grillparzer," in *Hofmannsthal and the Austrian Idea: Selected Essays and Addresses, 1906–1927*, trans. and ed. David S. Luft, Purdue University Press, Lafayette, 2011, 143.

13 See Gerhard Scheit, *Franz Grillparzer mit Selbstzeugnissen und Bilddokumenten*, Rowohlt, Hamburg, 1989; Josef Nadler, *Franz Grillparzer*, Liechtenstein Verlag, Vaduz, 1948; and August Sauer, *Franz Grillparzer*, Metzlerschen Buchhandlung, Stuttgart, 1941.

14 See Eva Wagner, *An Analysis of Franz Grillparzer's Dramas: Fate, Guilt, and Tragedy*, The Edwin Mellen Press, Lewiston, N.Y., 1992 on the persistent importance of these themes in Grillparzer's plays and the controversies that have surrounded them. For an overview of Grillparzer's work, see Gunter Schäble, *Franz Grillparzer*, Friedrich Verlag, Hanover, 1971.

15 See Hofmannsthal's account of Grillparzer's place in the Austrian literary tradition: "Schiller's dramas still take place in all the dominant countries, Grillparzer's all really take place in Austria. The Greek dramas have their setting in nowhere; in them is his homeland in timelessly idealized costumes. Of Grillparzer's other plays, four are set in Bohemia and the hereditary lands, one in Spain, which in a certain sense belongs to Austrian history, one in Hungary." Hofmannsthal, "Grillparzer's Political Legacy," in *Hofmannsthal and the Austrian Idea*, 76.

16 For a recent analysis of Grillparzer's dramas, see Brigitte Prutti, *Grillparzers Welttheater; Modernität und Tradition*, Aisthesis Verlag, Bielefeld, 2013. Prutti

emphasizes the sheer variety of Grillparzer's themes and approaches and his continuing significance for modern theater beyond the traditional question of Austrian identity.

17 He began *Des Meeres und Liebe Wellen* [The Waves of the Ocean and of Love] in 1820, although it did not appear until a decade later.
18 Birthe Hoffmann, *Opfer der Humanität: Zur Anthropologie Franz Grillparzers*, Deutscher Universitätsverlag, Wiesbaden, 1999. See also Clifford Albrecht Bernd, "Austrian Playwright or Weimarian Classicist?" in *Aneignungen, Entfremdungen: The Austrian Playwright Franz Grillparzer (1791–1872)*, ed. Marianne Henn et al., Peter Lang, New York, 2007, 117; Bernd emphasizes Grillparzer's exclusive concentration on a single character and Grillparzer's ability to give us "insight into the manner in which we, too, act out our lives—often, as Ottokar did, without realizing it."
19 Ivar Ivask, Introduction to Franz Grillparzer, *The Poor Fiddler*, trans. Alexander and Elizabeth Henderson, Frederick Ungar, New York, 1967, 8. See Walter Naumann, *Franz Grillparzer: Das dichterische Werk*, 2nd edition, W. Kohlhammer Verlag, Stuttgart, 1967, 42–64.
20 See Dagmar C. G. Lorenz, *Grillparzer: Dichter des sozialen Konflikts*, Böhlau, Vienna, 1986 and Heinz Politzer, *Grillparzer oder Das abgründige Biedermeier*, Verlag Fritz Molden, Vienna, 1972.
21 Literature is tied to a place and a time and a language in ways that can make it difficult for readers from other cultures and periods to appreciate, and this is especially true of theater. This can be true even of the greatest writers such as Shakespeare; as a poet of the theater, Grillparzer is in some ways comparable to Shakespeare (especially in his historical dramas), but he has never been favored with a great translator into English, as Shakespeare was in German. Grillparzer's commitment to the classical culture of Greece is also distancing for our time. Even audiences from Germany can be mystified by the language of a Nestroy play, and it is difficult to imagine how to convey this way of speaking to an English-speaking reader.
22 In 1990 Günther Nenning presented Grillparzer somewhat provocatively as "the undiscovered hero of postmodernism." See Ian F. Roe, *Franz Grillparzer: A Century of Criticism*, Camden House, Columbia, South Carolina, 1995, 126.
23 Hofmannsthal, "Grillparzer's Political Legacy," in *Hugo von Hofmannsthal and the Austria Idea*, 73. This sense of reality is the theme of Hofmannsthal's account.
24 Ibid., 74. Grillparzer and Stifter are sometimes regarded as old-fashioned, but many of their themes were not: women, ethnic minorities, non-elites, and outsiders.
25 Roe, *Franz Grillparzer*, 5 and passim.
26 On Austrian literature, see Franz Grillparzer, *Sämtliche Werke: Ausgewählte Brief, Gespräche, Berichte*, Vol. 3, Carl Hanser, Munich, 1964, 809–11.

27 Roe, *Franz Grillparzer*, 18. Wiese's comment was from 1948.
28 Ferdinand Kürnberger, *Literarischen Herzensachen: Reflexionen und Kritiken*, Verlag von L. Rosner, Vienna, 1877, 284.
29 Franz Grillparzer, *Sämtliche Werke*: Erster Band: Gedichte, Epigramme, Dramen I, 504. See also Vol. III, *Studien und Aufsätze*, 284: "To hell with theories."
30 Friedrich Nietzsche, "David Strauss: the Confessor and the Writer," in *Untimely Meditations*, ed. Daniel Breazeale, trans. R. J. Hollingdale, Cambridge University Press, Cambridge, 1997, 20. Nietzsche admired Stifter as well.
31 Grillparzer, *Sämtliche Werke*, Vol. I, 500.
32 Ibid.
33 Stifter's *Indian Summer* "constitutes, along with Grillparzer's most important creations—among them his still unknown diaries, which are full of substance like a mine—the strongest gift of Austria to Germany." See Hofmannsthal, "Stifter's Indian Summer," in *Hugo von Hofmannsthal and the Austrian Idea*, 151.
34 The term "*novella*" was important in nineteenth-century German literature, although the distinction from the short story no longer seems so compelling today. The most sensible definition seems to be that a *novella* is a "medium-length story," but it is often most easily indicated by the author's decision to use that term. I will not place a major emphasis on this distinction, but it was important in the nineteenth century, and the work done in this genre was a highpoint of German literature. See Martin Swales, *The German Novelle*, Princeton University Press, Princeton, 1977, 3.
35 See Franz Grillparzer, *The Poor Fiddler*, trans. Alexander and Elizabeth Henderson, intro. Ivar Ivask, Frederick Ungar, New York, 1967. See Introduction, 5–25.
36 Cited by Ivar Ivask in his introduction to the novella, 20–1.
37 See Naumann, *Franz Grillparzer*, 111–28 and Hermann Bahr, *Österreichische Genius: Grillparzer—Stifter—Feuchtersleben*, Bellaria Verlag, Vienna, n.d.
38 Roy C. Cowen, "The History of a Neglected Masterpiece: *Der arme Spielmann*," in *Grillparzer's Der arme Spielmann: New Directions in Criticism*, ed. Clifford Albrecht Bernd, Camden House, Columbia, S. C., 1988, 9.
39 See Adalbert Stifter, *Sämtliche Erzählungen nach den Erstdrucken*, ed. Wolfgang Matz, Deutscher Taschenbuch Verlag, Munich, 2001 and Wolfgang Matz, *Adalbert Stifter oder Diese fürchterliche Wendung der Dinge: Biographie*, Carl Hanser Verlag, Munich, 1995. For comprehensive studies of Stifter in English, see Eric A. Blackall, *Adalbert Stifter, A Critical Study*, Cambridge University Press, Cambridge, 1948 and Martin and Erika Swales, *Adalbert Stifter: A Critical Study*, Cambridge University Press, Cambridge, 1984.
40 Moriz Enzinger, *Adalbert Stifters Studienjahre (1818–1830)*, Österreichische Verlagsanstalt, Innsbruck, 1950.
41 See William Johnston on Stifter's contribution to Josephinism and Reform Catholicism: "Stifter's conviction that Christian love provides the sole basis of social

good recalls Bolzano's ethic. For these Bohemian contemplatives, education must touch heart as well as head, an ideal that Thun tried to carry out at the Ministry of Education." See William Johnston, *The Austrian Mind: An Intellectual and Social History 1848–1938*, University of California Press, Berkeley, 1972, 279.

42 On Stifter's writing about the urban world of Vienna, see Vance Byrd, "The Politics of Commemoration in *Wien und die Wiener*" (1841–1844), *Journal of Austrian Studies*, Vol. 47, No. 1 (2014), 1–20.

43 Adalbert Stifter, *Bunte Steine, Späte Erzählungen*, ed. Max Stefel, Adam Kraft Verlag, Augsburg, 1960, 6.

44 See Greiner, "Denken wie der Wald," 61.

45 Helena Ragg-Kirby, *Adalbert Stifter's Late Prose: The Mania for Moderation*, Camden House, Rochester, N.Y., 2000, 11. See also Martin Tielke, *Sanftes Gesetz und historische Notwendigkeit: Adalbert Stifter zwischen Restauration und Revolution* and Sebald's thoughtful, though demanding, essay on Stifter in W. G. Sebald, *Die Beschreibung des Unglücks: Zur österreichischen Literatur von Stifter bis Handke*, Residenz Verlag, Salzburg, 1985.

46 See Walter Weiss, "Stifters Reduktion," in *Adalbert Stifter und die Krise der Mitteleuropäische Literatur: Ein italienisch-österreichisches Colloquium*, ed. Paolo Chiarini, Bulzoni Editore, Rome, 1987, 3.

47 Hermann Broch, *Hofmannsthal and His Time*, ed. and trans. Michael Steinberg, The University of Chicago Press, Chicago, 1984, 127.

48 See Adalbert Stifter, *Die Mappe meines Urgrossvaters: Letzte Fassung*, Nachwort Alexaner Stillmark, Manese Verlag, Zurich, 1997.

49 Stifter, "Abdias" in *Erzählungen*, 403. The English translation does not seem to include these reflections of an African on realizing his dream of going to Europe. See "Abdias," in Adalbert Stifter, *Brigitta*, trans. Helen Watabe-O'Kelly, Angel Books, London, 1990, 21–95.

50 Sebald, "Bis an den Rand der Natur: Versuch über Stifter," in *Die Beschreibung des Unglücks*, 24.

51 This also includes his own *Witiko*. The importance of calm in Stifter's work recalls Grillparzer's emphasis on composure. Grillparzer aimed for a quality that was prominent in Hofmannsthal's understanding of the Austrian tradition: "Grillparzer holds mind and feeling together: when they are in harmony, the rare times, he calls this composure, and he knows no higher concept than this." Hofmannsthal, "Address on Grillparzer," in *Hofmannsthal and the Austrian Idea*, 142.

52 Schorske's discussion of *Indian Summer* was the one point in his book when he reached back before the liberal era, writing an important reading of Stifter's best known novel.

53 In *Adalbert Stifter's Late Prose: The Mania for Moderation*, Ragg-Kirby emphasizes the role of collecting in Stifter's *Nachsommer*, especially its contribution to the mood of calm.

54 Ulrich Greiner, "Denken wie der Wald," *Die Zeit*, Nr. 43, 20.Oktober 2005, 60.
55 Quoted by Fritz Krökel in the Nachwort to *Witiko*, Deutscher Taschenbuch Verlag, Munich, 1986, 885.
56 Swales and Swales, *Adalbert Stifter*, 29.
57 Friedrich Nietzsche, "On the uses and disadvantages of history for life," *Meditations,* 91.
58 See Jethro Bithell, *Modern German Literature 1880–1950*, Meuthuen & Co., London, 1939, 74–86 and passim. Terms such as "naturalism," "realism," and "impressionism" can be vague, inadequate, and overlapping; indeed, these terms often say as much about the commentators as about the writers under review. Bithell emphasizes the similarities between naturalism and decadence, and he includes Saar with decadence. At a time when these terms seemed to matter to critics, Bithell conceded that symbolism, neo-romanticism, and impressionism amounted to virtually the same thing—which was not too far from decadence. It is difficult to be sure which allusions and assumptions commentators have in mind when they use these terms. Strangely, Nietzsche dominates Bithell's chapter on Bahr to Dehmel. The turn from realism to a variety of modernisms concentrated on the means of representation rather than on what was represented, as Hermann Broch emphasized.
59 This is Schorske's discrimination of generations within the liberal era.
60 We might almost say that it is a parlor game among people in this field to debate whether a particular intellectual is German or Jewish or liberal.
61 Broch, *Hugo von Hofmannsthal and His Time*.
62 Marie von Ebner-Eschenbach's father was Count Dubsky, an influential Moravian nobleman, who was married to a number of women, many of whom died in childbirth, including Marie's mother.
63 See *Briefwechsel zwischen Ferdinand von Saar und Maria von Ebner-Eschenbach*, ed. Heinz Kindermann, Wiener Bibliophilen-Gesellschaft, Vienna, 1957.
64 Anzengruber's *Der Pfarrer von Kirchfeld* and Rosegger's *Als ich noch der Waldbauernbub war* are both very spiritual books, which are critical of a rigid, controlling Catholicism.
65 On the writers of the high liberal era, see Karlheinz Rossbacher, *Literatur und Liberalismus: Zur Kultur der Ringstrassenzeit in Wien*, J & V, Salzburg, 1992.
66 Saar's view of history sometimes echoes Schopenhauer, whom he admired. See *Das Erzählerische Werk*, Amandus-Verlag, Vienna, 1959, Vol. I, 241. Here the protagonist in "Der Exzellenzherr" expresses his love for the study of history "in which the unavoidable necessity of everything that happened and happens, as well as the nothingness and dreamlike quality of human existence, comes to consciousness."
67 Daniela Strigl, *Berühmt sein ist nichts: Marie von Ebner-Eschenbach: Eine Biographie*, Residenz Verlag, Vienna, 2016, 13. It is understandable that

commentators have thought of her over the past century as old-fashioned, although Strigl and others have argued for a more modern reading.

68 Schnitzler is best known for his subtle portrayal of psychological and sexual themes in his plays—such as *Reigen, Lieutenant Gustl,* and *Professor Bernhardi*—but also for his novel, *Der Weg ins Freie,* where he portrayed the social world of young Jewish men and women around the turn of the century. See Reinhard Urbach, *Arthur Schnitzler,* trans. Donald Daviau, Frederick Ungar, New York, 1973. On Hofmannsthal as a young man, see Gotthart Wunberg, *Der frühe Hofmannsthal: Schizophrenie als dichterische Struktur,* Kohlhammer Verlag, Stuttgart, 1965.

69 On Jews in this period, see Beller, *Vienna and the Jews 1867–1938,* and Le Rider, *Modernity and Crises of Identity.*

70 On Schnitzler's later work, see Felix W. Tweraser, *Political Dimensions of Arthur Schnitzler's Late Fiction,* Camden House, Columbia, S. C., 1998. On Hofmannsthal's essays after 1906, see *Hugo von Hofmannsthal and the Austrian Idea.*

71 Leopold von Andrian *Der Garten der Erkenntnis,* S. Fischer Verlag, Frankfurt am Main, 1970.

72 Letter from Saar to Andrian in Andrian, *Der Garten der Erkenntnis,* 66. Saar would not have had such difficulties with Schnitzler.

73 It is fitting that Andrian should later have become a diplomat for the Habsburg Monarchy. See William D. Godsey, Jr., *Aristocratic Redoubt: The Austro-Hungarian Foreign Service on the Eve of the First World War,* Purdue University Press, West Lafayette, 1999.

74 Young Vienna introduced a different attitude toward literature before what is usually called "modernism" in English literature.

75 See Judith Ryan, *The Vanishing Subject: Early Psychology and Literary Modernism,* The University of Chicago Press, Chicago, 1991. Ryan notes some of Bahr's most important articles (20): "The New Psychology" (1890), "Beyond Naturalism" (1891), "The Unsalvageable Self" (1904), "Impressionism" (1904). See Hermann Bahr, *Zur Überwindung des Naturalismus: Theoretische Schriften 1887–1904,* ed. Gotthart Wunberg, Kohlhammer Verlag, Stuttgart, 1968. Bahr was important as a public figure and an advocate for the ideas of the avant garde. See Donald G. Daviau, *Hermann Bahr,* Twayne Publishers, Boston, 1985.

76 For a recent discussion of modernism in the Habsburg Monarchy, see Scott Spector, "The Habsburg Empire" in *The Cambridge Companion to European Modernism,* ed. Pericles Lewis, 2011, chapter 4. See also Judith Ryan, *Rilke, Modernism, and the Poetic Tradition,* Cambridge University Press, Cambridge, 1999.

77 These novels are grounded in irony, which provides a way both to accept tradition and to overcome it—much like Musil's attitude toward the ego. Marjorie Perloff has recently written about "Austro-modernism," although her framework and approach are different from mine. See *The Edge of Irony: Modernism in the Shadow*

of the Habsburg Empire, The University of Chicago Press, Chicago, 2016. Perloff emphasizes the Monarchy as a whole, the aftermath of the First World War, and the contributions of Jewish writers.

78 Arthur Schopenhauer, "On Some Forms of Literature," in *The Art of Literature*, trans. T. Bailey Saunders, Macmillan, New York, 1900, 57.
79 Kassner was himself a slightly older figure of this generation.
80 See Luft, "Schopenhauer, Austria, and the Generation of 1905," in *Central European History*, March 1983, 53–75.
81 Nietzsche's impact on young minds in Central Europe around 1900 was nearly as catastrophic as his own vision of the death of God. But it was also inspiring and productive in a way that was quite different from the 1890s.
82 Nietzsche, *Schopenhauer as Educator*, 11. Nietzsche cites Emerson on the dismantling of Western culture and its conventions. *"A new degree of culture would instantly revolutionize the entire system of human pursuits."* See Nietzsche, *Schopenhauer as Educator*, 109.
83 He was born in Jačin, near Prague, but he spent most of his life in Vienna. Like Wittgenstein and Broch, Kraus came from a wealthy industrial family,
84 One of his most noteworthy achievements was to revive the work of Nestroy; Kraus and Nestroy shared the radical capacity for wit and criticism.
85 Karl Kraus, *The Last Days of Mankind: The Complete Text*, trans. Fred Bridgman and Edward Timms, Yale University Press, New Haven, 2015.
86 *The Kraus Project: Essays by Karl Kraus*, trans. and annotated Jonathan Franzen, assisted by Paul Reitter and Daniel Kehlmann, Farrar, Straus and Giroux, New York, 2013, 3–4. It takes a team of outstanding writers to make Kraus seem readable and contemporary in English.
87 See David S. Luft, *Eros and Inwardness in Vienna: Weininger, Musil, Doderer*, University of Chicago Press, Chicago, 2003.
88 Robert Musil, *Young Törless*, trans. Eithne Wilkins and Ernst Kaiser, in *Robert Musil: Selected Writings*, ed. Burton Pike, Continuum, New York, 1986, 2.
89 The fruitfulness of this period is evident in the number of important figures I will not discuss here—from Stefan and Arnold Zweig to Franz Werfel, from Rudolf Kassner to Georg Trakl and Alfred Kubin.
90 Robert Musil, *The Man without Qualities*, trans. Eithne Wilkins and Ernst Kaiser, Martin Secker and Warburg Ltd, London, 1954, Vol. I, chapter 8, 34. See *Robert Musil and the Crisis of European Culture: 1880–1942*, University of California Press, Berkeley, 1980.
91 Musil, *The Man without Qualities*, Knopf, Vol. I, chapter 109, 575–7.
92 He was interested in ethical experiences, experiences of feeling. This was already apparent in his early fiction: *Young Törless* and *Vereinigungen*.
93 Musil, "Political Confessions of a Young Man," in *Precision and Soul*, 33–4.

94 Musil, "The German as Symptom," in *Precision and Soul*, 150.
95 Ibid.
96 Musil, "The Religious Spirit, Modernism, and Metaphysics," in *Precision and Soul*, 22.
97 Musil, "Moral Fruitfulness," in *Precision and Soul*, 39.
98 Musil, *The Man without Qualities*, trans. Sophie Wilkins, 271.
99 Ibid., 271.
100 Ludwig Wittgenstein, *Tractatus Logico-Philosophicus*, trans. C. K. Ogden, intro. Bertrand Russell, Routledge and Kegan Paul, New York, 1978 [original: 1922], proposition 6.421.
101 Musil, "Sketch of What the Writer Knows," in *Precision and Soul*, 64.
102 Musil, "Mind and Experience," in *Precision and Soul*, 149.
103 Ibid., 147.
104 Musil, "Commentary on a Metapsychics," *Precision and Soul*, 56. Musil's *The Man without Qualities* might be seen as a literary exploration of Mach's advice that the ego must be given up, even that the male ego must be given up. Musil was well beyond the liberal ego—to the point of satire and reduction. He had moved past Freud's reactions to this as well—again in the playful way of satire. Kafka was working in the same vineyard.
105 Broch's *Sleepwalkers* was itself an account of the decline of values in the modern world, which was focused on the importance of the ethical.
106 Broch, *Hofmannsthal and His Time*, 96. He contrasts Hofmannsthal's concern with "ethicality" to Rilke's emphasis on "sacredness."
107 Ibid., 172. Broch calls the "Chandos Letter" Hofmannsthal's "break with aestheticism." This work of fiction portrays the loss of connection between the self and the external world, the loss of the confidence to name. According to Broch the young Hofmannsthal was able to "achieve complete identification with the object" (119), that is, the union of the ego and the world.
108 Ibid., 97.
109 Broch, *Hofmannsthal and His Time*, 27, citing Broch, Letter to Aldous Huxley, May 10, 1945 in *Briefe II*, 449ff.
110 Hofmannsthal, "The Written Word as the Spiritual Space of the Nation," *Hugo von Hofmannsthal and the Austrian Idea*, 160–1.
111 Writing in 1927, Hofmannsthal used the term "conservative revolution" in this essay; he seemed to be calling for a return to the Renaissance and Reformation, before the separation of Austria from the rest of German history, that is, before the division between Protestants and Catholics.
112 *The Sleepwalkers* is an amazing book, an intellectual and social history of Germany in the nineteenth and twentieth centuries that describes all social strata and analyzes the disintegration of values in modern culture. Broch took Germany as

his model in *The Sleepwalkers* as Musil did in his *The German as Symptom*, but both were aiming at an understanding of the modern world, whether in Broch's value-theory or in Musil's portrayal of Austria as the most modern state of all.

113 Hannah Arendt, "Einleitung," in *Dichten und Erkennen*, Vol. 6 of Broch's *Gesammelte Werke*, 5.

114 Theodore Ziolkowski calls Broch's book on Hofmannsthal "a symbolic autobiography." Theodore Ziolkowski, *Hermann Broch*, Columbia University Press, New York, 1964, 4. See also Broch on Virgil: Hermann Broch, *The Death of Virgil*, trans. Jean Starr Untermeyer, Random House, New York, 1945 [1972]. On Broch's life and work, see *A Companion to the Works of Hermann Broch*, ed. Graham Bartram et al., Camden House, Rochester, NY, 2019.

115 Broch emphasized that there was no longer a morality or great conceptual structure to rely on. He adapted his theory of the specialization of values from Hofmannsthal, and Weininger had a great impact on Broch. Weininger demolished the inherited conception of God as a man who created the world and called for a new spirituality.

116 See Manfred Durzak, *Hermann Broch*, J.B. Metzlerische Verlagsbuchhandlung, Stuttgart, 1967; Paul Michael Lützeler, *Hermann Broch: Eine Biographie*, Suhrkamp Verlag, Frankfurt am Main, 1986; and Donald L. Wallace, *Embracing Democracy: Hermann Broch, Politics and Exile, 1918–1951*, Peter Lang, Oxford, 2014. Lützeler calls Broch "to a certain extent a philosopher who strayed into literature" (*Hermann Broch*, 111).

117 Broch, *Hofmannsthal and His Time*, 28.

118 See Robert Musil, "Address at the Memorial Service for Rilke in Berlin," in *Precision and Soul*, 248, 243, 238.

119 Rainer Maria Rilke, *The Notebooks of Malte Laurids Brigge*, trans. Burton Pike, Dalkey Archive Press, Champaign, 2009.

120 *Rilke's Book of Hours: Love Poems to God*, trans. Anita Barrows and Joanna Macy, Riverhead Books, New York, 1997, 122.

121 See Rilke, *The Notebooks*, 5: "the desire to have a death of one's own is becoming ever rarer. In a short while it will be just as rare as a life of one's own." Or, "one dies one of the deaths employed by the institution" (6). Some lines might have been written by Kafka: "There are people who wear a face for years, of course it wears out, gets dirty, cracks in the folds, stretches like a glove one has worn on a journey" (3).

122 See Frank Wood, *Rainer Maria Rilke*, University of Minnesota Press, Minneapolis, 1958, 21. Wood cites Rilke's comment on moving beyond stereotypes and clichés: "And this is called a dog and that is called house/and here it begins and there it ends."

123 *Rilke's Book of Hours*, 58.

124 Rilke, *The Notebooks*, 13–14.
125 Ibid., 15–16. He was conscious of how long it took to ripen into a poet: 13: "One should hold off and gather sense and sweetness a whole life long, a long life if possible, and then, right at the end, one could perhaps write ten lines that are good."
126 Ibid., 17.
127 Ibid., 38: "it is not impossible to see everything differently and still go on living …. I still have not become accustomed to this world, which to me seems good. What should I do in another one?"
128 Jorge Borges suggests that Kafka's gift for inventing intolerable situations is the reason for "the primacy of his stories over his novels." As cited in Stanley Corngold, *The Commentator's Despair: The Interpretation of Kafka's Metamorphosis*, Kennikat Press, Port Washington, NY, 1973, 87. These intolerable situations also require the protagonist to justify himself.
129 Broch, *Briefe von 1929: bis 1951*, Rhein Verlag, Zürich, 1957, 374.
130 Wilhelm Emrich, *Franz Kafka: A Critical Study of His Writings*, trans. Sheema Zeben Buehne, Frederick Ungar, New York, 1968, 8, 11–12.
131 Benno Wagner, "No One Indicates the Direction," in *Kafka's Selected Short Stories*, trans. and ed. Stanley Corngold, W. W. Norton, New York, 2007, 302.
132 "On the Tram," 34 of *The Penal Colony: Short Stories and Short Pieces*, trans. Willa and Edwin Muir, Schocken Book, New York, 1977, 35–6.
133 Kafka, "Clothes," in *The Penal Colony*, 36.
134 Kafka, "The Sudden Walk," *The Penal Colony*, 27–8. On Kafka's stories and short pieces, see Emrich, *Franz Kafka*.
135 The year 1912 was the turning point for Kafka as a writer—that is, *The Judgment*, *Penal Colony*, and *The Metamorphosis*.
136 Peter Gay, *Modernism: The Lure of Heresy: From Baudelaire to Beckett and Beyond*, W. W. Norton, New York, 2008, 219.
137 Rilke, *Notebooks*, 1912, 276.
138 Heinz Politzer, *Franz Kafka: Parable and Paradox*, Cornell University Press, Ithaca, 1962.
139 *The Diaries of Franz Kafka: 1910–1913*, ed. Max Brod, trans. Joseph Kresh, Schocken Books, New York, 1948, 26.

Chapter 5

1 The conception of intellectual history as a field developed largely out of the histories of Germany and France—and out of the Anglo-American tradition—and it was aimed primarily at the social sciences. The degree to which Austrian thought

does not fit these preconceptions can be frustrating. The difficulty of locating Austria in the field of modern European intellectual history is apparent in the absorption of Austria into Germany in many of the standard accounts of twentieth-century European intellectual history. See, for example, H. Stuart Hughes, *Consciousness and Society*, Knopf, New York, 1958. On modern understandings of social science, see also Geoffrey Hawthorn, "Sociology and the Idea of Social Science," in *The Cambridge History of Philosophy 1870–1945*, ed. Thomas Baldwin, Cambridge University Press, Cambridge, 2003, 245–52.

2   For a thoughtful discussion of the variety and history of such umbrella terms, see "Introduction: Writing the History of Social Science," in *The Cambridge History of Science*, Volume 7: *The Modern Social Sciences*, ed. Theodore M. Porter and Dorothy Ross, Cambridge University Press, Cambridge, 2003, 1–10. Porter and Ross are attracted to the term "human sciences" or "*sciences humaines*," but settle on the modern English usage of "social sciences." They also note that it is the psychologists who have most favored the term "human sciences," which seems appropriate to a discussion that emphasizes economics and psychoanalysis. "The human sciences" was a favored term around 1950 as the period of this book came to an end. See Karl Acham, ed., *Geschichte der österreichischen Humanwissenschaften*, Passagen Verlag, Vienna, 2003, 6 volumes.

3   Austrian intellectuals were not strongly oriented to historical disciplines in the way that many German intellectuals were: they were not only resistant to Hegel, but they did not for the most part think in terms of objective mind in Wilhelm Dilthey's sense either.

4   John Boyer emphasizes the "long-term deficit in political theory" in the Austrian tradition, whether Liberal or Catholic. Boyer, *Political Radicalism in Late Imperial Vienna*, 6.

5   These are the two fields of Austrian social science that had the broadest impact on Western ideas. The degree to which knowledge about Austrian thought has been narrowly compartmentalized by fields is suggested by the title of a book that appeared not long ago: *Modern Applications of Austrian Thought*, ed. Jürgen G. Backhaus, Routledge, London, 2005. Despite the title, the book deals exclusively with economics.

6   The human sciences were not regarded as a coherent field in nineteenth-century Austria; indeed, the principal attempt to develop such a notion was conceived in the context of twentieth-century transatlantic studies. See Christian Fleck, *A Transatlantic History of the Social Sciences: Robber Barons, the Third Reich and the Invention of Empirical Social Research*, trans. Hella Beister, Bloomsbury Academic, New York, 2011.

7   Keith Tribe, *Strategies of Economic Order: German Economic Discourse, 1750–1950*, Cambridge University Press, New York, 1995, 3. Tribe's essays in this volume do not

discuss the German historical school, Austrian economics, or the social question that concerned Lorenz von Stein and Karl Marx.
8   See *Universität – Forschung – Lehre: Themen und Perspektiven im langen 20. Jahrhundert, 650 Jahre Universität Wien*, Vol. 1, Vienna University Press, Vienna, 2015. This volume concentrates, as the title suggests, on the twentieth century, and Thomas König's article on the social sciences is strongly oriented toward contemporary thought.
9   The Latin *cameralia* was the word for income from the crown domains and other resources. See Stollberg-Rilinger, *Maria Theresia*, 187.
10 On the role of neo-stoicism in the development of the early modern state, see Gerhard Oestreich, *Neostoicism and the Early Modern State*, trans. David McLintock, Cambridge University Press, Cambridge, 1982.
11 Albion Small, *The Cameralists: The Pioneers of German Social Policy*, The University of Chicago Press, Chicago, 1909, 481–596. Another key figure in the development of the field was Johann Heinrich Gottlob von Justi (1717–1771), who also worked for a time in Vienna, but is associated mainly with Leipzig and Berlin. See Small, 285–480. "Cameralism" is often understood broadly to refer to all public policy in German-speaking universities well into the nineteenth century. Keith Tribe characterizes it as a search for rationality and economic order. See Tribe, *Strategies of Economic Order*, 8–31. On Justi's role in the modernization of the Austrian state, see Adam Ulrich, *The Political Economy of J. H. G. Justi*, Peter Lang, Bern, 2006, 26–39.
12 On the history of "practical reasoning," see David F. Lindenfeld, *The Practical Imagination: The German Sciences of State in the Nineteenth Century*, The University of Chicago Press, Chicago, 1997, especially 1. It is helpful to bear in mind that practical reason is the opposite of theory.
13 Hanisch, *Der lange Schatten des Staates*. Hanisch argues "that Austria developed an especially strong state bureaucratic tradition, that modernizations frequently went out from above, that civil society could never quite free itself from the state."
14 Fritz Ringer does not have much to say about cameralism, the German historical school, or academic life in Austria, and his main argument is aimed at a phenomenon that was never dominant in Austria in the way it was in Germany. Austrian universities cultivated a very different style from the mandarin resistance to modernity described in *The Decline of the German Mandarins: The German Academic Community 1890–1933*, Harvard University Press, Cambridge, MA, 1969. Ringer's argument is focused on the imperial German academic community after 1890. On the centrality of sociology to this argument, see 162. "Modern German sociology was the true child of mandarin modernism …. It reflected the mandarins' characteristically pessimistic attitude toward modern social conditions." He is thinking here of Ferdinand von Tönnies, Georg Simmel, and Max Weber.

15 *Vom besten Staate* has now been translated into English. Bolzano outlines his understanding of reform and social change at the outset. See Bolzano, "On the Best State," 233–357.
16 Once the Holy Roman Empire had been abolished by Napoleon, Austrian cameralism diverged even more from other German states than it had before.
17 On the strong sense of the historicity of economic forms in German economics, see David Lindenfeld, "Grand Historical Narrative or Intellectual Strategy," in *The Historicity of Economics: Continuities and Discontinuities of Historical Thought in 19th and 20th Century Economics*, Springer Verlag, Berlin, 2002, 56–77.
18 Count Thun and Freiherr von Bruck (a key figure in the development of economic communities in Central Europe) brought Stein to Vienna.
19 Lindenfeld, *The Practical Imagination*, 204. Between 1850 and 1865, the "sciences which dealt with the state proper began to drift away from economics and statistics" (Lindenfeld, 197). What gradually emerged was a bifurcation into the social sciences (including economics and history) and the development of legal positivism, both civil law and administrative law (Lindenfeld, 204).
20 Ibid., 185.
21 Ibid., 193.
22 See Othmar Spann, *The History of Economics*, trans. Eden and Cedar Paul, W. W. Norton, New York, 1930, 278. This is a surprisingly readable account of the history of economics (from the immediate postwar era), where he notes that the existence of "a neo-liberal trend" was an indication that economics was "still talking the language of the eighteenth century."
23 Hans Kelsen, *A New Science of Politics*, ed. Eckhart Arnold, ontos verlag, Lancaster, 2004. See 11–15: Kelsen regarded himself as "a typical representative of positivism" within political science, and he defined positivism as "the principle of truthfully describing reality and explaining it on a strictly empirical basis, without having recourse to theology or any other metaphysical speculation." Spann adopted a "universalistic" approach to political theory that was directed against liberal individualism.
24 See Janek Wassermann, *Black Vienna; The Radical Right in the Red City, 1918–1938*, Cornell University Press, Ithaca, 2014.
25 On the Second and a Half International, see Julius Braunthal, *History of the International 1864–1914*, trans. Henry Collins and Kenneth Mitchell, Thomas Nelson and Sons, London, 1967–1980, 3 volumes.
26 See Rabinbach, *The Crisis of Austrian Socialism*, 7: "in the period after World War I, Austrian Socialism retreated from the contest for state power by building a political and cultural bastion in Red Vienna."
27 Otto Bauer, *The Question of Nationalities and Social Democracy*, original German in 1924, trans. Joseph O'Donnell, University of Minnesota Press, Minneapolis,

2000. A prominent idea that grew out of the Austrian experience was the notion of "nonterritorial national autonomy" (xxv).

28 See Ilona Duczynska, *Workers in Arms: The Austrian Schutzbund and the Civil War of 1934*, intro E. J. Hobsbawm, Monthly Review Press, New York, 1978. Duczynska emphasizes the confusion and uncertainty of the Socialist leadership.

29 See Rabinbach, *The Crisis of Austrian Socialism* and Norbert Leser, *Zwischen Reformismus und Bolschewismus: Der Astromarxismus als Theorie und Praxis*, Europa Verlag, Vienna, 1968. After emphasizing the vagueness and imprecision of discussions of Austromarxism, Helmut Gruber recommends using the word in two different senses: to refer to "a small group of Marxist theoreticians and intellectuals active in the decade before the war" or to refer to "the SDAP oligarchy of doers and reformers during the First Republic." And he rejects the view that there was any clear body of theory that united these two historical realities. See Gruber, *Red Vienna*, 30.

30 Both Left and Right wanted a stronger state and a more coherent sense of society than capitalism was able to provide.

31 See Klemens von Klemperer, *Ignaz Seipel: Christian Statesman in a Time of Crisis*, Princeton University Press, Princeton, 1972.

32 See Erich Voegelin, *Der autoriäre Staat: Ein Versuch über das österreichische Staatsproblem*, Verlag von Julius Springer, Vienna, 1936.

33 Marie Jahoda and Hans Zeisl, *Die Arbeitslosen von Marienthal*, S. Hirzel, Leipzig, 1933. Lazarsfeld is sometimes given as co-author with Marie Jahoda and Hans Zeisel. See also Christian Fleck, *Rund um "Marienthal": Von den Anfängen der Soziologie in Österreich bis zu ihrer Vertreibung* and the review by Mitchell G. Ash in *Contemporary Sociology*, July 1, 1992, Vol. 21, No. 4 (1990), 547–54.

34 *Paul F. Lazarsfeld: An Empirical Theory of Social Action: Collected Writings*, ed. Christian Fleck and Nico Stehr, trans. Hella Beister, The Bardwell Press, Oxford, 2011.

35 Paul F. Lazarsfeld, "The Sociology of Empirical Social Research," *American Sociological Review*, Vol. 27, No. 6 (December 1962).

36 See Bruce Caldwell, *Hayek's Challenge: An Intellectual Biography of F. A. Hayek*, University of Chicago Press, Chicago, 2004, 13. Caldwell's book is an excellent account of this whole tradition, including Menger.

37 In German-speaking universities, textbooks were written by young scholars.

38 The marginal theory of value asks about the value for the consumer of the next unit of a good rather than emphasizing labor or the other factors that go into the creation of a good. Neoclassical economics looks to formalize the mathematical regularities of marginal value.

39 Carl Menger, *Problems of Economics and Sociology (Untersuchungen über die Methode der Socialwissenschaften und der Politischen Oekonomie insbesondere)*, ed. Louis Schneider, trans. Francis J. Nock, University of Illinois Press, Urbana, 1963.

40 Menger argued for a different kind of economics from what the Germans had been doing in the nineteenth century; his work was more conceptual and abstract—and more methodologically self-conscious—but not notably mathematical. Although he contributed to the theory of marginal utility as it developed in the Austrian tradition, this was not his most important contribution and he did not emphasize it in his work. The other distinctive aspect of Menger's thinking, subjectivism, was also not entirely original in relation to the German historical school.

    On the influence of German economics on Menger's work, see Erich W. Streissler, "The Influence of German Economics on Menger and Marshall," in *Carl Menger and His Legacy in Economics*, ed. Bruce J. Caldwell, Duke University Press, Durham, 1990. On Menger's links to cameralism, see another essay in the same volume: Paul Silverman, "The Cameralist Roots of Menger's Achievement," 69–91. See also Allen Oakley, *The Foundations of Austrian Economics from Menger to Mises: A Critico-Historical Retrospective of Subjectivism*, Edward Algar, Cheltenham, 1997 on the importance of subjectivism rather than the free market as the key to Austrian Economics.

41 Unintended results are not usually emphasized by utopians, rationalists, and builders of models. Here Menger was making a point not about methodological individualism but about what can be known (or controlled). In this Menger was close to Burke and to the founders of the German historical school. See Caldwell's cautions about the term "methodological individualism" in Caldwell, *Hayek's Challenge*, Appendix B, where he recommends that we just stop using this vague term to describe Hayek's ideas. See also Barry Smith, "Austrian Economics and Austrian Philosophy," in *Austrian Economics: Historical and Philosophical Background*, ed. Wolfgang Grassl and Barry Smith, New York University Press, Washington Square, New York, 1986, 2–3. Smith emphasizes two distinctive qualities of Austrian economics: "the methodological and ontological centrality of the economic agent" and the "proposition that an economy presupposes consciousness."

42 Caldwell, *Hayek's Challenge*, 32. See 25: Caldwell explains that in this context "subjectivism" means "that *the subjective valuations placed by individuals on things that they believe will satisfy their needs are the origin of all economic activity.* Menger's commitment to subjectivism is clear from the opening chapter of *The Principles*, where he offers his definition of a good. Useful things are those things that are capable of being brought into a relation with those human needs that they can serve to satisfy …. Without people who (subjectively) evaluate the ability of goods to satisfy their own (subjectively) perceived needs, there literally would be no goods."

43 The book is in many respects dated, to the extent that few would disagree with its basic point: the value of distinguishing among economic theory, economic history, and economic policy.

44　As Musil pointed out, his distinction was not new with him, but only the ugly words. See Musil, "Sketch of What the Writer Knows," in *Precision and Soul*, 61–5.
45　Despite her sympathy for the Austrian School, Karen Vaughn argues "that there really is as yet no 'Austrian economics'" that is distinct from the neo-classical paradigm. Karen I. Vaughn, *Austrian Economics in America: The Migration of a Tradition*, Cambridge University Press, Cambridge, 1994, x. The title points to one of the ironies of this tradition: that Austrian Economics became more influential after it moved to the United States—and became American economics, as it were. See Vaughn's excellent article on knowledge and politics as the keys to Menger and Hayek's contributions. "The Mengerian Roots of the Austrian Revival," in Caldwell, ed., *Carl Menger and His Legacy*, 379–407.
46　Caldwell, *Hayek's Challenge*, 82.
47　We may say that this is the human being portrayed by the modernist novelists in Austria. Menger was concerned not just with subjectivity but with ontology, that is, with what the world is like.
48　Oakley, *The Foundations of Austrian Economics from Menger to Mises*, 38, citing Kirzner and others. See Raimondo Cubeddu, *The Philosophy of the Austrian School*, trans. Rachel M. Cost, née Barritt, Routledge, New York, 1993. The book approaches the principal Austrian economists—Menger, Mises, and Hayek—primarily as social and political theorists rather than as economists, and tries to draw out the implications of marginal utility and of a subjectivist view of human action.
49　Ibid., 55, citing Streissler.
50　While von Mises' seminar in Vienna influenced many Austrian economists, much of his most important work and influence came after the war in the United States. See Ludwig von Mises, *Human Action: A Treatise on Economics*, Yale University Press, New Haven, 1949. This is the English version of his ideas, although it is not simply a translation of the book he wrote a decade earlier in Swiss exile: *Nationalökonomie, Theorie des Handelns and Wirtschaftens*, Editions Union, Geneva, 1940.
51　Hayek's move to England as a young man intensified this British influence, but it also brought into focus themes which had been developing in Austrian thought since Menger—themes which set Austrians apart from many familiar German themes. A key issue is Hutchison's claim about Hayek's "methodological U-turn" in "Economics and Knowledge." See *Hayek's Challenge*, 3. Popper's influence on Hayek was also important in the years before the war.
52　F. A. von Hayek is best known in the United States for *The Road to Serfdom* and the ideological issues that emerged from the fascist era.
53　See Hayek, *The Counter-Revolution: Studies on the Abuse of Reason*, Liberty Fund, Indianapolis, 1952, 20–1. Hayek dates the modern, narrow usage from 1867.

54 Ibid., 23.
55 On French positivism, see Frank Manuel, *The Prophets of Paris*, Harvard University Press, Cambridge, 1962.
56 Ibid., 65.
57 The a priori that is so often referred to in Austrian economics is not what Kant meant by a priori. Austrian economists simply mean understanding general relationships and definitions rather than empirical particulars.
58 Hayek, *Counter-Revolution*, 41.
59 Ibid., 27.
60 See Ludger Lütkehaus, *"Dieses wahre innere Afrika": Texte zur Entdeckung des Unbewussten vor Freud*, Frankfurt am Main, 1989, 7–8: "das ungeheure Reich des Unbewussten, dieses wahre innere Afrika" is from Jean Paul, *Selina oder über die Unsterblichkeit der Seele* in his *Sämtliche Werke*, Abt. I, Bd. 6, Munich, Hanser, 1963, 1105–236; these words are from 1182.
61 See Michael Worbs, *Nervenkunst: Literatur und Psychoanalyse im Wien der Jahrhundertwende*, Europäische Verlagsanstalt, Vienna, 1983.
62 For a discussion of Freud's place in the history of psychiatry and psychotherapy, see Brian Farrell, "Sigmund Freud: Some Aspects of his Contribution," in *Intellectuals and the Future in the Habsburg Monarchy 1890–1914*, ed. László Péter and Robert B. Pynsent, Macmillan Press, London, 1988, 45–62. On some of the reasons for Freud's influence, see Stanley B. Messer and Nancy McWilliams, "The Impact of Freud and *The Interpretation of Dreams*," in *The Anatomy of Impact: What Makes Great Works of Psychology Great*, ed. Robert J. Sternberg, American Psychological Association, Washington DC, 2003.
63 Lionel Trilling, *Freud and the Crisis of Our Culture*, Beacon Press, Boston, 1955; Norman O. Brown, *Life against Death*, Wesleyan University Press, Middletown, CT, 1959; Herbert Marcuse, *Eros and Civilization: A Philosophical Inquiry into Freud*, Beacon Press, Boston, 1955, and H. Stuart Hughes, *Consciousness and Society*, Knopf, New York, 1955 all contributed to making Freud a dominant figure in American intellectual life in the 1950s. See also Philip Rieff, *Freud: The Mind of the Moralist*, Doubleday Anchor, Garden City, 1961 and *The Triumph of the Therapeutic: Uses of Faith after Freud*, Harper and Row, New York, 1966.
64 Peter Gay, *Freud: A Life for Our Time*, W. W. Norton, New York, 2006 is an important account of Freud's life and perhaps Gay's best book. See also Ernest Jones, *The Life and Work of Sigmund Freud*, 3 volumes, Basic Books, New York, 1953–1957 and Paul Roazen, *Freud and His Followers*, Signet, New York, 1971.
65 See John E. Toews' account of this transition in a paper for a conference in 1980 at the Pacific Coast Branch of the American Historical Association.
66 See Luft, *Eros and Inwardness in Vienna* and David S. Luft, "Science and Irrationalism in Freud's Vienna," *Modern Austrian Literature*, Vol. 23, No. 2 (1990),

89–97. Freud was, of course, not just an Austrian intellectual, but a European scientist and writer, who was at home in English, French, and Spanish as well as German, and drew on a classical education. He was what the Germans would call a *"Knotenpunkt"* or point of intersection of many different intellectual and scientific strands. As with Menger, the influences that shaped Freud's thought were international, coming in his case mainly from Germany and France and from fields that were not always aware of each other: research on sexuality, including childhood sexuality and homosexuality, ideas about the unconscious since Leibniz, medical research, and the new science of psychology, especially under the influence of Brentano.

67 Freud was exposed to Brentano's sophisticated approach to Christianity, but generally felt an attachment to positivism and civilization against what he regarded as the primitive superstitions of Roman Catholicism. He seems to have assumed that adopting the concept of God would change his understanding of causality.

68 The influence of Schopenhauer, Nietzsche, and philosophical irrationalism on the early Freud is well established, but it seems to have been after 1900 that Freud focused on reading Nietzsche's mature work. See Ronald Lehrer, *Nietzsche's Presence in Freud's Life and Thought*, State University of New York Press, Albany, 1995.

69 Much of Freud's contribution was to understanding the dynamics of the talking cure or the cure by love, including projection and transference. For the broad impact of these ideas on modern psychotherapy, see Jan Grant and Jim Crawley, *Transference and Projection: Mirrors to the Self*, Open University Press, Philadelphia, 2002.

70 Henri Ellenberger, *The Discovery of the Unconscious: The History and Evolution of Dynamic Psychology*, Basic Books, New York, 1970, 447–8. See also Frank J. Sulloway, *Freud, Biologist of the Mind: Beyond the Psychoanalytic Legend*, Basic Books, New York, 1979 and McGrath, *Freud's Discovery of Psychoanalysis*. For more on the unconscious before psychoanalysis, see L. L. Whyte, *The Unconscious before Freud*, Friedman, London, 1979 and Sebastian Gardner, "The Unconscious Mind," in *The Cambridge History of Philosophy 1870–1945*, ed. Thomas Baldwin, Cambridge University Press, Cambridge, 2003, 107–15. An important theoretical study of Freud's ideas is Paul Ricoeur, *Freud and Philosophy*, trans. Denis Savage, Yale University Press, New Haven, 1970.

71 A great deal of work has been done on Freud's invention of psychoanalysis, which culminated in *The Interpretation of Dreams*. See, for example, John E. Toews, "Historicizing Psychoanalysis: Freud in His Time and for Our Time," *The Journal of Modern History*, Vol. 63, No. 3 (September 1991), 504–45. Toews provides a thoughtful reconstruction of the origins of psychoanalysis and his critique of Gay's traditional approach to modern science. The key issues for Toews are Gay's commitment to a nineteenth-century scientific epistemology and his resistance to a more hermeneutic reading of Freud. The second half

of Freud's career has received less attention. Even *Three Essays on a Theory of Sexuality* deserves more attention than it has received, including the context of Otto Weininger's *Geschlecht und Character* and the discussions that followed its publication and Weininger's suicide. It seems likely that Weininger got some of his ideas from Freud and Hermann Swoboda, Weininger's friend who was a psychologist and a patient of Freud; Weininger and Plato more than Freud contributed to an ambience that influenced Musil's ideas in *The Confusions of Young Törless*.

72 Freud deserves more recognition for the thoughtful way he explored these relationships.
73 Bettelheim, *Freud and Man's Soul*. Bettelheim drew attention to the degree to which Anglo-American understandings of Freud depend on faulty and misleading translations. Freud was drawing here on a broader literary tradition, much like Musil. See chapter VIII, especially 58. Bettelheim's main point is that Freud's original language was not clinical, sterile, and abstracted from the everyday self.
74 Sigmund Freud, *Totem and Taboo*, trans. A. A. Brill, Vintage Books, New York, 1918.
75 Sigmund Freud, *Beyond the Pleasure Principle*, trans. James Strachey, Bantam Books, New York, 1959.
76 Sigmund Freud, *The Future of an Illusion*, trans. W. D. Robson-Scott, Doubleday Anchor, Garden City, New York, n. d.
77 Ibid., 77–8.
78 See Philip Rieff, *Freud: The Mind of the Moralist*, Doubleday, Garden City, N.Y., 1961.
79 Gay, *Freud: A Life*, 625.
80 *The Intellectual Migration: Europe and America 1930–1960* and H. Stuart Hughes, *The Sea Change: The Migration of Social Thought, 1930–1965*, Harper and Row, New York, 1975.
81 See Adolf Grünbaum, *Foundations of Psychoanalysis: A Philosophical Critique*, UC Press, Berkeley, 1984. These arguments seem unfruitful. More to the point is the question of what a science is—for any European intellectual. The standard definition at the time was a body of knowledge, but not always a lawful one, although Freud does not seem to have been very interested in such questions. Freud was more nearly a writer than a scientist, in twentieth-century terms.
82 There is a significant literature on this subject. See especially Juliet Mitchell, *Psychoanalysis and Feminism*, Pantheon, New York, 1974 and Judith Van Herik, *Freud on Femininity and Faith*, UC Press, Berkeley, 1982. The latter develops an important insight into the links between Freud's views of gender and religion, so that masculinity is coded as positive and Jewish, while femininity is negative and Christian. Masculine and Jewish also correspond to nineteenth-century liberalism.

After Cisleithanian Austria

1. The sharp break in 1938/1939 is not meant to extricate Austria from any political connection to Germany or to National Socialism, but to mark the end of a distinct period of intellectual history.
2. See Bauer, *The Question of Nationalities and Social Democracy*.
3. Austrians after 1945 came to think of themselves as a separate nation that was quite distinct from Germany, although it took some years for them to work out this understanding of their identity [See Thaler, *The Ambivalence of Identity* and Anthony Bushnell, *Polemical Austria: The Rhetorics of National Identity: From Empire to the Second Republic*, University of Wales Press, Cardiff, 2013]. Robert Menasse emphasizes that for Austrians after 1945 "it was imperative to maintain Austria's independence—especially vis-à-vis Germany—and by dissociating Austria from German culture and German language, to be reminded of Austrian state sovereignty." Robert Menasse, *Enraged Citizens, European Peace and Democratic Deficits*, trans. Craig Decker, Seagull Books, London, 2016, 65.
4. Dagmar C. G. Lorenz, "Austrian Jewish History and Identity after 1945," *Modern Austrian Literature*, 27, 3–4 (1994), 1.
5. See Hugo Bettauer, *Die Stadt ohne Juden: Ein Roman von übermorgen*, Gloriette Verlag, Vienna, 1922. By the 1980s Vienna became for Jews a symbolic place of return and commemoration, but this was no longer the same world. What emerged in this context was what Hillary Herzog calls "a self-consciously Jewish literature." Hillary Herzog, *"Vienna Is Different": Jewish Writers in Austria from the Fin de Siècle to the Present*, Berghahn Books, New York, 2011, 221.

Bibliography

A truly comprehensive bibliography of the field is difficult to imagine (though William Johnston's bibliography for *The Austrian Mind* comes to mind), but the titles cited here will be helpful to many readers.

A Companion to the Works of Hermann Broch. Ed. Graham Bartram, et al., Rochester, NY: Camden House, 2019.
Abrams, M. H. (1979). "How to Do Things with Texts," *Partisan Review*, Vol. 46, 566–88.
Alföldy, Géza. *Noricum*, trans. Anthony Birley, London: Routledge & Kegan Paul, 1974.
Agnew, Hugh Le Caine. *The Czechs and the Lands of the Bohemian Crown*, Stanford: Hoover Institution Press, 2004.
Allmayer-Beck, Johann Christoph. *Der Konservatismus in Österreich*, Munich: Isar Verlag, 1959.
Ammon, Ulrich. *Die deutsche Sprache in Deutschland, Österreich und der Schweiz: Das Problem der nationalen Varietäten*, New York: W. De Gruyter, 1995.
Anderson, Harriet. *Utopian Feminism: Women's Movements in fin-de-siècle Vienna*, New Haven: Yale University Press, 1992.
Andrian, Leopold von. *Der Garten der Erkenntnis*, Frankfurt am Main: S. Fischer Verlag, 1970.
Andrian-Werburg, Viktor Franz Freiherr von. *Osterreich wird meine Stimme erkennen lernen wie die Stimme Gottes in der Wüste: Tagebücher, 1839–1858*, ed. Franz Adlgasser, Vorwort Fritz Fellner, Vienna: Böhlau Verlag, 2011.
Aneignungen, Entfremdungen: The Austrian Playwright Franz Grillparzer (1791–1872). Ed. Marianne Henn et al., New York: Peter Lang, 2007.
Anne's Bohemia. Ed. Alfred Thomas, Minneapolis: Minnesota Press, 1998.
Anscombe, G. E. M. *An Introduction to Wittgenstein's Tractatus*, New York: Harper and Row, 1959.
Anzengruber, Ludwig. *Der Pfarrer von Kirchfeld*, Munich: Josef Berg, 1959.
Arendt, Hannah. "Einleitung," in *Dichten und Erkennen*, Vol. 6 of Broch's *Gesammelte Werke*, Zurich: Rhein Verlag, 1953, 5–42.
Arens, Katherine. *Empire in Decline: Fritz Mauthner's Critique of Wilhelminian Germany*, New York: Lang, 2001.
Arens, Katherine. *Vienna's Dreams of Europe: Culture and Identity beyond the Nation-State*, New York: Bloomsbury, 2015.
Ash, Mitchell G. *Gestalt Psychology in German Culture 1890–1967: Holism and the Quest for Objectivity*, Cambridge: Cambridge University Press, 1995.

Assimilation and Community: The Jew in Nineteenth-Century Europe. Ed. John Frankel and Steven J. Zipperstein, Cambridge: Cambridge University Press, 1992.

Aurelius, Marcus. *The Emperor's Handbook: A New Translation of the Meditations*, trans. C. Scot Hicks and David V. Hicks, New York: Scribner, 2002.

Austrian Economics: Historical and Philosophical Background. Ed. Wolfgang Grassl and Barry Smith, New York: New York University Press, 1986.

Bahr, Hermann. *Österreichische Genius: Grillparzer—Stifter—Feuchtersleben*, Vienna: Bellaria Verlag, n.d.

Bahr, Hermann. *Zur Überwindung des Naturalismus: Theoretische Schriften 1887–1904*, ed. Gotthart Wunberg, Stuttgart: Kohlhammer Verlag, 1968.

Banks, Erik C. *Ernst Mach's World Elements: A Study in Natural Philosophy*, London: Kluwer Academic Publishers, 2003.

Barclay, James R. "Franz Brentano and Sigmund Freud. A Comparative Study in the Evolution of Psychological Thought," diss., University of Michigan, 1959.

Barraclough, Geoffrey. *The Origins of Modern Germany*, London: Basil Blackwell, 1988.

Bartlett, Robert. *The Making of Europe: Conquest, Colonization and Cultural Change 950–1350*, Princeton: Princeton University Press, 1993.

Bartley, III, W. W. *Wittgenstein*, Philadelphia: J.B. Lippincott Company, 1973.

Basil, Otto, Herbert Eisenreich, and Ivar Ivask. *Das Grosse Erbe: Aufsätze zur österreichischen Literatur*, Graz: Stiasny-Verlag, 1962.

Bauer, Otto. *The Question of Nationalities and Social Democracy*, original German in 1924, trans. Joseph O'Donnell, Minneapolis: University of Minnesota Press, 2000.

Bauer, Roger. *Idealismus und seine Gegner in Österreich*, Heidelberg: Carl Winter, 1966.

Bauer, Roger. *La réalité royaume de Dieu: Études sur l'originalté du théâtre viennois dans le première moitié du IXe siècle*, Munich: Max Hueber Verlag, 1965.

Belke, Ingrid. *Die Sozialreformerischen Ideen von Josef Popper-Lynkeus* (1838–1921), Tübingen: J.C.B. Mohr, 1978.

Beller, Steven. *A Concise History of Austria*, Cambridge: Cambridge University Press, 2006.

Beller, Steven. *Vienna and the Jews 1867–1938, A Cultural History*, Cambridge: Cambridge University Press, 1989.

Benjamin, Walter. *Illuminations*, ed. Hannah Arendt, trans. Harry Zohn, New York: Schocken Books, 1969.

Bettauer, Hugo. *Die Stadt ohne Juden: Ein Roman von übermorgen*, Vienna: Gloriette Verlag, 1922.

Bettelheim, Bruno. *Freud and Man's Soul*, New York: Alfred A. Knopf, 1983.

Bithell, Jethro. *Modern German Literature 1880–1950*, London: Meuthuen & Co., 1939.

Black, Max. *A Companion to Wittgenstein's Tractatus*, Ithaca, NY: Cornell University Press, 1964.

Blackall, Eric A. *The Emergence of German as a Literary Language 1700–1775*, Cambridge: Cambridge University Press, 1959.

Blackall, Eric A. *Stifter, a Critical Study*, Cambridge: Cambridge University Press, 1948.

Blackmore, John T. *Ernst Mach: His Work, Life, and Influence*, Berkeley: University of California Press.

Bloch, Marc. "Toward a Comparative History of European Societies," in *Enterprise and Secular Change: Readings in Economic History*, ed. Frederic C. Lane and Jelle C. Riemersma, Homewood, IL: Richard D. Irwin, Inc., 1953, 494–521.

Bodi, Leslie. *Tauwetter: Zur Prosa der österreichischen Aufklärung: 1781–1795*, Frankfurt am Main: S. Fischer, 1977.

Bolzano and Analytic Philosophy. Ed. Wolfgang Künne, Mark Seibel, Mark Textor, Amsterdam-Atlanta: Rodopi, 1997.

Bolzano, Bernard. "From His Religious Teaching," in *Selbstbiographie*, Vienna: Wilhelm Braumüller, 1875.

Bolzano, Bernard. *Selected Writings on Ethics and Politics*, trans. Paul Rusnock and Rolf George, New York: Rodopi, 2007.

Bolzano, Bernard. *The Theory of Science: Attempt at a Detailed and in the Main Novel Exposition of LOGIC: With Constant Attention to Earlier Authors*, ed. and trans. Rolf George, Berkeley: University of California Press, 1972.

Bolzano, Bernard. *Theory of Science*, ed. and intro. Jan Berg, trans. Burnham Terrell, Boston: D. Reidel Publishing, 1973.

Bolzano, Bernard. *Über das Verhältnis der beiden Volksstämme in Böhmen: drei Vorträge*, Vienna: Wilhelm Braumüller, 1849. Lectures from the University of Prague in 1816; forward by Joseph Fesl.

Bolzano, Bernard. "Was ist Vaterland und Vaterlandsliebe?" in *Erbauungsschriften an die Jugend 1810*, Prague: E. W., 1850.

Bowman, William D. *Priest and Parish in Vienna, 1780–1880*, Boston: Humanities Press, 1999.

Boyer, John W. (2013). "Power, Partisanship, and the Grid of Democratic Politics: 1907 as the Pivot Point of Modern Austrian History," *Austrian History Yearbook*, Vol. 44, 148–74.

Boyer, John W. *Political Radicalism in Late Imperial Vienna: Origins of the Christian Social Movement 1848–1897*, Chicago: The University of Chicago Press, 1981.

Brady Jr, Thomas A. *German Histories in the Age of Reformations, 1400–1650*, New York: Cambridge University Press, 2009.

Braunthal, Julius. *History of the International 1864–1914*, trans. Henry Collins and Kenneth Mitchell, London: Thomas Nelson and Sons, 1967–80, 3 volumes.

Brentano, Franz. "Die vier Phasen der Philosophie und ihr augenblicklicher Stand" (1895) in *Vier Phasen der Philosophie*, ed. Oskar Kraus, Hamburg: Verlag von Felix Meiner, 1968.

Brentano, Franz. *Psychology from an Empirical Standpoint*, ed. Oskar Kraus, Linda L. McAlister, intro. Peter Simons, trans. Antos C. Rancurello, D. B. Terrell, and Linda L. McAlister, London: Routledge, 1973, 1995.

Breuilly, John. *Austria, Prussia and Germany, 1806–1871*, London: Pearson Education Limited, 2002.

Briefe an und von Josephine von Wertheimstein, selected by Heinrich Gomperz and edited by Robert A. Kann, Vienna: Verlag der Österreichische Akademie der Wissenschaften, 1981.

Briefwechsel zwischen Ferdinand von Saar und Maria von Ebner-Eschenbach. Ed. Heinz Kindermann, Vienna: Wiener Bibliophilen-Gesellschaft, 1957.

Broch, Hermann. *Briefe von 1929: bis 1951*, Zürich: Rhein Verlag, 1957.

Broch, Hermann. *Hugo von Hofmannsthal and His Time: The European Imagination, 1860-1920*, ed. and trans. Michael P. Steinberg, Chicago: The University of Chicago Press, 1984.

Broch, Hermann. *The Death of Virgil*, trans. Jean Starr Untermeyer, New York: Random House, 1945.

Broch, Hermann. *The Sleepwalkers*, trans. Willa and Edwin Muir, New York: Pantheon Books, 1947.

Brodbeck, David. *Defining Deutschtum: Political Ideology, German Identity, and Music-Critical Discourse in Liberal Vienna*, New York: Oxford University Press, 2014.

Brown, Norman O. *Life against Death*, Middletown, CT: Wesleyan University Press, 1959.

Bushnell, Anthony. *Polemical Austria: The Rhetorics of National Identity: From Empire to the Second Republic*, Cardiff: University of Wales Press, 2013.

Byrd, Vance (2014). "The Politics of Commemoration in *Wien und die Wiener*" (1841-1844), *Journal of Austrian Studies*, Vol. 47, No. 1, 1-20.

Caldwell, Bruce. *Hayek's Challenge: An Intellectual Biography of F. A. Hayek*, Chicago: University of Chicago Press, 2004.

Cameron, Euan. *European Reformation*, Oxford: Oxford University Press, 1991.

Čapek, Karel. *Talks with T. G. Masaryk*, trans. Michael Henry Heim, Chapel Hill: The University of North Carolina Press, 2014.

Carl Menger and His Legacy in Economics. Ed. Bruce J. Caldwell, Durham: Duke University Press, 1990.

Cartwright, Nancy, Jordi Cat, Lola Fleck, and Thomas. *Neurath: Philosophy between Science and Politics*, New York: Cambridge University Press, 1996.

Cavell, Stanley. *Must We Mean What We Say? A Book of Essays*, New York: Charles Scribner's Sons, 1969.

Chamberlain, Houston Stewart. *Foundations of the Nineteenth Century*, trans. John Lees, New York: John Lane Company, 1914, 2 volumes.

Chrislock, Carl Winston. "Reluctant Radicals: Czech Social Democracy and the Nationality Question 1914-1918," diss., Indiana University, 1971.

Coen, Deborah R. *Vienna in the Age of Uncertainty: Science, Liberalism, and Private Life*, Chicago: Chicago University Press, 2007.

Coffa, J. Alberto. *The Semantic Tradition from Kant to Carnap: To the Vienna Station*, ed. Linda Wessels, Cambridge: Cambridge University Press, 1991.

Cohen, Gary B. *Education and Middle-Class Society in Imperial Austria: 1848-1918*, West Lafayette: Purdue University Press, 1996.

Cohen, Gary B. *The Politics of Ethnic Survival: Germans in Prague, 1861–1914*, 2nd edition, Revised, West Lafayette: Purdue University Press, 2006.
Cohen, Michael (July 2001). "Was Wittgenstein a Plagiarist?" *Philosophy*, Vol. 76, No. 297, 451–9.
Corngold, Stanley, *The Commentator's Despair: The Interpretation of Kafka's Metamorphosis*, Port Washington, NY: Kennikat Press, 1973.
Coudenhove-Kalergi, Count Richard. *An Idea Conquers the World*, London: Hutchinson & Co., 1953.
Crary, Alice and Rupert Read, *The New Wittgenstein*, New York: Routledge, 2000.
Cubeddu, Raimondo. *Philosophy of the Austrian School*, trans. Rachel M. Cost, née Barritt, New York: Routledge, 1993.
Curtius, Ernst Robert. *European Literature and the Latin Middle Ages*, trans. Willard R. Trask, New York: Harper and Row, 1963.
Curtius, Ernst Robert. *Kritische Essays zur europäischen Literatur*, Bern: Francke Verlag, 1963.
Dahrendorf, Ralf. *Society and Democracy in Germany*, Garden City, NY: Anchor Books, 1969.
Das österreichische Deutsch. Ed. Peter Wiesinger, Vienna: Böhlau Verlag, 1988.
Das zeitlose Wort. Ed. Joseph Strelka, Vienna: Stiasny Verlag, 1964.
Daviau, Donald G. *Hermann Bahr*, Boston: Twayne Publishers, 1985.
David, Zdeněk V. *Finding the Middle Way: The Utraquists' Liberal Challenge to Rome and Luther*, Baltimore: The Johns Hopkins University Press, 2003.
David, Zdeněk V. *Johann Gottfried Herder and the Czech National Awakening: A Reassessment*, Pittsburgh: The Center for Russian and East European Studies, 2007.
David, Zdeněk V. (2008)."Masaryk a rakouská filosofická tradice: Bolzano a Brentano," *Filosoficky cašopis*, Vol. 56, 345–61.
David, Zdeněk V. *Realism, Tolerance, and Liberalism in the Czech National Awakening: Legacies of the Bohemian Reformation*, Baltimore: Johns Hopkins University Press, 2010.
Deák, István. *The Lawful Revolution: Louis Kossuth and the Hungarians 1848–1849*, London: Phoenix Press, 2001. Original edition: Columbia University Press, 1979.
Deak, John. *Forging a Multinational State: State Making in Imperial Austria from the Enlightenment to the First World War*, Stanford: Stanford University Press, 2015.
Deleuze, Gilles and Félix Guattari. *Kafka: Toward a Minor Literature*, trans. Dana Polan, Minneapolis: University of Minnesota Press, 1986.
Demetz, Peter. *Auf den Spur Bernard Bolzanos: Essays*, Vienna: Arco Wissenschaft, 2013,
Denis, Ernest. *Georges de Podiébrad*, Vol. 1 of *Fin De L'indépendance Bohème*. Paris: Armand Colin et Cie, 1890.
Der Briefwechsel B. Bolzano's mit F. Exner. Ed. Eduard Winter, Prague: Königliche Böhmischen Gesellschaft der Wissenschaften, 1935.
Deutsch-Österreichiche Literaturgeschichte: Ein Handbuch zur Geschichte der deutschen Dichtung in Österreich-Ungarn. Ed. Johann Willibald, Jakob Zeidler, and Eduard Castle, Vienna: Carl Fromme, 1937, 4 volumes.

Dickson, P. G. M. *Finance and Government under Maria Theresia 1740–1780*, Oxford: Oxford University Press, 1987, 2 volumes.
Die Habsburgermonarchie: 1848–1918, Vol. IX/part 2. Ed. Helmut Rumpler and Peter Urbanitsch, Vienna: Österreichischen Akademie der Wissenschaften, 2010.
Die österreichische Zentralverwaltung. Ed. Thomas Fellner and Heinrich Kretschmayr. This gigantic work began to appear in 1907. The volumes reached to 1867 in 1971, completing the record of the central administration.
Diversity and Dissent: Negotiating Religious Difference in Central Europe, 1500–1800. Ed. Howard Louthan, Gary B. Cohen, and Franz A. J. Szabo, New York: Berghahn Books, 2011.
Dobrovský, Josef. *Geschichte der böhmischen Sprache und Literatur*, Halle Salle: M. Niemeyer, 1955.
Duczynska, Ilona. *Workers in Arms: The Austrian Schutzbund and the Civil War of 1934*, intro E. J. Hobsbawm, New York: Monthly Review Press, 1978.
Dummett, Michael. *Origins of Analytic Philosophy*, Cambridge: Harvard University Press, 1994.
Dunkel, Harold B. *Herbart and Education*, New York: Random House, 1969.
Durzak, Manfred. *Hermann Broch*, Stuttgart: J.B. Metzlerische Verlagsbuchhandlung, 1967.
Eder, Karl. *Der Liberalismus in Altösterreich: Geisteshaltung, Politik und Kultur*, Vienna: Verlag Herold, 1955.
Ellenberger, Henri. *The Discovery of the Unconscious: The History and Evolution of Dynamic Psychology*, New York: Basic Books, 1970.
Emrich, Wilhelm. *Franz Kafka: A Critical Study of His Writings*, trans. Sheema Zeben Buehne, New York: Frederick Ungar, 1968.
Enzinger, Moriz. *Adalbert Stifters Studienjahre (1818–1830)*, Innsbruck: Österreichische Verlagsanstalt, 1950.
Erdmann, Karl Dietrich. *Die Spur Österreichs in der deutschen Geschichte: Drei Staaten zwei Nationen ein Volk?* Zurich: Manesse Verlag, 1989.
Evans, R.J.W. *Austria, Hungary, and the Habsburgs: Essays on Central Europe, c.1683–1867*, New York: Oxford University Press, 2006.
Evans, R.J.W. (2004). "Language and State Building: The Case of the Habsburg Monarchy," *Austrian History Yearbook*, 35, 1–17.
Evans, R.J.W. *The Making of the Habsburg Monarchy 1550–1700: An Interpretation*, Oxford: Oxford University Press, 1979.
Evans, R.J.W. *Rudolf II and His World: A Study in Intellectual History: 1576–1612*, Oxford: Thames and Hudson, 2nd edition, 1997.
Farrell, Brian. "Sigmund Freud: Some Aspects of His Contribution," in *Intellectuals and the Future in the Habsburg Monarchy 1890–1914*, ed. László Péter and Robert B. Pynsent, London: Macmillan Press, 1988, 45–62.
Festschrift für Hans Eggers: Zum 65. Geburtstag. Ed. Herbert Bakes, Tübingen: Max Niemeyer, 1972.

Fichtner, Paula Sutter. *The Habsburg Monarchy, 1490–1848: The Attributes of Empire*, New York: Palgrave Macmillan, 2003.

Finch, Henry Leroy. *Wittgenstein-The Early Philosophy: An Exposition of the Tractatus*, New York: Humanities Press, 1971.

Fischer, Kurt Rudolf. "Franz Brentano's Philosophy of *Evidenz*," diss., University of California, Berkeley, 1964.

Fleck, Christian. *A Transatlantic History of the Social Sciences: Robber Barons, the Third Reich and the Invention of Empirical Social Research*, trans. Hella Beister, New York: Bloomsbury Academic, 2011.

Fox, Robert. *Science without Frontiers: Cosmopolitanism and National Interests in the World of Learning: 1870–1940*, Corvallis: Oregon State University Press, 2016.

Franz, Georg. *Liberalismus: Die deutschliberale Bewegung in der Habsburgischen Monarchie*, Munich: Verlag Georg D.W. Callwey, 1955.

Freud, Sigmund. *Beyond the Pleasure Principle*, trans. James Strachey, New York: Bantam Books, 1959.

Freud, Sigmund. *Civilization and Its Discontents*, trans. James Strachey, New York: W. W. Norton, 1962.

Freud, Sigmund. *The Future of an Illusion*. Trans. W. D. Robson-Scott, Garden City, New York: Doubleday Anchor, n.d.

Freud, Sigmund. *Group Psychology and the Analysis of the Ego*. Trans. James Strachey, n.d.

Freud, Sigmund. *Three Essays on a Theory of Sexuality*, New York: Basic Books, 1962.

Freud, Sigmund, *Totem and Taboo*. Trans. A. A. Brill, New York: Vintage Books, 1918.

Fuchs, Albert. *Geistige Strömungen in Österreich 1867–1918*, reprint with an intro. by Friedrich Heer, Vienna: Löcker Verlag, 1949/1984.

Gagliardo, John G. *Germany under the Old Regime: 1600–1790*, New York: Longman, 1991.

Gay, Peter. *Freud, Jews, and Other Germans*, New York: Oxford University Press, 1978.

Gay, Peter. *Freud: A Life for Our Time*, New York: W. W. Norton, 2006.

Gay, Peter. *Modernism: The Lure of Heresy: From Baudelaire to Beckett and Beyond*, New York: W. W. Norton, 2008.

Gentz, Friedrich. *Betrachtungen über die französische Revolutuion: nach dem Englischen des Herrn Burkes*, Berlin: bei Friedrich Vieweg der älteren, 1794.

German Philosophy since Kant. Ed. Anthony O'Hear, Cambridge: Cambridge University Press, 1991.

Geschichte der österreichischen Humanwissenschaften. Ed. Karl Acham, Vienna: Passagen Verlag, 1999, 6 volumes.

Glettner, Monika. *Die Wiener Tschechen um 1900: Strukturanalyse einer nationalen Minderheit in der Grossstadt*, Munich: Oldenbourg Verlag, 1972.

Godsey, Jr., William D. *Aristocratic Redoubt: The Austro-Hungarian Foreign Service on the Eve of the First World War*, West Lafayette: Purdue University Press, 1999.

Goffman, Daniel. *The Ottoman Empire and Early Modern Europe*, Cambridge: Cambridge University Press, 2002.

Good, David F. *The Economic Rise of the Habsburg Empire, 1750–1914*, Berkeley: UC Press, 1984.
Grant, Jan and Jim Crawley. *Transference and Projection: Mirrors to the Self*, Philadelphia: Open University Press, 2002.
Greiner, Ulrich. "Denken wie der Wald," *Die Zeit*, Nr. 43, 20. October 2005.
Greiner, Ulrich. *Der Tod des Nachsommers*, Munich: Carl Hanser Verlag, 1979.
Grillparzer, Franz. *Sämtliche Werke*, Stuttgart: Cotta, 1893, 20 volumes.
Grillparzer, Franz. *The Poor Fiddler*, trans. Alexander and Elizabeth Henderson, intro. Ivar Ivask, New York: Frederick Ungar, 1967.
Grillparzer's Der arme Spielmann: New Directions in Criticism. Ed. Clifford Albrecht Bernd, Columbia, SC: Camden House, 1988.
Gruber, Helmut. *Red Vienna: Experiment in Working-Class Culture 1919–1934*, New York: Oxford University Press, 1991.
Grünbaum, Adolf. *Foundations of Psychoanalysis: A Philosophical Critique*, Berkeley: California University Press, 1984.
Gubser, Michael. *Time's Visible Surface: Alois Riegl and the Discourse on Historicity and Temporality in Fin-de-siècle Vienna*, Detroit: Wayne State University Press, 2004.
Hacohen, Malachi Haim. *Karl Popper—The Formative Years, 1902–1945: Politics and Philosophy in Interwar Vienna*, New York: Cambridge University Press, 2000.
Haller, Rudolf. "Brentanos Spuren im Werke Masaryks," *T.G. Masaryk und die Brentano-Schule*, ed. Josef Zumr and Thomas Binder, Filozofický ústav Československé akademie věd, Prague, 1992, 10–20.
Haller, Rudolf. *Questions on Wittgenstein*, London: Routledge, 1988.
Haller, Rudolf. *Studien zur österreichischen Philosophie: Variationen über ein Thema*, Amsterdam: Rodopi N.V., 1979.
Hanisch, Ernst. *Der lange Schatten des Staates: Österreichisch Gesellschaftsgeschichte im 20. Jahrhundert*, Vienna: Ueberreuter, 1994.
Hantsch, Hugo. *Die Geschichte Österreichs*, Vienna: Styria, 1937–1950, 2 volumes.
Harrison, Thomas. *1910: The Emancipation of Dissonance*, Berkeley: California University Press, 1996.
Hayek, F. A. von. *The Road to Serfdom*, London: Routledge, 1944.
Hayek, F. A. von. *The Counter-Revolution of Science Studies on the Abuse of Reason*, Indianapolis: Liberty Press, 1952.
Heer, Friedrich. *The Intellectual History of Europe*, trans. Jonathan Steinberg, Garden City, New York: Anchor Books, 1968, 2 volumes.
Heer, Friedrich. *Land im Strom der Zeit: Österreich gestern, heute, morgen*, Vienna: Verlag Herold, 1958.
Heindl, Waltraud. *Gehorsame Rebellen: Bürokratie und Beamte in Österreich, 1780 bis 1848*, Vienna: Böhlau Verlag, 1991.
Hellyer, Marcus. *Catholic Physics: Jesuit Natural Philosophy in Early Modern Germany*, Notre Dame: University of Notre Dame Press, 2005.
Hermann, A. H. *A History of the Czechs*, London: Allen Lane, 1975.

Hertz, Deborah. *Jewish High Society in Old Regime Berlin*, New Haven: Yale University Press, 1988.
Hertz, Heinrich. *The Principles of Mechanics Presented in a New Form*, trans. D. E. Jones and J. T. Walley, New York: Dover, 1956.
Herzog, Hillary. *"Vienna Is Different": Jewish Writers in Austria from the Fin de Siècle to the Present*, New York: Berghahn Books, 2011.
Heymann, Frederick G. *George of Bohemia: King of Heretics*, Princeton: Princeton University Press, 1965.
Heymann, Frederick G. *John Žižka and the Hussite Revolution*, Princeton: Princeton University Press, 1955, reissued in New York by Russell & Russell, 1969.
Himmelfarb, Gertrude. *Lord Acton: A Study in Conscience*, Chicago: University of Chicago Press, 1952.
Hobsbawm, Eric. *On History*, New York: The New Press, 1997.
Hochman, Erin. *Imagining a Greater Germany: Republican Nationalism and the Idea of Anschluss*, Ithaca, NY: Cornell University Press, 2016.
Hoffmann, Birthe. *Opfer der Humanität: Zur Anthropologie Franz Grillparzers*, Wiesbaden: Deutscher Universitätsverlag, 1999.
Hofmannsthal, Hugo von. *Hofmannsthal and the Austrian Idea: Selected Essays and Addresses, 1906–1927*, trans. and ed. David S. Luft, West Lafayette: Purdue University Press, 2011.
Hofmannsthal, Hugo von. *Reden und Aufsätze*, volumes 1–3 in *Gesammelte Werke*, ed. Bernd Schoeller and Rudolf Hirsch et al., Frankfurt am Main: Fischer Taschenbuch, 1979–1980.
Hohendahl, Peter Uwe. *Building National Literature: The Case of Germany, 1830–1870*, trans. Renate Baron Franciscono, Ithaca, NY: Cornell University Press, 1989.
Holton, Gerald. *Science and Anti-Science*, Cambridge: Harvard University Press, 1993.
Hösler, Joachim. *Von Krain zu Slowenien. Die Anfänge der nationalen Differenzierungsprozesse in Krain und der Untersteiermark von der Aufklärung bis zur Revolution 1768 bis 1848*, Munich: Oldenbourg Verlag, 2006. http://www.worldstandards.eu/cars/driving-on-the-left/
Hughes, H. Stuart. *Consciousness and Society*, New York: Knopf, 1958.
Hughes, H. Stuart. *The Sea Change: The Migration of Social Thought, 1930–1965*, New York: Harper and Row, 1975.
Husserl, Edmund. "The Crisis of the Sciences," in *The Crisis of European Sciences and Transcendental Phenomenology: An Introduction to Phenomenological Philosophy*, trans. and intro David Carr, Evanston: Northwestern University Press, 1970.
Ingrao, Charles W. *The Habsburg Monarchy 1618–1815*, 2nd edition, Cambridge: Cambridge University Press, 2000.
Jacob, Margaret C. *Living the Enlightenment: Freemasonry and Politics in Eighteenth-Century Europe*, New York: Oxford University Press, 1991.
Jäger-Sunstenau, Hanns. "Die adelte Judenfamilien im vormärzlichen Wien," diss., Vienna 1950.

Jahoda, Marie, Lazarsfeld, and Zeisel. *Die Arbeitslosen von Marienthal*, Leipzig: S. Hirzel, 1933.
Janik, Allan and Stephen Toulmin. *Wittgenstein's Vienna*, New York: Simon and Schuster, 1973.
Jelavich, Barbara. *Modern Austria: Empire and Republic 1815-1986*, New York: Cambridge University Press, 1987.
Johnston, William M. *Der österreichische Mensch: Kulturgeschichte der Eigenart Österreichs*, Vienna: Böhlau Verlag, 2010.
Johnston, William M. *The Austrian Mind: An Intellectual and Social History, 1848-1938*, Berkeley: University of California Press, 1972.
Johnston, William M. *Zur Kulturgeschichte Österreichs und Ungarns 1890-1938: Auf der Suche nach verborgenen Gemeinsamkeiten*, trans. Otmar Binder, Vienna: Böhlau Verlag, 2015.
Jones, Ernest. *The Life and Work of Sigmund Freud*, New York: Basic Books, 1953-1957, 3 volumes.
Judson, Pieter M. *Exclusive Revolutionaries: Liberal Politics, Social Experience, and National Identity in the Austrian Empire, 1848-1914*, Ann Arbor: University of Michigan Press, 1996.
Judson, Pieter M. *The Habsburg Empire: A New History*, Stanford: Stanford University Press, 2016.
Kafka, Franz. *The Metamorphosis, in the Penal Colony, and Other Stories*, trans. Willa Muir and Edwin Muir, New York: Schocken Books, 1977.
Kafka's Selected Stories. Trans. and ed. Stanley Corngold, New York: W. W. Norton, 2007.
Kaminsky, Howard. *A History of the Hussite Revolution*, Berkeley: University of California Press, 1967.
Kann, Robert A. *A History of the Habsburg Empire, 1526-1918*, Berkeley: University of California Press, 1980.
Kann, Robert A. *A Study in Austrian Intellectual History: From Late Baroque to Romanticism*, New York: Frederick A. Praeger, 1960.
Kann, Robert A. *The Multinational Empire: Nationalism and Reform in the Habsburg Monarchy 1848-1918*, New York: Columbia University Press, 1950, 2 volumes.
Keller, R. E. *The German Language*, Atlantic Highlands, New Jersey: Humanities Press, 1978.
Kelsen. Hans. *A New Science of Politics*, ed. Eckhart Arnold, Lancaster: ontos verlag, 2004.
Kieval, Hillel J. *Languages of Community: The Jewish Experience in the Czech Lands*, Berkeley: University of California Press, 2000.
Kieval, Hillel J. *The Making of Czech Jewry: National Conflict and Jewish Society in Bohemia, 1870-1918*, New York: Oxford University Press, 1988.
King, Jeremy. *Budweisers into Czechs and Germans: A Local History of Bohemian Politics, 1848-1948*, Princeton: Princeton University Press, 2002.
Kiss, Endre. *Der Tod der K.u.k. Weltordmung in Wien: Ideengeschichte Österreichs um die Jahrhundertwende*, Vienna: Böhlau, 1986.

Kiss, Endre. "Über Wiens Bedeutung für die essayistische Periode des jungen Georg Lukács," in *Die Östereichische Literatur: ihr Profil von der Jahrhundertwende bis zur Gegenwart (1880–1980)*, ed. Herbert Zeman, Graz: Akademische Druck, 1989, part 1, 371–83.

Kissinger, Henry. *A World Restored*, Boston: Houghton Mifflin, 1957.

Klagge, James C. *Wittgenstein in Exile*, Cambridge, MA: MIT Press, 2011.

Klemperer, Klemens von. *Ignaz Seipel: Christian Statesman in a Time of Crisis*, Princeton: Princeton University Press, 1972.

Knapp, Vincent J. *Austrian Social Democracy, 1889–1914*, Washington, DC: University Press of America, 1980.

Koethe, John. *The Continuity of Wittgenstein's Thought*, Ithaca, NY: Cornell University Press, 1996.

Kořalka, Jiří. *František Palacký (1798–1876): Der Historiker der Tschechen in österreichischer Vielvölkerstaat*, trans. Kořalka with Helmut Rumpler and Peter Urbanitsch, Vienna: Verlag der Österreichischen Akademie der Wissenschaften, 2007.

Kraft, Victor. *The Vienna Circle: The Origin of Neo-Positivism*, trans. Arthur Pap, New York: Philosophical Library, 1953.

Kraus, Karl. *The Last Days of Mankind: The Complete Text*, trans. Fred Bridgman and Edward Timms, New Haven: Yale University Press, 2015.

Kraus, Oskar. *Franz Brentano; zur kenntnis seines lebens und seiner lehre*, Mit Beiträgen von Carl Stumpf und Edmund Husserl, Munich: Oskar Beck, 1919.

Křen, Jan. *Die Konfliktgemeinschaft: Tschech und Deutsche 1780–1918*, trans. Peter Heumos, Munich: Oldenbourg Verlag, 1996.

Kühlmann, Wilhelm. *Gelehrtenrepublik und Fürstenstaat*, Tübingen: Max Niemeyer Verlag,1982.

Kürnberger, Ferdinand. *Literarischen Herzensachen: Reflexionen und Kritiken*, Vienna: Verlag von L. Rosner, 1877.

LaCapra, Dominick. *Rethinking Intellectual History: Texts Contexts Language*, Ithaca, NY: Cornell University Press, 1983.

Landes, David S. *Unbound Prometheus: Technological Change and Industrial Development in Western Europe from 1750*, Cambridge: Cambridge University Press, 1969.

Landoon, H. C. Robbins. *1791: Mozart's Last Year*, New York: Schirmer Books, 1988.

Lapointe, Sandra. *Bolzano's Theoretical Philosophy: An Introduction*, New York: Palgrave Macmillan, 2011.

Lazarsfeld, Paul F. (December 1962). "The Sociology of Empirical Social Research," *American Sociological Review*, Vol 27, No. 6, 757–67.

Le Rider, Jacques. *Modernity and Crises of Identity: Culture and Society in Fin-de-Siècle Vienna*, trans. Rosemary Morris, New York: Continuum, 1993.

Lehner, Ulrich. *Enlightened Monks: The German Benedictines, 1740–1803*, Oxford: Oxford University Press, 2011.

Lehrer, Ronald. *Nietzsche's Presence in Freud's Life and Thought*, Albany: State University of New York Press, 1995.
Lentze, Hans. *Die Universitätsreformen des Ministers Graf Leo Thun-Hohenstein*, Vienna: Hermann Böhlaus Nachf, 1962.
Leser, Norbert. *Zwischen Reformismus und Bolschewismus: Der Austromarxismus als Theorie und Praxis*, Vienna: Europa Verlag, 1968.
Lesky, Erna. *The Vienna Medical School of the 19th Century*, Baltimore: Johns Hopkins University Press, 1976.
Lhotsky, Alphons. *Geschichte des Instituts für österreichische Geschichtsforschung 1854-1954*, Graz: Hermann Böhlaus Nachf, 1954.
Lindenfeld, David F. "Grand Historical Narrative or Intellectual Strategy," in *The Historicity of Economics: Continuities and Discontinuities of Historical Thought in 19th and 20th Century Economics*, ed. Heino Heinrich Nau and Bertram Scheffold, Berlin: Springer Verlag, 2002, 56-77.
Lindenfeld, David F. *The Practical Imagination: The German Sciences of State in the Nineteenth Century*, Chicago: The University of Chicago Press, 1997.
Lindenfeld, David F. *The Transformation of Positivism: Alexius Meinong and European Thought, 1880-1920*, Berkeley: UC Press, 1980.
Lindner, Dolf. *Der Mann ohne Vorurteile, Joseph von Sonnenfels 1733-1817*, Vienna: Oesterreichischer Bundesverlag, 1983.
Lipset, Seymour. *Political Man: The Social Bases of Politics*, Garden City, NY: Doubleday and Company, Inc, 1960.
Literaturgeschichte Österreichs. Ed. Herbert Zeman, Graz: Akademische Druck- u. Verlagsanstalt, 1996.
Lorenz, Dagmar C. G. (1994). "Austrian Jewish History and Identity after 1945," *Modern Austrian Literature*, Vol. 27, No. 3, 1-17.
Lorenz, Dagmar C. G. *Grillparzer: Dichter des sozialen Konflikts*, Vienna: Böhlau, 1986.
Louthan, Howard. *Converting Bohemia: Force and Persuasion in the Catholic Reformation*, Cambridge: Cambridge University Press, 2009.
Luft, David S. (1992). "Austria as a Region of German: 1900-1938/1945," *Austrian History Yearbook, Vol. XXIII*, 135-48.
Luft, David S. (2007). "Austrian Intellectual History and Bohemia," *The Austrian History Yearbook*, Vol. 38, 108-21.
Luft, David S. (Winter 2007). "Cultural Memory and Intellectual History: Locating Austrian Literature," *Studies in Twentieth and Twenty First Century Literature*, Vol. 31, No. 1, 30-51.
Luft, David S. *Eros and Inwardness in Vienna: Weininger, Musil, Doderer*, Chicago: The University of Chicago Press, 2003.
Luft, David S. *Robert Musil and the Crisis of European Culture: 1880-1942*, Berkeley: University of California Press, 1980.
Luft, David S. (March 1983). "Schopenhauer, Austria, and the Generation of 1905," *Central European History*, in *Central European History*, Vol. 16, No. 1, 53-75.

Luft, David S. (1990). "Science and Irrationalism in Freud's Vienna," *Modern Austrian Literature*, Vol. 23, No. 2, 89–97.
Lütkehaus, Ludger. *"Dieses wahre innere Afrika": Texte zur Entdeckung des Unbewussten vor Freud*, Frankfurt am Main: Fischer, 1989.
Lützeler, Paul Michael. *Hermann Broch: Eine Biographie*, Frankfurt am Main: Suhrkamp Verlag, 1986.
Lützow, Franz von. *Bohemia: An Historical Sketch*, London: Dent and Sons, 1939.
Macartney, C. A. *The Habsburg Empire, 1790–1918*, New York: The Macmillan Company, 1969.
Mach, Ernst. *Contributions to the Analysis of Sensations*, trans. C. M. Williams, Chicago: Open Court, 1897.
Mach, Ernst. *Knowledge and Error: Sketches on the Psychology of Inquiry*, ed. Erwin N. Hiebert, Dordrecht: D. Riedel Publishing, 1976.
Mach, Ernst. *The Analysis of Sensations and the Relation of the Physical to the Psychical*, trans. C. M. Williams, revision Sydney Waterlow, New York: Dover, 1959.
Mach, Ernst. *The Science of Mechanics: A Critical and Historical Account of Its Development*, trans. Thomas J. McCormack, London: Open Court, 1942.
Major Figures of Austrian Literature: The Interwar Years 1918–1938. Ed. Donald G. Daviau, Riverside: Ariadne Press, 1995.
Mandelbaum, Maurice. *History, Man, & Reason*, Baltimore: The Johns Hopkins Press, 1971.
Manuel, Frank. *The Prophets of Paris*, Cambridge: Harvard University Press, 1962.
Marcuse, Herbert. *Eros and Civilization: A Philosophical Inquiry into Freud*, Boston: Beacon Press, 1955.
Masaryk, Tomaš. *The Meaning of Czech History*, ed. René Wellek, trans. Peter Kussi, Chapel Hill: The University of North Carolina Press, 1974.
Matysik, Tracie. *Reforming the Moral Subject*, Ithaca, NY: Cornell University Press, 2008.
Matz, Wolfgang. *Adalbert Stifter oder Diese fürchterliche Wendung der Dinge: Biographie*, Munich: Carl Hanser Verlag, 1995.
McGuinness, Brian. *Young Ludwig: Wittgenstein's Life, 1880–1921*, Oxford: Clarendon Press, 2005 (1988).
McGrath, William J. *Freud's Discovery of Psychoanalysis: The Politics of Hysteria*, Ithaca, NY: Cornell University Press, 1986.
Meinecke, Friedrich. *The Age of German Liberation, 1795–1815*, trans. Peter Paret and Helmuth Fischer, Berkeley: University of California Press, 1977.
Meister, Richard. *Entwicklung und Reformen des Österreichischen Studienwesens*, Teil I; Abhandlung. Vienna: Hermann Böhlaus Nachf., 1963.
Melton, James Van Horn. *Absolutism and the Eighteenth-Century Origins of Compulsory Education in Prussia and Austria*, New York: Cambridge University Press, 1988.
Melton, James Van Horn. *The Rise of the Public in Enlightenment Europe*, Cambridge: Cambridge University Press, 2001.

Menasse, Robert. *Enraged Citizens, European Peace and Democratic Deficits*, trans. Craig Decker, London: Seagull Books, 2016.

Menger, Carl. *Problems of Economics and Sociology (Untersuchungen über die Methode der Socialwissenschaften und der Politischen Oekonomie insbesondere)*, ed. Louis Schneider, trans. Francis J. Nock, Urbana: University of Illinois Press, 1963.

Messer, Stanley B. and Nancy McWilliams. "The Impact of Freud and *The Interpretation of Dreams*," in *The Anatomy of Impact: What Makes Great Works of Psychology Great*, ed. Robert J. Sternberg, Washington, DC: American Psychological Association, 2003.

Michler, Werner. *Darwinismus und Literatur: Naturwissenschftliche und literarische Intelligenz in Österreich, 1859–1914*, Vienna: Böhlau Verlag, 1999.

Michler, Werner, Wendelin Schmidt-Dengler. "Germanistik in Österreich: Neuere deutsche und österreichische Literatur," in *Geschichte der österreichischen Humanwissenschaften*, ed. Karl Acham, Vienna: Passagen Verlag, 2003, Vol. 5, 193–228.

Miller, Perry. *The New England Mind: From Colony to Province*, Cambridge: Harvard University Press, 1953.

Mises, Ludwig von. *Human Action: A Treatise on Economics*, New Haven: Yale University Press, 1949.

Mises, Ludwig von. *Nationalökonomie, Theorie des Handelns and Wirtschaftens*, Geneva: Éditions Union, 1940.

Mises, Richard von. *Positivism: A Study in Human Understanding*, New York: Dover Publications, 1951 (1968), trans. Jerry Bernstein and Roger G. Newton with von Mises; based on *Kleines Lehrbuch des Positivismus: Einführung in die empiristische Wissenschaftsauffassung*, The Hague: Van Stockum and Zoon, 1939.

Mitchell, Juliet. *Psychoanalysis and Feminism*, New York: Pantheon, 1974.

Modern Applications of Austrian Thought. Ed. Jürgen G. Backhaus, New York: Routledge, 2005.

Molisch, Paul. *Vom Kampf der Tschechen um ihren Staat*, Vienna: Wilhelm Braumüller, 1929.

Monk, Ray. *The Duty of Genius*, New York: The Free Press, 1990.

Morscher, Edgar. *Bernard Bolzano's Life and Work*, Vienna: Akademia Verlag, 2008.

Morscher, Edgar. *Das logische An-sich bei Bernard Bolzano*, Salzburg: Verlag Anton Pustet, 1973.

Müller, Adam. *Die Elemente der Staatskunst: Sechsunddreisig Vorlesungen*, Berlin: Haude & Spenersche, 1936 [original edition: 1806–1809].

Musil, Robert. *Beitrag zur Beurteilung der Lehren Machs*, diss., Berlin, 1908.

Musil, Robert. *The Man without Qualities*, trans. Eithne Wilkins and Ernst Kaiser, London: Martin Secker and Warburg Ltd, 1953–1960, 3 volumes.

Musil, Robert. *The Man without Qualities*, trans. Sophie Wilkins, New York: Knopf, 1995, 2 volumes.

Musil, Robert. *Precision and Soul: Essays and Addresses*, co-trans. and ed. Burton Pike and David S. Luft, Chicago: University of Chicago Press, 1990.

Musil, Robert. *Young Törless*, trans. Eithne Wilkins and Ernst Kaiser, in *Robert Musil: Selected Writings*, ed. Burton Pike, New York: Continuum, 1986.
Nadler, Josef. *Franz Grillparzer*, Vaduz: Liechtenstein Verlag, 1948.
Nadler, Josef. *Literaturgeschichte Österreichs*, Linz: Österreichischer Verlag für Belletristik und Wissenschaft, 1948.
Naumann, Walter. *Franz Grillparzer: Das dichterische Werk*, 2nd edition, Stuttgart: W. Kohlhammer Verlag, 1967.
Nicolson, Harald. *The Congress of Vienna; a Study in Allied Unity, 1812–1822*, London: Constable & Co., 1946.
Neurath, Otto. *Empiricism and Sociology*, ed. Marie Neurath and Robert S. Cohen, Dordrecht: Reidel, 1973.
Nietzsche, Friedrich. *Beyond Good and Evil: Prelude to a Philosophy of the Future*, trans. Walter Kaufmann, New York: Vintage, 1989.
Nietzsche, Friedrich. *Schopenhauer as Educator*, trans. James W. Hillesheim and Malcolm R. Simpson, South Bend: Regnery/Gateway, 1965.
Nietzsche, Friedrich. *Untimely Meditations*, ed. Daniel Breazeale, trans. R. J. Hollingdale, Cambridge: Cambridge University Press, 1997.
Nipperdey, Thomas. *Deutsche Geschichte 1800–1866: Bürgerwelt und starker Staat*, Munich: C. H. Beck, 1994.
Nosek, Vladimir. *Spirit of Bohemia: A Survey of Czechoslovak History, Music, and Literature*, New York: Brentano, 1927.
Nyíri, J. *Am Rande Europas: Studien zur österreich-ungarischen Philosophiegeschichte*, Vienna: Böhlau Verlag, 1988.
Oakley, Allen. *The Foundations of Austrian Economics from Menger to Mises: A Critico-Historical Retrospective of Subjectivism*, Cheltenham: Edward Elgar, 1997.
Oestreich, Gerhard, Brigitta Oestreich, and H. G. K. Königsberger, *Neostoicism and the Early Modern State*, trans. David McLintock, Boston: D. Reidel Publishing, 1982.
Ort, Thomas. *Art and Life in Modernist Prague: Karel Capek and His Generation, 1911–1938*, New York: Palgrave Macmillan, 2013.
Palacký, Franz. *Geschichte von Böhmen: grösstentheils nach Urkunden und Handschriften*, Prague: Kronberger und Weber, 1844–1867, 5 volumes.
Pannwitz, Rudolf. *Der Geist der Tschechen*, Vienna: Verlag "Der Friede," 1919.
Parker, Geoffrey et al. *The Thirty Years War*, 2nd edition, New York: Routledge, 1997.
Paul F. Lazarsfeld: An Empirical Theory of Social Action: Collected Writings. Ed. Christian Fleck and Nico Stehr, trans. Hella Beister, Oxford: The Bardwell Press, 2011.
Paul, Jean. *Selina oder über die Unsterblichkeit der Seele* in his *Sämtliche Werke*, Abt. I, Bd. 6, Munich: Hanser, 1963, 1105–236.
Pech, Stanley Z. *The Czech Revolution of 1848*, Chapel Hill: The University of North Carolina Press, 1969.
Perloff, Marjorie. *The Edge of Irony: Modernism in the Shadow of the Habsburg Empire*, Chicago: The University of Chicago Press, 2016.

plato.stanford.edu/entries/intentionality.

Poli, Roberto, "The Brentano Puzzle: An Introduction," in *The Brentano Puzzle*, ed. Roberto Poli, Brookfield, United States: Ashgate, 1998, 1–13.

Politzer, Heinz. *Franz Kafka: Parable and Paradox*, Ithaca, NY: Cornell University Press, 1962.

Politzer, Heinz. *Grillparzer oder Das abgründige Biedermeier*, Vienna: Verlag Fritz Molden, 1972.

Popp, Adelheid. *The Autobiography of a Working Woman*, trans. E. C. Harvey, Chicago: F. G. Browne and Co., 1913.

Popper, Karl. *The Logic of Scientific Discovery*, London: Hutchinson, 1959.

Popper, Karl. *The Open Society and Its Enemies*, Princeton: Princeton University Press, 1963, 2 Vols.

Přibram, Karl. *Conflicting Patterns of Thought*, Washington, DC: Public Affairs Press, 1949.

Přihonsky, František. *New Anti-Kant or Examination of the Critique of Pure Reason*, according to concepts laid down in Bolzano's *Theory of Science*, Bautzen, 1850 in *New Anti-Kant*, ed. and trans. Sandra Lapointe and Clinton Tolley, New York: Palgrave Macmillan, 2014.

Prinz, Friedrich. *Prag und Wien 1848: Probleme der nationalen und sozialen Revolution in Spiegel der Wiener Ministerratsprotokole*, Munich: Verlag Robert Lerche, 1968.

Prutti, Brigitte. *Grillparzers Welttheater: Modernität und Tradition*, Bielefeld: Aisthesis Verlag, 2013.

Pulzer, P. G. J. *The Rise of Political Anti-Semitism in Germany and Austria*, New York: John Wiley and Sons, 1964.

Rabinbach, Anson. *The Crisis of Austrian Socialism: From Red Vienna to Civil War, 1927–1934*, Chicago: The University of Chicago Press, 1983.

Raeff, Marc. *The Well-Ordered Police State: Social and Institutional Change through Law in the Germanies and Russia 1600–1800*, New Haven: Yale University Press, 1983.

Ragg-Kirby, Helena. *Adalbert Stifter's Late Prose: The Mania for Moderation*, Rochester, NY: Camden House, 2000.

Rancurello, Antos C. *A Study of Franz Brentano: His Psychological Standpoint and His Significance in the History of Psychology*, New York: Academic Press, 1968.

Redlich, Oswald. *Rudolf von Habsburg: Das deutsche Reich nach dem Untergang des alten Kaisertums*, Innsbruck: Neudruck der Ausgabe, 1903, Scientia Verlag Aalen, 1965.

Reitter, Paul (Autumn 2003). "Karl Kraus and the Jewish Self-Hatred Question," *Jewish Social Studies*, New Series, Vol. 10, No. 1, 78–116.

Reitter, Paul. *The Anti-Journalist: Karl Kraus and Jewish Self-Fashioning in Fin-de-siècle Europe*, Chicago: University of Chicago Press, 2008.

Reynolds-Cordileone, Diana. *Alois Riegl in Vienna 1875–1905: An Institutional Biography*, Burlington, VT: Ashgate, 2014.

Ricoeur, Paul. *Freud and Philosophy*, trans. Denis Savage, New Haven: Yale University Press, 1970.
Rieff, Philip. *Freud: The Mind of the Moralist*, Garden City: Doubleday Anchor, 1961.
Rieff, Philip. *The Triumph of the Therapeutic: Uses of Faith after Freud*, New York: Harper and Row, 1966.
Rilke, Rainer Maria. *The Notebooks of Malte Laurids Brigge*, trans. Burton Pike, Champaign: Dalkey Archive Press, 2009.
Rilke's Book of Hours: Love Poems to God. Trans. Anita Barrows and Joanna Macy, New York: Riverhead Books, 1997.
Ringer, Fritz K. *The Decline of the German Mandarins*, Cambridge, MA: Harvard University Press, 1969.
Roazen, Paul. *Freud and His Followers*, New York: Signet, 1971.
Robert Zimmermanns philosophische Propädeutik und die Vorlagen aus der Wissenschaftslehre, Vienna: Der Österreichische Akademie der Wissenschaften, 1975.
Robertson, John. *The Case for the Enlightenment: Scotland and Naples, 1680–1760*, Cambridge: Cambridge University Press, 2005.
Roe, Ian F. *Franz Grillparzer: A Century of Criticism*, Columbia, South Carolina: Camden House, 1995.
Rosegger, Peter. *Als ich noch der Waldbauernbub war*, Rosenheim: Rosenheimer Verlaghaus, 2006.
Rossbacher, Karlheinz. *Literatur und Liberalismus: Zur Kultur der Ringstrassenzeit in Wien*, Salzburg: J & V, 1992.
Rothenberg, Gunther E. *Napoleon's Great Adversaries: The Archduke Charles and the Austrian Army 1792–1814*, London: B.T. Batsford, 1986.
Royal and Republican Sovereignty in Early Modern Europe. Ed. Robert Oresko et al., Cambridge: Cambridge University Press, 1997.
Rumpler, Helmut. *Eine Chance für Mitteleuropa: Bürgerliche Emancipation und Staatsverfall in der Habsburgermonarchie*, Vienna: Verlag Carl Ueberreuter, 2005.
Russell, Bertrand. *A Critical Exposition of the Philosophy of Leibniz*, Wolfeboro, NH: Longwood Academic, George Allen & Unwin Ltd, 1964.
Russell, Bertrand. *A History of Western Philosophy*, New York: Simon and Schuster, 1945.
Rutherford, Donald. *Leibniz and the Rational Order of Nature*, Cambridge: Cambridge University Press, 1995.
Ryan, Judith. *Rilke, Modernism, and the Poetic Tradition*, Cambridge: Cambridge University Press, 1999.
Ryan, Judith. *The Vanishing Subject: Early Psychology and Literary Modernism*, Chicago: The University of Chicago Press, 1991.
Ryle, Gilbert. *The Concept of Mind*, New York: Barnes and Noble, 1969 [1949].
Saar, Ferdinand von. Das *Erzählerische Werk*, Vienna: Amandus-Verlag, 1959, 3 volumes.

Sauer, August. *Franz Grillparzer*, Stuttgart: Metzlerschen Buchhandlung, 1941.
Sayer, Derek. *The Coasts of Bohemia*, Princeton: Princeton University Press, 1998.
Schäble, Gunter. *Franz Grillparzer*, Hanover: Friedrich Verlag, 1971.
Scheit, Gerhard. *Franz Grillparzer mit Selbstzeugnissen und Bilddokumenten*, Hamburg: Rowohlt, 1989.
Schmidt-Hartmann, Eva. *Thomas G. Masaryk's Realism: Origins of a Czech Political Concept*, Munich: R. Oldenbourg, 1984.
Schnitzler, Arthur, *Der Weg ins Freie*, Frankfurt: Fischer, 1990.
Schönwiese, Ernst. *Literatur in Wien zwischen 1930 and 1980*, Vienna: Amalthea Verlag, 1980.
Schopenhauer, Arthur. "On Some Forms of Literature," in *The Art of Literature*, trans. T. Bailey Saunders, New York: Macmillan, 1900.
Schorske, Carl E. *Fin-de-siècle Vienna: Politics and Culture*, New York: Alfred A Knopf, 1980.
Schwartz, Agatha and Helga Thorson. *Shaking the Empire, Shaking Patriarchy: The Growth of a Feminist Consciousness across the Austro-Hungarian Monarchy*, Riverside: Adriane Press, 2014.
Scott, Joan Wallach. *Gender and the Politics of History Gender and the Politics of History*, revised edition, New York: Columbia University Press, 1999.
Sebald, W. G. *Die Beschreibung des Unglücks: Zur österreichischen Literatur von Stifter bis Handke*, Salzburg: Residenz Verlag, 1985.
Seidler, Herbert (1970). "Die österreichische Literatur als Problem der Forschung", *Österreich in Geschichte und Literatur*, 14. Jahrgang, Heft 7, 354–68.
Seigel, Jerrold. *The Idea of the Self: Thought and Experience in Western Europe since the Seventeenth Century*, Cambridge: Cambridge University Press, 2005.
Seton-Watson, R. W. *A History of the Czechs and Slovaks*, Hamden, CO: Archon Books, 1965.
Sheehan, James J. *German History 1770–1866*, Oxford: Clarendon Press, 1989.
Shepherd, Gordon Brook. *The Austrians: A Thousand-Year Odyssey*, New York: Carroll & Graf Publishers Inc., 1996.
Sak, Robert. *Josef Jungmann: Život obrozence*, Prague: Vyšehrad, 2007.
Small, Albion. *The Cameralists: The Pioneers of German Social Policy*, Chicago: The University of Chicago Press, 1909.
Smith, Barry. *Austrian Philosophy: The Legacy of Franz Brentano*, Chicago: Open Court, 1994.
Sorkin, David (2002). *A Wise, Enlightened, and Reliable Piety: The Religious Enlightenment in Central and Western Europe, 1689–1789*, Oakes Institute Pamphlet, No. 1, University of Southampton.
Sorkin, David (1999). "Reform Catholicism and Religious Enlightenment," *The Austrian History Yearbook*, Vol. 30, 187–219.
Sorkin, David. *The Religious Enlightenment: Protestants, Jews, and Catholics from London to Vienna*, Princeton: Princeton University Press, 2008.

Sorrels, Katherine. *Cosmopolitan Outsiders: Imperial Inclusion, National Exclusion, and the Pan-European Idea, 1900–1930*, New York: Palgrave Macmillan, 2016.

Spann, Othmar. *The History of Economics*, trans. Eden and Cedar Paul, New York: W. W. Norton, 1930.

Spector, Scott. *Prague Territories: National Conflict and Cultural Innovation in Franz Kafka's Fin de Siècle*, Berkeley: University of California Press, 2000.

Spector, Scott. "The Habsburg Empire" in *The Cambridge Companion to European Modernism*, ed. Pericles Lewis, New York: Cambridge University Press, 2011, chapter 4.

Spiel, Hilde. *Fanny von Arnstein: Daughter of the Enlightenment 1758–1818*, trans. Christine Shuttleworth, New York: Berg, 1991.

Spiel, Hilde. *Vienna's Golden Autumn: From the Watershed Year 1866 to Hitler's Anschluss, 1938*, New York: Weidenfeld and Nicolson, 1987.

Sprachgeschichte des Neuhochdeutschen: Gegenstände, Methode, Theorien. Ed. Andreas Gardt et al., Tübingen: Niemeyer, 1992.

Srbik, Heinrich Ritter von. *Metternich: Der Staatsmann und der Mensch*, 3rd edition, Munich: Bruckmann, 1957.

Stadler, Friedrich. *Studien zum Wiener Kreis: Ursprung, Entwicklung und Wirkung des Logischen Empiricismus im Kontext*, Frankfurt am Main: Suhrkamp Verlag, 1997.

Stadler, Friedrich. *The Vienna Circle: Studies in the Origins, Development, and Influence of Logical Empiricism*, trans. Camilla Nielsen et al., Vienna: Springer Verlag, 2001.

Stadler, Friedrich. *Vom Positivismus zur "Wissenschaftlichen Weltauffassung": am Beispiel der Wirkungsgeschichte von Ernst Mach in Österreich von 1895 bis 1934*, Munich: Löcker Verlag, 1982.

Stern, J. P (1989). "Bolzano, Language and Nationalism," *Journal of European Studies*, Vol. 19, Part 3, 169–89.

Stern, J. P (January 1966). "Karl Kraus's Vision of Language," *The Modern Language Review*, Vol. 61, No. 1, 71–84.

Stieg, Gerald. *Sein oder Schein: Die Österreichische Idee von Maria Theresia bis zum Anschluss*, trans. from *L'Autriche: Une nation chimérique?* Vienna: Böhlau Verlag, 2016.

Stifter, Adalbert, *Brigitta*, trans. Helen Watabe-O'Kelly, London: Angel Books, 1990.

Stifter, Adalbert. *Bunte Steine. Späte Erzählungen*, ed. Max Stefel, Augsburg: Adam Kraft Verlag, 1960.

Stifter, Adalbert. *Der Nachsommer*, Zurich: Scientia AG, 1945.

Stifter, Adalbert. *Die Mappe meines Urgrossvaters: Letzte Fassung*, ed. Nachwort Alexaner Stillmark, Zurich: Manese Verlag, 1997.

Stifter, Adalbert. *Sämtliche Erzählungen nach den Erstdrucken*, ed. Wolfgang Matz, Munich: Deutscher Taschenbuch Verlag, 2001.

Stifter, Adalbert. *Witiko: Roman*, afterward by Fritz Krökel, Munich: Deutscher Taschenbuch Verlag, 2001.

Stollberg-Rilinger, Barbara. *Maria Theresia: Die Kaiserin in Ihre Zeit: Eine Biographie*, Munich: C.H. Beck, 2017.

Strigl, Daniela. *Berühmt sein ist nichts: Marie von Ebner-Eschenbach: Eine Biographie*, Vienna: Residenz Verlag, 2016.
Sulloway, Frank J. *Freud, Biologist of the Mind: Beyond the Psychoanalytic Legend*, New York: Basic Books, 1979.
Swales, Martin. *The German Novelle*, Princeton: Princeton University Press, 1977.
Swales, Martin and Erika. *Adalbert Stifter: A Critical Study*, Cambridge: Cambridge University Press, 1984.
Swoboda, Erich. *Carnuntum: Seine Geschichte und seine Denkmäler*, 3rd edition, Vienna: Hermann Böhlau, 1958.
Szabo, Franz A. J. *Kaunitz and Enlightened Absolutism, 1753–1780*, New York: Cambridge University Press, 1994.
Tassone, Biagio G. *From Psychology to Phenomenology: Franz Brentano's "Psychology from an Empirical Standpoint" and Contemporary Philosophy of Mind*, New York: Palgrave Macmillan, 2012.
Taylor, A. J. P. *The Habsburg Monarchy 1809–1918*, new edition, London: Hamish Hamilton, 1948.
Textor, Mark. *Brentano's Mind*, Oxford Scholarship Online, 2017.
Thaler, Peter. *The Ambivalence of Identity: The Austrian Experience of Nation-Building in a Modern Society*, West Lafayette, IN: Purdue University Press, 2001.
The Analytic Turn: Analysis in Early Analytic Philosophy and Phenomenology. Ed. Michael Beaney, New York: Routledge, 2007.
The Austrian Contribution to Analytic Philosophy. Ed. Mark Textor, New York: Routledge, 2006.
The Cambridge Companion to Brentano. Ed. Dale Jacquette, Cambridge: Cambridge University Press, 2004,
The Cambridge History of Philosophy 1870–1945. Ed. Thomas Baldwin, Cambridge: Cambridge University Press, 2003.
The Cambridge History of Science, Vol. 7: *The Modern Social Sciences*. Ed. Theodore M. Porter and Dorothy Ross, Cambridge: Cambridge, University Press, 2003.
The Culture of Power in Europe during the Long Eighteenth Century. Ed. Hamish Scott and Brendan Simms, Cambridge: Cambridge University Press, 2007.
The Diaries of Franz Kafka: 1910–1913. Ed. Max Brod, trans. Joseph Kresh, New York: Schocken Books, 1948.
The Enlightenment in Bohemia: Religion, Morality and Multiculturalism. Ed. Ivo Cerman, Rita Krueger, and Susan Reynolds, Oxford: Voltaire Foundation, 2011.
The Intellectual Migration: Europe and America 1930–1960. Ed. Donald Fleming and Bernard Bailyn, Cambridge, MA: Harvard University Press, 1969.
The Kraus Project: Essays by Karl Kraus. Trans. and annotated Jonathan Franzen, assisted by Paul Reitter and Daniel Kehlmann, New York: Farrar, Straus and Giroux, 2013.
The Letters of Sigmund Freud to Eduard Silberstein 1871–1881. Ed. Walter Boehlich, trans. Arnold J. Pomerans, Cambridge, MA: Harvard University Press, 1990.

The School of Franz Brentano. Ed. Liliana Albertazzi, Massimo Libardi, and Roberto Poli, Boston: Kluwer Academic Publishers, 1996.

Theodor Gomperz: Ein Gelehrtenleben im Bürgertum der Franz-Josefs-Zeit. Ed. Robert A. Kann, Vienna: Verlag der österreichischen Akademie der Wissenschaften, 1974.

Thienen-Adlerflycht, Christoph. *Graf Leo Thun im Vormärz: Grundlagen des böhmischen Konservatismus im Kaisertum Österreich*, Vienna: Hermann Böhlaus Nachf, 1967.

Thomson, S. Harris. *Czechoslovakia in European History*, Princeton: Princeton University Press, 1943.

Tielke, Martin. *Sanftes Gesetz und historische Notwendigkeit: Adalbert Stifter zwischen Restauration und Revolution*, Frankfurt am Main: Peter Lang, 1979.

Tribe, Keith. *Strategies of Economic Order: German Economic Discourse, 1750–1950*, New York: Cambridge University Press, 1995.

Trilling, Lionel. *Freud and the Crisis of Our Culture*, Boston: Beacon Press, 1955.

Tweraser, Felix W. *Political Dimensions of Arthur Schnitzler's Late Fiction*, Columbia, SC: Camden House, 1998.

Ulrich, Adam. *The Political Economy of J. H. G. Justi*, Bern: Peter Lang, 2006.

Universität—Forschung—Lehre: Themen und Perspektiven im langen 20. Jahrhundert, 650 Jahre Universität Wien. Vienna: Vienna University Press, 2015, Vol. 1.

Urbach, Reinhard. *Arthur Schnitzler*, trans. Donald Daviau, New York: Frederick Ungar, 1973.

Urbach, Reinhard. *Wiener Komödie und Ihr Publikum: Stranitzky und die Folgen*, Vienna: Jugend und Volk, 1973.

Valjavec, Fritz. *Der Josephinismus: Zur geistigen Entwicklung Österreichs im achtzehnten und neunzehnten Jahhundert*, 2nd edition, Munich: R. Oldenbourg, 1945.

Van Herik, Judith. *Freud on Femininity and Faith*, Berkeley: UC Press, 1982.

Vaughn, Karen I. *Economics in America: The Migration of a Tradition*, Cambridge: Cambridge University Press, 1994.

Verdrängte Humanismus—verzögerte Aufklärung: Philosophie in Österreich. Ed. Michael Benedikt et al., Vienna: Turia and Kant, 1992, 4 volumes.

Vick, Brian E. *Defining Germany: The 1848 Frankfurt Parliamentarians and National Identity*, Cambridge, MA: Harvard University Press, 2002.

Vocelka, Karl. *Geschichte Österreichs: Kultur—Gesellschaft—Politik*, Graz: Verlag Styria, 2000.

Vocelka, Karl. *Glanz und Untergang der höfischen Welt: Repräsentation, Reform, und Reaktion im Habsburgischen Vielvölkerstaat*, Vienna: Ueberreuter, 2001.

Voegelin, Erich. *Der autoritäre Staat: Ein Versuch über das österreichische Staatsproblem*, Vienna: Verlag von Julius Springer, 1936.

Wagner, Eva. *An Analysis of Franz Grillparzer's Dramas: Fate, Guilt, and Tragedy*, Lewiston, NY: The Edwin Mellen Press, 1992.

Wallace, Donald L. *Embracing Democracy: Hermann Broch, Politics and Exile, 1918–1951*, Oxford: Peter Lang, 2014.

Wandruszka, Adam. *Geschichte einer Zeitung: das Schicksal der "Presse" und der "Neue Freie Presse" von 1848 zur Zweiten Republik*, Vienna: Neue Wiener Presse, 1958.

Wandruszka, Adam. *The House of Habsburg: Six Hundred Years of a European Dynasty*, trans. Cathleen and Hans Epstein, London: Sidgwick and Jackson, 1964.

Wangermann, Ernst. *Aufklärung und staatsbürgerliche Erziehung: Gottfried van Swieten als Reformator des österreichischen Unterrichtswesens 1781–1791*, Vienna: Verlag für Geschichte und Politik, 1978.

Wangermann, Ernst (2006). "An Eighteenth–Century Engine of Reform," *Austrian History Yearbook*, Vol. 37, 58–61.

Wangermann, Ernst. *The Austrian Achievement 1700–1800*, London: Harcourt Brace Jovanovich, 1973.

Was heist Österreich? Inhalt und Umfang des Österreichbegriffs vom 10. Jahrhundert bis heute. Ed. Richard G. Platschka, Gerald Stourzh, and Jan Paul Niederkorn, Vienna: Verlag der österreichischen Akademie der Wissenschaften, 1995.

Wassermann, Janek. *Black Vienna; The Radical Right in the Red City, 1918–1938*, Ithaca, NY: Cornell University Press, 2014.

Waugh, Alexander, *The House of Wittgenstein: A Family at War*, New York: Doubleday, 2008.

Wedberg, Anders. *History of Philosophy*, Vol. 3: *Bolzano to Wittgenstein*, Oxford: Clarendon Press, 1984.

Weininger, Otto. *Geschlecht und Charakter: Eine prinzipielle Untersuchung*, Munich: Matthes & Seitz Verlag, 1980 [reprint of the first edition, Vienna, 1903].

Weiss, Walter. "Stifters Reduktion," in *Adalbert Stifter und die Krise der Mitteleuropäische Literatur: Ein italienisch-österreichisches Colloquium*, ed. Paolo Chiarini, Rome: Bulzoni Editore, 1987, 3–27.

Weiss, Walter. "Thematisierung der 'Ordnung' in der österreichischen Literatur," in *Dauer im Wandel: Aspekte Österreichischer Kulturentwicklung*, ed. Walter Strolz, Vienna: Herder &. Co., 1975, 19–44.

Weiss, Walter. "Zum deutschen in der österreichischen Literatur," in *Tradition und Entwicklung: Festschrift Eugen Thurnher zum 60. Geburtstag*, ed. Werner M. Bauer et al., Innsbruck: Innsbrucker Beiträge, 1982, 47–58.

Wellek, René. *Essays on Czech Literature*, The Hague: Mouton & Co., 1963.

Wells, C. J. *German: A Linguistic History to 1945*, Oxford: Clarendon Press, 1985.

White, Hayden. *Metahistory: The Historical Imagination in Nineteenth-Century Europe*, Baltimore: Johns Hopkins University Press, 1973.

Whyte, L. L. *The Unconscious before Freud*, London: Friedman, 1979.

Williams, Raymond. *Culture and Society, 1780–1950*, New York: Columbia University Press, 1958.

Wingfield, Nancy M. *Flag Wars and Stone Saints: How the Bohemian Lands Became Czech*, Cambridge: Harvard University Press, 2007.

Winkelbauer, Thomas. *Ständefreiheit und Fürstenmacht: Länder und Untertanen des Hauses Habsburg im Kofessionellen Zeitalter*, Teil 2, Vienna: Carl Ueberreuter, 2003.

Winter, Eduard. *Die Sozial—und Ethnoethik Bernard Bolzanos*, Vienna: Verlag der österreichischen Akademie der Wissenschaften, 1977.
Winter, Eduard. *Frühhumanismus: Seine Entwicklung in Böhmen und deren europäische Bedeutung für die Kirchenreformbestrebungen im 14. Jahrhundert*, Berlin: Akademie-Verlag, 1964.
Winter, Ernst. *Der Böhmische Vormärz in Briefen B. Bolzanos an F. Přihonský (1824–1848)*, Berlin: Akademie Verlag, 1956.
Wittgenstein, Ludwig. *Notebooks 1914–1916*, trans. G. E. M. Anscombe, Oxford: Basil Blackwell, 1961 (1969).
Wittgenstein, Ludwig. *Tractatus Logico-Philosophicus*, trans. C. K. Ogden, intro. Bertrand Russell, New York: Routledge and Kegan Paul, 1978 [original: 1922].
Wittgenstein, Ludwig and Friedrich Waismann, *The Voices of Wittgenstein: The Vienna Circle*, ed. Gordon Baker, trans. Gordon Baker et al., London: Routledge, 2003.
Wohl, Robert. *The Generation of 1914*, Cambridge: Harvard University Press, 1979.
Wolff, Larry. *The Idea of Galicia: History and Fantasy in Habsburg Political Culture*, Stanford: Stanford University Press, 2010.
Wood, Frank. *Rainer Maria Rilke*, Minneapolis: University of Minnesota Press, 1958.
Worbs, Michael. *Nervenkunst: Literatur und Psychoanalyse im Wien der Jahrhundertwende*, Frankfurt am Main: Europäische Verlagsanstalt, 1983.
Wunberg, Gotthart. *Der frühe Hofmannsthal: Schizophrenie als dichterische Struktur*, Stuttgart: Kohlhammer Verlag, 1965.
Začek, Josef Frederick. *Palacký: The Historian as Scholar and Nationalist*, The Hague: Joseph Frederick, 1970.
Zahra, Tara, *Kidknapped Souls: National Indifference and the Battle for Children in the Bohemian Lands, 1900–1948*, Ithaca, NY: Cornell University Press, 2008.
Zeman, Herbert. Ed. *Literaturgeschichte Österreichs*, Graz: Akademische Druck- u. Verlagsanstalt, 1996.
Zeyringer, Klaus. *Österreichische Literatur seit 1945*, Innsbruck: Haymon Verlag, 2001.
Zeyringer, Klaus/Helmut Gollner. *Eine Literaturgeschichte Österreich seit 1650*, Vienna: Studien Verlag, 2012.
Ziolkowski, Theodore. *Hermann Broch*, New York: Columbia University Press, 1964.
Zöllner, Erich. *Der Österreichbegriff: Formen und Wandlungen in der Geschichte*, Vienna: Verlag für Geschichte und Politik, 1988.
Zöllner, Erich. *Geschichte Österreichs: Von den Anfängen bis zur Gegenwart*, 8th edition, Vienna: Verlag für Geschichte und Politik, 1990.
Zweig, Stefan. *The World of Yesterday*. Intro. Harry Zohn, Lincoln: University of Nebraska Press, 1943/1964.
Zwischen Orpheus und Don Juan. Ed. Ernst Schönwiese, Graz: Stiasny Verlag, 1965.

Index

Abrams, M. H. 154 n.15
Absolutism 11, 23, 31, 37, 76, 106, 151 n.47, 155 n.23
Adler, Max 83
Adler, Viktor 48, 49, 121
Administrative Union (1749) 15, 30
aestheticism: in Austrian literature 54; opposition to rationalism 100. *See also* aesthetics; art
aesthetics, and ethics 86, 94, 103, 106, 109. *See also* aestheticism; art
Ammon, Ulrich 153 n.8
Analysis of Sensations (Mach) 72–4, 174 n.83, 174 n.85, 175 n.97
analytic philosophy: in Austrian culture 59–60; in Great Britain 24; importance of language in 1, 60, 65, 79, 137; origins of 60, 170 n.38. *See also* empiricism; psychology
Andrian, Leopold von 99–102, 184 n.71, 184 n.72, 184 n.73
Andrian-Werburg, Viktor von 10, 43, 143 n.36
anti-Semitism: and German nationalism 49; in German politics 49, 56–7; and internationalism 52; of Maria Theresa 37; of Weininger 50. *See also* Judaism
Anzengruber, Ludwig 48, 99, 183 n.64
Aquinas, Thomas 70
aristocracy: decline of 102; and freemasonry 38; and language 32–3; and religion 36; and the state 36. *See also* class
Aristotle, influence on Brentano 67, 69
art: art history 48; in Austrian culture 29; and internationalism 52; in Prague 61; in salons 42. *See also* aestheticism; aesthetics; music; theater
atomism: logical atomism 81, 176 n.116; Mach on 75; Wittgenstein on 80. *See also* materialism; physics
Attila the Hun 17

Auersperg, Count Anton Alexander von 43
Ausgleich 7, 11, 39, 46, 124
Austria: annexation by Germany 57; archduchy of 3, 14, 16, 144 n.41; cultural regions of 3, 5, 14, 84, 94, 140 n.2; empire of 9–10, 27, 39, 144 n.43, 147 n.11, 156 n.37, 157 n.46; geography of 2, 4, 7, 13, 46, 137, 167 n.2; origins of 60, 117, 168 n.6; political decline 49, 101; republic of 3, 14, 16, 51, 55–6, 137–8. *See also* Cisleithania; Holy Roman Empire; Graz; Innsbruck; Vienna
Austrian Enlightenment: and Catholicism 31, 36–7, 41, 154 n.18; defined 25, 34–5; and education 32, 35–6; outside of Vienna 38; role of bureaucracy in 34; role of German language in 31–5, 37. *See also* Habsburg Monarchy; Josephinism
Austrian state 4, 7, 11–12, 15–27, 30–3, 35, 38, 118, 121, 138, 151 n.47, 190 n.11, 198 n.3
authoritarian state 118–23
Avenarius, Richard 76

Babenberg Dynasty 10, 16–18, 148 n.16
Bahr, Hermann 49, 102, 181 n.37, 183 n.58, 184 n.75
Baltic states 140 n.7
Baroque: aesthetics of 49; and Austrian identity 22, 29; and Catholicism 26, 36
Battle of Lechfeld (955) 18
Battle of Mohács (1526) 19
Battle of Mohács (1687) 20
Battle of Solferino (1859) 45
Battle of White Mountain (1620) 15, 22
Baudelaire, Charles 95, 101
Bauer, Otto 121–2, 137, 191 n.27
Benedictines 34, 94, 154 n.18
Berlin: Hegel in 41, 61–2; intellectual exchange with Vienna 12, 41, 159 n.59;

salon culture in 42, 159 n.59. *See also* Germany; Prussia
Bettauer, Hugo 138, 198 n.5
Beyond Good and Evil (Nietzsche) 100
Beyond the Pleasure Principle 132–3, 197 n.75
Bilingualism 44, 159 n.62
Bismarck, Otto von 2, 34, 43, 46, 56, 110, 147 n.11
Blackall, Eric V. 32, 153 n.6, 181 n.39
Bohemia: Bohemian Enlightenment 60; Bohemian Reformation 19, 21, 149 n.27, 157 n.44; counter-reformation in 15, 22, 25; Czech migration into 44; geography of 7, 13; historical connections with Austria 15; intellectual contributions of 54; introduction of Christianity into 17; separation with Austria 18, 24, 30, 54–5. *See also* Holy Roman Empire
Böhm-Bawerk, Eugen von 49, 126
Bolzano, Bernard: advocacy of bilingualism in Bohemia 44; and analytic philosophy 59, 65, 84–5, 168 n.9, 170 n.37, 170 n.44; and the Austrian Enlightenment 39, 60, 92; Bohemian ties of 40, 63; influence on reform 62, 119; intellectual contributions of 60, 64, 84; on logic 60–2, 64–6, 84, 86; religious views of 60, 62; and Schlegel 42; and Seibt 38, 157 n.44; and Thun 45, 62, 66, 171 n.46; on truth and knowledge 64–5; and Zimmerman 44, 66, 171 n.46. *See also Theory of Science*
Bonaparte, Napoleon: Confederation of the Rhine 41, 43; and Prussia 38, 41; resistance to 41
The Book of Hours 112
Borges, Jorge 188 n.128
Born, Ignaz von 38
Boyer, John W. 157 n.40, 158 n.53, 163 n.102, 189 n.4
Brady, Jr., Thomas A. 149 n.29
Brentano, Franz: on consciousness 68, 70–1, 84; and Freud 48, 67, 69–71, 173 n.74; influence of 67–8, 71, 172 n.55, 196 n.66; and Mach 12, 48, 59, 69, 73–5, 78–9, 84, 86, 139; on meditation 67; and positivism 59, 196 n.67; on psychology 68–72, 75, 172 n.58, 173 n.65, 173 n.73, 173 n.75; and scientific methodology 68, 84; at University of Vienna 48, 67, 171 n.50. *See also Psychology from an Empirical Standpoint*
Breuer, Josef 71
Brno (Czech Republic) 49, 72, 152 n.1, 159 n.64. *See also* Czech Republic; Czechoslovakia
Broch, Hermann 12, 15, 49, 53–4, 57–8, 87–8, 96, 99, 101–4, 106, 110–11, 114–15, 162 n.87, 164 n.104, 166 n.132, 178 n.2, 182 n.47, 183 n.58, 183 n.61, 185 n.83, 186 n.105, 186 n.106, 186 n.107, 186 n.109, 186 n.112, 187 n.113–17, 188 n.129
Brown, Norman O. 134, 195 n.63
Brücke, Ernst Wilhelm 130
Budapest 55. *See also* Hungary
Bühler, Charlotte and Karl 122
Bukovina 4, 7, 157 n.46
bureaucracy: and education 24; and intellectual life 40; and language 34, 47; and modernity 24, 151 n.44; and reform 25
Burke, Edmund 42, 120, 125, 193 n.41. *See also Reflections on the Revolution in France*
Bushnell, Anthony 198 n.3

Caldwell, Bruce 123, 126, 192 n.36, 193 n.40, 193 n.41, 193 n.42, 194 n.45, 194 n.46
Calvinism: in Austria 21; in Bohemia 21–2; tolerance of 26. *See also* Protestantism
Cameralism 31, 37, 117–23, 135–6, 190 n.11, 190 n.14, 191 n.16, 193 n.40
Canetti, Elias 53, 58, 165 n.114
Čapek, Karel 143 n.34, 159 n.64, 164 n.111, 166 n.124
capitalism: and anti-Semitism 57; in intellectual pursuits 30–1; reactions against 48. *See also* economics
Carlsbad Decrees (1819) 41
Carnap, Rudolf: and analytic philosophy 85; founding of Vienna Circle 52; and Popper 82, 85
The Castle 113, 115

Catholicism: in Austria 21–2; of Bolzano 61; Catholic Right 56, 121; critique in twentieth century 49; and Enlightenment 31, 36, 41, 61, 154 n.18; and Habsburg Monarchy 22; and liberalism 47; of Schlegel 42; and social reform 25, 36, 148 n.22, 168 n.7; as source of conflict within Cisleithania 49; of Wittgenstein 77. *See also* clergy; Counter-reformation; papacy

censorship 26, 41–2, 152 n.54, 154 n.17. *See also* publishing

Chamberlain, Houston Stewart 51, 163 n.94. *See also Foundations of the Nineteenth Century*

Chamberlain, Neville 9, 57

Charlemagne 17

Charles IV 19–20, 148 n.18

Charles V 20–1

Charles VI 22, 150 n.39

Charles-Ferdinand University 38, 72

Christian Social Party 47, 49, 55, 122

Cisleithania: as basis of Josephinism 27, 30, 39–40, 45–6; division of 51; language in 31–2, 34, 39, 47. *See also* Austria; Vienna

Civilization and Its Discontents 133

Clark Lecture 131

class: Bolzano on 63; and the First World War 51, 55; and intellectual life 47, 54; and language 32; and liberalism 46, 100. *See also* aristocracy; economics; industrialization; middle class; peasantry

clergy: and education 36; and Josephinism 25, 27, 36; and language 40. *See also* Catholicism

Comenius, John Amos 21

communism 52, 57. *See also* economics

Community of fate 137

Compromise of 1867 7, 11, 39

Comte, Auguste 66, 69, 72, 120, 127

Concordat of 1855 45, 47

Confederation of the Rhine 41, 43

Congress of Vienna 42, 158 n.50

Conservative 29–30, 38–47, 53, 101, 125, 148 n.22, 186 n.111

cosmopolitanism: in German culture 3, 14, 33, 44, 84; and political participation 52; in Prague 19, 112. *See also* internationalism

Coudenhove-Kalergi, Richard von 164 n.103

Counter-Reformation: in Austria 15, 22, 25, 33; and the Thirty Years' War 22. *See also* Catholicism

The Counter-Revolution of Science 127

The Critique of Pure Reason (Kant) 64, 170 n.31

Czech language: and class 36, 44; in education 44; in intellectual life 11, 19, 30, 37, 54, 56, 138; and literature 37, 43, 157 n.47; and other languages 31, 34, 44, 47, 56; and religion 21; revival of 34, 37. *See also* language

Czech Republic 16, 23, 138. *See also* Brno; Czechoslovakia; Prague

Czechoslovakia 4, 12, 14, 16, 30, 56–7, 67, 122, 135, 137, 148 n.13, 160 n.64, 166 n.124, 172 n.54. *See also* Brno; Czech Republic; Prague; Slovakia

Dahrendorf, Ralf 4, 141 n.15

Danube 16–18, 65, 146 n.6, 148 n.16, 171 n.47

Darwinism, Social Darwinism 50. *See also* materialism; science

Das Gemeindekind 100

David, Zdeněk 149 n.22, 157 n.44, 160 n.64, 172 n.54

Death and the Fool 110

Decker, Craig 198 n.3

Der Brenner (Innsbruck) 55

Der Garten der Erkenntnis 101, 184 n.71, 184 n.72

Der Schwierige 111, 115

Descartes, René 61, 74, 170 n.38

Dichter 135, 180 n.20

Die Fackel 104

Die Welt (Klemm) 33

Dilthey, Wilhelm 9, 189 n.3

Dionysianism 49

Dobrovský, Joseph: and the Austrian Enlightenment 34; and Bohemian history 37; influence of 45; and language 155 n.29

Doderer, Heimito von 53, 58, 166 n.128

Ebner, Ferdinand von 55
Ebner-Eschenbach, Marie von 48, 50, 66, 99, 183 n.62
economics: depression of 48; reform of 125; study of 120. *See also* capitalism; class; communism; industrialization; labor; socialism
Eder, Karl 151 n.49, 160 n.70
education: and class 196 n.66; reform of 35–6, 45; and religion 35–6; role in Enlightenment ideology 24; role in reinforcing use of German language in Austria 32; Vienna Circle on 82; Wittgenstein on 78. *See also* schools; universities
ego: in Austrian literature 108; Mach on 74–5. *See also* psychoanalysis; self
Ehrenfels, Christian von 68, 172 n.54
Emerson, Ralph Waldo 109, 185 n.82
empiricism: Brentano on 59, 68, 70–1, 79, 84; and Josephinism 26; and positivism 48, 69, 79; as a product of the Enlightenment 59, 63, 85; and the Vienna Circle 59; Wittgenstein on 59, 78–9. *See also* objectivity; science
Emrich, Wilhelm 114, 188 n.130
Engels, Friedrich 119
Enlightenment: and Austrian culture 29, 138; and class 32; emergence in Austria 24, 41; and Habsburg rule 34, 37; and liberalism 37, 43; long-term influence of 35, 37; and reform 24, 31–3, 35–8; and religion 35–6; and science 32–4, 36–7, 63–4, 85
Erdmann, Karl Dietrich 159 n.60
Ernst Mach Society 82
Ethical Movement 82. *See also* ethics
ethics: Bolzano on 168 n.14, 169 n.28, 182 n.41; and literature 54; and modernism 102; Musil on 53, 106, 177 n.131; and religious reform 104; and science 109, 139; Wittgenstein on 54, 77, 86, 104, 106, 108–9. *See also* Ethical Movement; morality
Exner, Franz 48, 62, 66, 157 n.44, 170 n.41, 171 n.46

fascism 57
Fechner, Gustav 71, 73

Feigl, Herbert 82, 176 n.120
Felbinger, Johann Ignaz von 33, 35–6, 155 n.23
feminism: in Austria 50, 55, 135; and internationalism 52. *See also* gender; suffrage; women
Ferdinand I 43
Ferdinand II 22
Fesl, Joseph 62, 169 n.25, 171 n.46
Feuchtersleben, Ernst von 181 n.37
Fichte, Johann Gottlieb 41, 171 n.47
Ficker, Ludwig von 55
First Republic (Austria) 123, 137, 192 n.29
First World War: effects on Austrian intellectual life 30, 53; and national borders 18; Wittgenstein in 54, 77; and women 55
Fleck, Christian 122, 189 n.6, 192 n.33, 192 n.34
Fliess, Wilhelm 71, 129, 134
Foundations of the Nineteenth Century (Chamberlain) 51, 163 n.94
France: absolutism in 23; and Austria 21–2, 24, 41, 123; and the Enlightenment 7, 21, 24, 154 n.12; and Germany 7–8, 42, 53, 188 n.1, 196 n.66; positivism in 59, 72, 84, 127, 129, 195 n.55. *See also* French language; French Revolution
Francis II (Francis I of Austria) 38–9, 41
Franz Joseph 46, 107
Franz, Georg 152 n.52, 160 n.70
Franzen, Jonathan 105, 185 n.86
Frederick V 21
freemasonry 38, 156 n.35
Frege, Gottlob: and the foundations of analytical philosophy 65; influence of 77–9
French language 5, 8, 35, 130, 196 n.66. *See also* France
French Revolution 7, 26, 35, 38, 40–1, 93, 145 n.47, 156 n.38. *See also* France
Freud, Sigmund: and Brentano 48, 70–1, 196 n.67; and gender and sexuality 50, 55, 129; influence of 104, 129, 195 n.62, 196 n.66; and liberalism 54, 135, 139; at the University of Vienna 48, 101, 130–1
Friedjung, Heinrich 49
The Future of an Illusion 133

Galicia 3–4, 7, 11, 13, 16, 40, 124, 139, 142 n.25, 144 n.42, 144 n.43, 157 n.46, 177 n.129

Gay, Peter 114, 130, 188 n.136, 195 n.64, 196 n.71, 197 n.79

gender: critique of gender norms 50; and society 55. *See also* feminism; masculinity; sexuality; women

General Civil Law Code (1811) 39. *See also* law

Gentz, Friedrich von 42, 158 n.54

George, Stefan 111

German culture 1–3, 6–7, 10–12, 14–15, 32–4, 38, 41, 44, 47, 52, 57, 84, 111, 140 n.2, 140 n.7, 153 n.7, 165 n.121, 172 n.61, 198 n.3

German Democratic Republic 43

German language: in Austrian intellectual life 3, 7, 11–12, 22, 29, 31–5, 37, 39–41, 43–4, 47; and the Austrian state 7, 11, 21–2, 31–3, 35, 198 n.3; and class 30, 32, 47, 51; and education 32–5, 159 n.62; and the Enlightenment 7, 31–8, 138, 153 n.5; German literature 3, 6–7, 12–13, 32, 37–8, 54, 87–115, 145 n.47, 181 n.34; and religion 35; in science 32. *See also* Germany; language

German Mathematical Association 82. *See also* mathematics

German Physical Society 82

Germany: culture of 1–3, 5–7, 10–12, 14–15, 21, 29, 31–4, 38, 41, 44, 47, 52, 57, 84, 110–11, 140 n.2, 140 n.7, 144 n.41, 144 n.43, 153 n.7, 155 n.25, 165 n.121, 198 n.3; geography of 2, 7, 33; nationalism of 5–6, 13, 33, 41, 43–5, 49–52, 55, 57, 72, 93, 120; philosophy of 2, 6–7, 38, 44, 52, 57, 59, 63, 67, 84, 87, 137–8, 145 n.47, 168 n.8; religion in 15, 35–6. *See also* Berlin; German language; Prussia

Geschichte von Böhmen (Palacký) 44, 147 n.13, 160 n.66

Gestalt psychology 68, 84, 172 n.61. *See also* psychology

Ghengis Khan 17

God 36, 61–2, 98, 107, 112–13, 133, 173 n.74, 185 n.81, 187 n.115, 187 n.120, 196 n.67

Goethe, Johann Wolfgang von 7, 9, 32, 34, 41, 91–2, 94

Gomperz, Heinrich 75, 159 n.58

Gomperz, Theodor 162 n.83, 173 n.74

Gottsched, Johann Christoph 32–3

Graz (Austria) 39, 54, 68, 72, 143 n.30, 146 n.6, 152 n.1, 153 n.2, 161 n.81, 165 n.116, 174 n.92, 178 n.2, 178 n.4, 179 n.6. *See also* Austria

Great Britain, and Enlightenment 24

Grillparzer, Franz 9, 12, 39–40, 42, 46, 79, 87–98, 139, 157 n.45, 179 n.12, 179 n.15, 179 n.16, 180 n.18, 180 n.19, 180 n.21, 180 n.22, 180 n.23, 180 n.24, 180 n.26, 181 n.29, 181 n.31, 181 n.33, 181 n.35, 182 n.51

Group Psychology and the Analysis of the Ego 133

Grün, Anastasius. *See* Auersperg, Count Anton Alexander von

Günther, Anton 62

Habsburg Monarchy: administration of 10, 30; centralization of 39, 47; as focus of Austrian history 5, 10, 13, 15; and language 21–2; long-term influence of 45; and nationalism 5, 9, 22, 45, 158 n.52; origins of 5, 7, 11–12; reforms of 21. *See also* Austrian Enlightenment; Holy Roman Empire

Haeckel, Ernst 84

Hainisch, Marianne 55

Hamerling, Robert 66

Hanisch, Ernst 39, 157 n.42, 157 n.44, 161 n.77, 190 n.13

Hartmann, Eduard von 44, 71

Haskalah 43, 154 n.12, 159 n.57

Haugwitz, Count Friedrich Wilhelm von 23–4, 35, 150 n.41

Hayek, Friedrich August von 9, 53, 57, 72, 123–9, 192 n.36, 193 n.41, 194 n.45, 194 n.48, 194 n.51, 194 n.52, 194 n.53, 195 n.58

Hebbel, Christian Friedrich 42, 95–6

Hebrew 37

Hegel, Georg Wilhelm Friedrich: and idealism 6, 41–2, 64, 92; influence of 63–4, 84, 145 n.47; move from Bavaria to Berlin 41; *Phenomenology of Mind* 137

Heidegger, Martin 67, 84, 171 n.53
Heindl, Waltraud 151 n.44
Helfert, Joseph Freiherr von 43
Herbart, Johann Friedrich 66, 71, 171 n.46, 171 n.47
Hertling, Georg von 67
Hertz, Deborah 159 n.59
Hertz, Heinrich 78, 175 n.105. *See also* *The Principles of Mechanics*
Herzog, Hillary 198 n.5
High Liberal Era 46, 51, 98–9, 183 n.65
Hitler, Adolf 56–7, 111, 134, 166 n.129
Hofmannsthal and His Time 110, 162 n.87, 182 n.47, 183 n.61, 186 n.106, 186 n.109, 187 n.117
Hohenzollern 3
Holocaust 138
Holy Roman Empire: conflict with Bohemia 11, 15, 18, 20; and language 32; and nationalism 43; territory of 17. *See also* Austria; Bohemia; Habsburg Monarchy; Hungary; Moravia
hospitals 26. *See also* medicine
Human sciences 1–2, 4–6, 9, 12, 29, 33, 64, 117–36, 138, 145 n.46, 165 n.119, 189 n.2, 189 n.6
Hume, David 76, 78
Hungary: and Habsburg rule 19, 44; and language 40; and nationalism 16; separation with Austria 11, 24, 30, 46. *See also* Budapest; Holy Roman Empire
Hus, Jan 19
Husserl, Edmund: and Brentano 67, 70, 84; and contemporaries 65; on logic 65, 170 n.33; long-term influence 67, 84; on positivism 83
Hussites 19, 148 n.20. *See also* Utraquism

Idealism: Austrian reception of 92; Bolzano on 64; in Germany 12, 40–2, 59–60, 64, 67, 75, 78–9, 92, 171 n.46, 171 n.47. *See also* Romanticism
individualism: and liberalism 37, 43, 75, 100, 191 n.23; and science 120, 125, 127–8
industrialization, Second Industrial Revolution 51, 57, 102, 163 n.99. *See also* class; economics; labor; modernization
Innsbruck (Austria), schools in 39. *See also* Austria

Institute for Austrian Historical Research 43, 48
Intellectual history 1–17, 29–31, 34, 40–1, 44–5, 51, 57, 83, 85, 87, 92, 105, 117, 123, 129–36, 138–9, 140 n.1, 141 n.15, 141 nn.18–19, 142 n.20, 142 n.23, 143 n.28, 143 n.31, 145 n.48, 146 n.6, 147 n.12, 157 n.47, 163 n.97, 179 n.7, 188–9 n.1, 198 n.1
intellectuals: and culture 1–3, 12, 29, 41, 54, 57, 105, 159 n.59; and language 1–2, 7, 11, 15, 22, 29, 31–2, 53, 104, 137, 155 n.29; and liberalism 30, 49–51, 100; and science 2, 6, 9, 26, 29, 51, 75, 135; and society 52; and the state 32, 35, 121; in Vienna 1, 9, 12, 14, 32, 40, 42, 48, 54, 57, 61, 75, 129, 137–8
internationalism 52, 163 n.100. *See also* cosmopolitanism
The Interpretation of Dreams 129, 195 n.62, 196 n.71
Italy: Italian renaissance 19; nationalism in 45
Itzig, Daniel 42
Izenberg, Gerald 130

Jahoda, Marie 122, 192 n.33
James, William 68, 75, 131
Jesuits, reform of 21, 36
Jevons, William Stanley 126
Joseph II (Holy Roman Empire): and the Enlightenment 24–5; and reform 25–6, 151 n.47, 156 n.38
Josephinism: Bolzano and 62; defined 25, 27, 152 n.54; and intellectual life 26, 30, 40–5; and language 39–40, 44; legacy of 26, 38–9; and religion 36; and the state 38–9, 41, 45, 90. *See also* Austrian Enlightenment
Judaism: and culture 33, 42, 54, 162 n.86; and intellectual life 42–3, 137, 155 n.30, 159 n.59; and language 47, 159 n.62; and religious tolerance 42; and society 42; and Wittgenstein 77, 78, 174 n.93. *See also* anti-Semitism
The Judgment 188 n.135
Judson, Pieter 4, 11, 47, 141 n.13, 144 n.43, 146 n.4, 153 n.5, 154 n.16, 157 n.46, 160 n.67, 161 n.75
Jungmann, Josef 40, 43, 160 n.64, 160 n.67, 169 n.24

Kafka, Franz: and ideology 53–4, 114; and language 106; and the Prague Circle 54
Kant, Immanuel: Bolzano on 9, 60–1, 63–4, 80, 169 n.30, 169–70 n.31, 171 n.47; Brentano 70; and German culture 32, 84; and idealism 41, 59, 64; long-term influence of 64, 83–4, 139; and Mach 73–6; on noumenon 74; Wittgenstein on 7, 79–80. *See also The Critique of Pure Reason*
Kassner, Rudolf 53, 103–4, 109, 185 n.79, 185 n.89
Kaunitz-Rietberg, Prince Wenzel 23
Kelsen, Hans 49, 121, 191 n.23
Kierkegaard, Søren 55, 94, 165 n.116
Kieval, Hillel J. 44, 159 n.62, 162 n.86
Klemm, Christian Gottlob 33. *See also Die Welt*
Klimt, Gustav 50, 101
Klingenstein, Grete 141 n.10
Knies, Karl 119–20
Knowledge and Error (Mach) 76, 174 n.91
knowledge: communication of 64, 84; and empiricism 69–70; Kant on 64, 74; and phenomena 69, 74; and religion 36, 109. *See also* truth
Köhler, Wolfgang 68
Kolowrat-Liebsteinsky, Count Franz Anton von 41
Königgrätz (Sadowa) 46
Kraft, Victor 82–3, 177 n.123
Kralice Bible 21
Kraus, Karl: and contemporaries 185 n.86; influence on Wittgenstein 78; intellectual contributions 54; and language 53, 104–6, 165 n.112
Kremsier 45, 72
Křen, Jan 16, 147 n.10, 156 n.37
Kubin, Alfred 49, 185 n.89

labor: strikes 53, 56; and women's rights 91, 96. *See also* class; economics; industrialization
LaCapra, Dominick 175 n.100
language: and analytic philosophy 1, 60, 65, 79, 137; and bilingualism 44; crisis of 53; and education 32; and Enlightenment 7, 29, 31–4, 37; equality of 44; and intellectual life 7, 11, 15, 19, 22, 29, 155 n.29; Musil on 53, 56, 106; reform of 19, 35, 47; and religion 15, 21; and the state 32, 34; and the Vienna Circle 79; Wittgenstein on 53, 79–81, 86, 106. *See also* Czech language; German language; literature
Latin 11, 19, 21, 32, 34, 35, 40, 149 n.24, 190 n.9
law 39, 69, 71, 118, 119, 121, 125, 136, 191 n.19. *See also* General Civil Law Code
Lazarsfeld, Paul 53, 122, 192 n.33
Leibniz, Gottfried Wilhelm 60–1, 70, 98, 145 n.47, 168 n.7, 196 n.66
Leitha River 4, 5, 7, 12, 15, 27, 46, 138
Leopold II (Holy Roman Empire) 24, 35, 38
Lessing, Gotthold Ephraim 7, 32, 41, 89, 159 n.57
Letter of Majesty (1609) 21
Lévinas, Emmanuel 70
liberalism: decline of 49; ideology of 43, 47, 92; liberal era 12, 26, 29, 30, 45, 46–51, 54, 66, 75, 86, 98–102, 106, 117, 130, 163 n.96, 182 n.52, 183 n.59; and nationalism 43, 45, 159 n.61; origins of 29–30, 42, 43, 45–9, 101, 130; and reform 45, 51, 117, 148 n.22; and religion 43, 104, 139; in Vienna 30, 47, 99, 101, 139; and women's rights 50, 99–100. *See also* social reform
Lindenfeld, David 191 n.19
Linz Program of 1882 49
literature: and culture 52, 54, 88, 106, 110; and Enlightenment 7, 32, 37, 38, 86, 110; and internationalism 52; and language 7, 32, 37, 106; and philosophy 1, 5, 6, 7, 54, 137; and politics 38, 51; in Prague 38, 54, 88, 137. *See also* language; publishing; Society for German Literature
Locke, John 86
logic: Bolzano on 60–1, 62, 64–6, 84, 86, 170 n.33; and positivism 59, 72, 76, 81, 83; Wittgenstein on 59, 65, 78–81. *See also* Polish School of Logic
Loos, Adolf 49
Lorenz, Dagmar 138
Louis II (Poland) 19
Louthan, Howard 150 n.33
Lower Austria 3, 18, 150 n.32, 161 n.72
Lueger, Karl 122

Luft, David 162 n.89, 162 n.93, 164 nn.105–6, 195–6 n.66
Lukács, Georg 55, 83, 104, 165 n.116
Luther, Martin 32, 33, 153 n.7
Lutheranism 19, 21–2, 26, 149 n.24, 150 n.33. *See also* Pietism; Protestant Reformation; Protestantism

Mach, Ernst: and atomism 75; and Brentano 12, 48, 59, 69, 73–5, 78–9, 84, 86, 139; on knowledge 73, 74, 76; long-term influence of 73, 75, 84; and philosophy of science 84; on reality 73–6; on sensation 69, 73–4, 83; and the University of Vienna 48, 72. *See also Analysis of Sensations; Knowledge and Error*
The Magic Flute (Mozart) 38, 156 n.36
The Magic Mountain 111
Mahler, Gustav 49
The Man without Prejudice (Sonnenfels) 37
The Man Without Qualities (Musil) 1, 51, 85, 101, 107, 109, 111, 115, 177 n.132, 186 n.104
Marcomanian 17
Marcus Aurelius 17, 148 n.15, 166 n.128. *See also Meditations*
Marcuse, Herbert 128, 134
Maria Theresa (Holy Roman Empire): anti-Semitism of 37; and education 36; and language 31, 33, 35; long-term influence 31; reforms of 23, 24, 25
Marty, Anton 67, 172 n.54
Marx, Karl 84, 96, 119, 125, 128, 130, 190 n.7
Marxism 76, 93, 121, 192 n.29. *See also* communism
Masaryk, Thomas 67, 172 n.54
masculinity 50, 197 n.82. *See also* gender
Masons 34
materialism 48, 49. *See also* atomism; Darwinism
mathematics: in education 82; and philosophy 67, 83, 95. *See also* German Mathematical Association; physics; science
Maudsley, Henry 71
Mauthner, Fritz 84, 164 n.108
Mayreder, Rosa 55

McGrath, William J. 49, 71, 130
McMahon, Darrin M. 141 n.18
medicine: funding of 26; schools of 31, 34, 118, 130. *See also* hospitals; Second Vienna School of Medicine
Meditations (Marcus Aurelius) 17, 148 n.15
Meinong, Alexius 67, 68, 70, 172 n.55
Meisel-Hess, Grete 55
Meitner, Lisa 55
Melton, James Van Horn 36, 155 n.23
memory 65, 70, 71, 76, 137
Menasse, Robert 198 n.3
Mendel, Gregor 49
Mendelsohn, Moses 42, 159 n.57
Menger, Carl 15, 48, 119, 120, 123–8, 192 n.36, 193 n.40, 193 n.41, 193 n.42, 194 n.45, 194 n.47, 194 n.48, 194 n.51, 196 n.66
The Metamorphosis 188 n.135
Methodius 18
Metternich, Prince Klemens von, political influence 41–2, 84
Meyrink, Gustav 49
middle class: and culture 47; and language 32; and the state 36. *See also* class
Mill, John Stuart 46, 66, 69, 70, 75, 162 n.92, 173 n.74. *See also On Liberty*
Miller, Perry 141 n.14
Mises, Ludwig von 126
Modern German language 1, 7, 29, 34, 138
modernism: and the arts 29, 52; Musil on 53; and society 24, 26
modernization: and class 119; and language 1, 7, 32, 138; and nationalism 43, 45; in Prussia 41; and reform 24, 25, 119, 122; of universities 45; and women's rights 55. *See also* industrialization
monasteries: and language 34; mediatization/secularization of 26
Monism 76, 84
Moore, G. E. 66, 77
morality: and the Enlightenment 35; and liberalism 101; and science 109. *See also* ethics
Moravia: and Czech culture 38; intellectual contributions of 11, 18, 36; and language 18, 21, 34, 37, 139; and nationalism 44, 49. *See also* Holy Roman Empire; Olomouc

Moyn, Samuel 141 n.18
Mozart, Wolfgang Amadeus 34, 38, 156 n.35. *See also The Magic Flute*
Müller, Adam 42
music, opera 89, 156 n.37. *See also* art; theater
Musil, Robert: biographical information on 107–10; Bohemian roots of 54; on chaos 108; on ethics 53; on ideology 56; influence of Mach on 75, 175 n.99; and language 53, 56, 106; role in Austrian intellectual history 9–10, 15, 85. *See also The Man Without Qualities*

the nation 111, 118, 121
nationalism: Bolzano on 92; complications of 44; and Enlightenment 32–3, 44, 92; and idealism 41; in Italy 45; and language 63; and liberalism 43, 45; resistance to 39, 41. *See also* patriotism
Neruda, Jan 160 n.67
Netherlands 27, 35, 150 n.41, 156 n.38
Neue Freie Presse (Vienna) 47, 48, 105
Neurath, Otto 82
Nietzsche, Friedrich 49, 50, 53, 57, 71, 74, 75, 92, 98, 103, 104, 107–12, 125, 130, 164 n.110, 165 n.116, 174 n.86, 183 n.58, 185 nn.81–2, 196 n.68. *See also Beyond Good and Evil*; *Schopenhauer as Educator*
Nikolsburg 37
Nipperdey, Thomas 40
nominalism: in Austrian philosophy 86; defined 86
The Notebooks of Malte Laurids Brigge 112
novel 15, 41, 87, 94–8, 99, 102–4, 106, 107, 111, 112–14, 139, 164 n.104, 182 n.52, 184 n.68, 184 n.77

Oakley, Allen 126, 193 n.40
object theory: Brentano's influence on 67–8, 70, 73; Mach on 73, 76; Meinong on 67, 68
objectivity: Bolzano on 61, 64, 66; Brentano on 66; and religion 62; role in Austrian intellectual history 85–6; Vienna Circle on 85–6. *See also* empiricism; rationalism
Old Liberalism 45, 160 n.70
Olomouc (Moravia) 37, 39. *See also* Moravia

On Liberty (Mill) 46
Open Society and Its Enemies (Popper) 57
Opera 48, 89, 137, 156
Oscar Wilde 100, 101
Otto I (Holy Roman Empire) 18, 147 n.11
Ottokar II (Bohemia) 15, 18
Ottoman Empire 19–20. *See also* Turkey
the Owl of Minerva 137

Palacký, František 40, 43, 44. *See also Geschichte von Böhmen*
Pan-Europeanism 163–4 n.103
papacy: challenges to 19; and the Jesuit order 36; papal infallibility 67, 171 n.52. *See also* Catholicism; Vatican
parliament: and intellectual life 46, 48; politics in 30; power of 30
Patent of Toleration 26, 36. *See also* religion
patriotism: Bolzano on 63; of Dobrovský 37. *See also* nationalism
Peace of Augsburg (1555) 21
peasantry: emancipation of 26, 45; and language 36, 72; Mach's origins as 72; mobility of 40; oppression of 22. *See also* class
The Penal Colony 188 nn.132–4
Perloff, Marjorie 184–5 n.77
Petrasch, Joseph Freiherr von 37
phenomenology: Austrian contributions to 59–60; Brentano's influence on 67–8, 74; Mach on 74; Wittgenstein on 59–60
philosophical irrationalism, defined 49, 196 n.68
physics: and atomism 80–1; Austrian contributions to 59–60; in education 61; Mach and 72, 73, 75, 76; Schlick and 82; and the Vienna Circle 76, 81, 82. *See also* atomism; mathematics; science
Piarists 61, 72. *See also* schools
Pietism 36. *See also* Lutheranism
Platonism 66
Poland: culture of 38, 144 n.43; participation in parliament 46; partition of 144 n.42, 157 n.46
Polish School of Logic 68. *See also* logic
political parties 49, 52, 56, 93, 108. *See also* politics

politics: Bolzano on 60, 63; and geography 2; in Hungary 11, 24, 30, 40, 161 n.72; and industrialization 43; and intellectual life 11, 30, 47, 56; and language 1, 40, 47; and religion 21, 26, 36, 60, 132, 134. *See also* political parties
Politzer, Heinz 115
pope. *See* papacy
Popp, Adelheid 50, 55
Popper, Karl: critique of German philosophy and politics 57; role in Austrian intellectual life 57, 85; and the Vienna Circle 57, 82, 86, 177 n.128. *See also Open Society and Its Enemies*
Popper-Lynkeus, Josef 72, 163
positivism: Brentano and 59, 66–9, 72, 196 n.67; Mach and 59, 72, 75, 76, 128; modest positivism 59, 167 n.3; in the nineteenth century 69, 75, 79, 131; and the Vienna Circle 59, 76, 81, 84; Wittgenstein and 59, 79, 81. *See also* Vienna Circle
Prague Circle 54
Prague: as capital city 19, 20; as cultural center 30, 40; language in 34, 137; universities in 30, 38, 39, 62, 72, 73, 169 n.25. *See also* Czech Republic; Czechoslovakia
Přemyslid princes 18, 90
The Primal horde 133
Prince Eugene of Savoy 22
The Principles of Mechanics (Hertz) 78, 175 n.105
Prinz, Friedrich 159 n.61
Project for a Scientific Psychology 131
Protestant Reformation, and language 33. *See also* Lutheranism; Protestantism
Protestantism: conflict with Catholicism 21, 61; and German culture 21; and Josephinism 36; and language 21, 33; and Wittgenstein 77. *See also* Calvinism; Lutheranism; Protestant Reformation
Prussia: annexation of Silesia 21, 23, 33; relations with Austria 3, 39, 41, 121. *See also* Berlin; Germany
Prussian Reform Movement 26, 35, 119
psychoanalysis; Brentano's influence on 67–9, 130; role in Austrian intellectual history 129–35. *See also* ego; psychology
Psychology from an Empirical Standpoint (Brentano) 67, 69
psychology: and atomism 80–1; Brentano on 68–72, 75, 172 n.58, 173 n.65, 173 n.73, 173 n.75; contributions by Austrian philosophy to 59, 67, 84, 143 n.31, 167 n.2, 167 n.5; effects of physiology on 69; Gestalt theory of 68, 84; influence of Leibniz on 61, 196 n.66; Mach and 73–6, 86. *See also* Gestalt psychology; psychoanalysis
publishing: of Brentano 67; censorship of 154 n.17; and the Ernst Mach Society 82; and language 35; of periodicals 37; for women 37. *See also* censorship; literature

rationalism: and intellectual life 51; and religion 61. *See also* objectivity
Rau, Karl Heinrich 119
Rautenstrauch, Franz Stephan 24, 36
reason: Bolzano on 63, 66; and literature 86, 135; and science 26
Red Vienna 122
Reflections on the Revolution in France (Burke) 42
Reformation. *See* Protestant Reformation
Reichsrat 30, 46, 49, 51. *See also* parliament
religion: Bolzano on 62; and the Enlightenment 35–6; and intellectual life 15, 35, 36, 109, 141 n.16; and language 15, 21; and politics 15–17, 21, 26, 60, 62, 76, 132, 134; and science 139, 141 n.16, 160 n.69; and sexuality 55, 134; toleration of 36, 152 n.54. *See also* Patent of Toleration; theology
Renaissance, influence in Central Europe 19, 20
Ricardo, David 124
Riegl, Alois 48
Rilke, Rainier Maria 9, 12, 15, 53, 54, 58, 88, 102, 103, 104, 106, 109, 111–15, 178 n.3, 178 n.6, 187 n.122
The Road into the Open (Schnitzler) 48
Robinson, Paul 130
Roman Catholic Church 47, 49, 89

Romania 23
Romanticism: in England 145 n.47; and the Enlightenment 41, 42; in Germany 6, 7, 9, 13, 40–1, 92, 106, 142 n.23, 145 n.47; as separate from Austrian philosophy 6, 41, 142 n.23, 158 n.51. *See also* Idealism
Roscher, Wilhelm 119
Rosseger, Peter 48
Rothschilds 42
Rudolf I (Holy Roman Empire): military victories of 22; rule of 18–19
Rudolf II (Holy Roman Empire); deposition of 21; and Prague 20
Russell, Bertrand: and analytic philosophy 65; influence on Wittgenstein 77, 80; and Meinong 70
Russia, emancipation of serfs 26. *See also* Soviet Union
Ryan, Judith 184 n.75

Saar, Ferdinand von 42, 48, 66, 99, 100, 102, 183 n.58, 183 n.66, 184 n.72
Saiko, George 53
saints' days 36
Saint-Simon, Henri 72, 119, 127
salons: and intellectual life 40, 42, 159 n.59; role of women in 42; in Vienna 42; of Wittgenstein 78
Salzburg 7, 54, 156 n.35
Sartre, Jean-Paul 70
Savigny, Friedrich Karl von 120, 125
Saxony: Brentano's citizenship in 67; influence of 67
Schiller, Friedrich 32, 34, 41, 92, 179 n.15
Schiller Festival 49
Schlegel, Friedrich 42, 158 n.51
Schlick, Moritz, and the Vienna Circle 52, 82
Schmoller, Gustav 120, 124
Schnitzler, Arthur 48, 49, 50, 51, 98, 100, 101, 102, 184 n.68, 184 n.72. *See also The Road into the Open*
Schoenberg, Arnold 101
Schönerer, Georg Ritter von 57
schools: funding of 26; and language 39; reform of 33; and women 50. *See also* education; Piarists
Schopenhauer as Educator (Nietzsche) 59, 185 n.82
Schopenhauer, Arthur: influence on Weininger 50, 78; influence on Wittgenstein 78, 79–80; and psychology 71; role in Austrian philosophy 77–81, 167 n.2. *See also The World as Will and Representation*
Schorske, Carl 49, 50, 51, 99, 101, 102, 130, 163 n.98, 182 n.52, 183 n.59
Schrifttum 111
Schumpeter, Joseph 49, 126
Schuppe, Wilhelm 76
Science: Bolzano on 59, 62–6, 84, 168 n.15, 170 n.33; Brentano on 59, 68, 69, 71, 84, 168 n.15, 196 n.66; and education 24, 82; and Freud 71, 130, 133, 135; Mach and 72–7, 83, 84, 128, 174 n.95; and Scientific Societies 34, 38; Social Sciences 4, 6, 9, 12, 51, 52, 57, 82, 117–20, 122, 124, 127, 128, 135, 188–9 n.1, 189 n.2, 189 n.5, 190 n.8, 191 n.19; and the Vienna Circle 59, 81–3, 139, 174 n.95, 177 n.128; Wittgenstein on 80, 81, 84, 86. *See also* empiricism; Darwinism; mathematics; physics
Sealsfield, Charles (Karl Anton Postl) 43
Secession of 1897 49
Second Republic (Austria) 137, 166 n.129
Second Vienna School of Medicine 48. *See also* medicine
Second World War, influence on intellectual life 145 n.46
Seibt, Karl Heinrich 38, 157 n.44, 160 n.64
self 41, 74, 132. *See also* ego
sensation: and knowledge 73, 74; and reality 74; and science 69, 73, 74, 83
sexuality: and intellectual life 55, 129, 135; and society 50, 55; of Weininger 50, 78; of Wittgenstein 78. *See also* gender
Siege of Vienna (1687) 20, 150 n.35
Silesia 21, 23, 33, 36
Simons, Peter 60, 68, 168 n.9
The Sleepwalkers 111, 115, 164 n.104, 186 n.112
Slovakia: in Czechoslovakia 4, 12, 14, 16, 30, 56, 57, 67, 122, 135, 137, 160 n.64; relationship with Bohemia 11, 14, 16. *See also* Czechoslovakia
Small, Albion 118, 190 n.11
Smith, Adam 124
Social Democratic Party 49, 121

Social realism 99, 102
social reform: and education 24, 36, 45; funding of 26; and intellectual life 19, 26, 30; and Josephinism 25–7; and language 19, 47; and modernization 24, 119, 122; and the state 62, 119. *See also* liberalism; suffrage
socialism: effects on intellectual life 10, 48; and internationalism 52; and liberalism 52; in Vienna 55, 122; and the Vienna Circle 82, 86. *See also* economics
Society for German Literature 32. *See also* literature
Sonnenfels, Joseph von: and the Austrian Enlightenment 32, 34; early life 37; and language 35. *See also The Man without Prejudice*
Sorkin, David 35, 155 n.22
soul, psychology and 69, 71
Soviet Union, Austrian emigration to 51–2. *See also* Russia
Spann, Othmar 118, 121, 122, 191 n.22, 191 n.23
Spiel, Hilde 58, 159 n.59
Spinoza, Baruch 61
Spirituality 45, 54, 55, 103, 107, 112, 187
Stein, Lorenz von 119, 190 n.7, 191 n.18
Steinberg, Michael 111
Steiner, Rudolf 83
Stieg, Gerald 140 n.8
Stifter, Adalbert: Bohemian roots of 40, 94; and Enlightenment 39, 139; on the relationship between Austria and Bohemia 15
Streissler, Erich W. 126, 193 n.40
Studies in Hysteria 131
Stumpf, Carl 67, 68, 84, 171 n.52, 175 n.99
Subjectivism 125, 193 n.40, 193 n.42
suffrage: and class 51; and political turmoil 30, 52; of women 55. *See also* feminism; social reform
Suleiman the Magnificent 20
Suttner, Bertha von 49, 55
Swieten, Gerard van 24, 25, 35, 36
Swieten, Gottfried van 25, 35
Switzerland 52, 58, 140 n.7, 142 n.25, 171 n.47

Technical University (Prague) 39
Thaler, Peter 166 n.126

theater, in intellectual life 40, 42, 47. *See also* art; music
theology 36, 82, 120, 191 n.23. *See also* religion
Theory of Science (Bolzano) 62, 64, 65, 170 n.31, 170 n.32
The Theory of the Novel 104
Thirty Years' War 22, 91, 96
Three Essays on the Theory of Sexuality 131
Thun, Count Leo: and Bolzano 45, 62, 66, 171 n.46; and University of Vienna 45, 66, 171 n.46
Timms, Edward 105
Toews, John E. 162 n.89, 195 n.65, 196 n.71
Tractatus-Logico Philosophicus (Wittgenstein) 79
Trakl, Georg 55, 185 n.89
Transleithanian 157 n.46, 161 n.72
Transylvania 20
The Trial 113, 115
trias model 43
Tribe, Keith 117, 189 n.7, 190 n.11
Trieste 149 n.31
Tristram Shandy 103
truth: Bolzano on 64, 66, 84, 86; correspondence theory of 67; and logic 61, 64, 84, 86; and objectivity 61, 64, 66, 128; and reality 74, 191 n.23; and reason 63. *See also* knowledge
Turkey 52. *See also* Ottoman Empire
Twardowski, Kazimierz 68, 70, 172 n.55

Unconscious 61, 70, 71, 73, 129, 131–4, 139, 196 n.66, 196 n.70
United Kingdom. *See* Great Britain
United States: abolition of slavery in 26; civil war in 15; definition of liberalism in 47; emigration to 57, 137; perspectives on Central European intellectual history 8, 130
Unity of Brethren 19, 21
universities: and class 50; language in 7, 32, 60; in Prague 30, 38, 39, 62, 72, 73, 169 n.25; in Prussia 35; reform of 30, 35, 45, 62; women in 50. *See also* education
University of Vienna: Brentano at 48, 67, 171 n.50; and intellectual life 30, 48, 51, 171 n.50; and language 30; Mach at

48, 72; reform of 30, 45, 62; Sonnenfels at 119; and women 50; Zimmerman in 48, 66, 171 n.46
utilitarianism: Bolzano and 62; in Britain 26
Utraquism: and language 44; origins of 44; and religious freedom 21. *See also* Hussites

Value vacuum 101, 103, 110
Vatican 45. *See also* papacy
Victorian England 137
Vienna Circle: Mach and 59, 76–7, 82, 84, 139, 174 n.95; origins of 81–3; philosophy of 12, 52, 57, 59, 80, 81–6, 139, 177 n.128; Wittgenstein and 12, 59, 77, 79, 81, 84, 85, 139, 176 n.119. *See also* positivism
Vienna: and Austrian identity 40, 55–6; Bolzano in 30, 40, 45, 59, 60–2, 64, 66, 80, 84, 139; class stratification in 47; Czech culture in 40; emigration from 52; geography of 138; Grillparzer in 9, 40, 42, 88–94; interest in sexuality at 50, 99; Jewish people in 42; Kraus in 54, 104–6, 175 n.103; and language 34, 37, 82, 84, 89, 137, 164 n.108; masonic lodges in 38; migration to 44, 56; move of capital from Vienna to Prague 20; newspapers in 47, 104; politics in 47, 51; role in intellectual life 12, 14, 30, 42, 48, 52, 54, 137; Romanticism in 41; salons in 42, 159 n.59; siege of 20, 150 n.35; Wittgenstein in 12, 59, 77–81, 84, 139. *See also* Austria; Cisleithania
Viennese Secession 101. *See also* Secession of 1897
Vocelka, Karl 146 n.6
Voegelin, Eric 53, 83, 122

Wagner, Benno 114, 188 n.131
Wagner, Richard 49, 51
Wagner Festival 49
Walras, Léon 126
Wangermann, Ernst 38

War of Austrian Succession (1740–1748) 23, 24
Wedberg, Anders 66, 168 n.9
Weininger, Otto: and contemporaries 54; Freud's influence on 197 n.71; on gender and sexuality 50; influence of 78; and science 75
Wells, C. J. 32
Wenceslaus I 23
Wertheimsteins 42, 48
Whitehead, Alfred North 77
Wieser, Friedrich von 126
Wiesinger, Peter 154 n.10
Williams, Raymond 141 n.14
Wittgenstein, Ludwig: and analytic philosophy 59, 65, 84; in Austrian intellectual history 15, 104; and ethics 54, 77, 86, 104, 106; and language 53, 79–81, 86, 106; life of 77–81, 105; on perception 77–81; and the Vienna Circle 12, 59, 77, 79, 81, 84, 85, 139, 176 n.119. *See also* Tractatus-Logico Philosophicus
Wolff, Christian 61
women: Bolzano on 62; in intellectual life 50, 55, 165 n.117, 165 n.119; publications for 37; and salon culture 42; suffrage for 55; at university 50; women's movement 50, 55. *See also* feminism; gender
World War I. *See* Second World War
World War II. *See* First World War
The World as Will and Representation (Schopenhauer) 78
Wyclif, John 19

Young Törless 101, 107, 185 n.92, 197 n.71
Young Vienna 49, 53, 99, 101, 102, 104, 106, 110, 129, 184 n.74

Zimmerman, Robert: poetry of 44; at University of Vienna 48, 66, 171 n.46
Zweig, Stefan 58, 164 n.106

www.ingramcontent.com/pod-product-compliance
Lightning Source LLC
Chambersburg PA
CBHW062144300426
44115CB00012BA/2032